LOST TOMBS

Studies in Egyptology

Editor: W V Davies, Deputy Keeper
Department of Egyptian Antiquities
The British Museum

Editorial adviser: A F Shore, Professor of Egyptology
University of Liverpool

Already published:

The Egyptian Temple; A Lexicographical Study
Patricia Spencer

The Administration of Egypt in the Old Kingdom; The Highest Offices and their Holders
Nigel Strudwick

Corpus of Reliefs of the New Kingdom from the Memphite Necropolis and Lower Egypt — Volume 1
Geoffrey Thorndike Martin

Problems and Priorities in Egyptian Archaeology
Edited by *Jan Assmann*, *Günter Burkard* and *Vivian Davies*

LOST TOMBS

A Study of Certain Eighteenth Dynasty Monuments in the Theban Necropolis

Lise Manniche

KPI

London and New York

First published in 1988 by
Kegan Paul International Limited
11 New Fetter Lane, London EC4P 4EE

Distributed by
Associated Book Publishers (UK) Ltd
11 New Fetter Lane, London EC4P 4EE, England

Routledge, Chapman and Hall Inc
29 West 35th Street
New York, NY 10001, USA

Printed in Great Britain by
Unwin Brothers Ltd., Woking, Surrey

ISBN 07103-0200-2

To the memory of Dr Labib Habachi

ACKNOWLEDGEMENTS

Over the past few years a great many institutions and private individuals have answered my queries about fragments of Theban tombs. I am much indebted to all of them: Avignon, Museum Calvet (G. de Loÿe); Berlin (E.), Ägyptisches Museum (H. Kischkewitz and K.-H. Priese); Berlin (W.), Ägyptisches Museum (B. Fay); Birmingham, City Museum and Art Gallery (P. J. Watson); Boston, Museum of Fine Arts (E. Brovarski and P. Lacovara); Bristol, Museum & Art Gallery (D. P. Dawson); Cambridge, Fitzwilliam Museum (J. Bourriau); Copenhagen, Ny Carlsberg Glyptotek (M. Jørgensen); Dresden, Staatliche Kunstsammlungen Dresden (H. Rost); Florence, Museo Archeologico (F. Nicosia); Jerusalem, The Israel Museum (D. Ben-Tor); Kingston Lacy, Bankes Collection, The National Trust (A. Mitchell); Lisbon, Museu Nacional de Arqueologia e Etnologia (F. J. S. Alves); Los Angeles, Los Angeles County Museum of Art (M. Smoot); New York, The Brooklyn Museum (R. A. Fazzini and J. Romano); The Metropolitan Museum of Art (C. Lilyquist and J. Wright); Paris, Musée du Louvre (J. L. de Cenival); Philadelphia, University Museum (D. O'Connor); Pisa, Università degli Studi di Pisa (E. Bresciani).

The British Library in London kindly allowed me to consult the records of the early travellers in their possession and to make tracings wherever necessary. The Faculty of Oriental Studies, University of Cambridge provided excellent working facilities and in addition entrusted me with a microfilm of the Hay MSS. During summer vacations I was granted full use of the library of the Carsten Niebuhr Institute, University of Copenhagen. Dr Lanny Bell made me welcome at the Oriental Institute, Chicago House in Luxor and allowed me to consult the outstanding library, including the collection of photographs, a similar service having been provided at the Oriental Institute in Chicago. At the Griffith Institute, Oxford Dr J. Málek instantly answered all my queries and placed all unpublished records at my disposal. Xerox copies of certain pages of the Wilkinson MSS, previously on loan to the Griffith Institute, were kindly provided by H. M. Colvin, St. John's College, Oxford, and by the Bodleian Library when the manuscripts were finally placed in this institution by The National Trust. Dr M. L. Bierbrier of the British Museum searched the archives of the museum for the history of the fragments in this collection, and Dr E. Leospo of the Museo Egizio in Turin promptly dispatched photographs and information on the many pieces in her care.

Dr J. van Dijk painstakingly copied the inscriptions on a statue in Leiden for me, and photographs of it were kindly provided by Dr M. J. Raven. Professor Dr J. Osing helped me out with deciphering the very difficult handwriting in the Lepsius MS, and Dr C. Traunecker, Centre Franco-Égyptien at Karnak, examined a particular site in the Theban necropolis for me before I was able to go there myself. With Dr R. G. Robins, Cambridge, I have had many discussions on painted fragments, notably a group which was eventually not included in the present work.

I would like to extend my thanks to the Egyptian Antiquities Organization for permission to visit a great many tombs at Thebes, in particular the President, Dr Ahmed Kadry; Dr Aly el-Khouly; the Chief Inspector for Upper Egypt, Mr Mohammed es-Sughayir; the Inspector at Qurna, Mr Mohammed Nasr; and the assistant inspectors Mr Nagi Gaafar, Mr Mohammed Ahmed Abdallah, Mr Taha Maamoun, Mr Reda Ali Mohammed, Mr Ibrahim Soliman and during my latest season Mr Sayed Aly Hegazy, as well as the chief guardians and assistant guardians of the necropolis who all went to considerable trouble to open tombs for me. Furthermore, I am indebted to Dr Mohammed Saleh, Director of the Egyptian Museum, for parting with a vital piece of information concerning the rediscovery of tomb no. C4, cleared while he was inspector at Qurna.

This work could not have been completed at the present time without the generous support I received from the British Council and the Carlsberg Foundation, Copenhagen, which allowed me three years of work without too many financial worries. Travel and other expenses were awarded by the Danish Research Council for the Humanities and Carl og Ottilia Brorsons Fond, Copenhagen, for a journey to the USA and Canada, and by Christ's College, the Thomas Mulvey Fund and the Chadwick Fund, all Cambridge, for a study tour to Egypt in 1983, the costs of the 1984 expedition being generously met by the Danish Research Council. Photographic expenses were covered by a contribution from the BA Travel and Research Fund, Christ's College.

My interest in painted fragments of Theban tombs was first aroused some ten years ago by Professor J. R. Harris, Durham (then Copenhagen). I am grateful for the encouragement he has given me over the years to pursue my studies in this field. I have benefited greatly from discussions with J. D. Ray, University of Cambridge; and to Dr G. T. Martin I owe a debt of gratitude, not only for searching for painted fragments for me during his own travels and for allowing me the use of his private library, but also for his never-fading interest in my work.

Introduction

'...when the saps of time shall have destroyed (the) integrity (of the wall-paintings), their legibility, and their brilliant hue future ages may tax our careless and sluggish nature, as we now do that of the Greeks and Romans, who saw the monuments of Thebes in all their glory; but stalked silently and stupidly by, hardly leaving us a notice of what they were, either in size, number, beauty, or appropriation. Mr Belzoni has done much; but the surface of Thebes is hardly scratched, its mine of diamonds remains unexplored.'
R. Richardson, *Travels along the Mediterranean and Parts Adjacent; in the Company with the Earl of Belmore during the Years 1816, 1817-18,* London 1822 (Vol. II, p. 78).

The Theban private tombs form a major source for our knowledge of Egyptian society. Ostensibly a great amount of work has been done in the necropolis over the past one hundred and sixty years of its modern history, and the bibliography for this area is among the most extensive in Egyptology. Many of the 415 or so decorated tombs have received a full publication, but for a great number only selected scenes have been made available, and a surprising amount remains to all intents and purposes unpublished. Some studies have dealt with the artistic and funerary aspects of tomb decoration, but there is a great deal of information still to be gathered from the lesser known and unpublished tombs. Moreover, there is another valuable primary source, the 'lost' tombs, utilized in the present study.

Before the creation of the Egyptian Antiquities Department early travellers were accustomed to remove portions of the wall-decoration of the Theban tombs, either for incorporation in their private collections of antiquities or for sale to the recently created national and provincial museums. Despite the efforts of the present Egyptian Antiquities Organisation this work of destruction still goes on, and it is a battle against time to record the decoration of the tombs before even more fragments disappear into private collections or are simply destroyed by inexpert handling. Once a fragment is out of context, it is often exceedingly difficult to re-assign the piece to its original position. This is the case with many of the fragments removed during the previous century.

The present study is concerned with a number of painted tombs of the Eighteenth dynasty which were visited by the early travellers, but the exact location of which is now unknown. The careful drawings and tracings made by these pioneers are apparently all that remains to show the appearance of these tombs. Some of the scenes represented are not found elsewhere in the necropolis, and others have special points of interest or unique details, linguistic, iconographic and religious, to offer. This very important material has not previously been used by scholars, and it has not been recognized that fragments of some of these vanished tombs can actually be traced to collections in museums and elsewhere.

To establish a connection between a fragment in a collection and one of the tombs described or drawn in the manuscripts of the early travellers is no straightforward task, for few of the museum fragments are actually represented by a drawing in the records. In fact, most of the pieces which prove to be relevant in the present study had been removed from the tombs before the walls were copied. But there are other means of linking a fragment with a tomb, such as the name of a person occurring on both, stylistic resemblance, or a common connection with some other source. All these matters will be demonstrated in the following pages.

For a number of tombs described and drawn by the early copyists no fragments appear to survive in the collections. However, the 'lost' tombs themselves are of such interest and importance that an attempt will be made to reconstruct their scheme of decoration on paper from the existing manuscript records. For this purpose a thorough study has been carried out of the distribution of a number of important scenes in typical tombs of the Eighteenth dynasty from which it emerges that a certain consistency was the general rule.

Chapters 3 to 12 of the present work formed my doctoral dissertation at Cambridge University, approved in 1985.

1 An Evaluation of the Number of Theban Private Tombs Now Lost

In order to estimate the full extent of the Theban necropolis during the New Kingdom and in particular during the Eighteenth dynasty a study of the extant tombs is by no means sufficient. Many tombs have not survived, and only a very small proportion of even these are dealt with in detail in our study of 'lost tombs'.

It is possible to gain an approximate idea of the total amount of lost tombs by examining the so-called 'funerary cones'. These are cone-shaped objects of baked clay which have at the circular, flat end a stamped impression including a name and title(s), and sometimes mentioning a relative, or short supplementary texts. Funerary cones are an essential element of New Kingdom tomb design at Thebes, and the presence of a cone is to all intents and purposes proof of the former existence of a tomb.

Purpose of the funerary cones

A great number(1) of cones with identical or varying stamps(2) were made for each tomb owner, and the cones were set as a frieze with the inscribed surface visible along the upper edge of the facade of the tomb, if possible extending round the corners, and sometimes also inserted under the pyramidion which covered the superstructure of the tomb. On the basis of some representations in Theban tombs and the presence in collections of 'corner stones' or wedges which bear impressions of the same stamp as the one used for the cones, Borchardt gave a full description of the cones as an element of funerary architecture.(3) Uninscribed cones of the Eleventh dynasty were found by Winlock *in situ* above the door of a tomb buried under the causeway leading to the temple at Deir el-Baḥri, (4) and there can be no doubt that this was how the cones were used from this early period and at least until Ramessid times. Most of the tombs in which an external view of the tomb is included in the wall-decoration are admittedly Ramessid, but there is nothing to indicate that the practise was in any way different during the Eighteenth dynasty, although the general appearance of the tombs was then slightly different.(5)

Few elements in Egyptian art are purely decorative, and a number of interpretations have been put forward as to the significance of these funerary cones. They were first mentioned by Champollion who thought that they might have served the same purpose as the Graeco-Roman wooden mummy labels. (6) Rhind saw some specimens apparently *in situ*, (7) and he suggested that their purpose was religious, memorial and ornamental.(8) Mariette thought that they were a kind of boundary stone, shaped like offering loaves, marking the territory of a prospective tomb owner.(9) Maspero,(10) later followed by Bruyère,(11) interpreted the cones as dummy offering loaves; others have preferred to regard them as imitations of pieces of meat.(12) Daressy viewed the cones as 'visitors' cards', left by devoted relatives.(13) Winlock, who was the first person in recent times actually to find cones *in situ*, apparently realizing that the cone-shape was less important than the circular area, suggested that they might represent the ends of the poles used for the roofing of houses. (14) Davies seemed partly to follow Borchardt in viewing them mainly as a decorative feature.(15) Recently Eggebrecht has put forward the interesting suggestion that the circular end of the cones is a representation of the sun's disc and that the presence of the cones enabled the deceased whose name they carried to partake in the solar cycle and thus gain eternal life.(16)

In the discussion emphasis has been laid either on the cone shape of the objects or on the visible, circular part, but little attention has been paid to their colour. A number of the cones show traces of red paint on the circular end,(17) but there is also evidence of blue(18) or white(19) having been applied. In Egyptian art it was generally established at an early date which colour any individual object represented was to have, and there are but few variations once colour conventions were laid down.(20) Loaves of bread are largely white,(21) meat is red, pottery is either red or blue, wood is most often red, though sometimes yellow, the sun's disc is red, and so on. It seems therefore that the Ancient Egyptians themselves had varying ideas as to what the cones were actually meant to represent. The accompanying texts on the cones frequently have to do with the adoration of the sun, and it seems safe to assume that to some at least this was the *raison d'être* of the cones. It also corresponds to the general idea behind tomb decoration as a whole, being instrumental in assuring eternal life for the tomb owner. It is less straightforward to provide an explanation for the blue and white cones. The white colour seems to cover the entire cone, not just the visible, circular end, suggesting rather strongly that the cones were by no means just a decorative feature.

Identification of funerary cones with known tombs

The elements available for an identification of funerary cones consists of 1) the name of the owner; 2) a nickname; 3) one or more titles; 4) name of father; 5) name of mother; 6) name of wife; 7) name of son (rare); 8) name of daughter (even more rare(22)). To a certain extent an excavation record may provide valuable information for an identification, as for example when the titles on cone and in tomb differ, but the presence of the cone in or near the tomb suggests the link.(23) On the other hand cones have sometimes been found at a considerable distance from where they presumably belonged.(24)

Some cones give only a name, others give two or more details which can be of use in an identification. In order to relate a cone to a known tomb a minimum of two common denominators must be required. The considerable number of titles often borne by each person and apparently used at random makes it no simple task. Furthermore each person sometimes had his cones impressed with two or more different stamps, giving variant titles and even different orthography of the name.(25)

For the New Kingdom it has been possible to link about 80 different cones with as many tombs (cf. Table I at the end of this chapter). For 325 New Kingdom tombs no cones seem to have been found, but a substantial number of tombs remain anonymous, or only the title of the tomb owner is left: 27 tombs of the Eighteenth dynasty(26) and 16 Ramessid tombs(27) are unaccounted for, and it remains a possibility that some of the cones came from one or more of these tombs. A careful scrutiny of the title of tomb owners which are not among those listed in the *Topographical Bibliography* may establish a few more links between cones and tombs.(28)

The date of funerary cones

The earliest funerary cones have been found in the Eleventh dynasty tombs mentioned above and in a tomb presumably belonging to Inyotef III.(29) These early cones are uninscribed and large, up to 52cm long. The size of the cones tends to decrease through the ages. In the Eighteenth dynasty the cones become very frequent. The earliest tomb for which a corresponding inscribed cone has been found is TT 345 belonging to a 'son' of Tuthmosis I.(30) Other cones can be linked with TT 67,(31) 71/353,(32) 179,(33) and TT 252(34) from the reign of Hatshepsut. Of early Eighteenth dynasty date are the cones belonging to TT 59,(35), 251,(36) 297,(37) 343(38) and 349.(39)

Among the as yet unprovenanced cones are some pertaining to officials of Tuthmosis I during his lifetime: a carrier of weapons (*ḫ'w*),(40) a senior steward,(41) and a steward and overseer of cattle.(42) Yet another cone-owner has been demonstrated to have functioned during the reign of this king.(43)

Cones from the mid-Eighteenth dynasty abound (cf. Table I), and among unprovenanced specimens there are many which can be dated to this period by the titles they carry, combined with a typically Eighteenth dynasty name as well as the size and style of the cone. After the reign of Amenophis III few cones are dated with certainty, except those belonging to TT 55(44) and 192(45) covering the reigns of Amenophis III-IV, TT 383 of Merymosi, viceroy of Kush and son of Amenophis III,(46) and TT 49 probably executed during the reign of Ay.(47) These figures must be seen against the amount of tombs prepared during the various reigns.

Some early authorities maintained that funerary cones were exclusive to the Eighteenth dynasty,(48) but this is by no means the case. Cones can be identified with known Ramessid tombs, other cones bear names and titles common in the Nineteenth and Twentieth dynasties, and wall-paintings of the tombs frequently show the cones in position as a frieze.(49) Nevertheless a surprisingly small number of cones can be related to existing, Ramessid tombs. It is evident from the figures given in Table II that the number of tombs had not declined during the Ramessid period. Yet only seven of these tombs yielded matching cones: TT 58,(50) 137,(51) 207,(52) 275,(53) 324,(54) 346,(55) and TT A6,(56) two of these being of the Twentieth dynasty.

Funerary cones dating from the Twenty-first dynasty have not been identified, but a few are connected with officials of rulers of the Twenty-second dynasty.(57) From the Twenty-fifth dynasty cones of Mentuemḥēt, the well-known fourth prophet of Amūn (TT 34) abound,(58) and others can be dated to the Twenty-sixth dynasty.(59) The proportion of cones from the Late Period seems consistent with the number of private tombs at Thebes at this time: there are few, but important, large tombs.

The geographical distribution of funerary cones

Just as certain elements of the decoration inside the tombs seem to be particular to the Theban necropolis,(60) the funerary cones decorating the facade appear to be mainly a Theban phenomenon. Almost all the cones with an excavation record have been found at Thebes. The exceptions are uninscribed cones found at Rizeiqât,(61) Armant,(62) Naqada,(63) and Abydos,(64) all of the Middle Kingdom. New Kingdom cones have been recovered at ʿAnîba,(65) possibly at Nagaʿ ed-Deir,(66) and at ed-Deir just north of Esna.(67)

The New Kingdom 'Egyptian' tombs at ʿAnîba seem to have been made either for Egyptian officials there (although the majority of these appear to have preferred to be buried in Egypt proper) or for the local people. Pennē, the deputy for Wawat whose painted tomb is the best preserved at ʿAnîba,(68) has not left us any funerary cones, but a certain ʿAnu had a tomb executed with pyramidion and funerary cones.(69) However, cones of his have also been found at Thebes.(70) Steindorff suggested that the ʿAnîba tomb was a cenotaph and that the real tomb was at Thebes.(71)

At ed-Deir inscribed cones of two individuals were found in a Middle Kingdom cemetery.(72) One set was large and painted white, the other small and unpainted. The title on one of the cones mentions *ʿgn*, the locality near which the cones were found.(73) Although the cones may be intrusive in the Middle Kingdom burials, they presumably belong to tombs in the neighbourhood and thus form an exceptional occurrence of funerary cones outside Thebes.

Some cones contain evidence of a possible Memphite connection. One belongs to Ḳenamūn, steward of the *prw-nfr*,(74) and two more square, stamped impressions to Nebwaʿ, his secretary, including Ḳenamūn's name and title.(75) The *prw-nfr* has been demonstrated to be the dockyard of Memphis.(76) Ḳenamūn may well have worked in this locality at some stage in his career, but his tomb was hewn at Thebes (TT 93). Although the cones bear a different title from those mentioned in the tomb, the cones were actually found at the tomb by Mond.(77) Nebwaʿ's tomb has not yet been found, but there are no compelling reasons why it should not also be somewhere in the Theban necropolis.

A third cone actually mentions the name of Memphis,(78) but by analogy with the case of Ḳenamūn one should probably look for the tomb of this person at Thebes. The cone is one of those allegedly found by Davies at Thebes, as were the cones mentioning the *prw-nfr*.

There are other cones which suggest that the occupation of the tomb owners kept them elsewhere than at Thebes. One was overseer of the granary of Monthu at Heliopolis (*ꜣIwnw*),(79), another was steward of the same god there,(80), and a third was *ḥꜣty-ʿ* of Monthu of Heliopolis,(81) and a fourth was inspector of works.(82) One person was in charge of the cattle of Ḥatḥor of Dendara *(ʾIwnt)* (83) Some officials presumably tarvelled around, being concerned with administrative functions both in the North and in the South, inspecting granaries,(84) counting cattle,(85) or loaves of bread,(86) or simply counting 'everything'.(87) All these persons possessed cones, almost all of which are known to have been found at Thebes. This corresponds with the fact that some of the officials whose tombs are located at Thebes also had titles which connected them with other parts of the country. There are the mayors of Aphroditopolis (TT 20), Thinis (TT 109) (88) and 'The Southern Lake and the Lake of Sobk' (TT 63), the governor of all Northern Lands (TT 239), the viceroys of Kush (TT 40, 289, 300, 383 and D1), and a number of officials attached to the granaries of the South and the North (TT 32, 46, 57 and 87).

It seems therefore that with very few exceptions funerary cones are restricted to the Theban necropolis. This fact makes the cones particularly useful and reliable as evidence of lost tombs in this area, just as painted tombs of New Kingdom date are also almost exclusively found at Thebes.(89) The two factors are not necessarily related, but it is a curious circumstance that the vast majority of the tombs for which cones have been found are indeed tombs with painted decoration. The reason for the absence or presence of funerary cones in any particular part of Egypt (or Nubia) is probably to be sought in the architecture of the tombs, and also in certain conventions established in a particular district. The Theban tombs are largely rock-cut, but so are those at el-Kâb, for example, and no cones have been found there. The tomb of Pennē at ʿAnîba and that of Kakemet at Asswân(90) were partly free-standing, painted tombs, but no cones have survived there either. It rather looks as if a rock-cut tomb with painted decoration provided the ideal conditions for the use of funerary cones, although this may be a coïncidence. The amount of tombs without cones and cones without tombs is too great for any statistics of this kind to be of serious value.

Distribution of tombs to which cones have been related

Within the Theban necropolis there is a certain pattern in the distribution of tombs for which cones have been found. The cones have by no means always been discovered in close proximity to the tomb to which they presumably belonged,(91) and never in recent times *in situ*. The vast majority of the tombs in question are on the slopes of the hill of Sheikh ʿAbd el-Qurna, almost six times as many as at Khôkha and Draʿ Abû el-Nagaʿ respectively (cf. Table III). At Deir el-Medîna only one tomb (TT 325) has yielded funerary cones,(92) and the identification of the tomb owner rests chiefly with the cones found in a pit nearby (no. 1089), others having been found elsewhere in the neighbourhood.(93) There are no titles on this cone inscribed for a man called Smen. Bruyère suggested that he might be identical with a certain Amenhotp, called Smen, a royal scribe whose funerary vases are now in Cairo.(94) Yet there are cones of this person in the corpus of Daressy(95) and of Davies & Macadam,(96) and it would seem that they are two different individuals.(97)

Two more cones have been found in the Deir el-Medîna area, both obviously out of context. Near TT 325 was found a cone of a certain Merymaʿet whose tomb was actually at Qurna,(98) and in pit no. 1089, along with cones of Smen, was found a cone belonging to

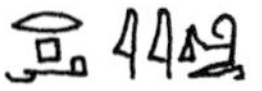 *ʾIrypʿt?*, unknown from other sources.(99)

It is significant that among the unprovenanced cones there is not a single one that is in any way connected with Deir el-Medîna. Titles pertaining to this community are usually very characteristic. On the basis of available evidence it would seem that the tombs at Deir el-Medîna were not normally provided with funerary cones. More than at any other section of the Theban necropolis the tombs themselves are designed to emphasize a kind of 'solar eternity',(100) and it may be that other elements in architecture and decoration superseded the use of cones as solar symbols. The amount of Ramessid tombs at Deir el-Medîna as compared to tombs of the Eighteenth dynasty (cf. Table II) may account for the absence of cones even as a decorative element, as cones do seem to decrease in number, but it does not explain their total absence. The reconstructions by Bruyère of the Deir el-Medîna tombs(101) do not allow for the presence of funerary cones. Bruyère himself suggested that ushabti figures took over the role of the cones.(102) But for some persons as least in other parts of the necropolis both cones and ushabti-figures have been found.(103)

When trying to estimate the amount of lost tombs on the basis of funerary cones one must keep in mind the fact that some tombs had double occupancy, and that two sets of cones would therefore ideally be expected for one tomb. Tombs deliberately planned for two owners are not very common outside Deir el-Medîna,(104) however, and the use of cones in this area is questionable. Seventeen tombs in the Theban necropolis were usurped by another person at some point sooner or later after the death of the first owner.(105) On the other hand some officials are known to have prepared more than one tomb during their life-time,(106) and in that case there might only have been one set of cones for two tombs.

A different problem is posed by the cones which bear a woman's name only. Non-royal women are not known to have made independent tombs in the New Kingdom.(107) There are nine cones belonging to women. Three of these have special titles: *ḥry mrt*(108) and *šmʿyt n ʾImn*.(109) The rest are designated as *ḥmt.f nbt pr*,(110) *ḥmt.f mrt.f*,(111) *snt.f mrt.f nbt pr*(112) or just *nbt pr*.(113) In spite of the personal pronoun *f* of the husband, his name is never mentioned. It has not been possible with any degree of certainty to identify any of these women with wives of known tomb owners. Presumably the cones of the wives belonged in the tomb with the cones of the husbands, just as husband and wife are elsewhere mentioned on one and the same cone. There seems to have been no prominent place left for unmarried women in the New Kingdom. But the fact that wives could have separate cones opens up a new range of possibilities for the use of funerary cones, and it may explain the many unprovenanced specimens. It may in fact have been possible not only for wives but also for relatives and friends to have cones inserted in the frieze of another person's tomb in order to obtain the same sort of eternal, solar life. If this was possible, the number of estimated 'lost' tombs would decrease dramatically.

For an estimate of the amount of tombs lost, based on the extant funerary cones, the situation may be summed up as follows:

1. Cones are an almost exclusively Theban phenomenon.

2. Cones of the New Kingdom can be isolated with a considerable degree of certainty.

3. Among the unprovenanced cones some may still belong in known tombs, the variety of titles and the scarce information on the cones often obscuring an immediate identification. Other cones may belong to anonymous tombs.

4. The amount of tombs with double occupancy, or usurped tombs (*i.e.* with the possibility of more than one set of cones) is to some extent made up for by the number of tomb owners who has more than one tomb (with the possibility of one set of cones for two or more tombs).

5. The number of tombs without cones is 327. The amount of cones without tombs is more than 400, *i.e.* about as many as there are known New Kingdom tombs in the necropolis.(114)

6. If one assumes that each cone represents a tomb there were in the New Kingdom about twice as many tombs as are known today. With the doubtful use of cones at Deir el-Medîna in mind the majority of cones is even more marked. If one assumes that each male cone owner possessed a tomb, the nine female cone owners having their cones inserted in the tombs of their husbands, this figure is slightly lower.(115) If on the other hand one assumes that it was possible for other male members of the family, or friends, to have their cones set up in the tomb,(116) it is not possible to estimate the amount of lost tombs on the basis of the funerary cones. The number may in that case be minimal.(117)

In any case the funerary cones represent a most valuable source, hitherto for the most part neglected, for the prosopography of the New Kingdom necropolis at Thebes. The following Tables summarize the information available so far.

Tomb No.	Location	Date	Daressy No.	Davies & Macadam No.
11	Draᶜ Abû el-Nagaᶜ	Ḥatshepsut/Tuthmosis III		257,263(118)
24	"	Tuthmosis III	83	
29	Qurna	Amenophis II	130	265
38	"	Tuthmosis IV	234	
45	"	Amenophis II		402
47	Khôkha	Amenophis III	207	406
48	"	Amenophis III	199	
49	"	Ay?	289	291
52	Qurna	Tuthmosis IV?	271	157
53	"	Tuthmosis III	180,213	
55	"	Amenophis III-IV	31	132-3
56	"	Amenophis II	14	
58	"	Dyn. XX	205	
59	"	early Dyn. XVIII		538-9
61	"	Tuthmosis III		355?,370
64	"	Tuthmosis IV	39bis	102
66	"	Tuthmosis IV	270	583
67	"	Ḥatshepsut	230	21,517-8
71	"	Ḥatshepsut	17-8	84,88
74	"	Tuthmosis IV		240
77	"	Tuthmosis IV		475
78	"	Tuthmosis III-Amenophis III		476
79	"	Tuthmosis III-Amenophis II	185	
80	"	Amenophis II		492
81	"	Amenophis I-Tuthmosis III	170	480-1
82	"	Tuthmosis III		128-9
84	"	Tuthmosis III	43,141	281,283
85	"	Tuthmosis III-Amenophis II	143	270
86	"	Tuthmosis III	38	100
87	"	Tuthmosis III	24,28, 103bis	89
88	"	Tuthmosis III-Amenophis II	20,27,164	201
92	"	Amenophis II		156
93	"	Amenophis II		432(119)
95	"	Amenophis II	160	390,400
96	"	Amenophis II	78	223-4
97	"	Amenophis II		42-4
99	"	Tuthmosis III		154
108	"	Tuthmosis IV		298
109	"	Tuthmosis III	73-4	109
110	"	Tuthmosis III		47
123	"	Tuthmosis III	249	368
137	"	Ramesses II		529
146	Draᶜ Abû el-Nagaᶜ	Tuthmosis III?		104
155	"	Ḥatshepsut/Tuthmosis III	102,110	139,182
162	"	Dyn. XVIII		12
164	"	Tuthmosis III	210	549
179	Khôkha	Ḥatshepsut		558
192	ᶜAsâsîf	Amenophis III-IV		140

TABLE I Tombs to which cones have been assigned (continued)

Tomb No.	Location	Date	Daressy No.	Davies & Macadam No.
200	Khôkha	Tuthmosis III/Amenophis II	4,13,166	4,22
201	"	Tuthmosis IV/Amenophis III	198	466
204	"	Dyn. XVIII		214
205	"	Tuthmosis III/Amenophis II?		350
207	"	Ramessid	231	
230	Qurna	Dyn. XVIII	150	292
246	Khôkha	Dyn. XVIII		229
249	Qurna	Tuthmosis IV?	115	153
251	"	early Tuthmosis III	68,178	367
252	"	Ḥatshepsut	16	120
260	Dra' Abû el-Naga'	Tuthmosis III?		61
275	Qurnet Mura'i	Ramessid	246	501
297	'Asâsîf	early Dyn. XVIII	45	73
324	Qurna	Ramessid		471
325	Deir el-Medîna	Dyn. XVIII		404
343	Qurna	early Dyn. XVIII		544
345	"	Tuthmosis I	132	247
346	"	Ramesses II	228	524
349	"	early Dyn. XVIII	272	311
367	"	Amenophis II	85	230
383	Qurnet Mura'i	Amenophis III	113	169-70,441
397	Qurna	Dyn. XVIII?		235
398	"	Dyn. XVIII	116	13,118-9
401	Dra' Abû el-Naga'	Tuthmosis III/Amenophis II?		266
A1	"	Dyn. XVIII	46	110
A3	"	New Kingdom	106	158
A5	"	Tuthmosis III/Amenophis II	104	148
A6	"	Tuthmosis III?(120)	12,165	14,396-7
A8	"	late Dyn. XVIII?(121)		204?,532,554
C1	Qurna	Amenophis III	144-5	314
C4	"	Amenophis III(122)	9	11
C6	"	Tuthmosis IV	194	

TABLE I (continued) Tombs to which cones have been assigned

Location	Dyn. XVIII	Ramessid	'New Kingdom'	Total
Draʿ Abû el-Nagaʿ	48	55	5	108
Deir el-Baḥri	1	0	0	1
Khôkha	32	29	1	62
ʿAsâsîf	2	14	0	16
Sheikh ʿAbd el-Qurna	110	37	0	147
Qurnet Muraʿi	6	12	1	19
Deir el-Medîna	6	47	0	53
Total	205	194	7	406

TABLE II Distribution of New Kingdom tombs in the Theban necropolis

These figures include the tombs without official numbers, Porter & Moss, *op. cit.*, I^2, 1, pp. 447-61 as well as three tombs in the files of the Griffith Institute to be included in a future edition of the *Topographical Bibliography*:

TT 412 Ḳenamūn, royal scribe. Tuthmosis III-Amenophis II (painted tomb).

TT A27 Say, royal scribe of the altar of the Lord of the Two Lands. New Kingdom

TT A28 Nakht(?). Twentieth dynasty.

The tomb of a certain Amenḥotp, chief physician is not included in that it has not yet been officially numbered as TT 415. For this tomb see Leclant in *Orientalia* 41, 1972, p. 263 (g).

The few tombs which are left undated in Porter & Moss have not been included, with the exception of TT A22 to which I have in a previous article assigned the date of the mid-Eighteenth dynasty. Usurped tombs are listed according to the date of the original owner.

Location	Dyn. XVIII	Ramessid	'New Kingdom'	Total
Draʿ Abû el-Nagaʿ	10	1	2	13
Khôkha	8	1	0	9
ʿAsâsîf	2	0	0	2
Sheikh ʿAbd el-Qurna	48	4	0	52
Qurnet Muraʿi	1	1	0	2
Deir el-Medîna	1	0	0	1
Total	70	7	2	79

TABLE III Distribution of tombs to which cones have been assigned

2 Decorated Fragments: Problems of Attribution

In order to attempt to ascertain the provenance of a fragment of the wall-decoration of a Theban tomb, it is relevant to examine briefly the types of decoration found on other monuments as fragments of these, out of context, might be mistakenly attributed to a Theban tomb.

Wall-decoration in Egypt is basically restricted to temples, secular buildings (houses and palaces) and tombs (royal and private). The main subjects of temple decoration are laid out in Tables IV-V, those of secular buildings in Table VI, the decoration of royal tombs in Table VII and private tombs in Table VIII, all to be found at the end of this chapter. These tables deal with New Kingdom material only (dynasties XVIII-XX).(1) The temple section relies mainly on evidence from Thebes and el-Amarna, whereas the tomb sections are intended to be complete, including sites over the whole of Egypt, Nubia, and the oases. An example of Egyptianizing wall-decoration from abroad is also included. As far as the royal tombs are concerned they are naturally limited to the Theban area, apart from the Royal Tomb at el-Amarna. The Memphite tomb of Ḥaremḥab, decorated before the owner became king, is a private tomb. Not every single detail of the decoration is included in the Tables; rather they reflect the main themes chosen to decorate the walls of the various categories of architecture.

Because of the particular nature of Egyptian representational art, which does not distinguish between the monumental and the minute, there is nothing in the dimensions of a given scene that can give a clue to its provenance, except in extreme cases. When utilizing photographs of fragmentary material (where indications as to dimensions are sometimes not available), or ancient drawings where this information has also been omitted, there is likewise no method of establishing the size of the original on purely iconographical grounds. Furthermore, large scenes can be found even on the fairly restricted space available on tomb walls, small ones on the bigger temple walls, and vice versa.

In the following we shall compare the decoration of private tombs with that of temples, royal tombs and secular buildings, material from the Amarna Period being treated separately, and finally comparison will be made between private tombs from various sites.

The decoration of temples as compared with the decoration of private tombs

Before we enter into the problems of tracing a fragment, the decoration of which might appear to suit private tomb and temple alike, mention should be made of the clues provided by the technique of decoration. It is highly desirable to ascertain whether a fragment is executed in relief or in painting. If it proves to be the latter the problem is reduced, in that the walls of the vast majority of temples were sculpted before being painted. The only examples of religious buildings with painted decoration likely to be mistaken for that of private tombs are the so-called 'chapelles des confréries' at Deir el-Medîna, votive chapels with painted decoration showing the king in front of a divinity; an example of what is possibly Amenophis I and Aḥmosi Nefertere; and a few other scenes of a mythological nature.(2) Part of the painted decoration of the temple of Amenophis III at Wadi es-Sebuᶜa(3) might possibly be mistaken for that of a royal tomb, whereas the Ḥatḥor chapel of Tuthmosis III at Deir el-Baḥri, though partly executed in painting, belongs thematically in a temple, not in a tomb.(4)

When a fragment is sculpted, the stone employed may provide a pointer to the nature of the monument from which it came, the stone used being to a certain extent the available local stone. The hills bordering the Nile Valley from Cairo to Esna are of limestone, whereas beyond that point they are of sandstone. The Theban tombs are thus cut in the local limestone, jambs of sandstone being sometimes added. The open courtyard tombs at Saqqâra, however, were built of mud brick, but the casing or interior revetment of slabs of stone, ca. 15cm thick, was also of limestone. Most temples were built of sandstone.(5) There are, however, a number of exceptions,(6) and this is where misattribution is most likely to occur, particularly where the style of decoration in a temple influenced the wall-decoration of neighbouring tombs. There is for example a remarkable similarity between the very fine decoration in bas-relief, once painted in bright colours, of the Eighteenth dynasty temples at Deir el-Baḥri and the quality of the relief in some of the tombs of the area.(7) If the subjects depicted overlap, *i.e.* could iconographically be part of a temple or a private tomb, it is exceedingly difficult to ascertain its provenance, unless a matching portion of the wall can be traced.(8)

When comparing Tables IV and VIII it is apparent that only a limited number of scenes usually found on the walls of private tombs are represented on the walls of temples, and in view of what has been said above regarding the material and technique employed, the chances of misattribution should therefore be reduced accordingly. In that the decoration of the walls of the temples or chapels built for the Aten at Thebes, el-Amarna and elsewhere do not conform to the pattern characteristic for the decoration of any other temple, its main features have been laid out in a separate table (Table V) to facilitate comparison with decoration found on other monuments at el-Amarna (see below).

Among the various scenes that decorate the walls of the tombs of private persons, only representations of the royal family, soldiers, foreigners and processions reflect the decoration of the temples.(9)

Representations of royalty

The most common picture of the reigning king in the Eighteenth dynasty tombs features the sovereign shown twice seated on either side of the doorway leading from the hall to the inner chamber(s) of the tomb.(10) The king sits on his throne in a kiosk, most frequently with the tomb owner bringing gifts, with scenes relating to his career as an official of the king on the adjoining portions of the walls. The scene with the king is always executed on a large scale, taking up the entire height of the decorated part of the wall. Scenes of this kind, with the king receiving attention from subordinates, are not to be found in temples, where the king is shown either actively performing various rituals, or receiving gifts, insignia or purification, but always from some higher authority, *i.e.* gods or goddesses.

On the other hand, the representation of the reigning king performing rituals before divinities is a subject which occurs sporadically in Theban private tombs. Where the divinity in question is one of the gods who normally have a temple of their own or are associated with the cult of other gods, cohabitating in their temples, there is nothing in the iconography of the scene which sets apart representations in tombs from those in temples.(11) If on the other hand the divinity is one of those not generally adored in a cult temple,(12) the scene is likely to belong on the walls of a tomb. In principle the option maybe a royal or a private tomb in both instances.

From an iconographical point of view representations of the deceased and/or deified kings in temples bear a certain resemblance to their counterparts on tomb walls. Rows of (statues of?) deceased kings such as those shown in the Festival Hall of Tuthmosis III at Karnak(13) and the mortuary temples of Ḥatshepsut,(14) Ramesses II(15) and III(16) are not unlike rows of kings seen in Ramessid private tombs.(17) If the context is descernible it will be seen that in temples the king responsible for the decoration is the main personage presiding over the representation, whereas in the private tombs it is the tomb owner who offers to the rows of deceased royalty.(18)

Representations of deceased royal persons other than the 'rows of kings and queens' are in the private tombs at Thebes mainly those of Amenophis I and/or Aḥmosi Nefertere shown with the tomb owner adoring or presenting gifts.(19) Most often the king and queen are seated on a throne, sometimes in a kiosk.(20) In the temples there is a greater choice of postures in the representations of deceased kings, but the main difference in the scene is that another royal person, rather than a private individual, performs the rituals in front of the deceased king. It should perhaps be noted that deceased royalties occur as such other than in their respective mortuary temples, for instance on the walls of the temple of Karnak, and Amenophis III represented himself as a god in his temple at Soleb while he was still living. A king offering to a deified predecessor(?) occurs only once in a private tomb.(21) This exception comes from a period of revision of conventional ideas in tomb decoration, and the idea was not generally followed up.

Scenes showing a young king or prince being suckled occur in private tombs as well as in temples, although not very frequently in the period with which we are concerned. The substantial difference between the representations is that in the temples the prince/king is always suckled by a goddess,(22) whereas in the tombs it is the wife or mother of the tomb owner who, as nurse to the royal children, was depicted in this capacity on the tomb wall.(23) There are admittedly two instances in the private tombs of a deity suckling a king, but from an iconographical point of view they are totally different, the goddess in question being a snake.(24) In the scenes in the tombs, reflecting a situation from real life, the infant sits on the lap of the nurse. In the temples on the other hand, where the intended message of the scene is purely ritualistic, the king is standing, his mouth being level with the breast of the goddess who is feeding him.

Where the evidence is fragmentary, and the figure of the person having the royal child on the lap cannot be identified, a representation of a male tutor with his royal charge may be in question. This motif occurs in a number of Theban tombs,(25) but never in temples, the reason being again the purpose of the decoration.

Representations of foreigners and soldiers

Scenes depicting foreigners in private tombs are of two kinds. Either they show tribute bringers coming to Egypt on a peaceful errand, portrayed on the walls of tombs belonging to viziers, governors or viceroys deputizing for the king, or the foreigners are prisoners of war being taken to Egypt to symbolize the king's victory. Tribute bringers occur only in tombs, not in temples, and defeated foreigners in tombs seem on present evidence to be restricted to the Memphite tomb of Ḥaremḥab. In the temples foreigners are shown on the vast areas of walls and pylons recording battles in foreign countries, or they are depicted after their defeat, being grasped by the hair by the king or led to the god, to whom the king attributes his victory. The only instance where foreigners are shown in a non-military context is in the reliefs at Deir el-Baḥri commemorating the expedition of Hatshepsut to the land of Punt.

Rows of bound prisoners surmounting 'name rings' mentioning foreign cities, or foreigners similarly shackled, frequently decorate the base of the king's throne, as shown in tombs as well as in temples. It is thus only when dealing with these symbolic representations of foreigners, or rows of prisoners of war, that there is a choice of provenance, and, as has been explained above, only if it is a question of a scene executed in relief. An important point to stress, however, is that any Ramessid representation is likely to belong to a temple. On the basis of present evidence such scenes appear to occur only in tombs of Eighteenth dynasty date.(26)

This also applies to scenes involving soldiers.(27) In tombs these come to an end at Thebes during the reign of Tuťankhamūn, at Saqqâra in the tomb of Ḥaremḥab. In temples the army is naturally present in battle scenes, and is thus linked with representations of foreigners, or in public processions, such as those taking place at the feasts of various gods. The army was also involved in the various non-military activities of Ḥatshepsut, depicted in her temple at Deir el-Baḥri. In the tombs at Thebes only the peaceful side of the soldiers' life is shown, the recruits being lined up for review or being present in tribute scenes. Again viceroys and governors, and also army scribes, have these scenes depicted in their tombs in connection with the record of their office or daily activities. Problems of attribution may thus arise where a fragment may stem from a tomb as well as from a temple, *i.e.* mainly where soldiers are lined up to accompany the presentation of tribute or in festival parades, and only if the representation cannot be dated to the Ramessid period.

Representations of musicians

With the exception of the Aten chapels to be discussed below, representations of musicians are not very frequent in temples, compared with the numerous examples from private tombs. The instruments shown are few,(28) and there is in fact no evidence of the existence of temple orchestras corresponding to the secular orchestras shown in the tombs. The groups of musicians with lutes depicted on the walls of the Luxor temple during the procession of the sacred boats at the Feast of Opet(29) are more likely to reflect an aspect of secular music than of religious music, but in that it is depicted on a temple wall it must be taken into consideration. At present it is a unique example. Temple music proper seems to have been restricted to vocal music accompanied by clapping and/or sistra, or consisted of a song performed by a harpist to his own accompaniment. The extant examples from temples are chiefly of Eighteenth dynasty date, but the material may not be representative. Similar scenes occur in private tombs of both Eighteenth dynasty and Ramessid date. Military music, including drummers and trumpeters, occurs in the orchestras defined above. Again the tombs provide examples from the Eighteenth dynasty,(30) the temples covering also the Ramessid period.

The decoration of Amarna temples as compared with contemporary tombs

Since Amarna art is so unmistakably characteristic its problems of attribution will be discussed in a separate paragraph. Fragments of tombs from el-Amarna itself are in museum collections.(31) In addition, certain tombs, now fragmentary, from the necropolis at Saqqâra(32) display characteristics of Amarna art, and a discussion is therefore relevant here.

In the Amarna Period(33) the types of decoration on the walls of tombs and temples overlap more than at any other period. Evidence from temples is as yet unusually fragmentary in that the tens of thousands of decorated blocks from the temples of the Aten at el-Amarna,(34) Karnak,(35) Luxor,(36) Madâmûd,(37) Memphis,(38) and possibly other places as well(39) were re-used in later buildings and have therefore become thoroughly, though not completely mixed up.

To distinguish between a fragment from an Aten temple and a fragment from a Memphite tomb or any other dressed fragment, the dimensions of the block may be decisive.(40) If it belongs to the category of blocks now known as *talatât*,(41) measuring ca. 52 x 22 x 26cm, and decorated on either the long or the shorter side,(42) there is little doubt that it came from one of the Aten chapels. Some of the blocks in collections have had part of the back cut away to make the block easier to handle, but the dimensions of the decorated surface are still characteristic. Blocks found at Hermopolis and originally belonging to the buildings at el-Amarna are generally cut in limestone,(43) as are other blocks from the north, whereas the Luxor, Karnak and Madâmûd blocks are with a few exceptions made of sandstone.(44)

The decoration on the walls of most of the tombs and all the temples in this period is in relief.(45) Both the temple and the royal palace were depicted on the walls of the tombs as well as on the walls of the temples, and even as the main subjects, so that in the case of fragments from tombs, and all the material from the temples, it is sometimes rather difficult to define the context of a scene.(46)

Several classifications of the scenes on the scattered blocks of the Aten temples have been made, some using isolated parts of scenes,(47) others attempting a more general enumeration.(48) In our Table V the classification has been adapted to the themes forming the main subject of this study, *i.e.* those in the private tombs, but due to the nature of the available material some items, *e.g.* the *talatât* and similar blocks, have had to be considered separately from their original context.

Because of the doubtful statistical value of the evidence from the sites as a whole, it is only relevant, within Table V, to compare the subjects represented on the blocks from Hermopolis and those from Karnak, and to compare the outcome with the subjects represented in the tombs. There is in fact only one striking difference in the themes depicted on the two groups of blocks: on the Hermopolis blocks scenes of the *ḥb-sd* are missing, not only those showing the king in the characteristic garment under the rays of the sun, but also those with the procession of the king in his carrying chair.(49)

A discussion of the private tombs at various sites will be found below, but a few remarks will be made here regarding the decoration of the private tombs at el-Amarna in relation to the decoration of the temples. Comparisons of subjects depicted have frequently been made when trying to reconstruct scenes out of the blocks from the temples. Most of the scenes on the walls of the temples are indeed reflected on the walls of the tombs: the royal family offering to the Aten; the king and queen in their chariots; the interior of the temple and of the palace; the military escort; minor officials and others adoring and bowing; musicians and the rejoicing crowd. Scenes not to be found in the tombs are - not unexpectedly - the king in the *ḥb-sd* and in coronation and foundation rites, and the king slaying an enemy, themes which conventionally belonged in religious buildings. Scenes not found in the temple are those focussed on a private person, offering or being rewarded, and representations of arts and crafts. The reason for the many royal scenes in private tombs is due to the status of the king and the royal family at this period, but it does not explain the influence of the decoration of private tombs on the walls of the temples (domestic scenes; private houses (admittedly the palace); crowds in the streets &c.) This requires a separate study which is not within the scope of the present work.

The Amarna Royal Tomb as compared with contemporary private tombs

The similarities between the wall-decoration of private and royal tombs will be discussed below. The decoration, though not the architecture, of the Royal Tomb at el-Amarna(50) is totally unlike any other royal tomb, and mention will therefore be made of it in connection with the aspects of Amarna wall-decoration mentioned above. The decoration of the Royal Tomb is very similar to the main themes in the private tombs and in the temples: the royal family worshiping the Aten being the main theme, with accompanying rows of courtiers, soldiers and foreigners. Desert animals greeting the rising sun form another detail that may be seen elsewhere at el-Amarna, but another theme emphasized in the Royal Tomb is unusual: mourning ceremonies for one of the princesses, occupying three large portions of the walls of rooms *alpha* and *gamma*. Apart from an isoloated instance in the tomb of Ḥuya (see below) nothing similar is to be found elsewhere at el-Amarna, and the only parallels are the details with the mourning women common to private tombs in the Eighteenth dynasty and the reign of Ḥaremḥab. The idea of representing the deceased during the funerary rites is not alien for a private tomb, but the entire conception of the scenes in the Royal Tomb and the fact that it is a royal, not a private tomb, is unique.

The decoration of houses as compared with the decoration of private tombs

Evidence of wall-decoration from houses and palaces is extremely fragmentary, in that comparatively little has been preserved of secular buildings, which were largely built of mud brick. The subjects of decoration laid out in Table VI must therefore be considered as incomplete.(51) The quality of the surviving material is sometimes so poor that it did not survive the initial discovery,(52) and few pieces found their way to museum collections. In that fragments consist chiefly of paintings on mud plaster, and for reasons explained below, any fragment, even if only a scrap, is nevertheless relevant for comparison in a study dealing with painted Theban tombs in a fragmentary state.

The sites of relevance as regards New Kingdom material are Malqata on the west bank of Thebes, the neighbouring village of Deir el-Medîna and the town of el-Amarna, the most spectacular pieces coming from the latter site.(53)

The close relation between the decoration of tombs and houses has previously been pointed out.(54) Here we are mainly concerned with the differences. The decoration of the royal palace at el-Amarna was executed in relief and painting alike, the relief scenes showing the royal family offering to the Aten, the wall-paintings featuring marsh landscapes, desert animals, or the royal family at leisure. The offering scenes, a unique scene with servants (painting),(55) and a detail with foreigners forming a border on a pavement (56) have parallels in the tombs and temples, desert animals being also depicted in relief in the Aten temples. In the official residence of one of the high officials there was an altar showing Akhenaten and Nefertiti worshiping the Aten,(57) and in one of the workmen's houses there is a close parallel to the banquet orchestras depicted on the walls of private tombs and in representations of the royal palace on the walls of the temple.(58)

Some of the themes displayed in the secular buildings at el-Amarna reflect the decoration found in the palace at Malqata: foreigners (on the pavement),(59) dancing Bes figures,(60) desert animals and birds, (61) details which, apart from the Bes figures, might well occur on the walls or ceilings of a Theban private tomb. There was at Malqata even a scene showing the king receiving foreigners, which must have been very much like an Eighteenth dynasty tomb painting.(62)

At Deir el-Medîna the dancing Bes figures are repeated,(63) and there are pictures of women in private situations,(64) which in spite of their iconographical similarity to the nursing scenes in the tombs are much more intimate, and in fact totally different. In one of the houses was found a painting showing part of a dancing woman playing the double oboe.(65) The context is lost, but the Bes figure tattooed on her thigh may place her either in the realm of women where this god was significant (conception, birth, &c.), or it may designate her status as a musician in some way. A representation of a person in a canoe adorned with the head of a duck(?) may also be related to the world of women.(66) In one instance a motif is common to tomb and house: a representation of the deified King Amenophis I.(67)

Most of the wall-decoration of the houses at Deir el-Medîna was painted, but lintels and jambs of stone show scenes that are identical to those in tombs: offering bringers; the deceased with his family; the deceased adoring. In such sculpted scenes there would in theory be nothing to distinguish fragments from a house (lintels or jambs) from those deriving from the walls of a sculpted tomb, but for the curious circumstance that all tombs at Deir el-Medîna have painted, not sculpted wall-decoration. The tombs too had jambs and lintels of stone, and the scenes depicted here are similar to those represented on jambs and lintels from the houses.

The decoration of royal tombs as compared with the decoration of private tombs

With the exception of the aforementioned Royal Tomb at el-Amarna it is rarely difficult to distinguish the wall-decoration of a private tomb from that of a royal tomb. The latter is largely concerned with the fate of the deceased, and, apart from large-scale representations of the king in the company of various gods, the several 'books' of the Netherworld,(68) listed in Table VII and the Litany of Rēᶜ were chosen to adorn the chambers.

The Eighteenth dynasty tombs and those of the Ramessid period differ, not only in their plan, but also in their style and subject of decoration. The Eighteenth dynasty tombs have sketched(69) or painted decoration, whereas the Ramessid tombs include relief cut in the rock or modelled on a layer of gypsum plaster. In the Eighteenth dynasty the theme is chiefly scenes from the Book of Imi-duat, and the king with the gods, the latter appearing for the first time on square pillars in the tomb of Amenophis II. The king with the gods henceforward becomes a standard motif, also in the Ramessid tombs. The king and gods are also shown on the upper part of the walls of the shafts. Characteristic for the Ramessid tombs is the Litany of Rēᶜ on the walls of the entrance corridor, and the Books of gates and Caverns spread over the walls of the inner chambers, with extracts from the Imi-duat, Book of Aker and Book of the Cow.(70) The ceilings have painted decoration with various astronomical subjects.

Of prime interest, in comparing the decoration of the private and royal tombs of the period, are the subjects which occur in both. These can be misattributed when in a fragmentary state.

A representation of the king may be difficult to place, in that the subject is by no means rare in private tombs. In royal tombs, the king is normally only present in his own tomb,(71) and as he would be shown several times it should be possible to trace the provenance of a fragment with some certainty.(72) The same applies to representations of the queen. The only example of a queen shown on the walls of her husband's tomb are a sketched figure in the tomb of Tuthmosis III and the representation of the queen in the tomb of Ay.

Funerary ceremonies in royal tombs are restricted to the Opening of the Mouth. If the royal mummy is recognizable, it should not be confounded with a scene from a private tomb. The Fields of Iaru occurs only once in a royal tomb, that of Ramesses III,(73) a curious tomb with several scenes unique for a royal tomb: scenes of provisions, tools and weapons, kitchen equipment, and even two harpists.

The tomb of Ay displays some equally atypical scenes, which may perhaps reflect the non-royal origin of the owner: fishing and fowling, spearing a hippopotamus,(74) and scenes from the Book of the Dead. Ay's wife accompanies him in some of the scenes, a detail reminiscent of the tradition of the private tombs. The scenes from this tomb and those from the tomb of Ramesses III should always be kept in mind when fragments of the aforementioned subjects are being considered.

A detail from the Book of the Dead should be pointed out here, as an example in a fragmentary state might perhaps be wrongly placed: four foreigners representing the races of the world as then known.(75) In a fragmentary state the figures might easily be mistaken for representations of tribute-bringers on the walls of private tombs.(76)

The decoration of private tombs at various sites

In the preceding pages the various possibilities for the misattribution of fragments of private tombs to other monuments with wall decoration have been outlined. The subject depicted and the technique of decoration (relief/painting) are the main criteria for deciding the provenance of a fragment. Within the private tombs we must now attempt to be more precise as to the site from which a fragment of a tomb wall might stem, since we are in the study of Lost Tombs concerned only with Theban tombs, and in particular those with painted decoration.

The principal subjects depicted on the walls of New Kingdom private tombs are laid out in Table VIII.(77) The most important sites are Thebes,(78) el-Amarna(79) and Saqqâra,(80) the provincial cemeteries with a few exceptions (el-Kâb, Asswân and Nagaᶜ Bogaᶜ) yielding surprisingly scanty evidence.(81)

We shall now briefly examine the similarities and differences in the decoration of the tombs in these areas, in particular Thebes and Saqqâra, as the tombs at el-Amarna are easily distinguishable from the rest due to the subjects depicted and the style of the representations. It should be borne in mind that the majority of the New Kingdom tombs from Saqqâra date from the end of the Eighteenth and the Nineteenth dynasties, and although the change in tomb decoration may have been instigated at Thebes, with Saqqâra adapting more slowly, it is in fact the Ramessid tombs at Thebes with which the majority of the Memphite tombs, for the most part represented by isolated blocks, should be compared.(82)

Representations of the reigning king are extremely common in the Theban tombs of the Eighteenth dynasty,(83) and also at el-Amarna, but only one instance seems to have survived at Saqqâra.(84) Deceased kings occur frequently at Thebes, but there is evidence of a similar subject at Saqqâra.(85) Queens are shown at Thebes and el-Amarna, and once at Saqqâra.(86) Royal children occur at Thebes and el-Amarna, and once at el-Kâb.(87)

Foreigners and the military are represented at all three major sites, and so is the deceased in office. Typically Theban are scenes with the deceased fishing and fowling in a canoe and hunting in the desert, subjects confined to the Eighteenth dynasty.(88) The fishing and fowling scenes are in Ramessid tombs at Thebes replaced by representations of the deceased fishing and fowling or netting birds from a chair at the bank of the river or lake.(89) Servants netting fish and fowl seem to have had a different significance.(90) They occur in the Eighteenth dynasty at Thebes, once at el-Amarna,(91) and possibly once at Saqqâra.(92)

Most other scenes of the so-called 'daily life' type(93) are to be found at all three major sites, some of them occurring in the provinces as well. The same applies to representations of the deceased offering to various gods,(94) whether or not these are depicted, and the common scene with rows of offering bringers.

As far as funerary ceremonies are concerned, with one exception(95) the voyage to Abydos is unique to Thebes, and the breaking of the pots seems to occur almost entirely at Saqqâra.(96) Excerpts from the Book of the Dead are to be found at both sites, and also at some of the provincial sites. The only reference to conventional funerary beliefs at el-Amarna occurs in the tomb of Ḥuya.(97)

In the subjects depicted in private tombs there are thus some important differences at the various sites, but on the other hand several subjects are common to both Thebes and Saqqâra. The technique of decoration, however, sets some of the Theban tombs apart, and possibilities of misattribution can be further reduced.

At Thebes the majority of the tombs are rock-cut. Where the local rock was of good quality, relief could be cut, otherwise the walls were covered with mud plaster and painted.(98) At el-Amarna most of the tombs have sculpted decoration,(99) and at Saqqâra all tombs discovered so far are also sculpted.(100) The Amarna tombs being easily identified, the choice of provenance for a fragment of wall-decoration with a scene belonging in a tomb lies chiefly between Thebes and Saqqâra, although some provincial cemeteries must also be considered.(101) According to the size and shape of a block it may be possible to determine whether a fragment comes from a rock-cut tomb (in that case presumably Thebes), or from an open-court tomb built of mud brick with a casing of limestone slabs, *i.e.* a Saqqâra tomb. The style of relief in the Saqqâra tombs is characteristic, and through comparison with reliefs known to have come from Saqqâra(102) it should eventually not be difficult to distinguish a Theban from a Memphite relief.

As regards tombs with painted decoration the choice is extremely limited and the problems of attribution therefore simplified. It is indeed exceedingly rare to find examples of tombs of New Kingdom date with painted decoration outside Thebes.(103) At Asswân, a Ramessid tomb forms one of the substantial exceptions. The tomb of Kakemet,(104) partly rock-cut, partly built of mud brick must surely have been decorated by Theban artists, as the style and subjects are identical to those found at Thebes. Another painted tomb comparable to a Theban tomb was once at Nagaʿ Bogaʿ,(105) and yet another at ʿAnîba.(106) The interesting example from Syria, note (81) above, should also be mentioned here.

In the light of what has been discussed above, it is reasonable to assume that a fragment of painted mud plaster which does not represent any of the subjects depicted on the walls of secular buildings or royal tombs, and which cannot be attributed to any of the very few temples or chapels with painted decoration, almost certainly derives from a Theban tomb.

SUBJECT	PM INDEX THEBES	DATE
KING:		
performing ritual before god	Ia,b,d,f-i,p,q	Dyn. XVIII-XIX
crowned	Ie,l,VIIIg	Dyn. XVIII-XX
purified	In	Ḥatshepsut-Ramesses IX
receiving offerings	Io	Dyn. XVIII-XX
deified	Iw	Amenophis I-Ramesses II
Amenophis I deceased	Iw	Ramessid<a>
with captives	Ic	Dyn. XVIII-XX
suckled by goddess	Iu	Ḥatshepsut-Ramesses IV
protected by god	Im	Amenophis II-Ramesses II
hunting in desert	(Iu)	Ramesses III<b>
cult statues of living king	It	Ḥatshepsut-Ramessid
rows of deceased kings		Ḥatshepsut-Ramesses III
QUEEN accompanying king	IIb	Ḥatshepsut-Ramesses III
ROYAL CHILDREN with one or both parents	IIa,b	Ramessid
HIGH OFFICIALS	IIIa-b,g	Ramessid<c>
MINOR OFFICIALS	IIIf	Ḥatshepsut-Ramessid
MUSICIANS AND DANCERS	IIIc-e	Ḥatshepsut-Ramessid
FOREIGNERS	IV	Dyn. XVIII-XX<d>
MILITARY	V	Dyn. XVIII-XX<d>
DIVINITIES	VI,IX (XIIa)	Dyn. XVIII-XX
PROCESSIONS	VIIIa-b	Dyn. XVIII-XX
RITUAL	VIIIc	Dyn. XVIII-XX
FOUNDATION CEREMONIES	VIIId	Tuthmosis III-Ramessid
ḤB-SD	VIIIe	Amenophis I-III
ANIMALS, sacrificial and sacred	X	Dyn. XVIII-XX<e>
EXPEDITIONS, not military		Ḥatshepsut, Tuthmosis III<f>

<a> only two instances
<b> only Medinet Habu
<c> mainly priests
<d> mainly in battle
<e> cf. PM index
<f> Botanical Garden, Deir el-Baḥri

TABLE IV showing a selection of scenes from New Kingdom temples

SUBJECT	MATERIAL	SITE
KING performing ritual	limestone	Heliopolis <a>
	limestone	Hermopolis
	sandstone	Madâmûd
	sandstone	Karnak
	sandstone	Luxor
in *ḥb-sd*	limestone	? <b>
	sandstone	Madâmûd
	sandstone	Karnak
in csrrying chair	sandstone	Madâmûd
	sandstone	Karnak
in chariot	limestone	Hermopolis
	sandstone	Karnak
in royal bark	limestone	Memphis<c>
	sandstone	Karnak
in coronation ceremony(?)	limestone	Hermopolis<d>
in foundation ceremony(?)	sandstone	Karnak<e>
slaying enemy	sandstone	Karnak<f>
QUEEN accompanying king	limestone	Heliopolis <a><g>
		Memphis<h>
	limestone	Hermopolis
	sandstone	Karnak
alone	sandstone	Madâmûd<i>
	sandstone	Karnak<j>
PRINCESSES accompanying one or both parents	limestone	Hermopolis
	sandstone	Madâmûd<k>
	sandstone	Karnak
in purification	limestone	Hermopolis<l>
alone in processions	sandstone	Karnak<m>
MILITARY incl. chariots	limestone	Heliopolis <a>
	limestone	Memphis
	limestone	Hermopolis
	sandstone	Madâmûd
	sandstone	Karnak
	limestone	Armant
FOREIGNERS, male	limestone	Hermopolis
	sandstone	Karnak<n>
female	sandstone	Karnak<o>
HIGH OFFICIALS (high priest)	sandstone	Karnak
MINOR OFFICIALS	limestone	Memphis
	limestone	Hermopolis
	sandstone	Karnak
PROCESSIONS, figures in	limestone	Hermopolis
	sandstone	Madâmûd
	sandstone	Karnak

TABLE V showing a selection of scenes represented on the walls of the chapels of the Aten (continued)

SUBJECT	MATERIAL	SITE
PERSONS adoring or bowing	sandstone	Madâmûd
	sandstone	Karnak
bringing offerings	sandstone	Madâmûd
	sandstone	Karnak
MUSICIANS	limestone	Hermopolis
	sandstone	Karnak
	sandstone	Luxor
WOMEN rejoicing	limestone	Hermopolis
DOMESTIC CHORES (cooking, sweeping &c.)	limestone	Heliopolis <a>
	limestone	Hermopolis
	sandstone	Madâmûd
	sandstone	Karnak
AGRICULTURE	limestone	Hermopolis
	sandstone	Karnak
ANIMALS, sacrificial	limestone	Heliopolis <a>
	limestone	Memphis<p>
	sandstone	Madâmûd
	sandstone	Karnak
in desert	limestone	Hermopolis
	sandstone	Karnak
BUTCHERING	sandstone	Madâmûd
	sandstone	Karnak
SHIPS (not royal)	limestone	Heliopolis <a>
	limestone	Hermopolis

<a> Cf. n. 39 to this chapter
<b> Fitzwilliam Museum block.
<c> Petrie, *Riqqeh and Memphis VI*, pl. 54, n.6
<d> Cooney, *Amarna Reliefs*, no. 5.
<e> *Akhenaten Temple Project*, 18:6.
<f> *Kêmi* 20, 1970, p. 190, fig. 2, cf. fig. 3; *MDAIAK* 22, 1967, pl. XVIII a,b.; *Orientalia* 42, 1973, pl. XXXVII(1).
<g> (queen? context unknown).
<h> *Riqqeh and Memphis VI*, pl. 54, no. 9.
<i> cartouche of queen next to those of the Aten.
<j> 'Nefertiti pillars'.
<k> unnamed, with female.
<l> Hamburg cat. no. 35.
<m> '*msw nsw*'.
<n> also as throne ornament.
<o> as throne ornament.
<p> *Riqqeh and Memphis VI*, pl. 54

SUBJECT	TECHNIQUE	SITE	DATE	COMMENT
ROYAL FAMILY posing	painting	el-Amarna	Amenophis IV	palace
adoring god	relief	el-Amarna	Amenophis IV	residen
	relief	el-Amarna	Amenophis IV	palace
KING AND PRINCESS(?)	relief	Deir el-Medîna	Dyn. XIX	<a>
AMENOPHIS I deceased	painting	Deir el-Medîna	Dyn. XIX	house
KING receiving foreigners	painting	Malqata	Amenophis III	palace
FOREIGNERS	painting	el-Amarna	Amenophis IV	palace
	painting	Malqata	Amenophis III	palace
OWNER and family	relief	Deir el-Medîna	Dyn. XIX	house<b
adoring gods	relief	Deir el-Medîna	Dyn. XIX	lintel
adoring cartouche	painting	Deir el-Medîna	Dyn. XIX	<c>
WOMEN nursing child	relief	el-Amarna	Amenophis IV	<d>
	painting	Deir el-Medîna	Dyn. XVIII-XIX	<e>
other	painting	Malqata	Amenophis III	palace<
MUSICIANS	painting	el-Amarna	Amenophis IV	house
	painting	Deir el-Medîna	Dyn. XIX	house
SERVANTS	painting	el-Amarna	Amenophis IV	palace
OFFERING BRINGERS	relief	Deir el-Medîna	Dyn. XIX	<g>
DIVINITIES: Bes dancing	painting	el-Amarna	Amenophis IV	house
	painting	Deir el-Medîna	Dyn. XVIII	houses
	painting	Malqata	Amenophis III	palace
Thoueris	painting	el-Amarna	Amenophis IV	house
Ḥatḥor nursing Ḥorus?	painting	Deir el-Medîna	Dyn. XVIII-XIX	house
HUNTING in the desert	painting	Malqata	Amenophis III	palace
BULL in papyrus	painting	Malqata	Amenophis III	palace
CALVES	painting	el-Amarna	Amenophis IV	palace
MARSH SCENE	painting	el-Amarna	Amenophis IV	palace
with person in canoe	painting	Deir el-Medîna	midDyn. XVIII	house<h
BIRDS: ducks	painting	el-Amarna	Amenophis IV	palace
	painting	Malqata	Amenophis III	palace
geese	painting	el-Amarna	Amenophis IV	palace
vultures	painting	Malqata	Amenophis III	palace
FISH	painting	Malqata	Amenophis III	palace
WHEAT AND FLOWERS	relief	el-Amarna	Amenophis IV	palace<

<a> Bruyère, *Rapport (1934-1935)*, fig. 122,p. 244.
<b> house: *ibid.*, fig. 12, pp. 44, 273.
<c> on false door: *ibid.*,pp. 196-7.
<d> found in palace *[sic]*: Brooklyn Museum 37.405.
<e> house. Cf. 'Ḥatḥor' below and references in the text of this chapter
<f> palace: cf. Tytus, *op. cit.*, fig. 10.
<g> Bruyère, *op. cit.*, fig. 12, p. 273.
<h> house: *ibid.*, p. 286, fig. 157.
<i> palace: *JEA* 22, 1936, pl. XX,3.

TABLE VI showing the subjects decorating the walls of houses

SUBJECT	SITE	DATE
KING and gods (embracing, leading &c.)	KV	Amenophis II-Ramesses VI<a>
	QV	Ramesses III
offering to gods	KV	Ḥaremḥab-Ramesses IX<a>
	QV	Ramesses III
receiving life &c. from gods	KV	Amenophis II-Tutʿankhamun<b>
with tree-goddess	KV	Tuthmosis III
fishing/fowling	KV	Ay
QUEEN accompanying king	KV	Tuthmosis III, Ay
with divinities	KV	Tausert
	QV	Ramesses II-III<a>
with tree-goddess	QV	Ramessid<c>
PRINCES	QV	Ramesses III
PRINCESS	KV	Tuthmosis III
FUNERARY CEREMONIES	KV	Tutʿankhamun-Ramesses III
LITANY OF RĒʿ	KV	Sethos I-Ramesses IV
IMI-DUAT	KV	Tuthmosis I-Ramesses IX
BOOK OF THE DEAD	KV	Ay-Ramesses IX<d>
BOOK OF GATES	KV	Haremhab-Ramesses VIII<a>
	QV	Ramesses II-III
BOOK OF CAVERNS	KV	Tausert-Ramesses IX<d>
	QV	?Tomb no. 36
BOOK OF AKER	KV	Ramesses III-VIII<d>
BOOK OF THE COW	KV	Sethos I-Ramesses VI
ASTRONOMICAL CEILING	KV	Sethos I-Ramesses IX
FIELDS OF IARU	KV	Ramesses III<e>
PROVISIONS	KV	Ramesses III

<a> *passim*
<b> also Merneptaḥ-Siptaḥ
<c> tomb no. 52
<d> infrequent
<e> rooms K and W.2

TABLE VII showing the subjects depicted on the walls of royal tombs

SUBJECT	PM INDEX THEBES	SITE	DATE
KING			
receiving gifts	1a	Thebes	Ḥat.-Amenophis III
		ʿAnîba	Ramesses VI
		Qasr Ibrîm	Tuth.-Amenophis II, Ramesses II
receiving foreigners and tribute		el-Amarna	Amenophis IV
	1b	Thebes	Tuth. III-Tutʿankhamun
receiving produce	1c	Thebes	Tuth. III-Amenophis IV
rewarding or appointing		el-Amarna	Amenophis IV
	1d	Thebes	Amenophis II-Ram. V
banqueting		el-Amarna	Amenophis IV
receiving bouquet	1e	Thebes	Ḥat.-Amenophis IV<a>
hunting in the desert	2g	Thebes	Amenophis II
adored as living	1f	Thebes	Tuth. III-Ram. IV
accompanied by deceased in ritual	1g	Thebes	Tuth. III-Sethos II
before divinities or deified kings		el-Amarna	Amenophis IV
	2b	Thebes	Amenophis III-Merneptah
		Qasr Ibrîm	Amenophis II
enthroned or standing	2a	Thebes	Tuth. III-Ramessid
		el-Kâb	Ramesses III-IX<b>
protected	2c	Thebes	Ḥat.-Ramesses V
before barks	2e	Thebes	Ramesses II-IX
cult statues of living king	2e	Thebes	Ḥat.-Amenophis III<c>
in funeral procession	2e	Thebes	Tuthmosis III-IV
in festivals	2e	Thebes	Ramesses II-IX<d>
royal barks	2f	Thebes	Tuth. III?-Ramesses II
Amenophis I deceased	3a1	Thebes	Ramessid<e>
other deceased kings	3a2,3b-c	Thebes	Ramessid<f>
		Saqqâra	Tutʿankhamun/Ḥaremḥab-Ramessid
child king suckled or nursed	4b	Thebes	Ḥat.-Amenophis III
in window of appearances		el-Amarna	Amenophis IV
		Thebes	Amenophis IV
in carrying chair		el-Amarna	Amenophis IV
QUEEN accompanying king		el-Amarna	Amenophis IV
	4a	Thebes	Ḥat.-Ramessid
rewarding		el-Amarna	Amenophis IV
	4a	Thebes	Ay
banqueting		el-Amarna	Amenophis IV
before divinities		el-Amarna	Amenophis IV
Aḥmosi Nefertere deceased	3a,b	Thebes	Aḥmosis-Ramessid
other deceased queens	3a2,3c	Thebes	Ramessid<g>
ROYAL CHILDREN with parents		el-Amarna	Amenophis IV
	4d	Thebes	Amenophis III
with nurses &c.	4c,d	Thebes	Tuthmosis III-IV
		el-Kâb	Dyn. XVIII<h>
deceased	4d	Thebes	Ramessid

TABLE VIII showing the subjects depicted on the walls of private tombs (continued)

SUBJECT	PM INDEX THEBES	SITE	DATE
FOREIGNERS		Saqqâra	Ḥaremḥab
		el-Amarna	Amenophis IV<i>
	5	Thebes	Amenophis I-Ramesses IX
MILITARY		Saqqâra	late XVIII-Ram<j>
		el-Amarna	Amenophis IV
	6	Thebes	Amenophis I-Tut.
DECEASED as official		el-Amarna	Amenophis IV
	7,8	Thebes	Amenophis I - Ramesses IX<k>
rewarded		Saqqâra	
		el-Amarna	Amenophis IV
	9	Thebes	Amenophis III-Ramesses V
		ʿAnîba	Ramesses IV
hunting in the desert	20	Thebes	Amosis/Amenophis I?-Amenophis II
		el-Kâb	Sebkḥotpe III?
fishing/fowling in canoe	17a	Thebes	Tuthmosis I-Amenophis III<l>
		el-Kâb	Sebkḥotpe III?
fishing/fowling/netting from land	17c	Thebes	Sethos I-Ram. III<m>
SERVANTS netting fish and fowl		Saqqâra?<n>	
		el-Amarna	Amenophis IV
	17e	Thebes	Amenophis I-III<o>
AGRICULTURE performed by labourers, incl. vintage		Saqqâra	Amenophis III-Ḥaremḥab <p>
		el-Amarna	Amenophis IV
	15,16	Thebes	Amosis-Merneptah<q>
		ʿAnîba	
		Bahriya	Dyn. XIX
DOMESTIC ANIMALS, incl. butchery		Saqqâra	Ramesses II
		el-Amarna	Amenophis IV
	18,19a-b	Thebes	Amenophis I-Ramessid<r>
SHIPS for transport of goods		Saqqâra<s>	
	10a	Thebes	Ḥat.-Ramesses II
DOMESTIC CHORES		Saqqâra	Amenophis IV
	13c,41a	Thebes	Tuth. III-Ram. II
		ʿAnîba	
		Bahriya	Dyn. XIX
BANQUET SCENES, incl. musicians and sitting groups at festivals		Saqqâra	end Dyn. XVIII
		el-Amarna	Amenophis IV<t>
	(24a)	Thebes	Tuth. I-Ram. II<r>
		el-Kâb	Dyn. XVIII
		Bahriya	Dyn. XIX

TABLE VIII (continued)

SUBJECT	PM INDEX THEBES	SITE	DATE
SINGLE HARPIST (or lutist)		Saqqâra	Ramessid<u>
		Thebes	Ḥat.-Ramessid
ARTS AND CRAFTS		Saqqâra	Amenophis IV-Ramessid
		el-Amarna	Amenophis IV
	13a-d	Thebes	Ḥat.-Ramesses IX
		el-Kâb	Sebkḥotpe III?
DECEASED offering to gods not depicted (often w. hymn)		Saqqâra	Sethos I<v>
		Nagaᶜ el-Mashâikh	Merneptaḥ
		el-Amarna	Amenophis IV
	28a-c	Thebes	Tuth. I-Ram. IV
		el-Kâb	Dyn. XVIII
DECEASED (& wife) before gods (excl. tree-goddess and Termuthis) cf. also 'funerary beliefs'		Saqqâra	end XVIII-Ram.II
		Zawiyet el-Mayitîn	Dyn. XVIII-XIX
		D. Durunka	Dyn. XVIII or XIX
		Deir Rifa	New Kingdom
		Abydos	Ramessid
		Rizeiqât	Dyn. XIX or XX
	28d-f	Thebes	Dyn. XVIII-XXI<w>
		el-Kâb	Dyn. XVIII-Ram. IX
		Asswân	Ramessid
		Nagaᶜ Bogaᶜ	Dyn. XVIII-XIX
		ᶜAnîba	Ramesses VI
		Bahriya	Dyn. XIX
TREE-GODDESS		Saqqâra	Ḥaremḥab-Ramessid
		Thebes	Amenophis II-Dyn. XXI<x>
		ᶜAnîba	Dyn. XIX or XX
TERMUTHIS		Thebes	Ḥat.-Ramessid
OFFERING BRINGERS		Saqqâra	Amenophis III-Ramesses II
		Zawiyet el-Mayitîn	Dyn. XVIII or XIX
		Thebes	Dyn. XVIII-Ram.
		el-Kâb	Dyn. XVIII
DECEASED offered to		Saqqâra	Amenophis III-Ramessid
	(34)	Thebes	Dyn. XVIII-Ram.
		el-Kâb	Amosis-Ram. IX
		Bahriya	Dyn. XIX
FUNERARY CEREMONIES		Saqqâra	Amenophis III-Ramessid
		Zawiyet el-Mayitîn	Dyn. XVIII or XIX
		Rizeiqât	Dyn. XIX or XX
		el-Amarna	Amenophis IV <y>

TABLE VIII (continued)

SUBJECT	PM INDEX THEBES	SITE	DATE
FUNERARY CEREMONIES (continued)	10b,31a-b,d-h	Thebes	Amosis-Ram.
		Asswân	Ramessid
		Naga‘ Boga‘	Dyn. XVIII-XIX
		Bahriya	Dyn. XIX
ABYDOS PILGRIMAGE		Saqqâra<z>	Ramesses II
	31c	Thebes	Tuth. I-Dyn.XXI
BREAKING OF THE POTS		Saqqâra	Ḥaremḥab-Ram.
		Thebes<zz>	Ramessid
FUNERARY BELIEFS (Fields of Iaru, weighing of the heart, &c.)		Saqqâra	end Dyn. XVIII-Ramessid
		D. Durunka	Dyn. XVIII or XIX
		Abydos	Dyn. XX
	22,35d,36a-d	Thebes	Ḥat.-Dyn. XXI
		Asswân	Ramessid
		Naga‘ Boga‘	Dyn. XVIII-XIX
		‘Anîba	Ramessid

<a> + one Ramesses II
<b> one only
<c> + one Ramesses II
<d> + one Tuthmosis III
<e> + 2-3 Dyn. XVIII
<f> + 2 Dyn. XVIII
<g> + one Tuthmosis III
<h> Paḥeri
<i> *JARCE* 8 (1968),27
<j> Edinburgh 1961.438
<k> mainly Dyn. XVIII
<l> also TT 217 (Ram. II); TT 23,157,158,216,331 (Ramessid)
<m> also TT 93 (Amenophis II)
<n> Leicester: PM III[2],p.758
<o> also TT 217 (Ram. II)
<p> Karlsruhe 1046?
<q> chiefly Dyn. XVIII
<r> mainly Dyn. XVIII
<s> Cairo 25.6.24.7 and others
<t> royal banquet
<u> East Berlin 20427
<v> Heidelberg 559
<w> rare in Dyn. XVIII
<x> mainly Ramessid
<y> only Ḥuya
<z> only Tia
<zz> only TT 44

TABLE VIII (continued)

3 Theban Private Tombs of the Eighteenth Dynasty: General Lay-out and Distribution of Scenes

The Theban tombs of the Eighteenth dynasty have certain features in common which distinguish them from tombs of other periods and, to some extent, from tombs in other places.(1) Within the tombs of the necropolis from this period there is, however, a great deal of variation in architectural design, distribution of scenes in the room or on the individual walls of the rooms, and the choice of scenes, the latter determined by a number of factors such as the occupation of the tomb owner and the space made available after the cutting of the rooms.

In order to derive any practical benefit from a comparison between the decoration of the tombs one must preferably choose a number of well defined scenes and examine how these motifs were dispersed in tombs of similar architectural design, with due consideration being given to the difference in time between the tombs of the early and late Eighteenth dynasty and the possible influence of the office of the tomb owner on the choice of decoration. In view of the fact that the tombs of Deir el-Medîna form a group apart,(2) they have been left out of this general comparison of tombs.

The tombs chosen for the investigation are those of the so-called 'T-shape', the only consistent type of tomb occurring through the dynasty. Ideally a tomb of this shape should comprise the following elements (excluding the forecourt and burial chamber(s)): 1) a transverse hall; 2) an elongated passage; and 3) an inner room with a niche or statue(s) at the rear wall. Some tombs do not completely conform to this pattern, either intentionally, or because they were left unfinished or are perhaps now destroyed, yet they have been included because the general idea behind the design, emphasized in the decoration, is the same. But in spite of any apparent similarities it must be stressed that there are many tombs which do not come within the category of T-shaped tombs and are totally different, although sometimes the individual scenes may occupy similar positions on the available wall space. For the purpose of the present study of fragmentary material with few plans available it must be kept in mind that there is always a strong possibility that the tomb dealt with is one of the many exceptions to what may cautiously be called the typical Theban tomb.

The scenes chosen for comparison are:

1) Representations of the reigning king in a passive rôle
2) Scenes connected with the office of the tomb owner (bringing in tribute, supervising temple workshops, being installed or rewarded, &c.)
3) The tomb owner offering on braziers, libating or adoring, represented at a large scale
4) The tomb owner fishing and fowling, occasionally combined with hippopotamus hunting
5) Hunting in the desert
6) Agricultural scenes
7) Vintage
8) The funeral procession and rites connected with it
9) The voyage to Abydos
10) Rites before the mummy (Opening of the Mouth)

As so many fragments of wall-decoration were apparently taken from 'banquet scenes' it would be tempting to include these in the study. But they present a problem, particularly when they are in a fragmentary state, as it may be difficult to distinguish between banquet scenes proper (rows of guests with attendants and musicians, pouring of drinks and presentation of unguent, necklaces, &c.) and seated persons being offered to, if only the seated persons survive. Such seated persons may occur almost anywhere in the tomb. Banquet scenes are often, though by no means always, to be found in connection with representations of the Feast of the Valley and the tomb owner offering as in 3) above.

Scenes showing 'offering bringers' have not been included, as they may occur in a number of different situations, such as accompanying the tomb owner libating or offering, in the bringing of produce from the fields or the marshes, in the funeral procession, or alongside a stela, false door or statue. In brief, they seem to be present wherever there was space left.

The positions of stelae and false doors have already been dealt with elsewhere,(3) and they are not immediately relevant for the present study.

In the following pages the tomb is viewed as seen on a plan. The 'right' and 'left front wall' are the walls on either side of the entrance door as seen from the doorway. The 'right' and 'left rear wall' are the opposite walls seen from the same position. The 'right' and 'left side wall' are the narrow walls of the transverse hall, uniting front and rear walls.

1) Representations of the reigning king in a passive rôle (4)

The king being the most important person in the scenes, the representation is on a large scale, and it is often connected with the office of the tomb owner, particularly if the latter was a military person or was involved in receiving tribute and taking it to his sovereign.

In forty-three of the T-shaped tombs the ruler is thus represented, and nearly always in the same part of the tomb: seated with his back to the doorway leading from the transverse hall to the passage. Quite often, though not always, he is shown on either side of the doorway.

This arrangement is apparent in a tomb from the reign of Ḥatshepsut (TT 73) and becomes more common in the reign of Tuthmosis III (TT 84, 86, 99, 110) and that of Amenophis II (TT 42, 85, 100, 200 and 56, 72, 88, 93, 96, 101, 143, 256, 367). In the reign of Tuthmosis IV it is very consistent in the large T-shaped tombs (TT 63, 64, 66, 74, 75, 76, 77). In the reign of Amenophis III such scenes are still abundant (TT 78, 90, 91, 116 and 48, 57, 120, 226), and they survive into the beginning of the reign of Amenophis IV (TT 55, 188) and even into that of Tutʿankhamūn (TT 40). TT 162, of no fixed reign, also has a representation of the king. It appears to date from the reign of Tuthmosis IV or that of Amenophis III.

In order to evaluate the extent to which this arrangement was common in T-shaped tombs, it should be compared with the number of T-shaped tombs in which no representation of the reigning king was found (in the following only tombs with completed or completely preserved decoration on the two walls in question have been included). During the early part of the dynasty, until the reign of Ḥatshepsut, five tombs are without it (TT 21, 125, 297, 343, 345) as opposed to one tomb (TT 73) depicting the sovereign. For the reign of Tuthmosis III there are twelve tombs without it (TT 22, 53, 81, 82, 87, 109, 121, 127, 130, 241, 251, 342) as opposed to four tombs with it. In the reign of Amenophis II only four tombs lack the king (TT 17, 80, 104, 143) as opposed to thirteen tombs with the king shown, whereas in the reign of Tuthmosis IV the figures are almost equal, six tombs lacking the king (TT 38, 52, 69, 147, 151, 276) as opposed to seven tombs showing the king. For the following reign of Amenophis III there are two tombs without the king (TT 253, 333), as opposed to nine tombs showing him. One tomb of each of the reigns of Amenophis IV, Ay and Ḥaremḥab lack representations of the king (TT 181, 49, 50) whereas two tombs from the time of Amenophis IV included them.

A few tombs have representations of the king in other parts of the monument, not at the doorway to the passage. TT 123 and 131 (temp. Tuthmosis III) depict the king to the left and right respectively of the entrance door. TT 256 (temp. Amenophis II) shows the king on the right side wall of the transverse hall, and in the contemporary TT 56 he is depicted at the extreme right end of the rear wall. TT 43 (temp. Tuthmosis III-Amenophis II) shows the king not only in the usual place, but also on the right side wall of the hall.

Some tombs which are not T-shaped also contain a representation of the sovereign.(5)

Although these statistics may be of limited use during the course of reconstructing a 'lost' tomb, they do give some indication as to which arrangements were within the limits of possibility. It is evident that the number of T-shaped tombs with representations of the reigning king is slightly higher than the number of tombs without such a scene (thirty-six + five with the king not shown at the doorway to the passage as opposed to thirty-two), and that the frequency with which the scenes occur accelerates in the reigns of Amenophis II, Tuthmosis IV and Amenophis III. This tendency must be seen against the development of the shape of the tombs in general, as the above comparison was made between T-shaped tombs only. From the reign of Tuthmosis III to and including the reign of Amenophis III the T-shape was far more common than any other shape (the figures for the four reigns are approximately 26/15, 29/1, 14/5 and 13/10). The obvious conclusion is that the above mentioned representation of the king was applied in T-shaped tombs in particular.

As far as can be ascertained the occupation of the tomb owner had some influence on whether a representation of the king should be included in the tomb or not. High officials tend to depict the king: the vizier (TT 55, 66, 100, 131), the mayor of the Southern City (TT 96, 162), some high ranking members of the Amūn clergy (TT 72, 75, 86, 120), the royal butler (TT 92, 101, 110, 188, but not TT 22) and other prominent members of the royal household (TT 43, 48, 64, 93, 192, 226, but not TT 21 (steward of Tuthmosis I) and TT 17 (the physician of the king)), as well as the royal heralds (TT 84, 201, but not 125 342) and members of the armed forces (TT 42, 74, 78, 85, 88, 90, 91, 200, 367) along with governors of the provinces (TT 63, 200, 239 but not 109).

On the other hand employees of the granaries rarely showed their relationship towards the king by representing him in their tombs (only TT 57 and 123, as opposed to TT 38, 81, 82, 87, 253, 297 which do not), and a childhood or youth spent in the royal harim as a *ẖrd n kȝp* was no obligation to include a scene of the king: he is shown in TT 56, 77 and 256, but not in TT 241 and 343.

A representation in a fragmentary state of the reigning king can thus be positioned with some certainty on the rear wall of the transverse hall of the tomb, on one or both sides of the doorway leading to the passage of a T-shaped tomb. Furthermore there is a strong likelyhood that the tomb from which such a scene stemmed was indeed a T-shaped tomb, and that it belonged to an official in the administrative scale, as noted above, although this is by no means a rigid rule.(6)

2) The office of the tomb owner

Almost half the tombs examined include a representation which bears a distinct relation to the office of the tomb owner. About sixty-three T-shaped tombs turned out to contain such scenes. Among the T-shaped tombs with complete decoration fourteen did not,(7) whereas nine tombs which do not come within the category of T-shaped tombs were found to show the owner in office. The few doubtful cases will be discussed below.

Although some occupations provided a more suitable motif than others, there seems to be a fair range of occupations represented. The subjects most frequently shown are those which come under the supervision of the vizier, priests of high rank and members of the militia: bringing of tribute, inspection of industries, and soldiers in various situations.

Soldiers(8) are shown in tombs from the reign of Ḥatshepsut until that of Amenophis III in the tombs of the military officials (TT 42, 74, 78, 85, 88, 90, 91, 200), royal heralds (TT 201, 342), chief stewards (TT 71, 93), a governor of the Northern Lands (TT 239), a mayor of the South Lake (TT 63), an overseer of the seal (TT 99), one vizier (TT 131) and an overseer of works (TT 77). They are often connected with the presentation of tribute (TT 42, 63, 71, 74, 78, 90, 99, 239). Tribute (9) occurs on its own without a large array of soldiers in tombs of viziers (TT 55, 100, 131), heralds (TT 84, 155), fan bearers (TT 188, 256), a viceroy (TT 40), an overseer of the treasury (TT 80), a first prophet of Amūn (TT 86) and a granary official (TT 81).

The supervision of industries is depicted fairly consistently in tombs of the members of the clergy of Amūn (TT 67, 75, 86, 95, 99, 125), and the vizier (TT 66, 100, 131), but also in that of a butler (TT 172), an overseer of the treasury (TT 276), and two sculptors (TT 181).

Scenes connected with harvesting and crops occur in a great number of tombs, but distinction should perhaps be made between the scenes that reflect the occupation of the tomb owner (transportation of grain, grain barges, measuring fields, recording grain in the granary or celebrating a harvest festival there) and the scenes which are part of general agricultural activities and which serve a different purpose (for these see below under 6)). Scenes of the first category are to be found in the tombs of officials of the granary (TT 38,(10) 57, 69, 253, 297, but not TT 82).

Scenes showing cattle are sometimes as difficult to determine as scenes of agriculture, as cattle occur in a context not necessarily connected with the occupation of the tomb owner, but as part of offerings. In the tomb of an overseer of cattle (TT 151) the cattle scene which is an elaborate one, is obviously dictated by the profession of the tomb owner. Recording of cattle appears also to have been part of the duties of the overseers of the granary (TT 57, 81, 87, 123) and was part of the supervisory work of the first prophet of Amūn (TT 86, 95). Its occurrence is less easy to explain in the tombs of a chief of bowmen (TT 357) and a fan-bearer on the right hand of the king (TT 76), but it is quite possible that the titles of the tomb owners have been incompletely recorded.

Among the more specific subjects which have a direct bearing on the tomb owner's work and responsibilities is the manufacture and display of gifts, including two obelisks, in the tomb of an 'overseer of works on the two great obelisks in the temple of Amūn' (TT 73); weighing metals in the tomb of the 'chief servant who weighs the silver and gold of the estate of Amūn' (TT 18); inspecting ships with produce in the tomb of the harbour master of the Southern City (TT 130); the consultation of a foreign prince in the tomb of a physician (TT 17); inspection of wine in the tombs of royal butlers (TT 110, 188, but not in TT 22 and 101); and the texts and pictures concerning the installation of the vizier (TT 29, 131) or steward (TT 93), or a scene connected with a specific mission abroad (TT 99).

The vast majority of the scenes discussed above are to be found in the transverse hall of the T-shaped tombs. In the sixty-three tombs examined only five were exempt from this rule (TT 42, 80, 123, 130, 172), two of these (TT 42, 123) having representations of this nature both in the hall and elsewhere. In all instances the second choice was the right or left wall of the passage.

In the hall the scenes can be positioned on any of the six available walls,(11) sometimes spreading over more than one wall. But only six representations were placed on either one or the other of the two narrow side walls, the scene spreading in almost all cases(12) to the adjoining front or rear wall. The scene is slightly more frequently represented on the rear wall than on the front wall, but there is no major preference for the right or left part of the tomb.(13) At no time during the dynasty was a particular position favoured.

Where representations of regiments of soldiers or foreigners with produce are concerned, it is the general rule that they move towards the king if he is present, which is indeed most often the case.

3) The tomb owner offering on braziers, libating or adoring(14)

The representation is on a large scale and shows the tomb owner offering to a god, who is not depicted but sometimes mentioned in an accompanying text (Amūn-Rēᶜ, Rēᶜ-Ḥarakhti, Osiris-Wennūfer). The scene has one advantage over all other scenes in that its position is absolutely rigid.(15) It occurs on the front walls of the transverse hall of a T-shaped tomb, on one or both sides of the entrance doorway. It is almost entirely confined to T-shaped tombs. Only eight tombs which are not strictly speaking T-shaped have a similar representation.(16) Forty-nine T-shaped tombs do, but on the other hand twenty-eight T-shaped tombs (of those with completely preserved decoration in the relevant part of the tomb) do not.

The motif occurs all through the dynasty from the reign of Tuthmosis I or slightly later (TT 21) to the beginning of the reign of Amenophis IV (TT 55), and its particular frequency in the tombs from the reigns of Tuthmosis III to Amenophis III must be seen against the frequency of T-shaped tombs during these reigns (see above, p. 34).

Ideally the scene comprised two symmetrical representations: the tomb owner offering on braziers and the tomb owner pouring ointment on offerings, facing the doorway. From the reign of Amenophis II the tomb owner is usually accompanied by his wife or, in two rare cases (TT 48, 181) by his mother, or by the prince of whome the tomb owner was the tutor (TT 64).

The scene showing the tomb owner offering on braziers is by far the most common and is usually shown on the right side of the door as seen from the entrance (TT 29, 38, 42, 43, 45, 56, 57, 64, 69, 74, 76, 77, 78(?), 79, 85, 86, 88, 90, 91, 93, 94, 96, 110, 147, 151, 162, 172, 200, 201, 226, 256, 343, 350), but sometimes it is depicted on the other (left) side of the door (TT 17, 20, 22, 57, 72, 74, 78(?), 91, 96, 99, 104, 108, 112, 130, 147, 162, 226, 367).

Offering on braziers is frequently shown alone without a counterpart on the other side of the doorway, whereas the alternative scenes rarely are so constructed (only TT 48, 181, both temp. Amenophis III). The motif is combined with pouring incense or ointment over offerings in some tombs (TT 38, 52, 55, 56, 64, 77, 93(?), 367), and with 'adoration' in a few others (TT 42, 151(?), 343). Offering on braziers on both sides of the doorway is to be found in TT 57, 74, 78(?), 96, 147, 162, 201, whereas two scenes showing only the pouring of ointment occurs in one tomb (TT 52).

Where the scene does not occupy the full height of the wall, it is positioned on the top half of the wall with offering bringers as a subscene, frequently with butchers included (TT 22, 38, 45, 52, 55, 57, 64, 74, 79, 88, 108, 162, 172, 181, 256, 367).(17)

4) The tomb owner fishing and fowling, occasionally including hippopotamus hunting (18)

The deceased fishing and fowling with his family on board a canoe is represented from the early part of the dynasty (TT 345, temp. Tuthmosis I) to the beginning of the reign of Amenophis III (only two tombs, TT 78 and 91, and the non-T-shaped TT 89 from the latter reign).

It is not to be confused with scenes depicting servants netting fish and fowl and similar activities. The motif occurs in thirty-six T-shaped tombs, and in eight tombs of a different architectural design.(19) Nine T-shaped tombs with completely preserved decoration do not contain scenes of fishing and fowling (TT 17, 50, 57, 110, 130, 147, 297, 343, 396). As the scene appears on a number of different walls of the tomb, there are several T-shaped tombs which may in fact have included it, but if the decoration of one of the possible walls has been destroyed or was left unfinished, it cannot be assumed that the scene was either absent or present in the tomb.

The fishing and fowling scene is a symmetrical representation of the two figures of the tomb owner facing each other with the papyrus thicket separating them. In the early part of the dynasty it may be combined with a representation of the tomb owner hunting a hippopotamus (TT 53, 82, 123, 125, 155, 164, 342) all from the reigns of Ḥatshepsut and Tuthmosis III.(20)

By far the most frequent position of the scene was on the right rear wall of the transverse hall (TT 11, 18, 21, 53, 82, 123, 127, 155, 164, 241, 342, 345 from the reigns of Ḥatshepsut and Tuthmosis III, TT 42, 100, 172 (temp. Tuthmosis III - Amenophis II), TT 92 from the reign of Amenophis II, and TT 52, presuambly from the reign of Tuthmosis IV). The opposite, right front wall was chosen three times (TT 73, temp. Ḥatshepsut, 72, 79, temp. Amenophis II), whereas four preferred the left front wall (TT 125, temp. Ḥatshepsut, 200, temp. Tuthmosis III - Amenophis II, 256, temp. Amenophis II, 91, temp. Amenophis III). The right side wall was chosen twice (TT 22, temp. Tuthmosis III?, and TT 104, temp. Amenophis II), whereas the owner of TT 104 in his second tomb (TT 80) preferred the left side wall.

The scene was moved to the passage in eight tombs, the middle part of the right wall (TT 84, temp. Tuthmosis III, 93, 96, temp. Amenophis II, 63, 66, 69, 77, temp. Tuthmosis IV), the inner part of the right wall (TT 78, temp. Amenophis III), or once to the left wall of the passage (TT 56, temp. Amenophis II).

All walls of the hall except the left rear wall thus provided a possible choice for a fishing and fowling scene. Where a hippopotamus was included, six chose the rear wall, one (TT 125) the left front wall.(21) In many tombs (TT 11, 18, 53, 77, 79, 82, 92, 127, 256) there is in a sub-scene a representation of vintage (cf. below 7)).(22)

5) The tomb owner hunting in the desert

The scene depicts the tomb owner hunting game in the desert either on foot or in a chariot. He is sometimes accompanied by servants, and once (TT 241) by his wife. It is to be found in tombs from the beginning of the dynasty (TT 21 from the reign of Tuthmosis I or slightly later) until the reign of Amenophis II, or possibly into that of Tuthmosis IV (TT 276), most scenes (thirteen out of the twenty-two tombs of all shapes) dating from the reign of Tuthmosis III.(23) It occurs chiefly in T-shaped tombs (seventeen examples), whereas only five tombs of a different plan have it.(24)

The tomb owner is represented hunting on foot in TT 11, 20, 53, 82, 93, 172, 241 and in chariot in TT 21, 56, 84, 123, 276, 432. In TT 155 the chariot is shown waiting for him. In TT 100, 131 and 256 the decoration is so fragmentary that the means of transport cannot be determined.

The wall most frequently chosen is the right wall of the passage at the extremity nearest the entrance door (ten examples). The corresponding part of the left wall was preferred once (TT 56), but in six instances the scene is to be found in the transverse hall, on the right end wall (TT 82, 131, 241); the right rear wall (TT 20, 100); or the right front wall (TT 53).(25)

Some of the T-shaped tombs from the early Eighteenth dynasty to the reign of Ḥaremḥab with completely preserved decoration do not include the hunting scene (TT 17, 50, 57, 69, 80, (85), 104, 121, 125, 127, 147, 343). To these may be added TT 63, 78, 110 the decoration of which is preserved in the parts of the tomb where the scene is likely to occur.

From this we may conclude that the hunting scene was not obligatory in the T-shaped tombs, but it was favoured during the reign of Tuthmosis III.(26) It could be placed on any wall of the hall and the passage, except on the left side wall, but it may be a mere coïncidence that no example is extant on this wall.

6) Agricultural scenes

This subject is to be found in about one third of the tombs (of all shapes) examined, from the early part of the dynasty (TT 21, 345, temp. Tuthmosis I) until the end (TT 255, temp. Ḥaremḥab(?)). The scenes comprise various stages of work in the field (hacking up the soil, ploughing, sowing, harvesting, carrying corn, threshing, winnowing and recording grain, sometimes with tree-felling and pulling flax included). Many of these scenes are now in a fragmentary state, and a detailed survey of the extent of the individual scenes is difficult. All the stages of the work are represented in the tombs from the reign of Tuthmosis III and on.(27)

Agricultural scenes occur in twenty-nine T-shaped tombs and in thirteen tombs of a different architectural plan,(28) whereas about eight tombs of T-shape with completed decoration omit it (TT 78, 82, 84, (85), 104, 110, 123, 396).

In twenty-five T-shaped tombs the scene is depicted in the transverse hall, most often on the left front wall (TT 18, 52, 56, 69, 86, 88, 121, 127, 241, 342), but also on the right front wall (TT 21, 57, 100, 101, 125, 143, 253), or on the left rear wall (TT 17, 53, 147, 345). It is once shown on the right rear wall (TT 162), the right side wall (TT 251), or on the left side wall (TT 38(29)). Of the four times the scene was moved into the passage, it occurs three times on the right wall (TT 63, 172, 200), and once on the left (TT 96).

In the above representation are not included those which apparently show only the measuring and recording of grain and which can be shown to relate to the tomb owner's office. This applies to the scenes in TT 297 (early Eighteenth dynasty), whose owner was counter of grain, and TT 131 (temp. Tuthmosis III), belonging to a vizier. One scene in this tomb shows heaps of grain, another the recording of grain in connection with the vizier's supervision of tax paying. Likewise TT 333 (temp. Amenophis III(?)) whose name and title is unfortunately lost; and TT 188 (temp. Amenophis IV) belonging to a royal butler who is represented recording produce for his king. It is interesting that in TT 57, belonging to the overseer of the granaries of Upper and Lower Egypt (temp. Amenophis III) there are two separate scenes on both front walls of the hall, one with work in the field, the other recording grain(30).

Although many a high official in the service of the king may well have been given a piece of land, and may for this reason be represented supervising work in the field, the significance of the scene lies not so much in representing the owner in one of his possible functions. Rather it has to do with the obsession of the Egyptians to ensure a constant supply of food in the Hereafter, supplementing the actual offerings which might be neglected, and the offering lists and offerings represented on the walls of the tomb. Only where the representations have a direct bearing on the tomb owner's main occupation can it be taken to relate to real life, and should thus be referred to section 2) of this chapter.(31)

As far as the position of agricultural scenes is concerned, there is no marked preference all through the dynasty, but it is most frequently placed on one of the walls of the transverse hall of the T-shaped tombs.(32)

7) Vintage

The subject, including picking grapes, treading them, and bottling the wine, sometimes with an offering to the serpent-goddess Termuthis (Renenwetet), occurs in a number of tombs(33) from the beginning of the reign (TT 15 (early Eighteenth dynasty) and TT 155 (temp. Ḥatshepsut and Tuthmosis III)) to the end (TT 49, temp. Ay(?)), but very sparsely towards the latter part (after Tuthmosis IV only in TT 90 (temp. Tuthmosis IV - Amenophis III), 188 (temp. Amenophis IV) and 49).

Twenty-five T-shaped tombs include the scene, seven tombs of a different plan likewise,(34) whereas the scene is absent in fourteen T-shaped tombs among those with completely preserved decoration (TT 17, 21, 50, 57, 69, 78, 80, (85), 104, 123, 125, 147, 253, 343). To begin with its position is invariably on the right rear wall of the hall (TT 11, 18, 53, 82, 86, 127, 155, 318, 342 (all temp. Tuthmosis III) and the slightly later TT 100), and this is taken up later in four tombs (TT 52, 276 (temp. Tuthmosis IV(?)), 90 (temp. Tuthmosis IV - Amenophis III), and 261 ('Eighteenth dynasty'(31))). The exceptions are TT 22 (temp. Tuthmosis III) which has it on the right side wall, as does also TT 200 (temp. Tuthmosis III - Amenophis II), and two tombs which place it on the right front wall (TT 79, 88 (temp. Amenophis II)). One tomb owner chose the left front wall of the hall (TT 256, temp. Amenophis II), while the contemporary TT 96 preferred the left rear wall, and another (TT 181, temp. Amenophis IV) the left side wall. Four tombs moved the subject to the passage on the right wall (TT 172, temp. Amenophis II, 66 and 77, temp. Tuthmosis IV) or the left wall (TT 56, temp. Amenophis II).

The scene presumably served the same purpose as the agricultural scenes, although in a few instances it may be related to the occupation of the tomb owner, like a butler, a steward, or a member of the clergy of Amūn in charge of temple magazines. This distinction may perhaps be relevant when it comes to the position of the scene in the tomb, although no particular pattern is at present immediately obvious. The subject is frequently represented below as a sub-scene or in close proximity to the fishing and fowling scene(36) (out of the thirty-two tombs of all shapes this happens in twenty-one instances).

Only four tombs represent the scene in the left part of the hall or passage. There is thus a strong probability that a vintage scene would be placed in the right part of the tomb, preferably on the right rear wall of the transverse hall, and presumably in connection with the fishing and fowling scene, although there are significant exceptions to this arrangement.

8) The funeral procession

The procession to the tomb and the rites connected with it(37) was a subject hardly to be excluded in the scheme of decoration, as there is scarcely a single tomb of those with completely preserved decoration that omits it.(38) It is to be found in fifty-two T-shaped tombs and in seventeen others(39) throughout the dynasty.

In the T-shaped tombs it is almost invariably placed on the left wall of the passage, in such a way that the figures move towards the right, into the tomb (TT 17, 20, 21, 29, 42, 53, 56, 57, 59, 61, 62, 63, 66, 69, 71, 72 75, 78, 80, 81, 82, 84, 92, 100, 104, 110, 112, 120, 121, 123, 125, 127, 130, 147, 151, 155, 162, 172, 200, 224, 256, 276, 333, 342, 343, 397). In ten tombs the right wall of the passage was preferred (TT 29, 56, 71, 72, 75, 80, 121, 130, 151, 162). In four tombs the scene is to be found in the transverse hall on the right side wall (TT 139, temp. Amenophis III), on the left side wall (TT 55, 181, temp. Amenophis III and IV, in the latter spreading to the left rear wall). In three tombs the scene was moved to the left wall of the innermost chamber (TT 87, 99, temp. Tuthmosis III) and to the left and right front wall (TT 96(40)). The figures almost always move into the tomb. As most representations are to be found on the left wall of the passage it happens that most figures in the funeral procession face right.(41)

The funeral procession often shares the wall with a representation of the voyage to Abydos (TT 17, 21, 53, 63, 75, 78, 81, 100, 104, 123, 125, 127, 130, 139, 147, 162, 343), or it is depicted in close proximity to it (TT 96).(42) The Abydos voyage, normally being on the lower part of the wall, has often suffered considerable damage, and there may be other tombs from which the scene has now disappeared.

As has already been demonstrated elsewhere, with the exception of the procession to the embalming house and the dragging of the coffin, the funeral procession and the rites depicted on the walls of the tomb do not necessarily correspond to what actually took place at a funeral in the Eighteenth dynasty.(43) Rather it is an exemplification of the general wish of the tomb owner to have a burial like that of his forefathers. The episodes depicted appear to be taken from representations from the Middle Kingdom, in turn based on scenes from the Old Kingdom.

9) The voyage to Abydos

The ritualistic voyage to Abydos is depicted in twenty-three T-shaped tombs, and in nine tombs of a different architectural plan,(44) whereas it was omitted in at least six T-shaped tombs with completely preserved decoration (TT 56, 66, 82, 84, 318 and TT 85, a T-shaped tomb with a transverse hall branching off from the passage) and TT 176, the decoration of which is extant where the scene might have been).

It is shown right through the dynasty, and is usually in close proximity to the register depicting the funerary rites (in at least twenty-five tombs of the altogether thirty-two tombs which include the scene). With very few exceptions it is therefore placed in the passage on the left wall (TT 11, 17, 21, 50, 53, 63, 77, 78, 81, 100, 104, 123, 125, 127, 147, 162, 343), or occasionally on the right wall (TT 57, 69, 75, 130). In one tomb (TT 96) it has been moved to the right wall of the inner room,(45) and in another it is represented on the right side wall of the hall (TT 139).(46)

The remarks on the direction of the figures in the funerary procession to a certain extent apply to the representations of the voyage to Abydos, in that the outward journey is represented as going toward the interior of the tomb, the homeward journey, with sails unfurled, emerging from the innermost part of the tomb.

10) Rites before the mummy

The various episodes of the rites of the Opening of the Mouth(47) are represented in thirty-four T-shaped tombs and in eight tombs of a different plan(48) from the beginning of the dynasty (TT 21, 343) until the reign of Tut'ankhamūn (TT 40), but by far the greater part of the representations date from the early and middle part of the dynasty to and including the reign of Amenophis II. A number of T-shaped tombs omit the subject (TT 57, 63, 66, 81, 85, 147, 253, 318, as well as TT 172, the decoration of which is extant where the scene might have been). In some tombs the rites are being performed not before the actual mummy, but before a statue of the tomb owner, notably in the later tombs (TT 130,(temp. Tuthmosis III(?)), 42, 100, 200 (temp. Tuthmosis III - Amenophis II), 169, 367 (temp. Amenophis II), 69 (temp. Tuthmosis IV(?)) and 40 (temp. Tut'ankhamūn)).

The scene is most frequently shown on the right wall of the passage (TT 11, 21, 62, 82, 83, 125, 127, 130, 343 (including the reign of Tuthmosis III), 100, 140, 200 (temp. Tuthmosis III - Amenophis II), 17, 72, 80, 92, 104, 169 (temp. Amenophis II), 78 (temp. Amenophis III); once on both the right and left wall (TT. 53, temp. Tuthmosis III); and three times on the left wall alone (TT 84, 224 (temp. Tuthmosis III) and 42 (temp. Tuthmosis III - Amenophis II)). It was moved to the inner room twice (TT 99, temp. Tuthmosis III, and 96, temp. Amenophis II), on the right and left walls respectively. In some tombs the subject is to be found in the transverse hall, sometimes on one or both sides of a stela(49): TT 130 (temp. Tuthmosis III(?), 90, 139 (temp. Amenophis III) all on the right side wall; TT 56, 367 (temp. Amenophis II) and 108 (temp. Tuthmosis IV(?)) on the left side wall; and TT 48 (temp. Amenophis III) on the right front wall. In TT 94 (temp. Amenophis III(?)) there is, in addition to the representation in the passage, another on a pillar in the transverse hall. The mummy or statue is usually facing in the opposite direction. The direction of the figures may thus give a clue to the position of the scene in the tomb.

To sum up, the scenes connected with the funerary ceremonies, whether real or not, are most frequently to be found in the passage of a T-shaped tomb, with the funeral procession and the voyage to Abydos on the left and the ceremonies of the Opening ofthe Mouth on the right. But although this is a general rule, there are many exceptions.

4 Lost Tombs Visited by the Early Travellers: Miscellaneous Tombs

In this study we are particularly concerned with 'lost' tombs which have to all intents and purposes disappeared today but about which a substantial amount of information can be gathered from the largely unpublished manuscripts of the early travellers. These tombs form the majority of those listed in the *Topographical Bibliography* I^2,1, pp. 447-61, where bibliographical references are given for individual scenes. Among the tombs there mentioned are also some which were apparently not known by the early travellers, but which were discovered late in the Nineteenth century or by the beginning of the Twentieth: TT A3, A7, C2, C10, C12 and D3. To these should now be added TT A27 and A28.(1)

The remaining New Kingdom tombs are the following: TT A4-5, A8-26, B1-2, C1, C4-9, C11, C13, C15 and D1-2, altogether thirty-five tombs,(2) known, copied or described by Wilkinson, Hay,(3) Burton, Cailliaud, Champollion, Rosellini, Lepsius and other early travellers. In some tombs only a few inscriptions were copied, in others whole walls, some even in colour.

Of these tombs eleven are Ramessid and therefore not dealt with in the present study: A6, A12, A14-18,(4) A23, A26, B1 and C7.

Among the remaining twenty-four tombs some remarks will be made in this section concerning the tombs which are not dealt with in detail below, either because the material is too sparse, as is unfortunately often the case, or because the tombs have been discussed elsewhere. The dates assigned by Porter & Moss are revised in a number of instances in the present study. Objects such as funerary cones, stamped bricks, ushabtis &c. are included in the discussion, and monuments cited in various volumes of the *Topographical Bibliography* are here brought together under the names of the individual owner. Certain names, cited by Porter & Moss, are also amended where necessary.

<u>TT A5</u>
'Mr Salt's tomb'; fragment Louvre E 13101
<u>Owner:</u> Neferḥotep, overseer of the granary of the Lord of the Two Lands, counter of grain of the North and the South.
<u>Family:</u> son Maḥu; daughters Sennūfer and Tawert.

Bibliography: *Description de l'Égypte. Antiquités,* ii, pl. 44 [7]; Hay MSS 29822,41,(5) 43-4,(6) 76; 29824,19 verso-20; Burton MSS 25644, 123-4; Wilkinson MSS v.110 [top left, bottom left, right], 111, 130 [right]; xvii.H.17 [bottom]; *id. Manners and Customs* i.307 (No. 30) = ed. Birch i.204 (No. 35); ii.6 (No. 77), 167 (No. 147), 275 (No. 209) = ed. Birch i.282 (No. 96), i.393 (No. 168), i.465 (No. 234); iii.2 (No. 318) = ed. Birch iii.257 (No. 567); Rosellini MSS 284,G 63 (No. 56); Cailliaud, *Voyage à Méroé,* ii, pl. 74 [2], 75 [1,2], cf. *texte* iii, pp. 292-8; *id. Arts et métiers,* pls. 35 and 37; Ledrain, *Les monuments*, pl. 3; Keimer in *RdÉ* 4, 1940, pp. 49-58; Vandier, *Guide* (1948), pl. 14 [lower],p. 64; (1970), pl. 18,p.84; S. Donadoni, *I protagonisti della Storia Universale* 58, p. 55, fig. 1; *La vie au bord du Nil* (Calais 1982), no. 1 with colour pl.; *Naissance de l'Écriture* (Paris 1982), no. 301.

Funerary cones: Daressy, *Recueil*, no. 104; Davies & Macadam, *Corpus* no. 148.

Description: The scenes copied by Cailliaud have been published more than once and his work studied by Keimer. Nevertheless some points can be further elucidated and will be discussed here.

Keimer was uncertain as to whether Cailliaud himself had detached the piece of wall-painting which is now in the Louvre.(7) This matter can be cleared up by turning to a source which seems to have been ignored by Keimer. Giovanni d'Athanasi was an eye-witness to many of the undertakings of the more illustrious travellers who left accounts of their discoveries in Egypt. 'Yanni's' observations throw a rather different light on some of the incidents, and what he has to say of the way in which Cailliaud obtained his fragment does not reflect flatteringly on the French scholar:

> In 1822, on M. Caillot's return from Mount Lexaar to Cairo, I invited him out of civility to my house, together with his travelling companion to pass some sociable hours in the evening. After supper we amused ourselves for a long time conversing on various matters of antiquity; - on the discoveries which we had made, and especially on that of a tomb which I had just opened, and in which there were some beautiful designs, representing the different processes of agriculture, and a hunt, in which were several animals of different kinds, and an archer who was letting fly an arrow at a bird. M. Caillot, on the recital of all that I had been telling him, became extremely anxious to visit this superb tomb, and intreated me to conduct him to it. I replied that, apprehensive lest the tomb should be spoiled by the Arabs, I had caused a door to be put up which should conceal it from observation until Mr. Salt returned, in order that he might see it untouched; and that it was impossible for me to conduct him to it that evening, but promised him to do so on the following day. Accordingly I did accompany him to the spot; where after having inspected the tomb, he requested permission to make drawings of different objects which pleased him most in it. To this I readily consented, and went away leaving him the key. But now to see how M. Caillot repaid me for all my kindness. Not satisfied with having copied to his heart's content whatever caught his fancy, he sent a messenger to Luxor, on the opposite bank of the river, to procure some iron tools, with which he forthwith set to work, detaching the crust of the wall into

> pieces which he began sending to his house. My Arabs, who were working in the excavations not far from the spot, having recognized the embellishments of the tomb forced them away from the men who were carrying them off; and one of them without loss of time, hurried to the tomb and demanded of M. Caillot of whom he had obtained permission to take away the embellishments in this manner. On this enquiry, M. Caillot seized a piece of iron and threw it at the head of my Arab who had come to warn him of his error; but the latter without being disconcerted, answered his attack in the same fashion, snatching from him at the same time all his implements, as well as the designs which he had just been detaching from their places, and which he brought to me. I was almost out of my senses on learning the ungenerous manner in which this gentleman had requited me of my civility; But out of pure pity I forgave him. It is almost inconceivable how he could have brought himself to publish anything relating to facts which do him so much discredit; I can only account for it by supposing that he did not expect that he whom he had so impudently calumniated would one day have an opportunity of replying to him.((8)

The tomb in question is most certainly our TT A5 in which Cailliaud made several drawings and, as it turned out, also removed at least one piece,(9) which he must have succeeded in spiriting away before he was discovered. Furthermore the tomb was known as 'Mr Salt's tomb', and d'Athanasi had clearly opened it on his account. But he was not the first person to enter it in modern times: it would seem that the members of Napoleon's expedition had already been there and drawn one figure, which is one of the very few from a private Theban tomb to be included in the *Description de l'Égypte*.(10)

The reference by Hay to some animals in the hunting scene being 'cut out by Salt' cannot at present be verified. Hay's information stemmed from Piccinini.(11) Hardly any fragments of hunting scenes are known to have come to collections.(12) Salt had obviously not seen the tomb at the time Cailliaud began cutting it to pieces. When Hay saw it some two years later, it was 'much filled up and destroyed', (13) and the inner room was 'filled to the top'.(14) From the few drawings made by Hay it is clear that the tomb had suffered severe destruction since Cailliaud saw it.

The scenes mentioned and copied by Cailliaud include 1) fishing and fowling; 2) a banquet scene; 3) hunting in the desert; 4) vintage &c. Yet another subject, 5) agriculture was referred to by d'Athanasi and Hay.

When the first edition of the *Topographical Bibliography* appeared, the distribution of the scenes was somewhat different from the arrangement suggested in the second edition. The latter would appear to be the more correct.(15) But perhaps an even more precise idea of the tomb can be obtained.

According to Hay,(16) the tomb had two chambers, all of the above mentioned scenes being in the first room, as the second chamber was inaccessible. 'To the right' in the first room was the banquet scene. 'At the end' the tomb owner was shown hunting in the desert. The position of the fishing and fowling scene is not indicated, but Hay then goes on to describe 'on the left side of the chamber' the agricultural scenes, from which we may perhaps assume that the fishing and fowling was to the right.

1) Fishing and fowling (Ill. 1)

The copy by Cailliaud is fairly good for its time, though by no means a facsimile when compared with the extant fragment of the scene in the Louvre. The length of the scene was 250cm, its height being 78cm. The Louvre fragment preserved the top border, and as would be expected, the subject belongs on the top part of a wall. Fishing and fowling can be positioned on virtually all walls of the hall of a T-shaped tomb,(17) except apparently the left rear wall, and also in the passage. The scene being wider than any of the others copied by Cailliaud, one would have expected it to have been positioned in a passage or corridor, but as Hay had access to it, it must have been in the first chamber, and probably in the right part.

2) Banquet

The orchestra occupied a square portion of the wall, 43cm wide and about the same in height (Ills. 3,4). The musicians face left, presumably towards a representation of the tomb owner and his wife, the banqueting ladies perhaps following to the right and/or below, apparently facing away from the tomb owner and his wife, or, if the scene belonged in the context of the Feast of the Valley, in the same direction as a large scale representation of the tomb owner offering.(18) In this case the scene would belong on the right front wall of the hall, the fishing and fowling scene taking up the right rear wall. The width of the right front wall would thus have to be the same as the opposite wall, ca. 25ocm.

The banqueting lady being sick, as well as her companions (Ill. 5), were drawn by Hay, Burton and Wilkinson and published by the latter, but without the inscriptions. In Burton MSS 25644,123 [top] the lady is named as *Kiꜣti*, her neighbour as ...*kt*. Wilkinson MSS v.110 [top left] copied the signs as *Nbiwti* and ...*tkt*. Hay omitted the hieroglyphs, but added two more ladies on the right (MSS 29822,76).(19)

3) Hunting in the desert (Ill. 6)

The dimensions of this scene were not indicated by Cailliaud, but in the copy it is slightly more wide than high. As the scene includes a main register as well as a subscene, there was probably nothing to add below.

Hunting in the desert occurs either in the hall of a T-shaped tomb, almost always in the right part, either front, rear or side wall,(20) or on the right wall of the passage, near the entrance. This hunting scene was probably on the right side wall of the hall, cf. Hay's remarks above.

4) Vintage &c. (Ill. 2)

The vintage is here combined with bringing of produce and punishment of workmen, as well as scribes recording. The entire scene was 200cm wide and 52cm high. The subject was not mentioned by Hay. It must have been positioned on either the front or rear wall of the hall. If the chamber was symmetrical we would expect the wall to be 250cm wide, as the fishing and fowling wall. A representation of the tomb owner inspecting, at a larger scale, taking up the height of two registers, presumably on the left, would bring this wall to about 250cm. Vintage often occurs as a sub-scene to fishing and fowling, and it is possible that this was also the arrangement in our tomb.

5) Agriculture

D'Athanasi refers to 'different processes of agriculture',(21) Hay to 'the common subject of grain being put in heaps & the quantities noted by the clerks in the usual way',(22) in other words the conventional detailed representation of workmen in the field. This subject may have shared the wall with the vintage scene mentioned above, or perhaps it was on the opposite wall. According to Hay, it was definitely in the left part of the hall.(23)

An inscription copied by Rosellini (MSS 284,G 63) suggests the existence of a scene not mentioned by any of the other travellers quoted above:

(MS)

... Tm n Wsỉr nṯr ꜥꜣ n Ḥtḥr ḥrỉ(t) tp smyt ỉmntt n ꜣInpw nb tꜣ ḏsr n Wpwꜣwt šmꜥ n ... nb ỉs (ỉ?)n ỉmy-r šnwty n nb tꜣwy ḥsb ỉt n šmꜥw mḥt mḥ ỉb mnḫ n nb.f Nfrḥtp mꜣꜥ ḫrw ḫr nṯr ꜥꜣ

'... Atum, to Osiris, great god, to Ḥatḥor, mistress of the western desert, to Anubis, Lord of the Sacred Land, to Wepwaut of the South, to... lord of the tomb (by) the overseer of the granaray of the Lord of the Two Lands, counter of grain of the South and the North, splendid trusted one of his lord, Neferḥotep, justified for the great god.'

Presumably *rdỉt ỉꜣw* is to be restored at the beginning of the text. Perhaps the inscription was to be found in the entrance doorway (in that case on the right jamb), being part of the prayer addressed to gods not depicted. The inscription is important in that it gives the full titles of Neferḥotep.

The tomb was described by d'Athanasi as a 'superb tomb' and with 'beautiful designs'. (25) Hay says that 'the style of painting is careful, equal to the 1st tomb [*sc.* TT 155] and the drawing is good'.(26)

Date: Probably temp. Tuthmosis III - Amenophis II.

Location: Draꜥ Abû el-Nagaꜥ, on the main hill, close to and south of TT A4, which was a few paces south of TT 155 and below TT 255, which is higher up on the hill.

TT A8

Lepsius tomb no. 4

Owner: Amenemḥab, royal scribe, steward in the mansion of Amenophis I on the west of Thebes, overseer of the granary of Amūn.

Family: father Maḥu, ... of Amūn; mother Kanuro, songstress of Amūn; wife Tanefer(t), songstress of Ḥatḥor, mistress of .(27)

<u>Bibliography</u>: Lepsius, *Text*, iii, p. 238, 239 [top right]; statue group of deceased, mother and wife: Leningrad, State Hermitage Museum 740, N. Landa & I. A. Lapis, *Egyptian Antiquities in the Hermitage*, Leningrad 1974, no. 51 (with full bibliography). Cf. also Lieblein, *Dictionnaire*, no. 1646.
<u>Funerary cones</u>: Davies & Macadam, *Corpus*, nos. 532 and 554.
<u>Description</u>: Record (by Lepsius) of only one wall-painting remains: the rear wall of the hall with two scenes: deceased offers to Osiris and Nephthys, and deceased, wife and parents(?) adore Amenophis I and Aḥmosi Nefertere in a kiosk.

Some of the texts were copied by Lepsius:

... in Wsir [mḥ ib n nṯr nfr?] sš nsw mꜣꜥ mr.f imy-r pr m Ḥwt Ḏsrkꜣrꜥ ḥr imntt Wꜣst imy-r šnwty n ʾImn ḥꜣty-ꜥ ʾImnmḥb mꜣꜥ ḫrw n niwt ḏd.f ind ḥr.k ḫnty ʾImntt Wnnfr ḥkꜣ ꜥnḫw ... n mwt.f Nwt mst nṯrw wr m nṯrw tpy m psḏt ity ir st Rꜥ rdiw n.f

'by Osiris [trustworthy one of the good god?], true royal scribe whom he loves, steward of the temple of Amenophis I on the west of Thebes, overseer of the granary of Amūn, mayor of The Town, Amenemḥab. He says, "Greetings to you the foremost in the West, Wennufer, ruler of the living... of his mother Nut, who bore the gods, the great one among the gods, the first in the Ennead, the sovereign who created the throne of Rēꜥ, to whom was given..."'

No texts of Amenophis I and Aḥmosi Nefertere were copied, but Lepsius does mention that the queen had yellow complexion.
<u>Date</u>: Porter & Moss date the tomb to the Eighteenth or Nineteenth dynasty, but in the index (p. 477) it is listed as an Eighteenth dynasty tomb. In Helck, *Materialien*, where the tomb owner is mentioned on pp. 31, 33, 88 and 158, the date is given as Eighteenth(?) dynasty. The style of the statue-group certainly suggests a late Eighteenth, post-Amarna date, the wigs, for example, being not unlike those found around the reign of Ḥaremḥab.(28) The two wall-scenes in the tomb do not give a certain clue to the date. Representations of the deified queen Aḥmosi Nefertere and her son, Amenophis I begin to become a regular feature in the tombs during the reign of Amenophis III,(29) and they are quite frequent in Ramessid tombs. Representations of the deceased with or without his family adoring Osiris, Isis and Nephthys are not rare in Ramessid tombs, but with one exception(30) they appear to be non-existent in Eighteenth dynasty tombs, and Nephthys appearing alone, *i.e.* without Isis is not known in a funerary context. Maybe there was a counterpart showing Osiris with Isis.

Among the personal names connected with this tomb only that of the tomb owner's mother is out of the ordinary. The name 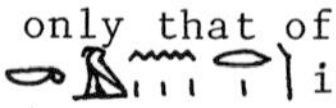 is transcribed variously in the *Topographical Bibliography* as Kanuro (TT A8) or Kenro (TT 54). As a man's name it is known from the early

Nineteenth dynasty (TT 54, cf. 'Kenro' of TT 178) and several times at Deir el-Medîna.(31) As a woman's name it seems only to occur in this place.(32) In that it belongs to a person a generation older than the tomb owner, this might perhaps oblige us to consider an early Ramessid date for the tomb. On the other hand a certain detail in the text on the statue is reminiscent of the late Eighteenth dynasty: on the back pillar the gods are asked to grant the deceased a 'firm corpse' in the necropolis, to go about outside the tomb and 'to see the Aten' in the morning. This same expression occurs in the tomb of Ḥaremḥab.(33) All things considered the tomb would appear to belong at the very end of the dynasty.

Personalia: The titles on the cones correspond very closely to the titles on the statue-group and those recorded in the tomb:

tomb: *sš nsw mȝʿ mr.f ỉmy-r pr m ḥwt Ḏsrkȝrʿ ḥr ỉmntt Wȝst ỉmy-r šnwty n ʾImn ḥȝty-ʿ n nỉwt*
cone 532 *sš nsw mȝʿ mr.f ỉmy-r pr m ḥwt ʾImnḥtp ḥȝty-ʿ m Wȝst*
statue col. A *sš nsw mȝʿ mr.f ỉmy-r pr m ḥwt Ḏsrkȝrʿ ỉmy-r šnwty n ʾImn ḥȝty-ʿ n nỉwt*
cone 554 *sš nsw mȝʿ mr.f ỉmy-r šnwty n ʾImn ḥȝty-ʿ n nỉwt*
statue col. Γ *sš nsw mȝʿ mr.f ỉmy-r šnwty n ʾImn m ʾIpt-swt ḥȝty-ʿ n nỉwt*

'True(34) royal scribe, his beloved, steward in the house of Amenophis I on the west of Thebes/ overseer of the granary of of Amūn (at Karnak), mayor of Thebes'.(35)

The statue-group was presented to the Leningrad museum from the Duke of Leuchtenberg in 1852, *i.e.* not long after Lepsius had visited the tomb.

Location: The tomb was at Draʿ Abû el-Nagaʿ, on the main hill a little higher than TT 12.

In 1906 Chassinat found a cone belonging to a counter of grain, overseer of the granary of Amūn, Amenemḥeb near a tomb of a certain  at Draʿ Abû el-Nagaʿ.(36) This person is not listed as a tomb owner in the *Topographical Bibliography*. If Daressy's copy is defective, as it sometimes happened, he may be identical with 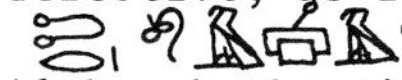Tharwas, the owner of TT 239, a tomb not far from TT 12. Although the titles differ slightly, the Amenemḥeb on the cone found by Chassinat may be the same as the owner of TT A8, and in that case there would be another link between this tomb and the area around TT 12.

TT A9

Lepsius tomb no. 3

Owner: name and title unknown.

Bibliography: Lepsius, *Text*, iii, p. 238.

Description: A painted tomb with a scene showing 'adoration of Amenophis II'.(37) The cartouches were cut out on 21 November 1844 and were still lying about on the following day (Lepsius, *loc. cit.*).

Date: temp. Amenophis II.

Location: Below TT A8, near TT 12 on the main hill of Draʿ Abû el-Nagaʿ.

TT A10

Champollion tomb no. 50 ter

Owner: 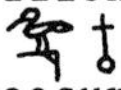 Ḏḥoutnūfer, hereditary prince, royal scribe, overseer of the treasury, chief lector priest in the embalming house *(pr nfr)*.

Family: father 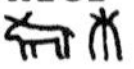 Kamosi, judge; mother 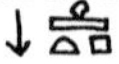 Senḥotp; wife 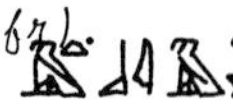 Tabia; son 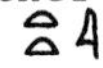 Teti, *waᶜb*-priest of Amūn.

Bibliography: Champollion, *Not. descr.* i, p. 542-3. Lintel and jambs: Florence Mus. 2576, 2598a,b, Alinari photo. 43846 (lintel); Petrie, Ital. photos. 207 [right], 249 [right] (parts of jambs). Texts, Schiaparelli, *Mus. arch.* I, pp. 341-4 [1607-8]; Berend, *Principaux Monuments*, pp. 77, 94-5; names, Lieblein, *Dictionnaire*, nos. 765, 784, cf. Supp. pp. 968, 970. See Rosellini, *Breve notizie*, pp. 32-3 [25], 38 [38], 48 [48]; Migliarini, *Indication succinte*, pp. 18-9, 29-30.

Funerary cone: Davies & Macadam, *Corpus*, no. 516.

Description: A fairly large tomb 'without sculpture', already filled up when Champollion saw it, with jambs and lintel lying on the ground. These were collected by Rosellini and came with his other antiquities to the museum in Florence.

The statement by Champollion that the tomb was 'without sculpture' may not necessarily mean that it was a painted tomb, but that no decoration whatsoever remained or was visible. Future discoveries may decide whether the tomb should be omitted from this work.

Personalia: The owner of this tomb shares name and titles with Ḏḥoutnūfer, owner of TT 80 and 104, who is apparently in some places called Ḏḥoutmosi.(38) But their family relationships show that they were two different individuals.

Location: On the main hill of Draᶜ Abû el-Nagaᶜ, lower part ('Au pied de la montagne, derrière le palais de Kourna [*sc.* the temple of Sethos I]').

Other monuments of the deceased: Stamped brick found rebuilt into the Ramesseum: J. E. Quibell, *The Ramesseum*, London 1898, p. 15, pl. 11.8.

The lower part of a kneeling statue in the Cairo Museum (Borchardt, *Statuen* III, no. 921, p. 155) of unknown provenance is by Helck(39) taken to belong to the 'other' Ḏḥoutnūfer. The back pillar is broken off just where the name of the mother would begin. The statue may equally well have belonged to the owner of TT A10. The title reads 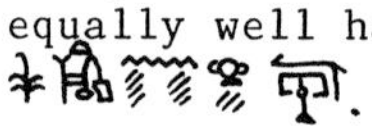.

TT A11

Champollion tomb no. 41

Owner: 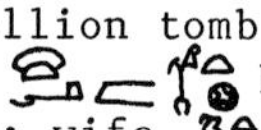 Khaᶜemwēset,... of Amūn.

Family: wife 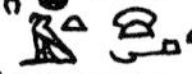Takhaᶜt; daughter 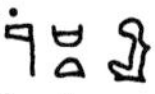 Ḥemtnūṯer, songstress of Ḥatḥor, mistress of ꜣIwnt; sons Neferḥotep and User; daughter 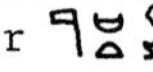  Ḥemtnūṯer-(ta-)Sheryt.

Bibliography: Champollion, *Not. descr.* i, pp. 534-5; Hay MSS 29822,45 and 29824,3 (ill. 7); Rosellini MSS 284,G54 (No. 42); Lepsius MSS 424.

Description: According to Hay this was 'a small tomb too much destroyed to copy', and only the right wall of the hall was described by the early travellers. It shows a scene entitled 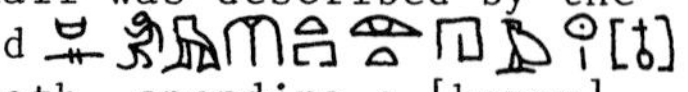 *ḥms m sḥt ỉrt hrw [nfr]* 'sitting in the booth, spending a [happy] day...' by the tomb owner and his wife. In Rosellini MSS 284,G 54 [lower] the inscription pertaining to the wife, presumably in this scene, is copied in more detail than in Champollion (the inscription runs from right to left, *i.e.* the lady would face right):

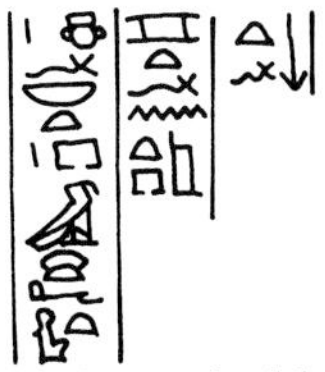

Their daughter presents them with a shallow drinking cup (white) and a napkin (white fringed with red). Behind her are nine women sitting on chairs and stools alternating [*sic*] with cushions, each nursing an infant (Ill. 8). Facing the 'first' woman and touching the boy called 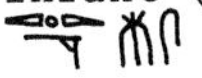 Minmosi(40) is a little girl, a second daughter of the tomb owner, called 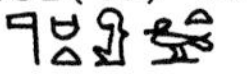 'Ḥemtnūṯer the younger'.(41)

Somewhere below this scene according to Hay are two torches with a lamp between, set on altars (Ill. 7).(42) The two sons were presumably also shown on this wall.

The scene showing the nine women nursing children is highly interesting. The word 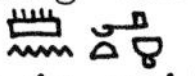 'nurse' occurs on this wall (Champollion, *loc. cit.*) and it is evident that the women, or at least one of them, were not the actual mothers of the infants. Champollion calls Minmosi the 'brother' of Ḥemtnūṯer-ta-Sheryt, but a justification for this statement is not given. The only other scene remotely like this one is the one in TT 56 (temp. Amenophis II), at present unpublished.(43) Userḥēt, the owner of this tomb, was 'child of the nursery', his wife a royal concubine. It is difficult to see anything but a royal connection in this scene. Single women nursing royal infants are occasionally depicted in Eighteenth dynasty tombs.(44)

A close scrutiny of Hay's faint pencil drawing shows that it is not just one nurse and one child shown in different situations. The child to the left, picking a bunch of grapes from a basket held by the woman, appears to be wearing a diadem with streamers. The child in the middle would seem to be a girl with short cropped hair and a diadem with one ornamental disc. This child also reaches to a bunch of grapes from a basket. The child to the right, suckling the breast of the woman, is obviously a boy, and he wears a side-lock and a diadem. The two children on the left wear necklaces and hold a lotus flower in one hand. The boy to the right has no necklace, and the nurse holds his flower.(45) The nurse looks the same in all instances, wearing a diadem with three discs visible and a lotus flower in front. The low chair on which she squats is decorated with a papyrus flower.

It would be logical to assume that the whole scene depicts one nurse, wife of the tomb owner,(46) with the nine children she once nursed. The children must have been high ranking, probably members of the royal family.

Date: Porter & Moss date the tomb to the 'New Kingdom'. Because of the non-existence of nursing scenes in Ramessid tombs,(47) and because of the shape of the candle corresponding to those depicted in the Eighteenth dynasty,(48) an Eighteenth dynasty date would be more accurate, presumably somewhere around the reign of Tuthmosis IV where nursing scenes have not yet come to an end and representations of candles are beginning to appear. If the infant Minmosi in the tomb, shown with royal(?) children, is the same as the Minmosi mentioned in n. (40) above, an earlier date is appropriate.

Personalia: The name of the tomb owner as given by Champollion and reproduced by Porter & Moss as 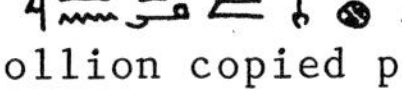 Amenkhaᶜemwēset is not otherwise known. Perhaps Champollion copied part of the title and

connected it with the name, a mistake which has been made even in recent times.(49) The name Khaʿemwēset was in use all through the New Kingdom, and 'Amūn' is more likely to be part of the title.
State of preservation: The paintings in the tomb were much blackened by smoke (Champollion and Rosellini), and the colours had changed, the red having turned brown (Hay).
Location: Near TT 161 'nearly under the ruined pyramid with a large arch'.

TT A19
Champollion tomb no. 50
Owner: an hereditary prince of Thinis, overseer of the prophets of Onuris, trusted friend of the Lord of the Two Lands.
Bibliography: Champollion, *Not. descr.* i, p. 541; Rosellini MSS 284,G60 verso (this latter reference was omitted in the *Topographical Bibliography*)
Description: A painted tomb 'of ordinary plan and on a fairly large scale' (Champollion), 'well painted, but... completely ruined' (Rosellini). According to Champollion the tomb was partly unfinished, but the paintings were large and magnificently executed. He saw a representation of a half-ruined garden beautifully painted, and he copied the titles, though not the name of the owner. Rosellini gave the full inscription which pertained to the tomb owner seated at an offering table, facing left:

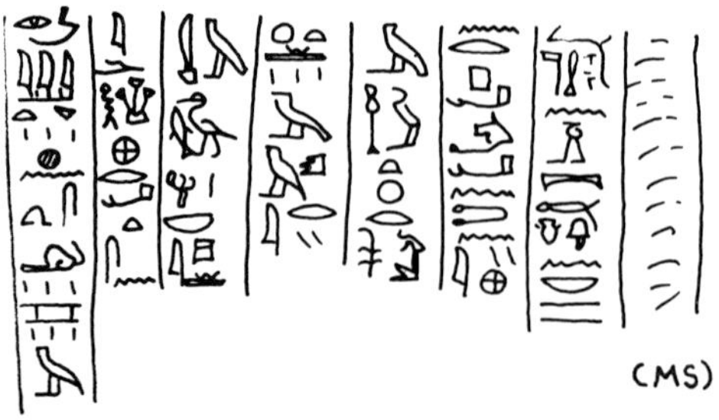

mꜣꜣ sḫwt ḫns pḥw m idḥw rdit snm ḥr nb ip ḫt m km iry m wḏt ḫr nsw n iry-pʿt ḥꜣty-ʿ n Ṯny imy-r ḥmw n ʾInḥrt mḥ ʾib mnḫ n nb tꜣwy...

'Viewing the marshlands, traversing the fens in the Delta marshes. Giving supplies from the master of accounts as a profit(50) of it as a command from the king to the hereditary prince and mayor of Thinis, overseer of the prophets of Onuris, splendid trusted one of the Lord of the Two Lands...'

The scene in question would seem to have shown the tomb owner inspecting various activities in the marshes and the delivery of produce from the area, due to him according to a decree from the king.
Date: In the *Topographical Bibliography* the tomb is undated. Helck(51) suggests that the owner is identical with a man with similar titles, but also anonymous, depicted in TT 93 of Ḳenamūn.(52) But Davies prefers to see in this latter person Min, the owner of TT 109, who bore the same titles. A third person has recently been suggested by van Siclen,(53) who identfies him with Amenḥotp, owner of a funerary cone for which no matching tomb has otherwise been found.(54) This

person functioned in the reign of Tuthmosis IV.(55) This latter identification certainly is the most attractive and substantial of the three.
Location: At Draᶜ Abû el-Nagaᶜ, Middle Valley (Shiq el-Ateiyât), on the north side towards the end.

TT A20
Champollion tomb no. 50 bis
Owner:  Panakht,(56) hereditary prince, overseer of the granary of Amūn.
Bibliography: Champollion, *Not. descr.* i, pp. 541-2.
Description: A vaulted tomb with a painted ceiling 'of a rare perfection' with 'grecque' pattern and facsimile wooden beams. On the left wall there was a picture of the deceased with two of his children, and the funeral procession with three *mww*-dancers preceding the oxen dragging the sarcophagus. On the right wall was the deceased again, and a half-effaced cartouche of King Amosis: 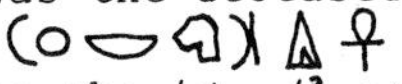 (57) 'To the right and left' and on the ceiling was the *ḥtp di nsw* formula and the name and the title of the tomb owner. The name of Amūn seems to have been erased, presumably during the Amarna Period.
Date: The tomb is dated to the reign of Amosis by Porter & Moss on the basis of the occurrence of the cartouche of this king in the tomb, and this may be so. Champollion says that the paintings are very much like the contemporary paintings (*sic*) at el-Kâb. These tombs had sculpted decoration, but they date from the beginning of the Eighteenth dynasty to the reign of Tuthmosis IV.
Location: The tomb was in the Middle Valley (Shiq el-Ateiyât), halfway down the south slope ('coté gauche du vallon, et à mi-coté').

TT A21
Champollion tomb no. 48
Owner: name and title unknown.
Bibliography: Champollion, *Not. descr.* i, p. 540.
Description: A small tomb with paintings of mediocre quality, probably, as Champollion indicates, the inner room of a tomb originally larger, but now lacking the hall. On the left was the funeral procession, on the right the Opening of the Mouth rites, and on the rear wall an uninscribed painted stela with horizontal lines.
Date: The tomb is left undated by Porter & Moss, but there can be no doubt that it is a New Kingdom tomb. Scenes of the kind described by Champollion are not known at Thebes prior to the New Kingdom. Likewise no post New Kingdom tombs with painted decoration on plaster are known at Thebes.

The numbers of the tombs described in Rosellini's notebook correspond fairly closely to those given by Champollion. Their tomb no. 49 is the same (=TT A22), and there is good reason to believe that Rosellini's tomb no. 48 = TT A21. His entry in MSS 284,G60 [upper] is as follows: 'Piccola e guasta in modo che non vi si trova più il nome del defunto - Sembra però che fosse un ajo del figlio di Memnone del quale si vede ancora il cartello

(MS)

Whatever the relationship between the tomb owner and the king, the cartouche certainly suggests a more precise date for this tomb.

Location: On south side of Middle Valley (Shiq el-Ateiyât), near summit and above TT A20 ('vers le sommet du plateau, au-delà du premier vallon et après notre maison de Kourna').

TT A22
Champollion tomb no. 49
Fragment: Louvre D60 (87 x 59cm).
Owner: 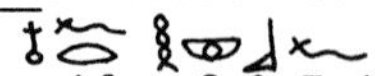 Neferḥabef, scribe, counter of grain.
Family: wife 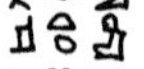 Esi.
Bibliography: Hay MSS 29822,46,47; 29824,20-1; 29853,107; 31054,136 [14]; Burton MSS 25644,141; Wilkinson, *Manners and Customs* ii.232 (No. 183)= ed. Birch, i.436 (No. 208); Wilkinson MSS v.158 [bottom left]; xvi,G,5 [left]; Champollion. *Not. descr.* i, p. 540; Rosellini, *Mon. civ.* 96 [4]; Rosellini MSS 284,G60 [lower]; de Rougé, *Notice sommaire*, p. 210 (no. 60); Perrot & Chipiez, *Histoire de l'art* i, pp. 791-2, pl. 12; Archives (Louvre) phot E.630; C. Boreux, *Antiquités égyptiennes* i, Paris 1932, p. 132; L. Manniche, 'Provenance of Louvre D 60', *GM* 29, 1978, pp. 85-8.
Description: Tomb of 'ordinary plan' (Champollion), presumably meaning T-shaped, with good paintings, one of which survives in the Louvre. On the rear wall was represented a banquet with musicians, described in some detail in Hay MSS 29824,20-1:

> '(In the feast ... the) 2 lines of guests are headed by a lady and gentleman of the same size & looking the same way, different from the large figures which are also represented in the usual manner - male and female servants attend as usual - and ... in one of the lines of male guests some have a thin garment that buttons (58) at the neck and sit on chairs, while others have the usual short kilt to the knees with a thin dress also that descends to the ancles (*sic*)... and sit on stools - but as to the distinction of rank there seem none as they follow alternately and are attended & served like the others.'

The extreme left part of these two registers can be seen on the fragment in the Louvre, along with two female musicians(59) and a girl with a shallow drinking cup in one hand and a pair of tiny vases (60) in the other. They face a heap of offerings and four unguent vases, to the left of which was undoubtedly the large scale representation of the deceased couple mentioned by Hay. An inscription (from here?) pertaining to the wife of the tomb owner was copied by Rosellini (MSS 284,G60 [lower left]). The hieroglyphs run from right to left:

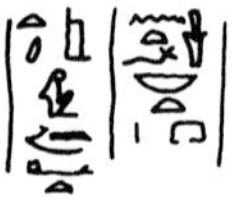 (MS)

Above the girl in the Louvre fragment remains another text:

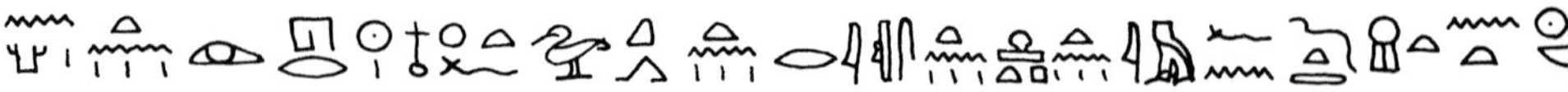

n kꜣ.tn ỉr hrw nfr ḫft ʿḳ.tn r ỉs.tn ḥtp.tn ỉm.f n ḏt ḫrt hrw nt rʿ nb

'To your *kas*! Spend a happy day when you enter your tomb, and rest in it through time, in the course of every day!'

At the lower edge of the fragment is the tip of a harp decorated with the head of the goddess Ma^{c}et.(61) The harpist and his instrument in the register below was destroyed when Hay saw it. The fragment belonged at the top part of a wall, as the polychrome top border shows.

In Hay MSS 29822,47, following the drawing of the previous scene, there is another drawing of a banquet scene which presumably belongs in this tomb (Ill. 9).(62) It shows in the top register a man seated on a stool with a lotus bud in one hand. A male servant pours water(?) over his other hand. Below, another man sits on a chair and smells a lotus flower. Behind him a male musician plays the oblique flute *(nây)*.(63) Hay says that these persons 'have no thin garment above the waist', as opposed to those described above.

Hay MSS 29824,21 mentions another subject depicted in the tomb which is not quoted by Porter & Moss: 'Traces of the subject of Grain may be made out with the clerks - a house & trees - besides apparently different trades which are not distinct.'

Date: The tomb was left undated by Porter & Moss. It is clearly of the Eighteenth dynasty. The bold lines, the large figures and vivid colours suggest a date around the reign of Tuthmosis IV. The head of Ma^{c}et decorating ladle-shaped harps occur in two other tombs of slightly earlier date (TT 29 and 100). Scenes of agriculture and arts and crafts would also fit a mid-Eighteenth dynasty date.

State of preservation: 'Almost completely destroyed & has been inhabited' (Hay). Rosellini says that the tomb was even more destroyed than the previous one (TT A21). The fragment in the Louvre, however, is well preserved and was apparently not blackened by smoke, or it has since been cleaned.

Location: 'On the side of a hill facing to the North, forming the South side of a small valley or inlet before arriving at the 3rd tomb [*sc.* TT A4] from Yanni's house(64)', *i.e.* on the south side of the Middle Valley (Shiq el-Ateiyât).

TT A25

Owner: name and title unknown.

Bibliography: Wilkinson MSS v.107 [upper].

Description: The only scene recorded from this tomb, which was inhabited when Wilkinson saw it, is part of an agricultural scene showing, to the left winnowing, in the centre a man driving a span of oxen round the threshing ground, and to the right a man with a fork at a heap of grain (Ill. 10).

Date: Judging from Wilkinson's sketch, the tomb appears to be of the Eighteenth dynasty. The scenes are obviously part of a larger representation, ploughing, sowing, harvesting presumably being shown on the adjoining portions of the wall. This rendering of the individual stages of the work in the field also points to an Eighteenth dynasty date, Ramessid representations of the subject being more summary.

Location: 'Near Hammam's house' (Wilkinson). Could this tomb be the same as TT A22?

TT B2

Champollion tomb no. 58

Owner: Amennofru, *wa^{c}b*-priest, carrier in front.(65)

Family: wife ʿAḥmosi.

Bibliography: Hay MSS 29821,82 (notes and drawing); 29858,318 (notes); Champollion, *Not. descr.* i, p. 557; Rosellini MSS 284,G48 verso (no.37).

Description: The left wall of the oblong room had a representation of the funeral procession with three (*sic* Rosellini) *mww*-dancers facing a man with a bowl of incense and the oxen dragging the sarcophagus. The accompanying text was copied by Rosellini:

(MS)

ỉrt snṯr wꜣḥ n.f tp.f - my mww
'Censing. He has placed his head...' - 'Come, *mww*-dancers!'

A minute sketch of the head of a dancer was included: 
Also on this wall were the Fields of Iaru with obelisks.

In the room was a brick arch (Ill. 11) on the jambs of which was an inscription mentioning Tuthmosis III:

(left) 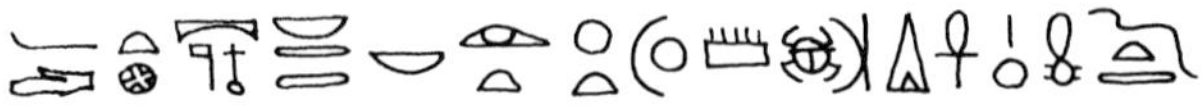

... *Bḥdt nṯr nfr nb tꜣwy nb ỉrt ḫt Mnḫprrꜥ dỉ ꜥnḫ mỉ Rꜥ ḏt*
'of Edfu, the good god, Lord of the Two Lands, lord of rituals, Menkheprurēꜥ, given life like Rēꜥ for ever.'

(right) 

The width of the opening was according to Hay 2.8ft, the thickness of the bricks 0.2ft. There was a gap between the rock ceiling and the arch. In the room behind this arch was a large offering list. This 'arrière cabinet' (Champollion) and the room with funerary scenes presumably correspond to the niche and inner room (passage) of a tomb which once also had a hall. Somewhere in the tomb Hay copied the names of the tomb owner and his wife ('hieroglyphs over the female figure':(66)

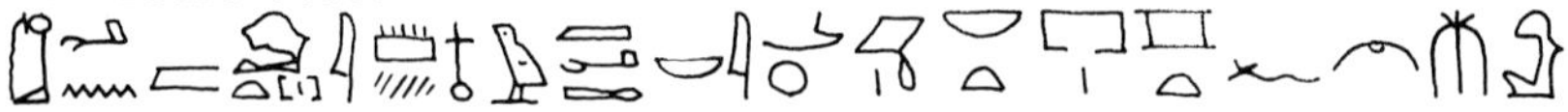

wꜥb rmn m ḥꜣt ꜣIm[n]nfrw mꜣꜥ ḫrw nb ỉmꜣḫw nbt pr mrt.f ꜣIꜥḥms
'The *waꜥb*-priest, carrier in front, Amennofru, justified, lord of veneration. The mistress of the house whom he loves, ꜥAḥmosi.'

State of preservation: 'The paintings destroyed since 1827' (Hay); but colours of paintings well preserved (Champollion). When Hay visited the tomb some years later (16th December 1832) the tomb had suffered further: '... Visited a tomb that is arched in brick & has the oval  It is under another - parts of which were drawn by me the 1st time I was at Thebes but now quite destroyed!' (MSS 29858,318).(67)

Date: Presumably temp. Tuthmosis III because of the presence of the cartouche in the tomb. Also Champollion compares the *mww*-dancers facing the oxen and the obelisks of the Fields of Iaru to those in the tomb at el-Kâb.

Location: In the Khôkha area, 'sur la colinne (*sic*) isolée de l'entrée de L'Assassif à gauche', according to Porter & Moss probably near TT 200. Champollion entered it through another ruined, painted tomb through an opening in the vaulted ceiling, well below the floor level of the tomb above. Rosellini described entering through a well.

TT C1
Lepsius tomb no. 34
Owner: Amenḥotp, overseer of carpenters of Amūn, chamberlain.
Family: father Iuti, chamberlain; wife Tiyi; brother Neferḥotep, *wa*ᶜ*b*-priest of Khons.
Bibliography: V. Loret, 'Le tombeau de l'Am-Xent Amen-hotep', *Mém. Miss.* i, pp. 23-32; Wilbour MSS 2 E,2; Piehl, *Inscr. hiér.* I Ser. 105-7 [C]; Hermann, *Stelen*, pp. 47 [middle] - 49 (from Loret); Helck, *Urk. IV*, 1936-8, cf. *Übersetzung*, pp. 385-6 [726]; D. Wildung, *Imhotep und Amenhotep*, Munich 1977, pp. 19-20 (8,1).
Funerary cones: Daressy, *Recueil*, nos. 144-5; Davies & Macadam, *Corpus*, nos. 314-5.
Description: This tomb was described and drawn in some detail by Loret, and a description is therefore omitted here.
Date: temp. Amenophis III.
Location: The tomb was visited by Lepsius, and by Wilbour (1880-90) and Loret, but it has since become lost. It was at Sheikh ᶜAbd el-Qurna, according to Porter & Moss near TT 252 and 103.
Other monuments of the tomb owner: 1) Brick, Berlin Mus. 1580: Lepsius, *Text* iii, p. 250; *Ausf. Verz.*, p. 449. 2) Built in block in the temple of Khons at Karnak showing the tomb owner following a princess: Borchardt in *ZÄS* 41, 1926, no. 40; Helck, *Urk. IV*, 1938 [bottom], cf. *Übersetzung*, p. 326 [near top]; cf. *Topographical Bibliography* II², p. 244. 3) Block statue found at Deir el-Baḥri, Pittsburgh, Carnegie Museum 2940/2,3: E. Naville, *XIth Dynasty Temple at Deir el-Bahri* iii, London 1913, pl. 9 [D], pp. 2-3; Helck, *Urk. IV*, 1939 [727], cf. *Übersetzung*, p. 326; cf. *Top. Bibl.* II², p. 394.

TT C5
Owner: unknown.
Bibliography: Hay MSS 29816,139-40.
Description: 'A small tomb... without roof' (Hay).

Hay copied part of one register showing a banquet scene (Ill. 12). The copy is done by *camera lucida* and the lines of the pencil are now very faint. The paintings were obviously much destroyed, undoubtedly due to their exposed state, but they appear to have been well executed with great attention to detail. To the left is a group of three women being served by a naked girl with necklace and hip belt. Then follows a group of four women. All the guests are seated on luxurious chairs and cushions with bold patterns. Some of them wear a fringed garment, the lavish folds of their tunics matching their elaborate jewellery. The wigs are decorated with unguent cones and garlands, and a horizontal line below ear level suggests some further decoration.

To the right was the female orchestra, sadly destroyed when Hay saw it. Two of the girls are shown dancing, one playing the lute, the other the lyre (the horizontal line at the elbow and the position of the right arm suggest that this was the girl's instrument). The two persons on the right are stationary.Their instruments are no longer extant. The foremost girl in the group which originally would have included more members than those shown in Hay's copy, would play the large, boat-shaped harp, the others double oboe and rectangular tambourine. A girl clapping her hands and singing may also have been included.

The garments of the two girls on the right look particularly ragged in Hay's copy. The uneven outline is no doubt to be interpreted as the edge of the yellow area at the top part of an otherwise plain white dress in vogue at the time,(68) the outline of the skirt being either erroneously omitted in the copy or invisible at the time the drawing was made. The two dancing musicians wear both a hip belt and a diaphanous garment.
Date: On the basis of the wigs and dresses a date around the reigns of Tuthmosis IV and Amenophis III seems most probable. The chairs and cushions are strongly reminiscent of the furniture represented on the banquet fragments in the British Museum to be discussed below. The execution of the scene, however, is markedly different from the style of these fragments.
Location: 'SW of Yanni's' (Hay), *i.e.* south west of TT 52 of Nakht.

TT C8
Champollion tomb no. 38
Fragment: lintel, University College London 14227.
Owner: Nakht, overseer of fowl-houses in the estate of Amūn.
Family: wife Irtnefert; mother , Taḥu, songstress of Amūn.
Bibliography: Champollion, *Not. descr.* i, pp. 532-3, 850; Rosellini MSS 284,G51-2. Lintel: J. E. Quibell & W. M. F. Petrie, *Catalogue of Antiquities from Thebes Exhibited in University College 1896*, 9 [16]; Weigall in *RT* 39, 1907, p. 220 [xi]; H. M. Stewart, *Egyptian Stelae Reliefs and Paintings from the Petrie Collection*, I London 1976, p. 52, pl. 42.2.

Description: A T-shaped tomb:
On the right front wall A (called 'left' wall by Champollion) is a representation of the tomb owner seated with a long stick in one hand, a cloth in the other. In front of him are offerings consisting of several loaves of bread, fowl, and bowls. Beyond him are in three registers(?): 1) a prostrate peasant and a servant receiving geese from two men leading flocks of these birds; 2) a scribe taking account of the geese, and a man being beaten on the shoulders; 3) another scribe counting three flocks of geese being taken to him. The text describing the entire scene is as follows:

sḫmḫ ỉb ỉrt bw nfr ỉrt ỉrw m ꜣpdw n ḥtp nṯr n ꞽImn šsp ꜣpdw nw tꜣ mḥ ỉn ỉmy-r...
'Rejoicing at doing something pleasant, taking account of the fowl of the divine offerings of Amūn. Receiving fowl from the north, by the overseer...' (here follow, according to Champollion, the titles of the deceased).

The scene thus depicts Nakht in his official capacity of overseer of the fowl-houses of the temple of Amūn.
On the other walls (positions not specified) were pictures showing 1) the tomb owner fowling with his family; 2) netting birds; 3) plucking geese; 4) agricultural scenes; 5) offerings &c. &c. (Champollion). Perhaps the inscription copied by Rosellini (MSS 284,G52) belonged here:

sḫmḫ ỉb šsp bw nfr ỉr(t) hrw nfr ỉn ỉmy-r h3y n ʾImn Nḫt ḥmt.f
nbt pr ʾIrtnfrt m3ʿt ḫrw

'Enjoying oneself receiving something good, spending a happy day by the overseer of the fowl-houses of Amūn, Nakht (and) his wife, mistress of the house, Irtnefert, justified.'

Another interesting inscription copied by Rosellini (MSS 284,G51) pertains to a scene showing the tomb owner offering to his forefathers:

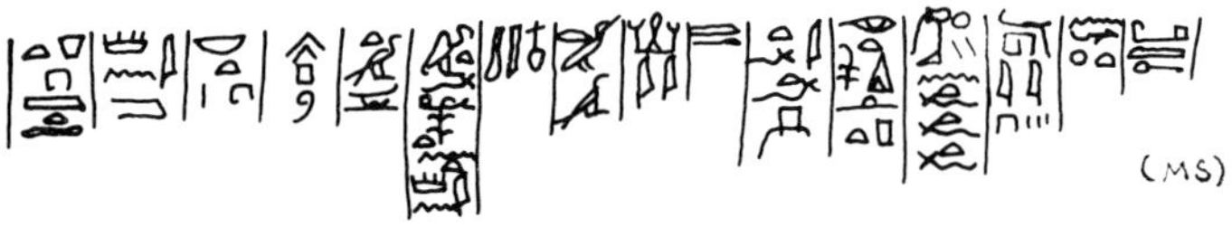

ỉrt ḥtp dỉ nsw wʿb sp sn n ỉtw ỉmy-r h3y Nḫt m3ʿ ḫrw
ỉt ỉt ỉm3ḫw m3ʿ ḫrw ḥm-k3 P3nfr m3ʿ ḫrw mwt.f šmʿyt nt ʾImn
T3ḥwḥpw nbt pr ʾImnmwsḫt m3ʿt ḫrw

'Making an offering which the king gives twice pure to (his) forefathers. The overseer of the fowl-houses Nakht, justified. - (His) grandfather, the venerable(69) justified. The soul priest Panūfer. His mother, songstress of Amūn, Taḥuḥepu.(70) The mistress of the house Amenemweskhet, justified.'

The accompanying scene would show Nakht facing left, offering to a row of relatives facing right

In the inner room was a representation of the tomb owner and his wife seated, with a young girl pouring a drink from two tiny vases into a drinking cup, both white. This was undoubtedly part of a banquet scene. Unfortunately no one copied this tomb, of which so much seems to have remained when Champollion visited it. But a fragment of the lintel remains, having been bought by Petrie at Thebes. It is of sandstone carved in shallow sunk relief, and shows Nakht and his wife adoring Osiris (the figure of the deity is lacking, but his name survives).

Date: The tomb is dated to the Nineteenth dynasty by Porter & Moss, a date repeated by Helck(71) and Stewart. But every single scene in the tomb is a typically Eighteenth dynasty scene, and the wig and dress point to the earlier half of the dynasty. The T-shape of the tomb supports this earlier date, although it does occur in Ramessid tombs. The detail of the girl pouring a drink from tiny twin vases also has parallels in the first half of the Eighteenth dynasty and not in the Ramessid period.

Location: The lower enclosure of Sheikh ʿAbd el-Qurna, according to Porter & Moss probably near TT 343. In the Rosellini MSS these two tombs are referred to on the same page (MSS 284,G52).

TT C9

In the first edition of the *Topographical Bibliography* I (1927), this tomb, then called 'nn', had more scenes than those listed in the present second edition. The 'tumbling girls, girl with dishevelled hair' in Hay MSS 29852,244-6 and 29822,71 have been taken out. Some tumblers (29852,246) are now to be found under TT 53(2), the rest (29852,244-5 and 29822,71) under TT 135(7).

The draughts playing scene which the second edition assigns to this tomb (Hay MSS 29852,243) has recently been shown to refer to TT 10.(72)

This leaves the ornamental vases (Hay MSS 29852,242), not three, as Porter & Moss say, but five, as proof of the existence of 'TT C9'. Two of these vases appear to be absolutely identical to two vases in TT 95, a tomb in which Hay is also known to have copied scenes.(73) Among the remaining three vases two are reminiscent of a set of vases in the same TT 95,(74) but in this tomb there are two vases lying in a shallow bowl, not just one, and the vases are provided with handles, the shallow bowl having an ornament at the bottom. The wall with vases is now very faded, and when seen by me in 1984 it was not immediately possible to identify the vases drawn by Hay with any of the other vases on the tomb wall. Perhaps we shall have to search the walls of another incompletely published tomb. In 1832(75) Hay spent several days tracing vases in a large tomb near his house, *i.e.* close to the house of Giovanni d'Athanasi near TT 52 of Nakht. The tomb he entered also had a 'large picture of cows'. The only tomb in that position containing both cattle and unusual vases is TT 131. Some of the vases were published by Vercoutter, *op. cit.* Perhaps the future publication of the tomb, proposed by Säve-Söderbergh, will enable us to identify the remaining vases.

The heading for the relevant section of Hay MSS 29852, including the subjects mentioned above, says 'Gourna. A tomb joining the one with a hunting subject [*sc.* TT 342]. Below my house'. This remark on an apparently misplaced page was presumably the cause of the confusion over this tomb in the past. The evidence rather points to the fact that 'TT C9' never existed.

TT C11

Lepsius tomb no. 86

Owner: Nebseny, overseer of the goldworkers of Amūn, overseer of all works of silver and gold and bronze at Karnak.

Family: father Nebmosi; mother Teti; wife Tanefert.

Bibliography: Lepsius, *Text*, iii, pp. 286-7.

Description: The texts of the two scenes showing recording of cattle and spearing a hippopotamus were copied by Lepsius:

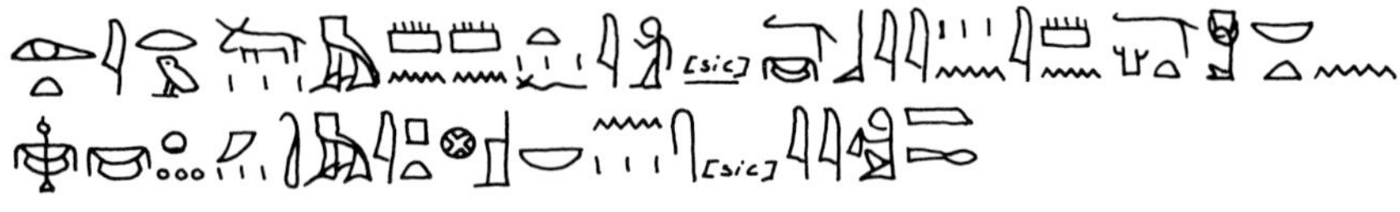

ỉrt ỉrw k3w mnmnt.f ỉn ỉmy-r nwbyw n ʾImn ỉmy-r k3t nbt n ḥḏ nbw ḥmt m ʾIpt-swt Nbsny m3ʿ ḫrw

'Taking account of his cows and cattle by the overseer of the goldworkers of Amūn, overseer of all works of silver, gold and bronze at Karnak, Nebseny, justified.'

[wḏꜣ ỉn](76) ỉmy-r nwbyw n ꜣImn Nbsny mꜣʿ ḫrw r stt ḥb r stw(77) r sḏꜣ ḥr.f m kꜣt Sḫt r wdn n nbt ḥb ỉr.s mrrt.f

'[Going out by] the overseer of the gold-workers of Amūn, Nebseny, justified, to shoot the hippopotamus, to walk about and to take recreation in the works of the Fen goddess, and to make offering to the Lady of hunting so that she may do what he wishes.'

Date: Porter & Moss date the tomb 'Tuthmosis III(?)'. This is undoubtedly correct, as all known hunting scenes showing hippopotamus hunting date from around this period.(78)
State of preservation: The name of Amūn was hacked out in some places, but it had been restored in ancient times. The damaged parts had been replastered and the hieroglyphs re-done in blue paint, the original hieroglyphs being polychrome. A varnish over the figures had blackened.
Location: Just east of TT 123 at Sheikh ʿAbd el-Qurna.

TT C13
Lepsius tomb no. 73
Owner: name and title unknown.
Bibliography: Lepsius, *Text*, iii, pp. 279-80.
Description: A very ruined painted tomb with a representation of a procession of people holding palm-branches. Lepsius mentions an 'Osiris' crown which has at the tip not a solar disc, but a round shape resembling , a yellow disc with red lines and green markings at the base. The crown was presumably worn by Osiris, and a representation of this god must thus be included among the few others recorded from the tomb (being omitted by Porter & Moss), presumably separate from the scene showing the procession.
Date: undated, but undoubtedly New Kingdom, though possibly Ramessid?

TT 15
Lepsius tomb no. 61
Owner: an overseer of the Two Houses of Gold, overseer of the Two Houses of Silver.
Bibliography: Lepsius MSS 352 [middle and lower].
Description: None, except for titles of deceased and name of Neferweben, son of ʿAmethu (TT 83).
Date: Porter & Moss have 'probably Eighteenth dynasty', which is presumably correct, in view of the presence of a son of ʿAmethu, who was vizier of Tuthmosis III.(79)
Location: 'Probably in plain.'

5 Tomb No. A4

As regards this tomb(1) we are exceptionally fortunate in having at our disposal a number of elements essential in an attempted reconstruction: descriptions and drawings by the early travellers; a sketched plan and indications of the measurements of the tomb; and actual fragments of the wall-decoration, now in a museum collection. In addition, part of the wall-decoration has an unusually close parallel in another tomb.

The starting point in the investigation was provided by the following three statements:

1) Hay MSS 29824,19: 'The 3rd tomb at Gourna - the whole of the right side of the chamber is destroyed and filled with rubbish - said to be carried off by Mr. Salt - on the left side is [*sic*] the remains of the feast much destroyed in an attempt to cut out pieces... The style of painting is very careful and may be considered equal with the hippopotamus tomb [*sc*. TT 155].'
Hay worked in this tomb from 30 May to 10 June 1826 (diary MSS 31054,135-135 verso).

2) Burton MSS 25638,48: 'Small catacomb opened by Yanni(2) East^{rn} End of the Mountain called Dra Aboo Negr Southern End.' MSS 25639,40: 'The small catacomb on the S side of Dra Aboo Negr. East.^{n} end, opened about 2 or 3 years since by Mr. Salt; -& cruelly defaced. The walls every where broken or cut - whole subjects destroyed for the sake of getting off pieces. One of the people thus employed must have been a dealer in hieroglyphics, as he has diligently effaced the names of the male & female proprietors, the lord and lady of the tomb. -He has been no indifferent traveller, but one whose particular study has been hieroglyphics.' Burton wrote this ca. 1824.

3) Porter & Moss, *Topographical Bibliography*, I^2,1 (1960), p. 447: 'A.4. Siuser 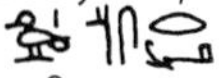 Scribe, Counter of the grain, Mayor of the Southern City, Overseer of the granary. Dyn. XVIII.'

The tomb in question is of the so-called T-shape (plan in Hay MSS 29824,19, cf. Ill. 13). It is evident from the above quotations that some pre-1824 traveller systematically cut out pieces from certain parts of the tomb.(3) On the other hand, judging from the sketches and drawings made, above all by Hay, other parts of the tomb, especially the inner room, were left fairly untouched. The person who attacked the tomb removed so much of the right part of the hall that nothing is mentioned by the early travellers as to the nature of the subjects depicted. Of the banquet scene, an ever-popular target on the part of dealers, enough was left for Burton to include one sketch.

The scenes remaining in good condition on the walls in the mid 1820s included the decoration of the two long walls of the inner room: on the left scenes connected with the burial of the deceased and funerary episodes, on the right the various rituals performed before the mummy of the deceased, with pictures 'in large'(4) of the deceased couple on either wall. In the left part of the hall there was a scene showing the tomb owner taking account of his cows, vineyard and fishery (no copies survive of this part of the wall, but it is mentioned by Burton), and a highly interesting scene representing goods being brought from Kush, being stacked by a whole regiment of women, supervised by men with sticks. In the top right corner of this latter scene there was a large scale picture of Siuser, *ḥ3ty-ʿ* of the Southern City, overseer of the granary, the person whom Porter & Moss take to be the owner of the tomb.(5) On the 'opposite' wall was the banquet scene, but it is not clear which of the two scenes was on the front and rear walls respectively. A picture of the deceased on the left jamb of the doorway between hall and inner room completes the selection of scenes recorded by the above mentioned early travellers.

A closer study of the wall depicting the rites before the mummy, as copied by Hay, reveals that the person for whom the ceremonies were performed was not Siuser, the mayor, but a man whose title was related to one of Siuser's titles, a scribe and counter of grain (or scribe of the accounts of grain), 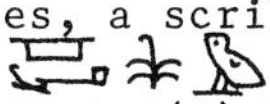 Wensu, whose name and title are repeated over and over again.(6) There is no Wensu mentioned in the fascicle of the *Topographical Bibliography* dealing with the Theban necropolis, but a man of that name is known from other sources (see below), and fragments of the tomb of a certain Wensu are at present in the Louvre.(7) They include a very large representation of agricultural scenes, now in five pieces, one large fragment of offering bringers and butchers in three registers, loading of grain onto boats from the top register of a wall, and geese in two registers. The style of these painted fragments appears to be identical to those drawn by Hay, and in the agricultural scenes there remain the name and title of the person presiding over the activities: Wensu, scribe of the Southern City.

It is possible to establish a connection between the Louvre fragments and Henry Salt. Some of them (8) are mentioned in the 1827 catalogue of the *Musée Charles X* by Champollion,(9) which was written when Champollion had acquired a collection of antiquities on behalf of the king of France. These objects had been sent to Leghorn by Salt. The lengthy negotiations concerning the sale were concluded during the summer of the previous year.(10) The collection in question was Salt's 'second collection',(11) formed during the years 1818-24. According to the statement written by Burton ca. 1824 the tomb of Wensu had been discovered two or three years previously. In 1822 Salt himself wrote: 'Yanni has also discovered some most interesting private tombs where most of the domestic scenes usually represented are as fresh as when they were painted.' (12) This statement presumably refers to our tomb among others.

Although the sources just quoted claim that the tomb had been opened in the early 1820's, an even earlier traveller describes a tomb which can only be TT A4 of Wensu.

The earliest record of any consequence concerning the private tombs at Thebes was given by L. M. Ripault who came up with the expedition of Napoleon in 1799-1800, but W. Hamilton, travelling in Egypt in 1801, is the first to give a description with enough details to enable us to identify some of the tombs he visited with known and numbered tombs.(13) One of them was beyond doubt TT A4. Among other scenes he describes the agricultural scene and specifically states that the tomb had 'nearly the same details as at Eleithias [*sc.* el-Kâb]'. As we shall see, this was true of the tomb of Wensu. Hamilton's description of the scene will be discussed *ad loc.* below. But he mentions other subjects which were only treated cursorily if at all by subsequent travellers: a hunting scene, not mentioned elsewhere; a fishing and fowling scene (referred to by Burton); preparing fish &c., not included in other descriptions. These subjects will all be discussed below.

In his general description of the tombs Hamilton included the banquet scenes. It is more than likely that his description was inspired by among others the banquet scene in TT A4 which was in a poor state when hay and Burton saw the tomb.

Hamilton's description takes back the modern history of the tomb of Wensu another twenty years. It is surprising that the tomb was left undisturbed during this span of time. It was obviously not suited for habitation, being too far from other dwellings, or the local residents would have taken it over and left their mark on the walls.

Scenes in the hall

1) The functions of the tomb owner

Incomplete drawings and descriptions of the wall, showing the tomb owner's office, were made by Hay, Burton and Wilkinson. Two subjects seem to have been depicted, one of them being a unique and highly interesting 'market scene', the other the inspection of farm produce.

The wall in question is either the left front or the left rear wall of the hall, opposite the wall showing the banquet. The interesting scene apparently depicting goods being bartered at a market or by the door-to-door method was copied by Hay in MSS 29822,21-22 on two pages, joining each other, but drawn at a slightly different scale by *camera lucida* (MSS 29822,21 verso has a duplicate drawing of the top left register). A substantial part of the middle register was destroyed, affecting the registers above and below (Ill. 14).(14) Burton (MSS 25644,125) copied the lower right part of the scene, with details not shown in Hay's drawing (Ill. 15). On the basis of Burton's drawing it is possible to identify a small drawing made by Wilkinson in 1828 (Ill. 16).(15)

The lower register shows on the left two groups of six and five women with open mouths and with unguent cones upon their heads, clapping their hands. The foremost group moves forwards. They are preceded by two women again with cones on their heads, carrying objects that can hardly be anything but rectangular tambourines,(16) in spite of the curious red loop at the upper edge.(17) Between them is a girl who seems to be dancing and who may be snapping her fingers. The text above them explains their exhilaration:

rmṯ Wꜣst m ḥꜥꜥwt m ršwt m nḏm ib gsw m bꜣk nḏm wrḥ m ꜥntiw ḫn n nhm ḏd

'The people of Thebes are in jubilation, in joy and pleased at heart; "ointment of sweet moringa oil, unguent of myrrh" are the joyful words they say.'

In the centre there is a group of three figures, one of whom, a man, turns towards the rejoicing women with a stick in his hand. At this point Burton's excellent drawing helps to identify the setting of the scene. It is clearly two rows of houses with a street between them.(18) Every single brick of the houses is marked, and they are the 'colour of crude brick or rather dark grey' to use Burton's phraseology. The left part of the far row of houses shows the roof supported by a papyriform column, and several pillars decorated with horizontal coloured bands, including yellow and blue. This is most certainly the detail which Wilkinson copied. The 'tower' shown in his drawing is, however, not in the drawing by Burton, the roof of the buildings here continuing at the same level. As a matter of fact, the 'tower' is not in Wilkinson's original drawing. But after he added it for his publication, subsequent scholars copied it. The window of the house next to the porch is similar to the window in Wilkinson's 'tower'. The curved line in the right part of his drawing in all probability corresponds to what is in Burton's drawing the outline of the basket being carried by the men in the lower part of the register.

To the right of the porch are apparently two connecting houses with vertical lines dividing them. The first house has one window (Wilkinsons's 'tower' window) and a door, the second house having a door, the jambs and lintel painted red, the door itself having a 'grey tint', according to Burton, 'w(hite)' according to Hay. Two small windows at different levels, suggesting the existence of two storeys, are set on either side of a larger one, with a fanlight above.

The second row of houses shows three large entrance doors and two small windows high up, the doors being in this instance red, the jambs and lintels grey.(19)

At the same level as the base of this latter row of houses are large figures to be visualized as walking in the street: a woman and a man are bargaining about some fish (the top part of the figures is destroyed), two men carry a huge basket of grain,(20) and two scribes follow with their palettes, one of them carrying a scroll.

On top of the lower row, *i.e.* where the street is, an inscription has been inserted among the figures, running from right to left, and explaining the scene:

sšmt rm(w) n rmt Wꜣst (m) pryt.sn m pꜣ ḥw rsfy n pꜣ ḥkꜣ
'Taking fish to the people of Thebes in their houses out of the food catch of the ruler.'(21)

The middle register, the central part of which was destroyed, depicts on the left three women walking to the left. One carries a piece of meat, the other two have sacks on their shoulders. A group of a dozen women with sacks, apparently empty, are being addressed by a man who turns towards them with a stick in his hand. Two women with unguent cones upon their heads arrange a heap of merchandise with four pink jars above. Hay coloured a few details in this drawing, and it is possible to identify grapes, cucumber and meat in the heap. Next to them more women are presumably occupied in the same way (they are partly destroyed).(22) The text above refers to the goods:

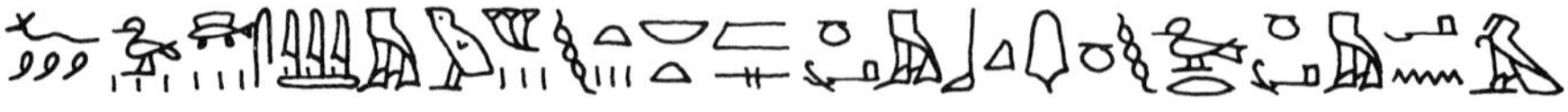

...[ỉw]f ꜣpdw rmw smw(t) bnrỉt nbt gsw m bꜣḳ wrḥ m ꜥntỉw
'meat, fowl, fish, all kinds of sweet herbs, ointment of moringa oil, unguent of myrrh.'

To the right of the destroyed portion of the wall there remains part of a heap of vegetables, including onions or leeks, cucumbers, a bird, and possibly loaves of bread. A scribe takes account of the proceedings, a sack like those used for clothes being deposited in front of him.

The top register shows on the left two women walking left with red sacks, a piece of meat hanging from the arm of one of them. They are followed by another with an unguent cone on her head and a piece of meat in her sack. Two groups of four and three women appear to be arguing with one of the inspectors. The woman on the left carry empty sacks, those on the right have their sacks filled up.(23) The man in the middle apparently also holds a sack. In the centre of the register a man confronts a row of nine women, holding aloft a stick. Two women behind him turn round with loaded sacks on their shoulders. Another man gives a hand with a sack next to a heap of sacks lying on the ground. The number and contents are presumably being taken down by a scribe whose name and title are given above:

sḥḏ sš m nỉwt rst Pꜣḳdw mꜣꜥ ḫrw
'The inspector and scribe (or: inspector of scribes?) of the Southern City, Paḳedu, justified.(24)

Above the women is the title of the scene:

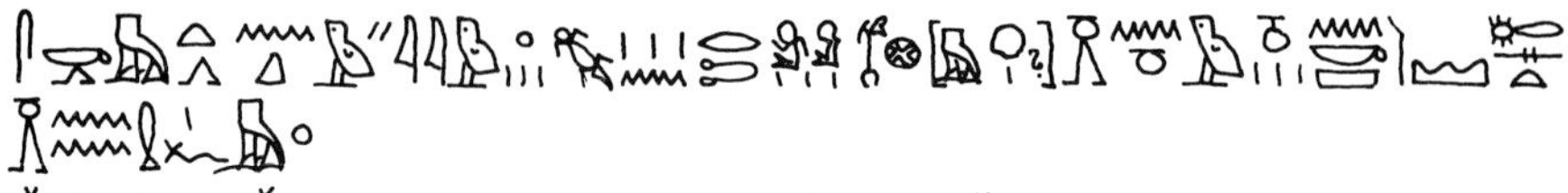

sšmt nḳyw ꜥšꜣw n rmṯ Wꜣst [m tp?] ỉnw n Kš ḫst ỉnn ḥm.f m ...
'Taking many notched sycomore figs(25) to the people of Thebes out of the best of(?) the goods from vile Kush which his Majesty brought from...'

The entire scene is being watched by the 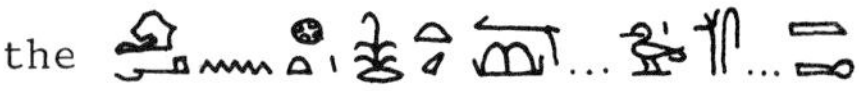 *ḥ3ty-ᶜ n nỉwt rst ỉmy-r šnwt ... S3wsr,* 'the mayor of the Southern City, overseer of the granary...(26) Siuser.'

The presence of the mayor of Thebes(27) lends an official air to the scene. One of the duties of the mayor was to collect the harvest tax consisting of grain, and in this he was assisted by the overseer and the scribes of the granary. But here he can hardly be shown in his capacity of tax collector, as grain has little to do with the representation. Taxes consisting of items like incense, oils, and fruit, of which there is in the scene a fair selection, were administered by the treasury.(28) It seems therefore that it is not an event connected with the delivery of tax that is represented. The goods consist chiefly of sycomore figs and ointments as well as vegetables, fish and fowl, and were it not for the presence of men with sticks, perhaps admonishing the women, one would have thought it a pleasant market scene. Also the goods(29) had apparently been provided hy the king. The sweet-smelling herbs and unguents contrast strangely with the presence of fish and meat, and the unguent cones worn by some of the women are a rather unusual detail outside banquet and offering scenes. It remains a fact that the occasion depicted was obviously a cause of jubilation for the inhabitants of Thebes, and that it had something to do with royal good-will. It seems reasonable to assume that the event depicted was the day on which one of the merchant ships or caravans of Tuthmosis III(30) returned from the South (Kush), inundating the city of Thebes with goods. These are shown being organized and sorted out under the supervision of the mayor, and with the assistance of the scribes, presumably including Wensu, the scribe of the granary, and that the goods were then taken round to be distributed to the inhabitants.(31)

According to Burton MSS 25639,40 there is a continuation of this scene, not mentioned by any of the other copyists: 'Upon the opposite wall [*sc.* of the banquet scene] where the house is, the lord is seen with the same sort of stick he always carries, & a mace in the other hand, standing & taking account of his cows, vineyard and fishery...' Burton then goes on to describe the market scene.

It is possible to estimate the approximate size of this wall. Burton gives the width of the hall as being about 17ft (5.18m), the height of the wall being about 7ft (2.13m). If we allow a minimum of 50cm for the doorway leading to the inner room, and assume that this opening was set in the middle (cf. Hay's sketched plan of the tomb, and considering the width of the agricultural scene to be described below) the width of the wall with which we are concerned would be a maximum of 2.34m. This means that the height of the wall was very roughly the same as its width. Thus we must conclude that any other representation on this wall must have been either above or below the market scene. Indeed, the fact that the hieroglyphic inscription in the lower register to the left turns from horizontal to vertical strongly suggests that this was the end of the wall.

In Hay's drawing the border line on the right continues beyond the lower register of the market scene, and it is therefore to be assumed that the 'cows, vineyard and fishery' are to be placed in the lower registers.(32) As this latter scene was still on the wall when Burton visited the tomb, there is little possibility of finding any fragments of it in the collections of Salt. But the description by Hamilton throws some light on the meaning of Burton's statement. Hamilton's remarks about the subject, beyond doubt referring to this tomb, will be quoted *in toto*:

'The fishing and fowling scenes are described as at Eleithias; but the water is here better expressed. There is also another method of fowling, which is by using decoy birds; the men hold two of these in their hands, and when the birds are come among the lotus-bushes, others knock them down with a stick, at one end of which is a serpent's head; perhaps this may have some allusion to a persuasion that prevailed in Egypt, that the eye of the basilisk could charm birds to stop their flight and fall into his mouth. Some are employed in carrying the produce of the farm into the granary; others are pounding or bringing in their wheat, drying and salting their fish; and some are preparing for the feast after the labours of the day, or the completion of the harvest.'(33)

It would seem that there were actually two scenes concerned with fishing and fowling one of which was similar to one at el-Kâb (Eleithias). In general such scenes are of two types: 1) the tomb owner fishing and fowling; 2) servants netting fish and fowl. The former is usually a large scale representation, whereas the latter is at a much smaller scale, suitable for a sub-scene. The two types frequently occur within the same tomb, but the difference in significance and execution must not be confused.

The fishing and fowling scene on the wall in question must be the one showing servants in action, partly because of the available space, and partly because it is connected with a scene showing the preparation of the catch. Such a scene is to be found in the tomb of Paḥeri at el-Kâb below the banquet scene.(34) Here the two lower registers show Paḥeri supervising 1) fishing, carrying fish, preparing fish and mending nets, and 2) catching fowl with a net, plucking the birds and storing them in jars.

The sub-scene in TT A4 may then be taken to comprise the following elements: 1) fishing and fowling with nets as in the tomb of Paḥeri (mentioned by Hamilton and Burton); 2) drying and salting fish as in the tomb of Paḥeri (mentioned by Hamilton);(35) 3) vintage, possibly as in the tomb of Paḥeri on the same wall as fishing and fowling, but there separated from it by two registers (mentioned by Burton); 4) cows (mentioned by Burton).

2) The agricultural scenes

The greater part of the wall showing agricultural activities is at present in the Louvre. It consists of the following pieces:

1) Five fragments showing the tomb owner presiding over work in the field (N 1431, cf. Ill. 17). The main agricultural scene has been published several times, cf. *Topographical Bibliography* I^2,2, p. 819. To this bibliography may be added the following: J. F. Champollion, *Le Musée Charles X*, Paris 1827, p. 99; E. de Rougé, *Notice sommaire des monuments égyptiens exposés dans les galeries du Louvre*, Paris 1876, p. 85; Vandier, *Guide* (1970), p. 25 (this is the first to give the provenance as 'de la tombe d'Ounsou'); M. Lambrino, *L'Égypte (Encyclopédie par l'image)*, Paris 1963, fig. p. 20 (part of top register); B. Romant, *Life in Egypt in Ancient Times*, Geneva 1978, p. 94 (colour).

2) Three barges being loaded with grain (N 1430, cf. Ill. 18), cf. Porter & Moss, *loc.cit* . To this may be added Champollion, *loc. cit.*; de Rougé, *loc. cit.*; J. Vandier, *Manuel d'archéologie égyptienne*, V,2, Paris 1969, fig. 362.
3) Possibly from here: geese in two registers, also in the Louvre (unpublished, cf. Ill. 19).

As mentioned above the connection between the fragments in the Louvre and TT A4 can be established by 1) the close similarity between the execution of the paintings on the fragments and the decoration in other parts of the tomb, as revealed by the copies by Hay and Burton; 2) the link with the tomb of Paḥeri at el-Kâb, which is apparent not only in the agricultural scenes, but also in the funeral procesison (see below); 3) the name and the title of the person inspecting the agricultural activities corresponding to those of the owner of TT A4; 4) the fact that Henry Salt was alleged to have removed portions of the walls from the tomb and the acquisition of the Louvre fragments from the Salt collection.

As far as the position of the agricultural scenes in the tomb is concerned there can be little doubt that they are to be placed in the right portion of the hall. The left part is taken up by the market and banquet scenes, and Hay explicitly says that the scenes in the right part were cut out by Salt, leaving not a trace to be described by subsequent visitors. But whether the scenes were once on the front or rear wall of this part of the hall remains uncertain.

The proportions of the wall in question, be it the front or the rear one, would be roughly 2.34m wide, with an average height of about 2.13m. The five fragments featuring the tomb owner inspecting work in the field have been assempled on one wall in the Louvre, but the fragments are not in their exact position. When re-arranged,(36) the complete picture measures about 2.35m, the agricultural scenes thus taking up the entire width of the wall and the height of the three registers (*i.e.* 68cm + bottom border lines). The bottom line is clearly visible on the four large fragments.

In the tomb of Paḥeri the grain barges belong on the same wall as work in the field. There they are to be found in a lower register. The fragment with the barges in the Louvre preserves part of a polychrome top border. It therefore belongs to the top register, possibly at the extreme right, as the corresponding (reversed) barges in the tomb of Paḥeri belong towards the left part of the scene.(37) The central part of the wall, more than half its entire height, is lost. One would expect a large scale representation of the tomb owner to the left, overlooking activities such as those depicted in the tomb of Paḥeri. The fragment with geese perhaps belonged on this wall.

The agricultural scenes show conventional activities as depicted in numerous other tombs of the Eighteenth dynasty. An unusual detail is the plough drawn by two men instead of a span of oxen. There is only one parallel known to me of a similar arrangement, namely in the tomb of Paḥeri at el-Kâb. As shown in Ill. 20 a great number of other figures in the scene are absolutely identical with those from the Louvre fragments,(38) others are very similar. As this state of affairs is also apparent in the decoration elsewhere in the tomb, the relation between the two tombs will be discussed in a separate paragraph below.

To the left is Wensu supervising the activities, staff in hand and seated on a stool. The inscription in front of him describes the scene (signs in brackets [] have been restored from the tomb of Paḥeri):

mꜣꜣ ỉtrw šmw ỉtrw prt ḥnwt nbt ỉrrt m sḫt ỉn sš n nỉwt rst Wnsw mꜣʿ ḫrw
'Seeing the season of summer and the season of winter and all the occupations done in the field by the scribe of the Southern City, Wensu.'

Above him offerings are laid out, bowls of fruit and loaves of bread, lotus flowers on stands, and a box with a necklace(?).

The lower register shows ploughing and sowing. Above the team of oxen and a man with a whip to the left is an inscription to be linked with the text above the following ploughman:

nfrwy prw n r.k pꜣy šrỉ hrw(39) *nfr šw m sdb* ...(40)
'How excellent is your exclamation, my child. The day is beautiful, free of worries...'

The exclamation referred to is omitted in the tomb of Wensu. In the tomb of Paḥeri it comes from one of the men pulling the plough: 'We are [hurrying up]. Fear not for the corn-fields, they are very good.'

Next follows another span of oxen, presumably without the plough(41) which is drawn by men while two others use their hand picks to hack up the crusty soil. Above them are written the words they say:

ỉw.ỉ r ỉrt ḥꜣw ḥr bꜣkw.ỉ n pꜣ sr grw
'Now, I shall do more than my work for the noble.'

In the tomb of Paḥeri this is the answer to a remark made by one of the other labourers, but omitted in the tomb of Wensu: 'Hurry up with the work, friend, and let us finish in good time'.

The second register from below shows to the left a tree and a man rippling flax and another carrying a bundle which a third man has tied. Next is shown pulling flax by four men and a woman. Above them are fragments of a inscription:

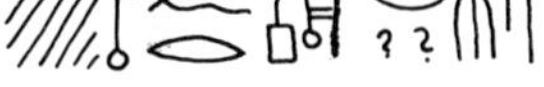 *nfr sš Nbms*(42)

A group of women face them. After the gap comes the harvest of grain, accompanied by an inscription giving the words of one of the girls (words in brackets [] are restored from Paḥeri):

ỉmỉ n.ỉ. wꜥt drt mk ỉỉ.n m mšrw m ỉr nꜣ n khsw n sf gr m pꜣ hrw
'Give me a handful!(43) Look, we shall be going back by twilight.(44) Do not do the evil tricks(45) of yesterday. Stop it today!'

Paḥeri does not give us any clue to this scrap of conversation, but one would imagine that 'yesterday's evil tricks' had to do with one of the girls contriving to return with a full basket, but with less effort put into the work.

The third register shows to the left the measuring of the fields by the tax collectors. A few hieroglyphs remain:

apparently giving a name followed by 'justified', and the name and title of the field measurer.

This subject is omitted in the tomb of Paḥeri which has winnowing instead. To the extreme right threshing and carrying grain in baskets is represented. The labourer in the tomb of Paḥeri carries his basket on his shoulders with the opening up, not over his head as his colleague in the tomb of Wensu.

The loading of the grain barges which must be placed near the top of the wall, separated from work in the fields by other rural activities, is accompanied by the following legend almost identical to the text in the tomb of Paḥeri:

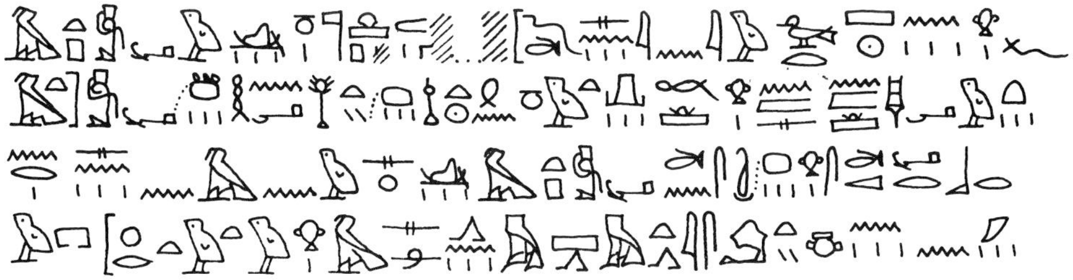

ꜣtp wsḫw nw ḥtp nṯr(46) [m ỉt bdt] [ḏd.sn ỉn ỉw wrš.n ḥr fꜣt] ỉt ḥnꜥ bdt ḥḏt šnwt mḥ ḥr gsgs ꜥḥꜣw n r.sn nꜣ n wsḫw ꜣtp dns ỉt ḥr sd r brw ḫr twtw ḥr ꜣs.n m šmt ỉs ḥꜣty.n n ḥmt
'Loading barges of the divine offering with barley and wheat. They say,"Must we spend all day carrying barley and white emmer? The granaries are full, heaps are pouring over the opening. The barges are heavily laden, the grain is spilling out. But one hurries us to go. Is our heart of copper?(47)"'

The description by Hamilton of this wall mentions swine, a detail seen in the tomb of Paḥeri but not extant among the remaining fragments of the tomb of Wensu, and introduces a detail not mentioned elsewhere:

'... there is likewise the same [*sc.* as at el-Kâb] representation of a farmyard and stock of a rich landed proprietor and breeder of cattle. Here is likewise introduced a herd of swine; and in a neighbouring compartment are two very animated bull-fights, in which these animals are bellowing aloud, as they furiously attack each other with their horns and hoofs.'(48)

In the tomb of Paḥeri there is a scene showing a bull covering a cow,(49) but no actual bull fight. The cattle must be inserted between the loading of boats in the top register and the agricultural activities in the three lower registers.

3) The banquet scene

Where the banquet scene is concerned we must rely almost entirely on the description by Burton (MSS 25639,40) and one of his drawings (MSS 25638,48, cf. Ill. 21 [upper]).(50) All that Hay has to say (MSS 29824,18) is that 'on the left is *[sic]* the remains of a feast much destroyed in [an] attempt to cut out pieces.' At least this gives an approximate position of the scene as being somewhere in the left part of the hall. According to Burton it was on the 'opposite' wall of the scene with the houses and market described above.

As to the general lay-out of the scene Burton says that 'the females are sitting as usual separate from the males'. They have unguent cones upon their heads and lotus flowers in their left hands bent to their breasts, and on their heads: 'those who have the full blown lotus on their head have the bud in hand & so alternately'. The women sit on 'block, lionlegged stools'. The men sit on 'solid green seats. They also have the lotus in their hands, but not upon the head. All have green necklaces - None have bracelets...'

Details include a female attendant offering unguent from a tall vase to a guest and arranging it on the head of the guest. A female offers a shallow bowl to a woman, while three kneeling women clap their hands (cf. Burton's drawing). Below servants, including a 'naked female' are bringing in provisions. The tomb owner and his wife are not described, but the grapes on the table of offerings in front of them are 'admirably done, & have all the bloom on them & appear in relief'.

It is tempting to try and match unprovenanced banquet scenes in collections with this wall, of which however more seems to have been destroyed than carried away. But to prove a connection will be exceedingly difficult, as the only drawing made of this wall is the one by Burton. When searching for suitable fragments one must necessarily only include those that have a long history after their removal from the tomb, *i.e.* those which have been on the market since the early 1820's, and comparatively few qualify in this respect. One piece might just conceivably fulfill the requirements. In 1947 the collection of Moïse Levi de Benzion was sold by auction. Some of the fragments of wall-decoration in this lot will be discussed in another part of this study. Suffice it to say that they are linked with fragments known to have been removed from a Theban tomb around 1820. When we are looking for part of a banquet scene dating from the reign of Tuthmosis III a certain fragment in the de Benzion collection immediately springs to mind. A photograph of it was published by Keimer in 1953.(51) It shows five male guests and three servants, two male and one female, and they might just fit Burton's general description: 'solid seats', 'green necklaces', 'no bracelets', 'lotus flowers on their heads but not in their hands'. It must be born in mind that in case this piece stems from TT A4, it was presumably removed before Burton visited the tomb, and he would have described what remained of a related scene. Among the unpublished pieces in the de Benzion collection there may well be others that could be fitted into this context, if only we knew where they were now.

Other scenes in the hall

4) Fishing and fowling

The passage in Hamilton, quoted above p. 68, clearly refers to a large scale representation of fishing and fowling, a frequent motif in the T-shaped tombs of this period. The scene was usually positioned on the right rear wall of the hall. As this applies in particular to the tombs of the reign of Tuthmosis III, we can assume that this was the position of the scene in our tomb as well, the opposite, right front wall being thus taken up by agricultural scenes.

Fishing and fowling often had vintage as a sub-scene. But according to Burton this subject was depicted on another wall in this tomb.(52)

5) Hunting in the desert

Hamilton describes a hunting scene in this tomb which was omitted by the other travellers:

'The same hand that had succeeded so well in this scene [*sc.* the bulls mentioned above] was probably employed to depict in the same grotto an Egyptian hunt, where the Laird of the estate is in his car drawn by two horses, exactly resembling the war-chariot of the monarch in the battle-scenes, armed with his bow and arrows, and attended by his servants on foot. The mountains of the desert before him are crowded with ostriches, stags, wolves, leopards, porcupines. The oescher plant(53) is the only shrub which seems to enliven the scene with any symptoms of vegetation. The interest excited by this singular picture is not a little heightened by the consideration of the changes that must have since taken place in the brute inhabitants of the neighbourhood.'(54)

Most hunting scenes in the tombs date from the reign of Tuthmosis III and occur in T-shaped tombs. The position of the scene is either on the right wall of the passage, which is not feasible in our tomb as this wall is taken up by another subject, or else in the right part of the hall. As the decoration of both the front and rear walls have already been accounted for, the hunting scene must have been positioned on the right side wall (as in three other contemporary tombs).(55)

6) Offering bringers and butchers

The fragment in the Louvre (N 1393, cf. Ill. 22) undoubtedly comes from this tomb and can only belong somewhere in the hall. In the *Topographical Bibliography* I^2,2, p. 819 the fragment is wrongly described as showing a man watching agricultural scenes, including ploughing and butchers. The Louvre card for this fragment assigns this number to the fragment showing two rows of offering bringers and, in the top register, a butchering scene. The fragment has been mentioned by the following: Champollion, *loc. cit.*; de Rougé, *loc. cit.*; Boreux, *op. cit.* II, p. 414; Vandier, *Guide* (1961), p. 20; Lambrino, *op. cit.*, fig. p. 21 (the offering bringers); two details were published by Romant, *op. cit.*, p. 99 [upper and lower] (colour).

On the basis of Hamilton's description of 'carrying the produce from the farm into the granary' this fragment with 'offering bringers' may perhaps be the fragment referred to. It is 65.5cm high and would be able to be fitted in, the available space being: total height of wall 2.13m (according to Burton) less the height of the market scene (which was calculated to being 1.10m) less the top border and an empty space at the bottom (ca. 30cm in all). This leaves some 70cm unaccounted for. But it is difficult to arrange the three registers of offering bringers with the other rather elongated subjects on this wall.

Another possibility would be to place the offering bringers below the hunting scene, a frequent arrangement. But the produce they bring include other items than those which would be the result of a hunting expedition.

However, the butchers may provide a decisive clue as to the position of the scene. They frequently occur in connection with scenes related to the Feast of the Valley, in particular near a large scale representation of the tomb owner offering on either side of the entrance doorway, often next to the banquet.

Scenes in the inner room

1) Funerary ceremonies

The elements available for a reconstruction of this wall are as follows:

1) a sketch by Hay (MSS 29824,18, 18 verso, cf. Ill. 23) with an enumeration of the individual groups depicted on the wall; a few details drawn by *camera lucida* (MSS 29822,23,36 and MSS 29853,105, cf. Ills. 24-6), some with details in colour.

2) a description by Burton (MSS 25639,40), with drawings of a few groups (MSS 25638,49,50, cf. Ill. 27), some with more details than those found in the Hay MSS.

3) a water colour of one detail (lake with trees) by Wilkinson (MSS v.130 [bottom]).

4) indications of measurements of the wall by Burton (MSS 25639,40).

5) for comparison a wall depicting similar scenes in the tomb of Paḥeri (Tylor & Griffith, *Paheri*, pl. V). The individual groups in this tomb are to a large extent identical with those in TT A4, judging from the available drawings of the latter. Portions missing from the tomb of Paḥeri may be restored from the contemporary tomb of Rekhmirēᶜ.(56)

No fragments of this wall seem to be found in museums or other collections.

In MSS 29824,18,18 verso Hay gives the general lay-out of the individual registers, followed by a brief enumeration of the groups of figures represented. It is apparent that to a considerable extent these are identical with those in the tomb of Paḥeri, although the order of events varies. TT A4 is the more complete.(cf. Ills. 28 and 31).

The beginning of the first register(57) is similar to Paḥeri: a lector priest in front of a shrine, the two 'Kites' in a boat with their backs to a shrine, the boat being drawn by a man (Paḥeri has three men drawing the boat), met by a priest with a scroll and with his back to two shrines. Then the two tombs differ, in that Paḥeri introduces the *ḥ̮bt*-dancers whereas TT A4 has another lector priest and two men carrying a box (Paḥeri has four men carrying), with two female figures below and a priest censing.

The subjects depicted in a lower register in the tomb of Paḥeri are represented in the subsequent part of the first register in TT A4: four men guarding the coffin during its travel across the river or along a canal, and, omitted in Paḥeri, unloading the coffin. Then follows a pond with trees surrounded by eight slaughtered cows(58) (again omitted in Paḥeri), and four armless figures in an enclosure, (59) in Paḥeri to be found in a lower register, and in Rekhmirēᶜ called  *nṯrw r ᶜw wrw* 'the gods at the great gates.'

The second register shows the 'Nine Friends' (Paḥeri has only two), a lector priest and a female (in Paḥeri called the 'Older Kite'), following the mummy on a bier and preceded by another female figure (in Paḥeri called the 'Younger Kite'); the mummy is drawn on a sledge by two oxen and four men (Paḥeri has only two men) with in between three men with raised arms, a priest with an incense burner and a water jar (Paḥeri omits the latter) and another figure, partly destroyed. TT A4 then takes up subjects which also occur in one or the other of the two lower registers in Paḥeri: a priest reading from a scroll in front of a shrine, two *mww*-dancers in a vaulted structure, palm trees beside a pond(60), two trees of unspecified variety and a set of vases, followed by four closed shrines and a larger figure of Osiris in an open shrine(61) (the figure of Osiris, though not his insignia, is reversed in Paḥeri). Hay indicates that this is the end of the register.

It is evident from Hay's description and the available illustrations that the three upper registers in TT A4 were incomplete. As far as the third (middle) register is concerned it appears to be continuous for the right three-quarters of the representation, the gap occurring on the extreme left and actually extending into the registers above.(62) The scenes show the hacking up of soil near a shrine (not in Paḥeri, but restored from Rekhmirēᶜ), a female facing a lector priest, two kneeling figures in a boat (the foremost is in Rekhmirēᶜ the *ỉmỉ-ḫnt*), a shrine, another lector priest in front of a shrine(63) (partly destroyed) with a small figure on the right, yet another lector and a boat with three kneeling male figures in front of a square object sailing towards a hawk on a standard and two rows of four shrines,(64), the foremost four closed, the remaining four showing three bearded deities and one with a jackal's head.

The disposition of the upper two registers is less straightforward. It seems certain from Hay's detailed drawing of a section combining two of them that the *ḫbt*-dancers preceding the coffin dragged by three men fit below the scene showing the mooring of the boat (MSS 29822,23). To the left in the fourth register was according to Hay a kneeling figure in a boat with a haunch of beef and a pot. Hay's sketch of this group is not very clear, but presumably a scene like the one in Rekhmirēᶜ (65) is meant, and this has therefore been inserted in the reconstruction. Then follows a building with a roof supported by four slender columns, in front of which are two small figures holding what Hay calls 'knives', but which are probably clappers.(66) A priest(67) censes before another man, and then comes the *tekenu*(68) dragged by three men. The nature of the object on the sledge was by Hay described as 'a large green case ... This may be The Green Bag!' What Hay refers to here is not obvious to me. At this point Hay goes on: 'The rest [*sc.* figures] are destroyed... the sarcophagus and dancing men follow'. On the sketch Hay scribbled: 'part is damaged, then follows the dancing men which I have drawn.' The texts above the two scenes in his drawing(69) prove that there was no continuous scene beyond this point, and the figures would thus neatly conclude the two top registers on the right, a large area being destroyed about the middle of the registers.

In the top register there is a shrine in a boat with an incense cup on a tall stand in front of it, a kneeling man at the stern and two men rowing with one oar at the helm. They go towards another hawk on a standard. A man with two paddles runs towards a shrine (the man is rendered in water-colour in Hay MSS 29853,105,(cf. Ill. 26), and two kneeling female figures (in Paḥeri called the two 'Kites') with little round jars (drawn by Hay in MSS 29822,36, cf. Ill. 25) facing four ponds.(70) Here ends Hay's sketch, but as described above, the right extremity of the register, drawn with the *ḫbt*-dancers(71) shows the hands and title of a lector priest, a partly destroyed kneeling figure in front of an offering table(72) with an ox and a bird with a severed head above,(73) and the mooring of the boat containing the coffin.

Two spare *mww*-dancers facing a lector priest drawn by Hay in MSS 29822,36 (Ill. 25) present a problem, in that they cannot immediately be placed on this wall where, judging from Burton MSS 25639,40 they undoubtedly belong: 'The figures are seen in one place standing in a grotesque way, with high frames or caps upon their heads, upon one leg pointing at the roll, which a priest, who is reciting, holds in his hand.' A second pair of *mww*-dancers is not referred to in Hay's text. They can hardly go into the left part of the middle register as Hay says that much was destroyed here. The central portion of the fourth register seems to have been totally destroyed between the *tekenu* and the coffin on the sledge, and the only likely position is thus somewhere in the blank part of the upper register, although it is strange that Hay should have omitted these three persons in his descriptions - but all he has to say about the right part of the same register is that 'the rest is drawn with the dancing men of the line below'. I would therefore suggest that they be fitted in in the top register.

According to Burton's measurements in MSS 25639,40 this wall was about twice as wide as it was tall: 'The inner [room] is about 14ft by 6.6ft (4.27m x 2.13m)'. In order to accommodate the decoration suggested by Hay's description as being to the right of the five registers described above, Burton's measurements must be interpreted as taking into account the entire height of the wall, not only the decorated surface. The height of the five registers as reconstructed (Ill. 31) is already almost twice the width, thus suggesting that an undecorated area should be considered below.

The remaining portion of the wall at the far end of the room contained representations at a larger scale than the preceding five registers. Hay MSS 29824,19 says:

> 'At the end of these [*sc.* five registers] are the large subjects which fill up the wall - a kneeling figure before the green god with a table of offerings - fruit, vegetables, calf's head, goose - behind the deity a goddess with the hawk upon her head - Below a priest with the tyger(74) skin offers a similar offering to the above before the gentleman & lady, the latter embracing the former.'

The 'kneeling figure' before Osiris is no doubt the one copied by Hay in MSS 29822,40 (cf. Ill. 30), now mounted on the same page as at least one drawing from TT A5 and by Porter & Moss taken as belonging to the latter tomb. Apart from the wig, the figure is identical to the figure adoring Osiris in the tomb of Paḥeri.(75) The wig corresponds to the one worn by Wensu elsewhere.

In Hay MSS 29822,38 (cf. Ill. 29) there is a drawing of the upper part of a seated couple which may belong on this wall (*sic* also Porter & Moss). The direction of the figures is as would be expected, the couple facing the entrance of the tomb. Hay says that 'this last subject [*sc.* priest before couple] is repeated on the right side twice.' In MSS 29822,34,35 he gives water-colours of the three persons involved on the right side, and by reversing them and comparing them with the drawing of the couple mentioned above, we have a fairly good idea of the appearance of the couple and priest on the left side.

In the tomb of Rekhmirēᶜ a representation of the goddess of the necropolis is to be found in a different register from the one with Osiris. In the tomb of Wensu, according to Hay, a similar figure must be added behind that of Osiris.

Only two groups are mentioned as decorating this part of the wall, and they must have been really 'large' in comparison with the other figures. The Osiris scene was the upper one, and as lower registers often contain representations at a smaller scale compared to those above, I would allot the height of three of the five registers to the left to the representation of Osiris, goddess and kneeling man with offerings, the couple and the priest taking up the height of the two lower registers. It follows from this reconstruction that the portion to be added to the height of the wall in the reconstruction, comprising top and bottom border and an undecorated area just above ground level, should be approximately equivalent to the average height of one of the five registers.

2) Rites before the mummy

The greater part of the right wall of the inner room presents no major problems in a reconstruction, as reasonably good drawings and indications of positions of scenes are to hand in Hay MSS 29822,24-32 (drawings by *camera lucida*, cf. Ill 32), 34 (Ill. 34), 35 (Ill. 33) (water-colours). A priest with a mummy (in the second register from above, left part(76) was drawn by Burton in MSS 25638,48 [lower], cf. Ill. 9 [lower]. An ox, a goose, and some hieroglyphs (among others 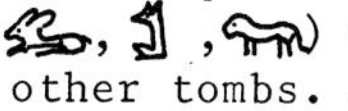 were drawn in colour on a sheet now among tracings from other tombs. Although they have a pencilled note saying 'from the 3rd tomb' they were not included in the *Topographical Bibliography*. On the same sheet, MSS 29853,131,(cf. Ill. 36) there were two more coloured drawings from the tomb (cf. below, p. 78).

When pieced together Hay's drawings form five registers, proportionally about the same size as those on the opposite, left wall, *i.e.* the width of the decorated part of the wall is just under twice the height. One large area spreading from the upper part of the bottom register to the very top was destroyed,(77) as well as one patch in the lower right corner extending over three registers, a small piece in the middle of the second register from the top, and a small part of the right end of the top register. The destroyed areas help to ascertain the sequence of the registers, and so do Hay's notes on the drawings, which clearly indicate '1st piece, upper line' and so forth. A side border line is drawn on the right (towards the entrance of the tomb). There is thus no doubt about the general lay-out of these five registers, which are dedicated to the ceremonies taking place in front of the mummy of the scribe and counter of grain, Wensu.

There are no scenes with rites before the mummy in the tomb of Paḥeri, presumably for reasons of space. In the tomb of Rekhmirēʿ the rites are performed in front of a statue of the deceased, and the order of events is rather different from TT A4.

On the left wall there remains to be filled in, according to Burton MSS 25639,40: 'the lord and lady... in large in 2 or 3 places.' Hay MSS 29824,19 says, referring to the representation of the couple and priest on the left wall: 'This last subject is repeated on the right side twice', and Hay drew one of these, showing the couple seated on a chair with a monkey eating from a basket full of fruit below (Ill. 33), and, in another drawing at a larger scale, the upper part of a priest clad in a panther skin (Ill. 34). A very similar group is to be seen on a wall in the tomb of Paḥeri (Ill. 35).(78) Apart from the different wig of the man and the position of his left arm the three persons are very similar indeed.

It is impossible to say whether the couple and priest drawn by Hay belong at the upper or lower part of the wall. The two representations must have been of unequal size, the smaller one presumably at the bottom. The two walls would in any case have been well balanced, the decoration being roughly of the same proportions.

On the sheet of paper referred to above (Hay MSS 29853,131) Hay drew the heads of a man and a woman which may be the second representation of the seated couple on this wall (Ill. 36). The head of the man is virtually identical to the one drawn on the opposite wall, except that it is reversed. The wig has blue and black stripes.(79) The woman, drawn separately, wears a black wig and lotus bud, and a red unguent cone. Her necklace is blue and green, and the colour scheme and style is very similar to the coloured drawing made by Burton of the ladies in the banquet scene. The possibility remains, however, that the two heads were copied from the banquet scene in the hall.

The episode on this wall are to be read from left to right, beginning in the top left corner. The rites before the mummy concern the ceremonies of the Opening of the Mouth, known from other sources. The scenes represented in the tomb of Wensu do not include all known rites, but they are among the most complete in the Theban necropolis.(80)

Top register

1) Preparing the mummy on its heap of sand (mostly destroyed).<1>

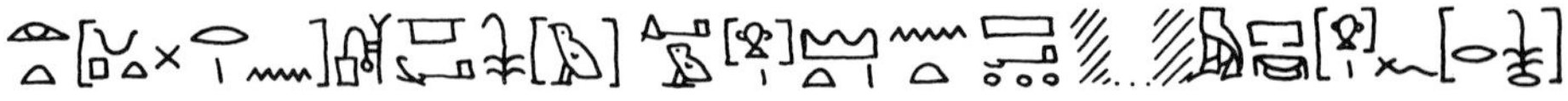

ỉrt [wpt r n] sš Wnsw dỉw [ḥr] ḫ3st nt šʿ... m pr nbw [ḥr].f [r rst]

'Performing [the Opening of the Mouth of] the scrine Wensu, placed [on] a mound of sand... in the house of gold, his [face towards the South].'

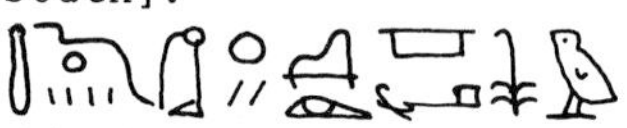

ḏd mdw sp 4 wʿb sp sn Wsỉr Wnsw

'Words to be said four times: "(You are) pure, (You are) pure, Osiris Wensu."'

2) The *sm*-priest pours water over the mummy, watched by the lector.<2>

ḏd mdw pḫr ḥꜣ.f m nmst 4 nt mw ḏd mdw sp 4 wꜥb sp sn sm ẖry-ḥb Wsir sš Wnsw mꜣꜥ ḫrw

'Words to be said going round behind him with the four *nmst*-jars of water. Words to be said four times: "(You are) pure, (you are) pure." The *sm*-priest. The lector. Osiris, the scribe Wensu, justified.'

3) The *sm*-priest pours water over the mummy, watched by the lector.<3>

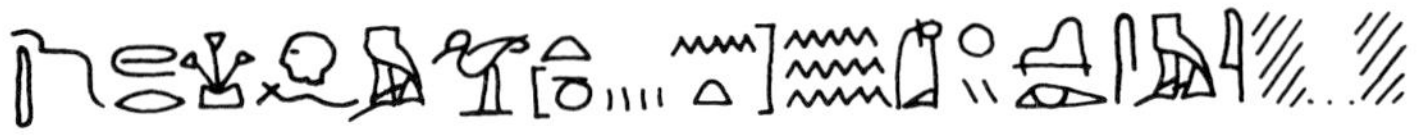

ḏd msw pḫr ḥꜣ.f m dšrt [4 nt] mw wꜥb sp sn Wsir sm i...

'Words to be said going round behind him with the [four] *dšrt*-vases [of] water: "(You are) pure, (you are) pure, Osiris". The *sm*-priest...'

4) The *sm*-priest with a bowl of incense before the mummy, watched by the lector.<6>

ḏd mdw sm pḫr ḥꜣ.f m sntr wꜥb sp sn Wsir sš ḥsb it [Wns]w mꜣꜥ ḫrw sm

'Words to be said. The *sm*-priest. Going round behind him with incense: "(You are) pure, (you are) pure, Osiris." The scribe and counter of grain, [Wens]u, justified. The *sm*-priest.'

5) The *smr*-priest with a bowl of incense before the mummy, watched by the lector.<4>

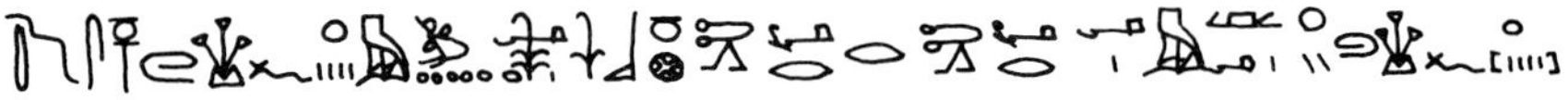

ḏd mdw smr pḫr ḥꜣ.f sp 4 m ṯꜣ 5 šmꜥ nḫb it r r it r ꜥ m wꜥ ꜥsp sn pḫr ḥꜣ.f sp [4]

'Words to be said. The *smr*-priest. Going round hebind him four times with five pellets of Upper Egyptian (natron) from Nekheb (el-Kâb): "Take (it) towards the mouth. Take (it) towards the arm with one arm. Repeat." Going round behind him [four] times.'

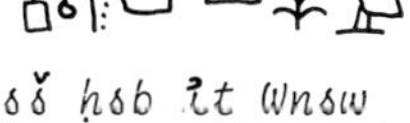

sš ḥsb it Wnsw

'The scribe and counter of grain, Wensu.'

6) The *smr*-priest with a bowl of incense before the mummy, watched by the lector.<5>

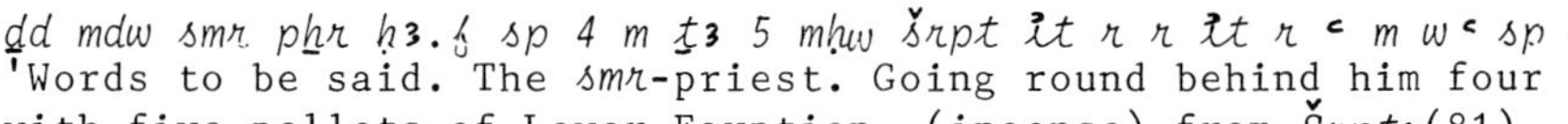

ḏd mdw smr pḫr ḥꜣ.f sp 4 m ṯꜣ 5 mḥw šrpt it r r it r ꜥ m wꜥ sp sn

'Words to be said. The *smr*-priest. Going round behind him four times with five pellets of Lower Egyptian (incense) from *Šrpt*:(81)

"Take (it) towards the mouth, take (it) towards the arm with one (arm). Repeat."'

7) The lector and three other priests before the mummy (no inscriptions).<8>

Second register from above
8) (Destroyed).(82)

9) The *(sm)*-priest opening the mouth of the mummy, watched by the lector. <14> <33>

wp r irty m ... wꜥb sp sn Wsir ḥꜣ.n.(i) n.k r.k r ḳsw.k... sw mꜣꜥ ḫrw
'Opening the mouth and the eyes with(?)(83)... "(You are) pure, (you are) pure, Osiris. I have adjusted your mouth to your bones." [Wen]sw, justified.'

10) The lector supervises a butcher killing the first bull.<19> <23>

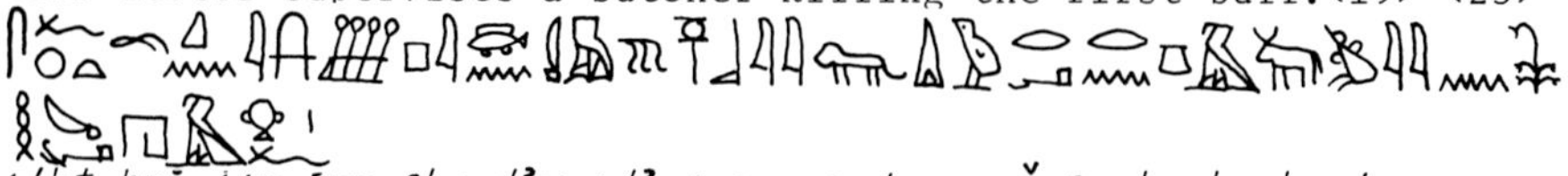

sfḫt ḳni ššp inm ꜥby diw rdi ꜥ r ngꜣ ṯꜣy n šmꜥw ḥw ḥꜣ ḥr.f
'Laying aside the *ḳni*-garment, taking the panther skin. It is placed. Giving a sign to the male *ngꜣ*-bull of Upper Egypt. Butcher! Tread upon it!'

11) Rites before the mummy (destroyed).

12) Opening the mouth with the *dwꜣ-wr*-adze (partly destroyed).<26>

ḏd mdw ššp biꜣ dwꜣ-wr ... m sp tpy dwn-ꜥ ... m sp snw
'Words to be said: "Receive the iron *dwꜣ-wr*... the first time, the *dwn-ꜥ*... the second time."'

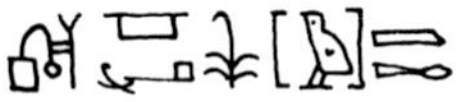

sš Wnsw mꜣꜥ ḫrw
'The scribe Wensu, justified.'

13) Opening of the eyes of the mummy (partly destroyed). <27>(?)

sm ḫry-ḥb irty ššp ... wp ... irty
'The *sm*-priest. The lector. (Your) eyes, receive... open...eyes.'

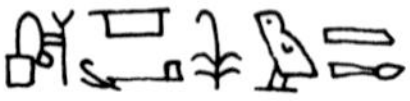

sš Wnsw mꜣꜥ ḫrw
'The scribe Wensu, justified.'

14) Finding the *sꜣ-mr.f* and entering the tomb.<31>

prt r ḥꜣ sm ẖry-ḥb smr gmt sꜣ-mr.f ꜥḥꜣ r-ẖnw is
'Going behind. The *sm*-priest. The lector. The *smr*-priest. Finding the *sꜣ-mr.f*. Standing within the tomb.'

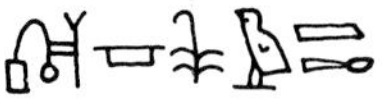

sš Wnsw mꜣꜥ ḫrw
'The scribe Wensu, justified.'

Third register from above
15) (Destroyed).

16) (Destroyed except for Wensu's title *sš* 'scribe').

17) Dressing the mummy (partly destroyed).<34>(?)

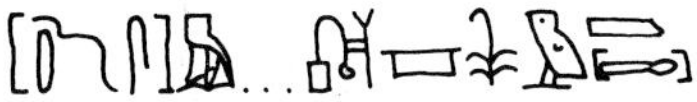

[ḏd mdw s]m ... sš Wnsw mꜣꜥ [ḫrw]
'[Words to be said. The *s*]*m*-priest... the scribe Wensu, justified.'

18) The *sm*-priest holds the *psš-kf* (instrument for opening the mouth) to the face of the mummy (no inscriptions, and partly destroyed).<37>

19) A priest offers a bowl of grains of incense(84) to the mummy (partly destroyed, no inscriptions except *sš Wn[sw]* 'The scribe Wen[su]').

20) The *sm*-priest holds a feather (= the eye of Horus) to the mummy.(39) (Partly destroyed, no inscriptions except *[Wn]sw mꜣꜥ ḫrw* '[Wen]su, justified'.)

21) The *sm*-priest supervising a butcher killing the second bull, with the older and the younger Kite watching (no inscriptions).<43>

22) Two priests holding a bowl with the heart of the bull (no inscriptions).<44>

23) The *sm*-priest presenting the haunch to the mummy, followed by a priest with the bull's heart in a bowl (no inscriptions).<44>

Fourth register from above
24) *sm*-priest with a haunch of beef before the mummy (mostly destroyed).<45>

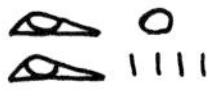 *irty sp 4*

'... the two eyes four times.'

25) (Destroyed).

26) Rite before mummy (mostly destroyed).

... *mw* ... [*Wnsw mꜣꜥ*] *ḫrw ḫr nṯr* [*ꜥꜣ*]
'... water. [Wensu], justified before the [great] god.'

27) The *sm*-priest presenting two strips of cloth(?) to the mummy (partly destroyed).<48>

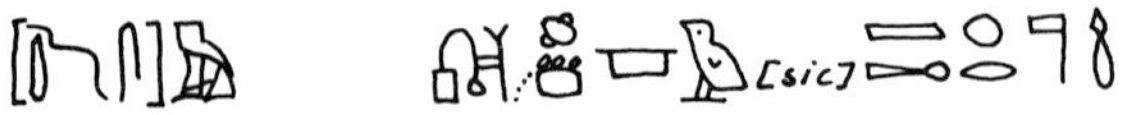

[*ḏd mdw s*]*m* ... *sš ḥsb it Wnsw mꜣꜥ ḫrw ḫr nṯr ꜥꜣ*
'[Words to be said. The *s*]*m*-priest... The scribe and counter of grain, Wensu, justified before the great god.'

28) The *sm*-priest(85) presenting a bowl of burning incense to the mummy.

ḏd mdw swꜥb m snṯr n Wsir sm
'Words to be said. Purifying with incense for Osiris. The *sm*-priest.'

[*Wn*]*sw mꜣꜥ ḫrw*
'[Wen]su, justified.'

29) A priest with a club and flail before the mummy (no inscriptions).

30) The *sm*-priest with a mace before the mummy (no inscriptions).<57B

31) A priest presenting the *mnḫt*-garment to the mummy, watched by the lector (partly destroyed).<50>

ḏd mdw sfḫt mnḫt ḫry-ḥb

'Words to be said. Laying aside the *mnḫt*-garment. The lector.'
Trace of Wensu's title  *sš* 'scribe'.

32) Rite before the mummy (almost totally destroyed. There remains )

Lower register
33) Six priests, including the lector, grouped in front of the mummy (partly destroyed, no inscriptions).

34) The lector and a priest with raised arms before the mummy (no inscriptions).

35) A kneeling priest with two *nw*-jars facing the mummy, with an offering list between them.<65>

The offering list is the so-called 'short offering list'(86) of the private tombs of the Eighteenth dynasty, and it includes the following items:

mw	'water'	
ḥtꜣ	'*ḥtꜣ*-bread'	
psn	'*psn*-bread'	
dpti	'*dpti*-bread'	
iwr	'meat'	
ꜣšrt	'roast'	
irp n	'1 cup oasis wine'	
Wḥꜣt		

špnty	'2 jugs beer'
šnt ḥnkt	
hꜣts	'4 *hꜣts*-bowls...'
... *bit*	'4 bowls honey'
[mw] d[šrt]	2 *dšrt*-jars water'
bd	'2 bowls natron'

To the left are traces of the text to be recited at the offering:

... *šsp* ... *dd mdw sp 4 Ḥr(?)* ...(87) *ḥr irt.k [s]m kbḥ*
'...receive... Words to be said four times. Horus(?)... on your eye. The [*s*]*m*-priest. Cool...'
To the right are Wensu's name and title:

sš ḥsb it [n pr] ꜥI[mn?] Wnsw
'The scribe and counter of grain [in the temple of Amun?], Wensu.'

36) The *sm*-priest addressing three squatting figures, watched by the lector.<73>

is grw tn sš Wnsw fꜣ.tn sw m(?) Ḥr m ḥnw wts.f tw m rn.k Skr
'Go you then. The scribe Wensu, carry him like(?) Horus on the *ḥnw*-bark. It supports you in your name of Sokar.'

37) The lector, the *sm*-priest, and two others facing one another (partly destroyed). The inscription continues above the three squatting men in the previous scene.

... *mdti* ... *m* ... *nb im*

... *fꜣ rf tn sw sš Wnsw rdi.n n.k Ḥr mstiw.f ẖr.k fꜣ.sn tw ẖnm.k im.sn*
'... carry him, the scribe Wensu. Horus has given you his children under you so that they can carry you, that you may unite with them.'

ink msw ꜣmst Ḥpy
'I am the children Amset and Ḥapy.'

38) The *sm*-priest and another in front of a shrine on a sledge (partly destroyed).<74>

r n fꜣt twt ḏd mdw in smrw 8 fꜣ sw
'Spell of carrying the statue. Words to be said by the eight *smr*-priests carrying him.'

Wensu, scribe and counter of grain

The fact that the mummy for whom the rites are performed in the inner room of TT A4 is that of the scribe and counter of grain, Wensu is conclusive proof that Wensu was the real owner of this tomb.

None of the early travellers gives any indication whatsoever of the decoration of the rear wall of the inner room, where one would expect to find a statue of the deceased, or a stela.(88) The tomb is a fairly small one, the width of the inner room being (according to Burton MSS 25639,40) about 6.6ft (1.98m). Part of the rear wall may have been taken up by one of the statues found carrying the name of the scribe Wensu. One was found at Karnak, but two presumably stem from the necropolis.

The National Museum of Antiquities in Leiden possesses a limestone statue of Wensu, scribe and counter of grain (Ill. 37),(89) ca. 41cm high, showing the person kneeling with a stela. The complete text of this little known statue is as follows:

Back pillar: 

imꜣḫy m niwt rst sš ḥsb [it m prʾIm]n Wnsw
'The honoured one in the Southern City, the scribe and counter of [grain of the temple of Amū[n], Wensu.'

Round the base: 

ḥtp di nsw ʾImn...[di.]f ssn(92) ṯꜣw m ʿntiw ḥr snṯr n sš Wnsw mꜣʿ ḫrw
'An offering which the king gives (to) Amūn that he [may give] a smell of myrrh and incense to the scribe Wensu, justified.'

ḥtp di nsw Wsir nṯr ʿꜣ nb tꜣ ḏsr di.f ḥtp ib m imntt nfrt n sš ʾI[mn] Wnsw mꜣʿ ḫrw
'An offering which the king gives (to) Osiris, great god, lord of the Sacred Land, that he may give happiness in the beautiful West to the scribe of A[mūn], Wensu.'

On the top surface of the stela:

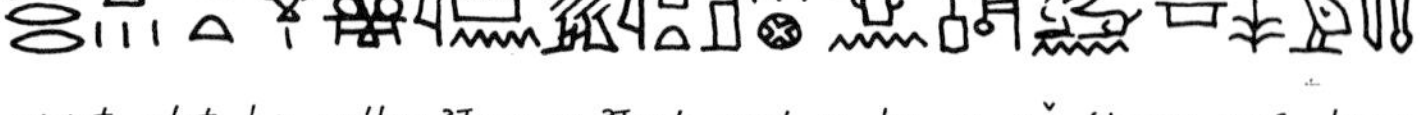

prrt nbt ḥr wdḥw ʾImn m ʾIpt-swt n kꜣ n sš Wnsw mꜣʿ ḫrw

'All (offerings) coming to the offering table of Amūn in Karnak to the *ka* of the scribe Wensu, justified.'
On the stela and dress:

dwꜣ rꜥ [nb nṯrw] m ḫꜥ.f ḫnt ẖt mwt.f in sš n niwt rst ꜣImn Wnsw mꜣꜥ ḫrw ḏd.f ind ḥr.k rꜥ m prw.k ... m ḥtp.k nfr sḏm.k nis.i ir.k ḏ[d].i ḥtp.k [n].i iw n.k ḥtpw [ḥr] spw nfr(w) irn.k n.i
'Praising Rēꜥ, [lord of the gods], when he comes forth from his mother's womb by the scribe of the Southern City (of) Amūn, Wensu, justified. He says, "Greetings to you in your...(94) coming forth and in your beautiful setting. May you hear me when I acclaim(95) you so that you can do what I say and be gracious [to] me. There are offerings for you [because of] the good occasions you have made for me."'

When Leemans was first faced with the reorganization of the Leiden collection, many of the labels stuck on the objects had fallen off because of damp conditions, but where they remained or could be restored with certainty, indications of the provenance of the objects were given in his catalogue. As far as this statue was concerned the information given is that it was 'de la collection de la dame M. Cimba, vendue à Livorne.'(96) There is sone evidence of a connection between this name and that of Salt which might suggest that the statue might have been found by him (or his agent) in the necropolis. The Cimba family was known to Salt in Cairo,(97) and it may be that the statue was somehow acquired through Salt.

In the Louvre there is another statue of Wensu, scribe of the granaries of Amūn, this time with his wife Amenḥotp (Ill. 39).(98) They are shown seated, and the group may have come from the tomb, being sold with Salt's second collection of antiquities along with the wall-paintings. On the statue the name of Amūn is hacked out, again indicating that the tomb was probably accessible during the heresy of the Amarna Period one hundred years after it was cut.

There is another statue of Wensu, scribe and counter of grain of Amūn.(99) It is 28cm high, of black granite and was found in 1902 near the sacred lake at Karnak. It shows Wensu with a scroll on his lap. The inscriptions on this statue give the names of his parents: his father 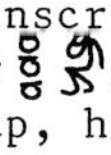 *Nw* or *Nwnw* and his mother  *Rnptḥtp*, along with that of Amenḥotp, his wife.(100)

Relationship with the tomb of Paḥeri

To revert to the very close similiarity between the tomb of Wensu and that of Paḥeri at el-Kâb it is impossible to establish any definite link between the two persons, such as a family relationship or an acquaintance resulting in one being depicted in the tomb of the other. One of Paḥeri's duties, as scribe of the grain, extended as far north as Ḥet-Ḥathor (presumably Dendara) and thus may have included the Theban area, and the two men must by virtue of their office have been acquainted, though what caused their tombs, about 83km apart, to be so similar is puzzling.(101) It is even difficult to establish if one of them was the prototype of the other. In the agricultural scene, for example, Paḥeri has the more complete text, but as far as the funeral ceremonies are concerned, Wensu is more explicit. There can be no doubt about the fact that they were decorated about the same time. Paḥeri's tomb is estimated to have been decorated in the beginning of the reign of Tuthmosis III. The two tombs bear some resemblance in style and subjects represented to the tomb of Rekhmirēᶜ, undoubtedly decorated during the reign of Tuthmosis III or the beginning of that of Amenophis II. In view of the presence of the mayor of Thebes in the tomb of Wensu (to be discussed below), there can be little doubt that the decoration of this tomb dates from the reign of Tuthmosis III.

Similarities in Egyptian tomb decoration have sometimes been pointed out by scholars, the best known examples being perhaps the musical scenes in TT 38 and 75(102) and the similarity in style between the paintings in the tombs of Menna (TT 69) and Pairi (TT 139).(103) But in the case of the tombs of Wensu and Paḥeri more than a *similarity* is involved: apart from the fact that the one tomb is painted, the other is in relief, a great number of individual figures are absolutely identical (cf. Ills. 20 and 28).(104) Either one was copied from the other, or they both copied the same original. Although there are examples of a grid being applied to a relief or painting in order to copy it, no trace of a 'pattern' book used by outline draughtsmen has yet been discovered.(105) The tombs of Wensu and Paḥeri strongly suggest that such a thing existed.(106) The variety in the arrangement of the subjects as a whole seems to indicate that whatever form the 'pattern' had (scroll, board or ostrakon(107)) it was fairly small, yet big enough to accomodate the height of a register. The span of juxtaposed, identical figures rather suggests a broad format, such as a scrol of papyrus or leather. In the contemporary royal tombs, particularly those of Tuthmosis III and Amenophis II, the wall-decoration was copied from a papyrus scroll. This is evident, not only from the style of the drawings made to look as if they were drawn with ink and brush, but also from the fact that the original scroll was sometimes torn, particularly at the beginning of the text and pictures, *i.e.* the part of the scroll which was the last to be rolled up and therefore the most vulnerable. Lacunae were left as such, or the draughtsman wrote 'found ruined' or the like.(108)

In order to overcome the technical difficulties in drawing identical figures and groups of figures on the walls of two tombs separated by a distance of some 80km, the draughtsman must have employed a similar 'book', containing subjects such as 'work in the field', 'funerary ceremonies' and 'priest before seated couple'. That he had more than one 'book' at his disposal is suggested by the banquet scene, for here the two tombs differ in the general lay-out as well as in the individual figures.(109)

Siuser, mayor of Thebes?

The whereabouts of the presumed tomb of the mayor Siuser remains unknown. It has not been identified among the tombs in the Theban necropolis, where a mayor of the town would most certainly have had his tomb cut. At first sight his name might seem a fairly common one, but it is a curious fact that no one else of that name seems to be known in Egyptological sources. This may point to a solution to the problem. In Hay's drawings the hieroglyphs are usually copied fairly accurately, but there is just the possibility that in copying the name of the person supervising the market scene Hay mistook one bird for another, or the ancient draughtsman may have made the mistake. When drawing up a list of mayors of Thebes during the reign of Tuthmosis III based on evidence from Theban tombs the result is that three persons held this office: ʿAmethu (TT 83) during the early years of the reign; his son User (TT 61 and 131) during the middle part; and the nephew of the latter, Rekhmirēʿ (TT 100) whose duties extended into the reign of Amenophis II. It is difficult to see how a person who was not a member of the family would have had an opportunity of breaking this succession of blood-related mayors.

All three mayors also functioned as viziers. It is just possible, though perhaps unlikely, that Hay copied *ṯꜣty* (vizier) as *sꜣ* (110) and that the person depicted is not an otherwise unknown mayor of Thebes called Siuser, but User, the well-known mayor and vizier, who was also represented in the tomb of Amenemḥēt (TT 82). Against this attractive solution speaks the fact that User does not seem to have borne a title connected with a granary.(111) It is therefore better to leave the question open.

6 Tomb No. A6

Tomb no. A6 was visited by Lepsius as the only one among the early travellers, but all he copied was the title of the tomb owner: *ỉmy-r sḫtỉw n nb tꜣwy* 'overseer of the peasants (or fowlers) of the Lord of the Two Lands.' Lepsius gave the tomb the number 6, and described it as being near to his no. 5 at Draᶜ Abû el-Nagaᶜ.(1) Virtually nothing has been recorded of the decoration of the tomb. It was presumably destroyed by the time Lepsius saw it. But a number of items from the tomb can be traced to collections in Europe and the USA.

In 1906 Gauthier excavated the east slope of the main hill of Draᶜ Abû el-Nagaᶜ, and he came across the tomb of an 'overseer of the peasants (or fowlers)' by the name of Ḏhoutnūfer, called Seshu.(2) A man of similar names, but with a different title: *sš ḥbw n ꜣImn*(3) or *sš [ḥsb] kꜣw ꜣpdw n pr ꜣImn* 'scribe and [counter] of cattle and fowl of the temple of Amūn'(4) was known from a number of funerary cones. Gauthier identified the owner of the cones with the owner of the tomb, undoubtedly rightly so.(5) But he assigned it to the date of the Twentieth dynasty. This has later been corrected to the reign of Tuthmosis III(?).(6)

According to Gauthier, the tomb consisted of 'a certain number of chambers' cut into the rock, and a shaft measuring 2x3m, being 10m deep. Two thirds down the shaft were two rooms, one at the south west corner, the other at the north east corner. In the upper chambers Gauthier found a fragment of painted limestone with the hardly legible name and title *ỉmy-r sḫtỉw Ḏḥwtynfr* 'overseer of the peasants (or fowlers), Ḏhoutnūfer'. In front of the tomb owner was *sꜣt.f mr.t.f...* 'his beloved daughter...'

In the first chamber Gauthier found a door jamb of an [overseer of] weavers(?) which most certainly did not belong here.(7) The only remains of the actual tomb would appear to be a fragment now in the Metropolitan Museum of Art, no. 15.2.4, a sandstone door jamb with the colours beautifully preserved (Ill. 39).(8) It measures 35cm across, and it shows in two registers the tomb owner and his wife, the top and lower part respectively missing. In both registers the tomb owner and his wife are shown seated between two framing borders. In the lower register the accompanying text remains:

sḫmḫ ỉb m33 bw nfr šsp ... sš ḥsb k3w 3pdw n ʾImn mḥ ỉb mnḫ n nb... Ḏḥwtynfr ḏd.n.f Sšw ḥmt.f mrt.f nt st-ỉb.f nbt pr Bnbw m3ᶜ(t) ḫrw

'Rejoicing seeing something pleasant, receiving... by the scribe and counter of cattle and fowl of Amūn, splendid trustworthy one of [his] lord (or 'the Lord of the Two Lands'), Ḏḥoutnūfer, called Seshu.(9) His beloved, favourite wife, mistress of the house, Benbu, justified.'

In the register above a man is shown offering(?) to the deceased couple.

In the shaft Gauthier found a fragment of a stela,(10) but there is nothing which enables us to identify the owner of the stela with the owner of the tomb. A statue also found in the tomb is equally difficult to identify.(11) But another statue, of unknown provenance, may have been the funerary statue which originally belonged in the tomb. It is now in the Louvre, no. AE/A55.(12)

The statue shows a seated couple in the conventional mid-Eighteenth dynasty pose. The inscriptions on the kilts identify the persons as 'the scribe and counter of cattle and fowl of Amūn, Ḏḥoutnūfer, called Seshu' and 'the mistress of the house, Benemb(13)'. There can be little doubt that this couple is identical to the owners of TT A6. The offering formular on the statue suggests that the statue was indeed the cult statue from the tomb: 'An offering which the king gives (to) Osiris, lord of eternity, that he may give all good and pure things to the *k* of the scribe and counter of cattle and fowl of Amūn, Ḏḥoutnūfer, called Seshu' and 'an offering which the king gives (to) Amūn that he may give all good and pure things to the *k3* of the mistress of the house, Benemb.' The name of Amūn appears to have been hacked out during the Amarna Period.

The father of Ḏḥoutnūfer is mentioned on one set of funerary cones.(14) He was an otherwise unknown scribe called  Mesu. A son and a daughter appear on two(15) stelae in Turin which came from the Drovetti collection.

One stela(16) was erected by his son, the scribe 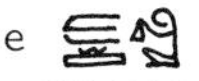 Maḥu to make his father's name live. A long self-laudatory text, translated in the previous publication, is given to Ḏḥoutnūfer to recite to Osiris who is represented in the top register. The stela was presumably positioned in the courtyard of the tomb. The second stela(17) shows Ḏḥoutnūfer, seated, with his daughter 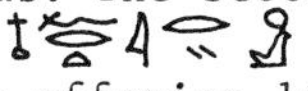 Nefertere, standing, in front of an offering table with an offering list depicted above. The accompanying text, also previously translated, mentions an offering to Rēᶜ-Ḥorakhty and to Osiris, and the wish to go in and out of the necropolis, returning to earth and seeing the sun disc. This stela obviously also belonged in a funerary context, *i.e.* the tomb.

The name of the wife occurs in a number of variations, but it probably still refers to the same person:

stela Turin no. 157 (no. 17) MMA jamb		(19)
stela Turin no. 153	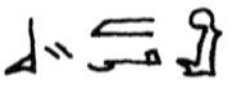	(20)
Louvre AE/A55		(21)

7 Tomb No. A13

Like the previous tomb this one appears to have been visited only by Lepsius who copied some of the inscriptions and described very briefly the scenes to which they belonged (MSS 425).(1)

The owner of the tomb was a certain Paimosi, not known from other sources, who was sealer of the storehouse of goods and a follower of the king in all foreign lands. His wife had the common name Sensonb, and a son of theirs was priest of Maᶜet. Unfortunately his name was not recorded, and we cannot relate him to the priests of Maᶜet discussed in the section dealing with TT C4. Judging from the scarcity of known priests of Maᶜet in the Eighteenth dynasty we may cautiously date TT A13 to the middle or later part of the dynasty where these priests do occur, but it is not possible to say which king benefitted from the services of Paimosi.

The tomb was at Draᶜ Abû el-Nagaᶜ, on the hill below Deir el-Bakhît, near a 'tomb of the hill of the brick pyramid of Piccinini [*sc.* TT A12].'

Judging from the text copied by Lepsius, the left wall of the entrance doorway had a representation of the tomb owner adoring the sun rising in the eastern horizon. The accompanying text describes the scene:

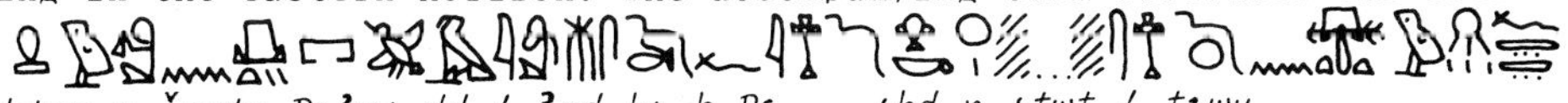

ḫtmw n šnwty Pꜣỉms ḏd.f ỉnḏ ḥr.k Rᶜ ... sḥḏ.n stwt.f tꜣwy

'The sealer of the storehouse, Paimosi. He says, "Hail to you, Rēᶜ... whose rays have enlightened the Two Lands."'

On the 'left side wall' (of the hall?) the wife of the tomb owner is named as 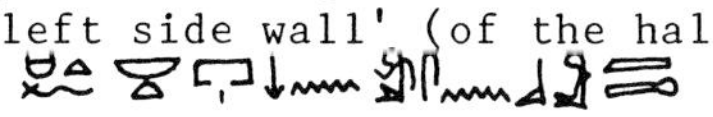 *ḥmt.f nbt pr Snsnb mꜣᶜ(t) ḫrw* 'his wife, mistress of the house, Sensonb, justified.' The inscription runs from right to left in a vertical line, so Sensonb was presumably facing right, towards the interior of the tomb.

On the 'right side wall' there was a representation of the tomb owner with the following titles:

...(?) nsw šms r nmtt nsw mḥꜥỉkr(2) ḥsy n ḥm.f mḥ ỉb n nb tꜣwy ḥsy n nṯr nfr ḫtmw n šnwt ỉnw Pꜣỉms mꜣꜥ ḫrw
'royal ..., following in the steps of the king, excellent one, praised by his Majesty, trustworthy one of the Lord of the Two Lands, praised by the good god, sealer of the storeroom of goods(3) Paimosi, justified.'

The text is written in vertical columns from right to left.

On one of the two rear walls (of the hall?) the tomb owner and his wife receive offerings. The inscription runs from left to right. The couple would therefore be facing left:

sḫmḫ ỉb m bw nfr šsp ꜣwt m ... ḥwt.f šms nsw ḥr ḫꜣst nbt Pꜣỉms ḥmt.f mrt.f nt st-ỉb.f nbt pr Snsnb mꜣꜥt ḫrw

'Enjoying seeing something pleasant, receiving gifts from ... his abode (by) the one who follows the king in all foreign lands, Paimosi. His beloved, favourite wife, mistress of the house, Sensonb, justified.'

'Above' their son, the 'priest of Maꜥet', was shown offering.

Next to the door(4) are three registers with a mummy in each. The door in question may be the door to an inner room, and the mummies part of the Opening of the Mouth ceremonies. But according to Lepsius one of the mummies is accompanied by the name of the wife of the tomb owner, and the wife does not normally appear in this ritual. Her name is written from right to left, hence the person to whom it pertains must have been facing right. We must conclude that the name, although written next to a mummy, presumably refers to a mourning widow facing it, and that the scene is to be placed on the left wall of an inner room, if such existed. A libation is performed in front of each of the mummies. In the upper register it is accompanied by the name (*sc.* of the tomb owner) only, in the middle register by that of the wife as described above, and in the lower register the name is illegible.

Adjoining the name of the wife is another brief inscription running in the opposite direction, the two together appearing thus:

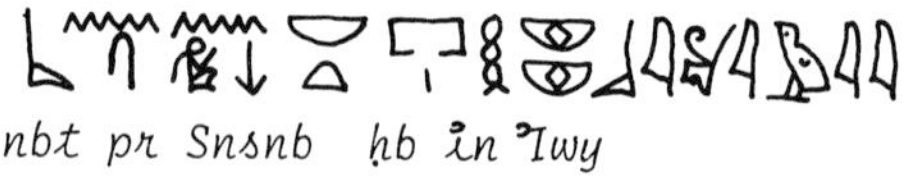

nbt pr Snsnb ḥb ỉn ꜥIwy

'mistress of the house, Sensonb. Mourning(?) by Iuy.'(5)

An inscription on the ceiling gives part of an offering formula repeating the name and title of the tomb owner

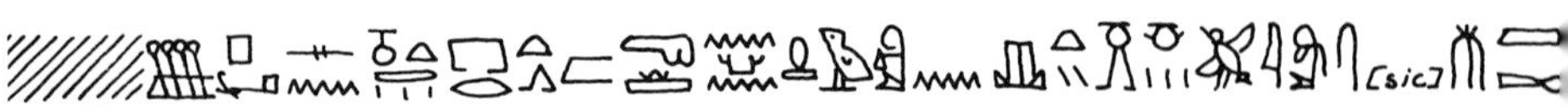

... šsp.sn t ḥnkt prt m bꜣḥ n kꜣ n ḫtmw n šnwty ỉnw Pꜣỉms mꜣꜥ ḫrw
'... may they receive bread and beer, and what comes forth into the presence, for the *kꜣ* of the sealer of the storehouse of the goods, Paimosi, justified.'

8 Tomb No. A24

This tomb was visited only by Wilkinson and Champollion. By the time Champollion went there, the once beautiful tomb had already fallen to pieces: 'tombeau jadis couverte de peintures executés avec un très grand soin et de belles couleurs; il en reste quelques fragments, sur les parois l'enduit de limon est tombé avec la peinture prèsque partout...' (*Not. descr.* I, p. 539). When Wilkinson saw it some years earlier, it was obviously in a much better condition. At least the fishing and fowling scene which he copied seems to have been fairly intact. Perhaps attempts were made between the two visits to cut out pieces, causing the plaster to come off the walls. Typical scenes, such as banquet, agriculture, and funerary ceremonies are nowhere described. The tomb had been subject to attack during the Amarna Period, but presumably only the usual mutilations were carried out.

The scenes copied and/or mentioned by the early travellers are to be found in the following : Wilkinson MSS ii,18 verso [right]; MSS v.215-7 [top]; *id.*, *Manners and Customs* ii.149 (No. 136), iii.41 (No. 336) = ed. Birch, i.381 (No. 156), ii.107 (No. 365); Champollion, *Not. descr.* I, pp. 539-40. For secondary publications cf. below.

According to Champollion the tomb was 'de moyenne grandeur, dans le plan ordinaire', and we may therefore take it that it was a medium sized T-shaped tomb, although no inner room is mentioned. It was located 'on hill of Pyramid called el-Mandara, near Hammam's' (Wilkinson MSS v.215), *i.e.* somewhere in the neighbourhood of the spot marked 'Q' on his map.(1) Champollion gave it the number 47 (C").

The owner of the tomb

The owner of the tomb was 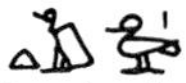 Simut, an important official in the reign of Amenophis III. He is known from a number of sources. His final rank was second prophet of Amūn,(2) but he had a variety of titles which will here be listed according to each source of information.

TT A24

 *ḥm nṯr 2-nw n ʾImn* second(3) prophet of Amūn

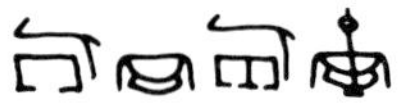 *ỉmy-r pr nbw ỉmy-r prwy ḥḏ* overseer of the House of gold and the House(s) of Silver

 *ḫtm ḫtmt nb(t) m ꜣIpt-swt* sealer of every contract in Karnak

 *ỉt nṯr ḥry sštꜣ m ... ḥry tp* god's father, in charge of the secrets in ...(4), chief

 *ỉmy-r pr rḫ ḏsr n Ḥwt-sr* knowing and special steward of the house of the noble(5)

 *sꜣ nsw tpy n [ꜣImn]* first king's son of [Amūn]

Ushabtis

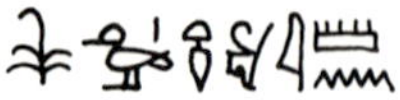 *sꜣ nsw tpy n ꜣImn*(6) first king's son of Amūn

 *ḥm nṯr 2-nw n ꜣImn*(7) second prophet of Amūn

Statue Cairo 1107(8)

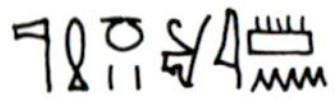 *ḥm nṯr 2-nw n ꜣImn* second prophet of Amūn

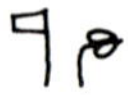 *wꜥb nṯr* waꜥb-priest of the god

 *sḏꜣwty bỉt* seal-bearer of the king of Lower Egypt

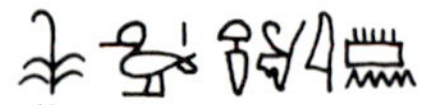 *sꜣ nsw tpy n ꜣImn* first king's son of Amūn

 *wꜥb n ḥꜣt n ꜣImn*(9) *wꜥb*-priest in front of Amūn

Soleb temple(10)

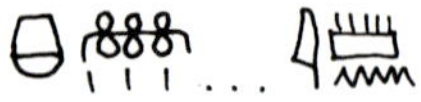 *ḫry-ḥb sꜣ 3... ꜣImn* lector, third phyle... Amūn

Jamb from Malqatta(11)

 *ḥm nṯr 4-nw n ꜣImn* fourth prophet of Amūn

 *sḏꜣwty bỉt* seal-bearer of the king of Lower Egypt

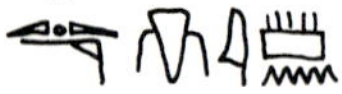 *smꜣ Mn ꜣImn* stolist of Min-Amūn

Statue Brussels(12)

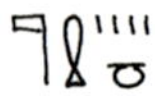 *ḥm nṯr 4-nw* fourth prophet

Statue Cairo 932(13)

 *wꜥb rmn m ḥꜣt ꜣImn* waꜥb-priest and carrier in front of Amūn

The wife of Simut accompanies him in the tomb as well as in the statues. She is

TT A24

 *šmꜥyt n ... Bꜣky* songstress of [Amūn], Baky

Cairo 1107

 *šmꜥyt n ꜣImn* songstress of Amūn

 *ḫkrt nsw* ornament of the king(14)

Cairo 932

 *šmꜥyt n ꜣImn* songstress of Amūn

A son is mentioned in the tomb. He is *it nṯr wꜥb ꜥwy Wsrḥꜣt* 'god's father, clean of hands,(15) Userḥēt.' He appears to be unknown from other sources. He, or another son, certainly had a family, for the statue in Cairo,1107,(16) was restored by a grandson *wꜥb ꜥꜣ rmn n ꜣImn ḥr sꜣ 2-nw Pꜣsr* 'great *waꜥb*-priest, carrier of Amūn,(17) in the second phyle, Paser.' The priestly titles ran in the family even through the Amarna Period during which Userḥēt and certainly Paser must have lived. The restoration of the statue done by Paser may perhaps be compared with the restoration of TT C4 performed by another grandson or nephew of an official of the reign of Amenophis III (cf. below). It suggests that much of the restoration work done in tombs and other non-royal monuments during the early Ramessid period was due to family relationships, not just ordinary piety towards a neglected divinity.

Description of the scenes

Most of the scenes mentioned can be placed on the walls of the hall of this tomb with some certainty. Champollion mentions three scenes, Wilkinson repeats one of these and supplies the remaining two. On the basis of the indications by Champollion, the direction of the hieroglyphs as copied by Wilkinson, and conventional tomb design the five scenes are to be positioned on the two front and rear walls of the hall.

Left front wall

This wall 'à gauche de la porte' had a representation of the tomb owner (with shaven skull) receiving offerings from his sons and servants.(18) The cartouche of Nebmaꜥetre was written next to his head. Champollion rightly suggests that the royal name was part of the title of Simut, but he does not mention any other hieroglyphs here.

Right front wall

'À droite de la porte' offerings were being brought ... *in sꜣ nsw tpy n...* 'by the first king's son of...', followed by ////////// *snt.f mrt.f n st-ib.f šmꜥyt...* 'his beloved favourite wife, songstress...' and a number of servants. One of these was (19) *sdm-ꜥš Šmsnfr* 'the servant Shemsnūfer'.(20) He carried a bunch of three papyrus flowers. Wilkinson (MSS v.215 [lower]) describes the scene as 'man bringing grapes on the table behind man of tb.'

From the directions of the hieroglyphs the tomb owner and his party were facing right, towards the entrance of the tomb. The entire scene was without question the offering scene in connection with the Feast of the Valley conventionally represented in this part of the tomb (cf. chapter 3, p. 37), showing the tomb owner offering or libating over a heap of offerings, followed by his wife and at least two men, one with grapes on a stand, the other Shemsnūfer with the papyrus plants.

Left rear wall (Ill. 41).

On the 'paroi de gauche' was a fishing and fowling scene which was copied and published in beautiful detail by Wilkinson (MSS ii.18 verso [right]; v.216,217 [upper] (the same scene copied twice); *Manners and Customs* iii,41 (No. 336) = ed. Birch, ii.107 (No. 365)). Although this motif is not found on the left rear wall in other tombs (cf. chapter 3, pp. 37-8), there can be little doubt that this was where it belonged in our tomb. Fishing and fowling is rarely represented in this period,(21) and this one must be one of the last examples.

Simut is shown fowling to the left. Onboard his canoe are also Userḥēt, his son (with side-lock), his wife, and an anonymous man and woman, presumably meant to be children. A cat is shown jumping up his knee. The inscription describing the activities is as follows:

sḫmḫ ỉb mꜣ bw nfr ỉrt smt m kꜣt Sḫt ḥsy n nbt ḥb ỉt nṯr wꜥb ꜥwy ḥry sštꜣ m ... ḥry-tp ỉmy-r pr rḫ ḏsr n Ḥwt-sr ḏd mḏt nṯry ḥmw nbw ḥwt ꜥꜣ ḥm nṯr 3-nw ... [mꜣꜥ] ḫrw

'Amusing himself, looking at pleasant things, taking part in the works of Sekhet(24) by the one beloved of Sekhet, praised by the mistress of hunting, the god's father, clean of hands, in charge of the secrets in...,(25) knowing and special steward of the *Ḥwt-sr*,(26) who gives divine unguent (to) all the servants of the palace(?),(27) the third(28) prophet..., justified.'

The woman standing behind the tomb owner in the boat is  *snt.f nbt pr ...y* 'his wife, mistress of the house [Bak]y.' The son is named as 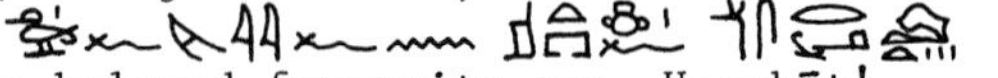 *sꜣ.f mry.f n st-ỉb.f Wsrḥꜣt* 'his beloved favourite son, Userḥēt'.

Above the scene showing the tomb owner spearing fish is the following legend

ḫns šꜣw hbhb sšw sḫmḫ ỉb stt mḥt m ḥmw ỉn mry Sḫt ḥm nṯr 3-nw n ꜣImn mḥ ỉb n nṯr nfr ỉmy-r pr nbw ỉmy-r pr ḥḏ ḫtm ḫtmt nb(t) m ꜣIpt-swt Sꜣmwt mꜣꜥ ḫrw

'Traversing the pools, penetrating the nesting places, enjoying himself spearing fish in the marshes by the one beloved of Sekhet, third(29) prophet of Amūn, trustworthy one of the good god, overseer of the House of Gold, overseer of the House of Silver, sealer of every contract in Karnak, Simut, justified.'

The woman behind him is 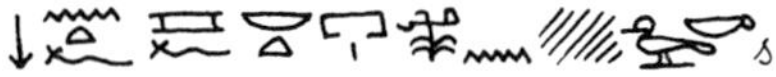 *snt.f mr(t).f nbt pr šmꜥytn...Bak[y]* 'his beloved wife, mistress of the house, songstress of [Amūn] Bak[y].' The son who accompanies him again has here got his full title: 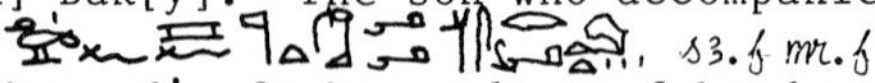 *sꜣ.f mr.f ỉt nṯr wꜥb ꜥwy Wsrḥꜣt* 'his beloved son, the god's father, clean of hands, Userḥēt.'

In connection with fishing and fowling, a sub-scene showing vintage is frequently represented (cf. chapter 3, pp. 40-1). As the frequency of fishing and fowling scenes decreased towards the reign of Amenophis III so did the vintage scenes. One such scene was in our tomb, and a detail of it was drawn and later published by Wilkinson (MSS v.215 [middle]; *Manners and Customs* ii.149 (No. 136) = ed. Birch, i,381 (No.

Porter & Moss take the scene to be 'right of door', presumably based on a remark by Champollion about Shemsnūfer carrying grapes. This however clearly refers to the offering scene on the right front wall and not to the vintage scene which Champollion omits.(30)

The detail copied by Wilkinson is more likely to belong to a once more complete scene on the same wall as the fishing and fowling scene. It shows two persons under the vines, one scaring away a bird with a sling (*sic* Wilkinson) or a club, the other picking a bunch of grapes. This latter is named as 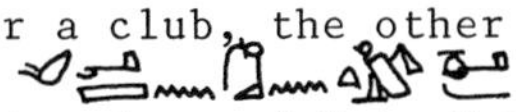(31) *sḏm-ʿš n wʿb n Mwt Mḥw* 'the servant of the *waʿb*-priest of Mut, Maḥu', the name referring either to the *waʿb*-priest or to the servant himself.(32)

Another name was written to the left of the scene, that of Shemsnūfer, known from the right front wall. As the hieroglyphs are written from right to left, Shemsnūfer would face right, watching the grape-gathering.

It may be appropriate to mention here a vintage scene described by one of the early travellers. The tomb to which it belonged remains unidentified. It was discovered by d'Athanasi and the scene in question drawn by Bonomi, but the drawing appears to be lost. D'Athanasi suggested that it might have been included in the Hay papers, but there is no drawing answering to the description in the Hay MSS. When d'Athanasi wrote, the tomb had already been destroyed by the Arabs. Although proof is lacking, it remains a possibility that the tomb was TT A24 which had the unusual detail of bird scaring in the vintage scene, which was according to d'Athanasi 'admirably detailed'. His description will therefore be quoted *in toto*.

> 'Amongst innumerable instances in which the manners and labours of the ancient Egyptians are exhibited in the contents of their tombs, I may mention the following as particularly interesting, namely, - a tomb in which the whole operation of grape-pressing for the purpose of making the wine is admirably detailed. I shall give a few words in description of this curious painting. In the first place is seen the frame-work, from which hang the grapes; then the men who are gathering them into baskets, and throwing them into the press. On each side of this press is a man standing upright and working the machine; beneath the press is a vessel to receive the liquor, and near to it a man on his knees filling vases, which he afterwards corks. At one side are seen two or three others who are carrying the corked vases to the storehouse, at the door of which is the master seated on a chair, with a clerk standing at his side, who, with an ink-bottle in his left hand, takes a note of the vases as they are brought in. In the last place is seen a servant, who having carelessly let fall a vase of wine, kneels before his master, kissing his feet, and in a suppliant manner asking forgiveness.
>
> When I found the above-mentioned tomb at Thebes, I begged Mr. Bonomi to take a drawing of it, and give me a copy to carry to Mr. Salt. To this he agreed, and promised to send my copy to me at Alexandria, where I was obliged to go some days subsequently; but I in vain awaited the arrival, and I think it must have fallen into the hands of Mr. Hay, who, I have no doubt, will publish it, with other drawings of the kind.

This curious tomb, I regret to say, no longer exists; the Arabs have destroyed it, according to their usual custom, in order to sell it piece-meal among travellers.'(33)

Right rear wall

To this wall we assign the scene showing the tomb owner supervising merchandise being brought from areas outside the Nile Valley (cf. Ill. 40).(34) The hieroglyphs as copied by Wilkinson run from right to left, therefore the tomb owner would be facing right. The scene showed 'man seated... men weighing in scales & scribes'. These latter would be facing left, towards the tomb owner inspecting.

The scene falls within the catagory of section 2 of chapter 3 above, representing the office of the tomb owner. The subject is most frequently represented on the front or rear walls of the hall in T-shaped tombs, and, where tribute is concerned, in connection with a picture of the reigning king, which is almost always shown on either side of the doorway leading to the inner room. Although there is no mention of such a representation of the king, he may have been there originally.

The inscription is as follows

m33 ỉnw wḥ3t ḫrpwt r ḥwt-nṯr n [Im]n m n3 n k3mw n ... m33 ỉnw nw W3w3t g3wt nw T3-Sty b3kt nbt rḫyt ʿš3t wrt ḫrpwt nsw nḫt nsw bỉt Nb-m3ʿt-rʿ

'Inspecting goods(35) from the oasis, taxes to the temple of [Amūn] from the vineyards of ...(36) Inspecting goods from Wawat, dues from Nubia, all revenues (from) a great many people, taxes of the victorious king, the king of upper and Lower Egypt, Nebmaʿetrēʿ...'

The position of one inscription, copied by Champollion in the tomb, remains to be identified:

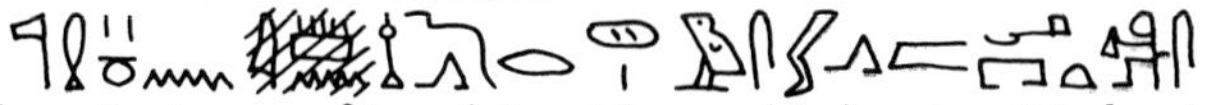

ḥm nṯr 2-nw n ʾImn ḥḏ r Nḫn ws(tn) rd m ʿt špst

'second prophet of Amūn who sets forth at dawn to Nekhen (Hierakonpolis), free of foot in the splendid room.'(37)

As Champollion usually writes from left to right in his book, it is not possible to determine the position of this inscription.

One of the statues of Simut and his wife, no. 1107 in the Cairo Museum 'of unknown provenance', appears from the inscriptions on it to have come from a funerary context, and probably from the tomb itself. One of the inscriptions(38) mentions the conventional funerary gods, including 'all the gods of the Underworld', and a prayer is made for 'a good burial after good old age and good life time, seeing his ancestors

The inscriptions were hacked out on the lap of the figures where the name of Amūn would have been, and later restored with hieroglyphs which make no real sense, at least as published.

9 Tomb No. C4

According to Burton this tomb was a 'small catacomb behind Yanni's house'(1) (MSS 25639,41 verso). Wilkinson also places it behind Yanni's (MSS v.140). Hay says that it was 'a tomb below Mons. Dupuy's house' (MSS 29852, on unnumbered page before p. 250, and referring to his tracings from the tomb on pp. 250-66). Prudhoe calls it a 'tomb at the end of the lower line' (Atlas A,19b). Champollion describes it as being 'situé sur la montagne' (*Not. descr.*, p. 520), and he gave it the number 31. Rosellini attributed the tomb to the father of the actual owner, who also occurs in it (MSS 284,G40). Lepsius called it no. 49 (*Text*, iii, p. 262). Porter & Moss conclude that the tomb was probably situated near TT 69 of Menna (*Topographical Bibliography*, I^2,1, p. 457).

This assumption proved to be correct. In the early 1960's the tomb was excavated by the Egyptian Antiquities Organization, after a donkey had fallen into a hole in the ground below a house now occupied by the Boghdady family. Mr Ahmed Sayed Hindi, followed by Mr (now Dr) Mohammed Saleh cleared and excavated the tomb and its shafts. A report on the work was deposited in the Inspectorate at Qurna, but was possibly misplaced when the office was transferred from the old Davies' house to Beit el-Medîna.

In March 1985 the tomb was re-entered by the present writer, who spent a week studying the remains. It is the only one among the 'lost' tombs to have been re-discovered, and a reconstruction of its scheme of decoration is greatly facilitated by the availability of factors which for most of the other tombs remain conjectural. However, very little survives of the actual decoration.

Mohammed Saleh correctly identified the owner of the tomb as being identical with the owner of tomb no. C4, the name and title occurring on fallen ceiling fragments; in a few inscriptions on a small scale from the walls; and on cones presently lying in the tomb. The ownership was thus never in doubt.

The tomb was visited by most of the early travellers who worked in these monuments. Hay made excellent tracings of many scenes, the Prudhoe MSS have useful sketches of parts of two walls,(1a) and Burton, Wilkinson and Rosellini copied selected scenes. The only lengthy description of the tomb is by Burton, written ca. 1824.

'The tomb was I believe opened a few years back & the faces &c of figures are not mutilated as in those opened some centuries back, & cut out by Christians, for after all it seems they have done more harm than the Arabs. The tomb had been plastered fresh by the family to whom it belonged, and the mud is plastered all over the paintings.' (MSS 25639,41 verso)

There is in fact ample evidence of this layer of modern mud plaster covering the paintings. A small patch of decoration extant on the east end of the right wall of the inner room was almost completely concealed by a layer of mud 0.5-1cm thick. Some of the fragments found lying on the floor showed a similar feature. Yet the early travellers managed to trace and draw in the tomb, and thus part of the decoration must have been exposed.

The tomb, which is of the common T-shape with a niche in the rear wall of the inner room, is in many places bared to the roughly cut walls of the rock. The mud plaster of the ceiling has fallen down everywhere, though chunks of it survive on the floor. Attempts have been made to cut out pieces of the wall-decoration. On the right front wall of the hall and the right wall of the inner room the chisel marks form a neat square in the remaining mud plaster which appears to have been applied in two coatings. The second layer, and with it the decoration, has disappeared along with the rest of the decoration of the walls. In the rear wall of the niche the right half of the decoration has been cut free, and as the niche had only one layer of mud plaster, the rock wall is exposed where the painting was removed.

Two shafts descend from either end of the hall, the northern one continuing eastwards, the southern shaft bending westwards into the mountain. At the inner corner of the right wall of the inner room a gap appears to another shaft. None of these shafts, which appeared to be empty, were entered by me. In the tomb itself were found fragments of several painted coffins of a date later than the date of the tomb, along with mummy wrappings, human remains and broken pots. Most of the fragments of wall-decoration were recovered from this heap which had probably been piled up in the inner room when the tomb was cleared.

Judging from Hay's tracings the visible scenes were in almost pefect condition, and Burton specifically says about a detail in the funerary procession that the colours are 'very perfect'. It has proved possible to assign fragments in a museum collection to this tomb, and the craftsmanship displayed here and in the fragments found in the tomb is indeed excellent.

The owner of the tomb and its date

The owner of TT C4 was the *waʿb*-priest of Maʿet, Merymaʿet. He is shown receiving offerings, introduced to the gods and working in the Fields of Iaru. His coffin is being dragged in the funeral procession, and one of the mummies represented is named as his. The ownership is thus beyond doubt.

Other members of the family of Merymaʿet are represented in the tomb, four generations in all. His father was the *waʿb*-priest of Maʿet, Sennūter, and his mother was called Ḥenutsha. The father of his father was the scribe of the wine-cellar of the House of the Morning,(2) Sennūfer. His son was also a *waʿb*-priest of Maʿet, called Pewaḥ. The wife of Merymaʿet was songstress of Amūn, but in the scene where she is represented, the inscription was either incompletely copied by Hay, or the sheet of tracing paper was lost, unless the lower part of the scene was destroyed. After the title follows an . A fragment found in the tomb shows traces of an to follow. However, this fragment (see below) is not the same piece which Hay copied, although it looks deceptively like it. When comparing the tracing of the fragment found in the tomb, made by me, with Hay's 1:1 tracing in his MSS 29852,266-7, it was found that it was at a different scale. The fragment must thus belong to another scene, though the inscription appears to be identical.

Six funerary cones belonging to Merymaʿet were found in the tomb,(3) and the name of the wife is here Maʿya, preceded by the title *nbt pr* 'mistress of the house' (Ill. 61[2]). However, somewhere in the tomb(4) Champollion copied *ḥmt.f nbt pr ꜣImnḥtp* 'his wife, the mistress of the house, Amenḥotp'. The other inscriptions copied by Champollion are from the aforementioned scene, where the wife of Merymaʿet is called 'songstress of Amūn, M...' Either the *ḥmt.f* is the wife of another person, or Merymaʿet had two different wives.

A sister of Merymaʿet is also represented in the tomb. Her name is Maʿyi(t). She may be his half-sister by his mother, for in the inscription accompanying the representation of Sennūṯer, Ḥenutsha and herself she is called 'her beloved, favourite daughter', referring to the mother only.(5)

A last member of the family is a skipper called Wesem.(6) He inserted an inscription in the tomb in which he claims to have re-opened the tomb. He is qualified as 'son of his daughter', an ambiguous statement, which could refer both to Merymaʿet and to his father Sennūṯer, both of whom are represented in the scene in which the inscription occurs. As Maʿyit is also present, one may perhaps assume that the reason why Wesem chose this particular scene for his inscription was that it showed his mother(?) and his grandfather. We do not know who his father was. The *f* in *is.f*, describing the tomb, would then still refer to Merymaʿet, as one would expect, but the *f* in *sꜣt.f* would refer to Sennūṯer in the picture. If this is the case, Wesem was the nephew of Merymaʿet. If on the other hand the *f* of *sꜣt.f* is taken to refer to Merymaʿet, Wesem would be two generations younger - he may then have been the son of Pewaḥ.

Yet another person is represented in the tomb. The secretary(?) of the temple, Panūfer, but his family relationship is not given.

The tomb can be dated with some certainty. The style of the paintings points to a date not much earlier than Tuthmosis IV and no later than Amenophis III. In Champollion's copy of the name of a wife called Amenḥotp, the Amūn element seems to have been erased,(7) indicating a date earlier than the Amarna Period.

The same proved to be the case in a fragment of wall-decoration extant on the south jamb of the entrance doorway. The tomb owner and a woman are shown with a hymn including the name of Amun (Ill. 61 [3]). A close scrutiny of the wall revealed that the group and preceding signs were painted on a separate lump of gypsum which had not received adequate grounding, for the colours were very pale (bluish green), the border lines between the signs showing similar characteristics. On the other hand the Atenists ignored the name of Amūn in our Ill. 43, for which a very similar fragment (Ill. 57 [5]) was found to have no alterations, and the name of Amūn *(sic)* in the title of Merymaᶜet in the Fields of Iaru (Ill. 46).

A stela from the temple of Maᶜet at Karnak was dedicated to this goddess by a *waᶜb*-priest of Maᶜet, called Merymaᶜet.(8) The stela bears the cartouche of Amenophis III. Few *waᶜb*-priests of Maᶜet of the Eighteenth dynasty are known,(9), and the name of Merymaᶜet is not very common.(10) The identity of the owner of TT C4 and the person who erected the stela is therefore fairly certain, and the tomb must have been decorated during the reign of Amenophis III, or just possibly that of his predecessor if the stela was cut a number of years after the tomb.

The date of the tomb makes the statement of the skipper Wesem particularly interesting. As Wesem was one or perhaps two generations younger than Merymaᶜet he must have lived into the following reign, and possibly beyond it.Wesem says that he 'renewed the tomb anew having found it closed.' The word 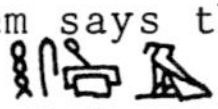 *ḥsꜣ*, describing the state in which he found it, is not mentioned in the *Wörterbuch,* but it is now included in the list of additions given by Andreu & Cauville,(11) referring to an ostrakon mentioned by Janssen.(12) It is here used of a box which someone is being asked to open. Janssen compares the word with Demotic *ḥsis* which is used of a tomb, and he suggests a connection with *ḥsꜣ* 'cord'. Renewal of monuments was usually performed when the monument in question had fallen into disrepair, being ruined, or the like.(13) The tomb of Merymaᶜet appears to have been locked up at some point. If the relatives had still been around, there would have been no purpose in closing the tomb, and if the family had died out, the tomb would have been left unattended. But it was *ḥsꜣ*, 'secured with a string?' as if the arrangement were temporary. Although no traces of the family of Merymaᶜet have been recovered at el-Amarna, it is tempting to imagine that this is where they went. If the skipper Wesem was the nephew of Merymaᶜet he would have been well advanced in age by the time he restored the tomb, but as we have seen, it is just possible that he was the grandson of Merymaᶜet, and in that case he would have been considerably younger.

The decoration of the tomb

As mentioned above the tomb is T-shaped (Ill. 60 [1]) and of medium size, the average height of the walls being about 2m. For the size of the individual walls see below. In reconstructing the decoration of the walls the tracings by Hay are particularly helpful, not only because they are excellent copies, but also because they are facsimile and thus 1:1. Similar tracings were made by me of the few patches of decoration remaining on the walls and of all the decorated fragments found on the floor, some of them being very small.

To the early travellers the tomb was known as the tomb 'with the bunch of grapes in the frieze' (Burton MSS 25639,41 verso and 25644,83). Five fragments of an upper frieze were found in the tomb (Ill. 60 [2]. All the fragments have pendant lotus flowers, but one of the fragments show the dark blue and black outlines of bunches of grapes. The base border in both rooms was the 'palace facade' with red, green and blue design on a white background. The border was remarkably well preserved. In some places a black area was visible at floor level (Ill. 61[4]).

Entrance, south jamb (Ills. 60[3] and 61[2]).

The lower third of a representation of a man and a woman remains in good condition on this wall, facing the rising sun and presumably shown adoring Amūn-Rēᶜ whose name occurs in the accompanying hymn. A similar text in TT 140 provides some of the missing signs.(14)

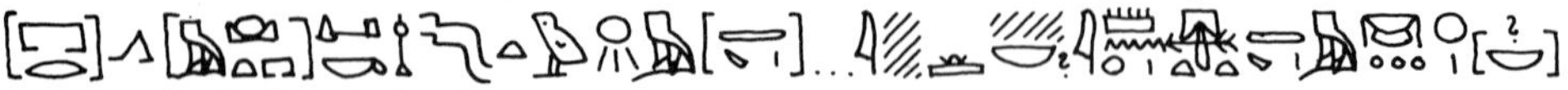

... *[pr] [m ꜣḫt] dỉ.k ḥḏdwt m [tꜣ]* ... *ỉ* ... *ꜣImn-Rᶜ stwt tꜣ m nwb rᶜ [nb?]*

'... [coming out] [of the horizon]. May you give light on [earth] ... Amun-Re the rays. The earth is like gold every day(?).'

Hall, right front wall

The large section of a wall drawn for the Prudhoe MSS (Atlas A,19a), with details drawn by other early travellers, can be assigned to this wall with some certainty. According to Rosellini a representation of this nature was to be found in exactly this position: 'In fondo alla alta parete destra entrando, il defunto siede & siede più basso accanto a lui la sua sorella' (MSS 284,G40). A conventional position of the subject of the Feast of the Valley in the main upper register was on one of the front walls of the hall, and there is ample room for all the available elements, with space left for a representation of the tomb owner offering next to the doorway, if such a scene existed. A further point in favour of the emplacement of the scene on this wall will be mentioned below.

There are two registers copied in the Prudhoe MSS, the top register showing to the left a man offering to a seated couple and a standing girls, and, to the right, a seated couple being approached by four girls with sistra and bouquets. The lower register shows the supervision of work in the field, the tomb owner and a young woman being seated in a booth to the left with two registers of agricultural activities in front of them.

We shall discuss the lower register first. Apart from the drawing in the Prudhoe MSS, other copies of part of this scene were made by the early travellers. Hay made a tracing of the two persons in the booth(MSS 29852,266-7, cf. Ill. 43), and Rosellini made a less accurate drawing of the same scene (*Mon. civ.* 133 [2]). Wilkinson drew the ploughing and felling of trees (MSS v.140 [lower middle], cf. *Manners and Customs* 2. Ser. i.46 (No. 425) = ed. Birch, ii.394 (No. 468)), and Champollion copied some of the hieroglyphs (*Not. descr.* p. 845, cf. p. 520), as did Lepsius (*Text*, iii,262).

The title of the scene is as follows

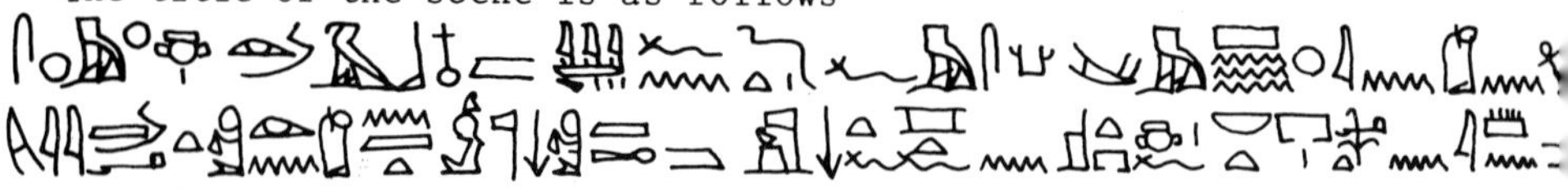

sḫmḫ ỉb mꜣꜣ bw nfr m sḫwt.f n ḏt.f m skꜣ m šmw ỉn wᶜb n Mꜣᶜt Mrymꜣᶜt ỉr.n wᶜb n Mꜣᶜt Snnṯr mꜣᶜ ḫrw m ẖrt-ntr snt.f mrt.f n st-ỉb.f nbt pr šmᶜyt n ꜣImn M...

'Rejoicing at seeing something pleasant in his fields of his estate, ploughing during the *šmw*-season by the *waᶜb*-priest of Maᶜet, Merymaᶜet, son of the *waᶜb*-priest of Maᶜet, Sennūṯer, justified in the necropolis; (and by)his beloved,favourite wife, mistress of the house, songstress of Amūn,...'

A fragment very similar to part of this text was found in the tomb, showing not only part of the left vertical border in green, white and red, with a sliver of yellow to the left, but also the signs 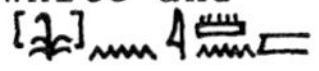 with a small part of the following sign, undoubtedly , the name of the wife being thus obviously identical to the name on the cones, Maʿya. The hieroglyphs are now grey, but were originally black. There are no signs of the name of Amūn having been tampered with. As mentioned above, p. 101, the size of the fragment appears to be incompatible with Hay's 1:1 tracing of the scene on the wall. The fragment would therefor seem to stem from another part of the tomb with a representation of Maʿya.

Merymaʿet with shaven skull wears a white tunic, a collar of green and blue leaves, and bracelets, also green and blue.(16) He sits on a stool with lattice bracing painted white and holds in his hand a black stick with a red and yellow tip.(A similar stick, but again at a different scale, appears on one of the fragments found in the tomb, cf. Ill. 59 [10a-b]). In the other hand he clasps a fully blown lotus flower, held to the nose of his wife. She is dressed in a white rippled garment with a loose part slung over her right arm. She has an elaborate necklace, two bracelets on either arm, and on top of her heavy wig she wears a floral band and a lotus bud. She is barefoot, whereas her husband wears sandals. She sits on a very low black chair,(17) her left hand posed on her husband's knee, and a duckling resting in her right hand. The skin of Merymaʿet is the conventional red, that of his wife yellow. The booth in which they spend the day has a slender papyriform column with a lotus bud attached to the capital.

The scene in front of them is divided into two registers. In the top register a heap of offerings is displayed to the left, including loaves of bread, a basket of fruit(?), fowl, and three receptacles (or possibly pieces of cloth?). The agricultural activities read from right to left: felling trees, hacking up the soil, ploughing with oxen and sprinkling the seed. In the field there is a lake with fishes. Part of the wall was destroyed, but next to the offerings part of the winnowing scene remains, apparently performed by men. A few hieroglyphs seem to be left above.

Little is left of the lower register. To the extreme right a man squats before a large, square object (stacked flax or papyrus?). To the extreme left there is a man drawn at a large scale, appearing to be taking account of something, now lost. His name remains above: 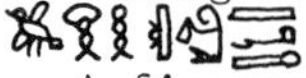 *P3w3ḥ m3ʿ ḫrw* 'Pewaḥ, justified'.

A figure like the one of Pewaḥ would usually supervise the recording of produce, in this case grain, and, if the tiny fragment on the right represents stacking flax, the recording of this commodity as well. We may thus tentatively restore heaps of grain being measured in barrels, and possibly flax harvest, in this missing part of the register. The actual harvest of grain, a favourite subject in contemporary tombs, was not copied by the early travellers, but fragments of it were found in the tomb: two good matching pieces and one very small one (Ill. 56 [1a-c]). It is to be regretted that the rest was not recovered, for the remaining scene is admirably painted.

Two men, represented in the 'layering' technique appearing in the reign of Tuthmosis IV,(18) grasp the tall straw with their left hands and are about to lift the sickle to chop off the heads of grain. Only one sickle seems to be drawn, being made of red wood with a cutting edge shaped like molars of a paler red. A large succulent weed with red flowers stands in their way. Behind them two girls bend over to collect the ears of grain in their baskets. A foot in the air, wearing a black sandal, reveals what was to follow: the stacking of the ears of grain in huge baskets where the contents need squeezing in to the extent that the field labourer has to jump high in the air to do so. It is to protect his feet during landing in the stubble that he wears the sandals. An identical detail can be seen in TT 57 of Khaꜥemḥēt(19) and in another fragment to be discussed in chapter 11.

It must remain an open question whether this harvesting detail continued the register drawn in Prudhoe MSS to the right, or whether it went below. But there is tangible evidence to show that the detail may have belonged on this wall. The harvest fragment is a palimpsest consisting not just of two layers of paint, but of two layers of gypsum plaster a few mm thick, each with a separate layer of painted decoration. Where the top layer of gypsum has come off near the lower edge of the two larger fragments, a black base line at a different level is apparent. It was not possible to pursue the investigation further lest the harvest scene should be destroyed. In a fragment of another scene to be discussed below, the alteration seems to be restricted to a re-placement of the same subject, not a change of motif. Although the reason for this procedure remains a mystery, the alterations in the harvest scene may be of a similar nature and simply consisted of lowering the base line.

The original layer of gypsum in the larger harvest fragments thus reveals a tiny part of the decoration in the lower register, now completely disappeared under the final top layer of gypsum. The upper part of a papyrus flower proves that there was indeed another register below, possibly a row of offering bringers moving towards the representation above. Small fragments of such persons were found in the tomb, but as they do not show any trace of the double layer of gypsum they probably belonged on another wall. But the double layer of gypsum is apparent in the 'palace facade' decoration at the base of the wall near the entrance doorway. Here most of the original layer is extant, but patches of the second layer remain with the same 'palace facade' decoration painted on it (Ill. 61[5]).

In the top register to the left offerings are being presented to the family of Merymaꜥet (Ill. 45).(20) The inscriptions identifying them are

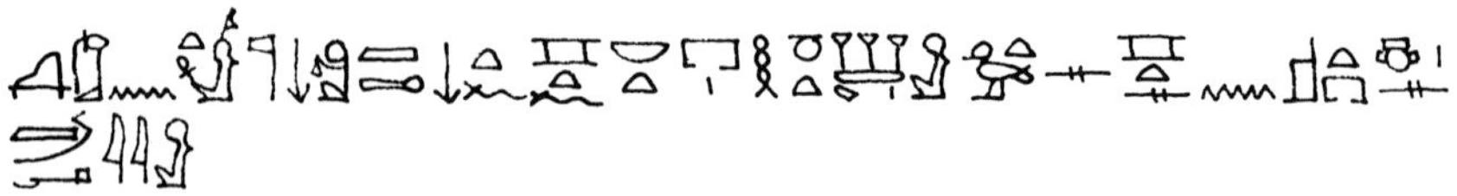

Wsir wꜥb n Mꜣꜥt Snnṯr mꜣꜥ ḫrw snt.f mrt.f nbt pr Ḥnwtšꜣ sꜣt.s mrt.s n st-ib.s Mꜣꜥy(t)

'Osiris, *wꜥb*-priest of Maꜥet, Sennūṯer, justified; his beloved wife, mistress of the house, Ḥenutsha; (and) her beloved, favourite daughter, Maꜥyi(t).'

All wear fine white garments and ornaments similar to those described above, but Sennūṯer wears no shirt. The necklace of Ḥenutsha consists of rows of black beads. She and her husband wear tall unguent cones. Maʿyit has a bunch of flowers in one hand and in the other a cluster of blue fruits or flowers, not immediately identifiable. Sennūṯer holds a kerchief in one hand, the other reaching to an offering table piled with loaves of bread, baskets of fruit (black circles on green background), a piece of meat and a bird, a cos lettuce and a lotus flower with two buds. A man with shaven head and long kilt presents him with a bouquet. The inscription immediately above and behind him was admirably copied by Hay, but when tracing the text above the offering table, the paper seems to have moved, and the signs are indistinct. The following can be made out:

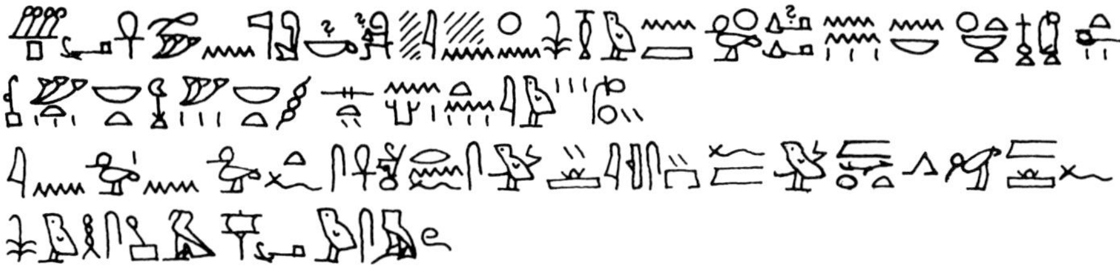

šsp ʿnḫ n nṯr.k(?) šps(?) ʾI[m]n [...] ḥsw n Mȝʿt sȝ(t) Rʿ dd.n n.k(?) ḫt nbt nfrt wʿbt ḥnkwt rnpwt nbt ḫȝwt nbt nḏm sty n kȝ.tn iw.w wʿb sp sn in sȝ n sȝt.f sʿnḫ rn.f smȝwy is.f m mȝw m-ḫt gm.f sw ḥsȝ Wsm

'Receiving the bouquet of your(?) noble(?) god Amūn...(21) praised by Maʿet, daughter of Rēʿ. We(22) give to you(23) all good and pure things, vegetables, all herbs and sweet smelling plants for your *kȝ*, they being twice pure. It is the son of his daughter who lets his name live renewing his tomb anew having found it closed, the skipper Wesem.'

The latter remark is an interesting statement, which we discussed above.

In horizontal hieroglyphs above the bouquet presented by the man is written 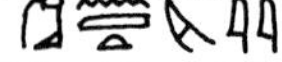 *wʿb n Mȝʿt Mrymȝʿ(t)* '*waʿb*-priest of Maʿet, Merymaʿe(t)'. The identity of the offering bringer is thus seemingly questionable. From the distribution of the hieroglyphs it seems possible that at some point they were altered. The 'renewal text' could not possibly have been written when the tomb was first decorated, but must naturally be a later addition. I am inclined to think that the name of Merymaʿet was originally written in the vertical column behind the head of the offering bringer, and that it is indeed Merymaʿet who is depicted, offering to his father, and that Wesem changed the text, yet did not want to suppress the name, and squeezed it in above the bouquct.(24)

Adjoining this scene is another, only preserved in the drawing in the Prudhoe MSS, with some names given by Lepsius (MSS 305 [bottom]) and scraps of text, and sistrum and *menat* drawn by Wilkinson (MSS v.141 [top right]). The Prudhoe drawing is reproduced in Ill. 46.

The tomb owner Merymaʿet, justified, is seated with a woman like the one in the previous scene. They are not wearing unguent cones. Facing them are four women. The first gives a *menat* to Merymaʿet, while in the other hand she holds a sistrum. The following two women carry a sistrum in one hand and a lotus in the other. The arm and sistrum of a fourth woman is visible in the Prudhoe drawing, indicating that there was indeed a continuation of this wall, featuring the Feast of the Valley.

In Wilkinson's drawing of sistrum and *menat* (cf. Ill. 46) the girl holds the sistrum higher that she does in the Prudhoe sketch. The accompanying text was partly(?) copied by Wilkinson:

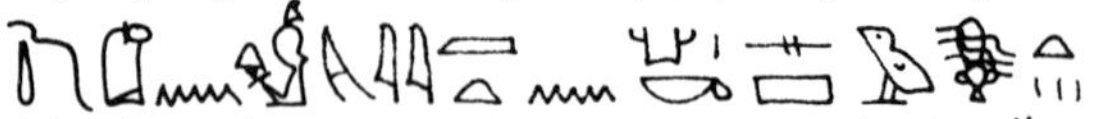

ḏd mdw wꜥb n Mꜣꜥt Mrymꜣꜥt n kꜣ.k(25) *sšwt*

'Words to be recited: " *wꜥb*-priest of Maꜥet, Merymaꜥet, to your *ka* the sistra...'

A passage in Burton MSS 25639,41 verso mentions women with sistra, presumably the same drawn for the Prudhoe MSS: 'Priests & priestesses with sistrum bouquets *[sic]*, bird &c are seen on the opposite wall [to the one with the funeral procession, cf. below]'. There is reason to believe that part of this scene has been preserved to this day in a fragment in Florence (no. 2471).

This fragment (Ill. 47) was acquired by Rosellini and is mentioned in the catalogues of the collection,(26) and it was recently published by S. Donadoni, *Arte egizia*, Turin 1975, colour plate facing p. 18. As it was acquired along with a fragment from TT 78 it has long been thought to come from the same tomb. However, this has been shown not to be the case,(29) though an alternative provenance has not been suggested. Several factors indicate an attribution to the tomb of Merymaꜥet.

The fragment shows a man facing left with a very large bouquet, followed by a woman, partly destroyed, with two smaller bouquets, and preceded by another woman, the back outline of the wig only being preserved. The man is described as

sꜣ.f wꜥb n Mꜣꜥt Pꜣwꜣḥ

'His son, *waꜥb*-priest of Maꜥet, Pewaḥ.'

Above them is part of a hieroglyphic inscription:

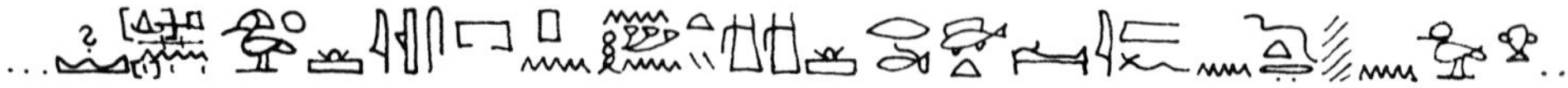

... *dỉ.sn ꜣḫ ỉs pn n ḥnty rwḏt ḫꜣt ỉm.f n ḏt.. n sꜣ ḥr*

'... may they give that this tomb be useful for ever and the body firm in it for always...'(28)

The title of the *waꜥb*-priest of Maꜥet is not at all frequent, as already mentioned. The first mention of a *waꜥb*-priest of Maꜥet occurs in the tomb of Rekhmirēꜥ,(29) but whether a Theban temple was meant is not certain. A Maꜥet temple was built by the Ramessids and Nektanebos I at Karnak-North, incorporating blocks of an earlier building erected by Amenophis III.(30) In the list of members of the staff of this temple given by Helck(31) only two persons can safely be attributed to the Eighteenth dynasty: the owner of TT C4 (and of the funerary cones), and his father. The only other person is Pewaḥ from the fragment in Florence. As both our Merymaᶜet and his father held the title, it seems logical to assume that the sacerdotal occupation ran in the family, and that Pewaḥ was the son of Merymaᶜet. To sustain further this idea, it is significant that a man of a certain standing, to judge from the scale at which he is represented, also named Pewaḥ, was depicted in the agricultural scene on the same wall. In all probability he is the very same person.

Although the sequence of scenes and details of scenes drawn by the early travellers is by no means conclusive proof of two neighbouring drawings stemming from the same tomb, it is nevertheless significant that Wilkinson, who drew this particular offering bringer on MSS v.141 [top middle], placed other drawings from TT C4 on the same page of his notebook [top right] and [top left], as well as on his p. 140 (cf. our Ill. 46).

The style of painting in the Florence fragment has a strong similarity to the style of the paintings in the tomb as reflected in Hay's facsimile copies. This is perticularly evident in the treatment of the mouth, with fully outlined lips, in the floral collar and bracelets, and in details of the garment (knot and wavy lines along the waist). A final proof of the provenance of Florence 2171 is its dimensions. According to Schiaparelli (repeated by Brack) the fragment measures 51.5x34.5cm.(32) The register as measured on Hay's tracing is 61cm high (not including the top border). On the Florence fragment the lower part of the legs is missing, and although part of the top border is included, the missing portion may easily account for the discrepancy in measurements given by otehrs.

There is thus little difficulty in placing the fragment on this wall, perhaps just joining the Prudhoe drawing, if the wig of the woman in the fragment belongs to the woman whose arm appears in the drawing. The fragment would have been *in situ* when Wilkinson and Burton saw it. As we have seen, Rosellini certainly had access to this tomb, and he presumably took this fragment and two more with him. These other fragments will be discussed below.

The right front wall of the tomb itself shows chisel marks in the remaining plaster where a fragment 43cm high and 36cm wide has been cut out, perhaps successfully. The upper edge of the square is 20cm from the ceiling, the right edge ca. 143cm from the doorway. The Florence fragment with Pewaḥ is too large to fit in here, and the position of the square on the wall is too far to the north, according to the drawing in the Prudhoe MSS. An attempt must therefore have been made to cut out the head of one of the ladies with sistra. The area to the right of the square is now bared to the rock, and there is no other trace left on the wall of the destruction caused by the removal of the fragment in Florence.

In Wilkinson's notebook, next to the drawing of Pewaḥ with the bouquet, there is another little sketch showing two offering bringers, also turned towards the left, one of them carrying a bowl, the other a bird (Ill. 46). Although Burton mentions someone carrying a bird after the row of women with sistra, the two offering bringers in Wilkinson's sketch, designated as priests, seem rather to belong on the wall with the Opening of the Mouth, particularly since the foremost of the two figures appears to be carrying a heart in a bowl, a common detail in the funerary rites.(33) This drawing will therefore be discussed below.

The height of the top register, as measured on Hay's facsimile tracings, is 61cm, that of the second register with the couple in the booth is 51cm, to which must be added a few centimeters for the missing feet. Altogether the two registers took up about 115cm of the wall. If the harvest fragment is added below, with a fourth register of offering bringers as the bottom register, the total height of the decorated surface would be about 165cm. The base frieze being about 39cm, the additional top frieze would bring the total surface thus far accounted for to the height of the actual wall, which is about 216cm. The width of the wall is about 380cm. Hay's tracing of Meryma^{c}et's family measures 100.5cm, and the total width of the known decoration, with the Florence fragment added immediately after the arm of the sistrum player in the Prudhoe MSS, is about 250cm.

Hall, left front wall

The tomb of Meryma^{c}et is unusual in that the funeral procession was moved from the conventional position in the passage (inner room) to a wall in the transverse hall, which caused certain problems in the reconstruction of the scheme of decoration before the actual size and shape of the tomb was known.

Two registers were drawn for the Prudhoe MSS (Ill. 49), and the width of the scene, which appears to be the total width, was estimated to about 350cm. The width of the walls of the inner room is only about 296cm. It is evident from the directions of the figures that the scene was in the left part of the tomb, enabling the procession to move towards the interior. Burton's description is to some extent of little help, for he claims that the wall was 'opposite' to the wall with the Feast of the Valley, which is clearly impossible, especially as he adds that the mummy carried in procession was 'at the north end'. This leaves us with only one solution for this scene: the left front wall of the hall, which may perhaps be interpreted as being on the 'opposite [side of the doorway to the] wall' with the Feast of the Valley.

The wall itself has the base border intact with a few very small patches of gypsum plaster left just above. In one of the patches, about 165cm from the doorway, a bluish colour can be distinguished, and a faint horizontal line, once black, with a yellow area with faint red lines above. According to Burton 'the lower compartments [below the funeral procession] [are] defaced, but have had boats &c.' (MSS 25639,41 verso).

The voyage to Abydos is very frequently represented below the funerary procession, and as we shall see below, there is yet another pointer to such an arrangement in this tomb. A fragment found on the floor (Ill. 57 [3]) shows part of a boat on a strip of water of exactly the same width as the traces on the wall, and although the fragment belonged to a register which was not a lower register, very little doubt remains that however unorthodox the arrangement, this was where the scene was located in the tomb of Meryma^{c}et.

Apart from the registers drawn for the Prudhoe MSS (Atlas, A,19b), Burton drew the mourners and a Kite (MSS 25638,70,71 (for the latter cf. Ill. 48)) and gave a description of the wall (MSS 25639,41-2), while Wilkinson drew isolated details of the procession (MSS v.180 [bottom], 181 [bottom right], 140 [middle], cf. *Manners and Customs* 2. Ser. ii.418 (No. 501), 1 Ser. ii.123 (No. 114) = ed. Birch, iii. 449 (No. 634), i.362 (No. 134), cf. our Ills. 50-1).

Burton's description agrees to some extent with the drawing in the Prudhoe MSS, and however brief and vague, it gives valuable clues as to part of the wall-decoration omitted by all copyists.

The upper register shows from left to right: three out of the 'Nine Friends', followed by another priest; the coffin on a sledge, adorned with bouquets, drawn by six men and followed by a male mourner supported by another man, the inscription identifying the coffin as belonging to

 *Wsἰr(?) wᶜb n Mꜣᶜt Mry[mꜣᶜt] mꜣᶜ ḫrw*

'Osiris(?), *waᶜb*-priest of Maᶜet, Mery[maᶜet],(34) justified.' Another coffin on a sledge follows, attended by two women in the boat and the two Kites, , presumably referring to the younger Kite, although Wilkinson has for , and the older Kite ; a person in a lomg garment; a destroyed patch, and six men holding the rope attached to four oxen and an attendant (according to Burton two of the oxen are red, the other two white). Preceding the coffins is the *tekenu* with the face visible, drawn by three men and a lector priest joining them. The entire procession is led by a man with floral offerings, and it is directed towards the goddess of the west.

The second register shows three more of the 'Nine Friends', two men carrying a mummy on a couch, a man with a chair, two men with chests, one of them holding a fan, two large and two small men with stands supporting jars, and a group of female mourners. There is an inscription above them:

rmy n pꜣ wᶜb wrd ᶜḏ n.k sp sn

'Weeping for the *waᶜb*-priest without wearing. Welcome, welcome.'

Burton adds in a vertical column *pꜣ.n nb(?)* 'our lord(?)' (MSS 25644,83). A group of nine men, some with stems of papyrus, carry an elongated object, apparently folded at one end, possibly a long sheet, and they are preceded by three more offering bringers. The procession is headed towards a building, drawn accurately by Wilkinson (Ill. 51). Above the door is written *pr nfr*, a designation for the funerary workshop.(35)

In his enumeration of the figures in the procession Burton also mentions a 'priest reading precedes, & another in a tyger's skin [*sc.* panther skin] with libations and incense - before whom are the two mummies, held in an upright position by 2 men (shorn) & drest as priests. The principal female mourner kneels at the feet of the foremost & rods (as those carried in procession by the priests) twisted round with leaves &c and ornamented by flowers of Lotus? stand before each'.

A fragment in Florence (No. 2472, cf. Ill. 52) answers to the latter part of this description. In style it is extremely similar to the one from the wall described above, and it was acquired at the same time. It was published in the catalogues of the collection,(36) and in recent times in A. Galvano, *L'arte egiziana antica*, Milan 1938, fig. 65. Along with the fragment mentioned above, it was for many years taken to come from TT 78. A conclusive proof of its provenance is the fact that the names of Merymaᶜet and Pewaḥ occur on it.

The fragment shows the two mummies as described above. There is a pile of offerings behind the female mourner, and a wavy line above indicates that the mummies were being purified, cf. Burton's 'priest with libations'. The texts are as follows:

(before the mummy)

ỉmꜣḫy ḥr Wsỉr wꜥb Mrymꜣꜥt

'the venerable one for Osiris, *waꜥb*-priest Merymaꜥet.'

(behind the head of the foremost priest)

sš šꜥt(?) ḥt nṯr Pꜣnfr

'secretary(?) of the temple, Panūfer'

The second man is the

wꜥb n Mꜣꜥt Pꜣwꜣḥ

'*waꜥb*-priest of Maꜥet, Pewaḥ'.

To the right in the fragment the border line is visible, showing that the scene was at the very extremity of the wall. At the lower edge there remains a small section of the scene below with a light shelter with columns of papyrus and the top part of columns of hieroglyphs. The nature of the scene, now lost, may be inferred from Burton's description. Following the mention of the mummies, Burton goes on to say: 'The lower compartments defaced, but have had boats &c.' From this we may assume that the voyage to Abydos was represented here, and that there were at least two more registers. In other Theban tombs there is in connection with the representation of the voyage to Abydos a booth with offerings, and sometimes an empty chair in it, with mourners and priests in front.(37) The shelter on the Florence fragment seems to be just such a building. As one of the two papyriform columns comes down in the middle of it, no person would have been depicted there, as he would have been partly hidden by it, or *vice versa*, and there may not even have been a chair. Presumably a number of vases and other provisions were housed in the shelter.(38) The hieroglyphs pertaining to the scene are 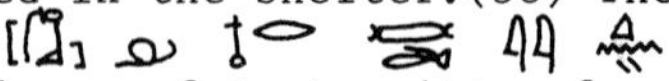 which are obviously the beginning of columns of text written from left to right.

The fragment from the tomb with a boat on a strip of water no doubt stems from a scene showing the various stages of the voyage to Abydos of which Wilkinson copied one detail (MSS v.140 [lower middle], cf. Ill. 46). (39) The boat heads to the right, with a small figure at the stern of the boat probing the depth of the water with a stick. The arm of a sailor(?) can just be made out on his left. On the bank of the river the boat is greeted by two figures, represented in the same layered fashion as the harvesters. Part of their speech remains above, written from left to right in black between red dividing lines:

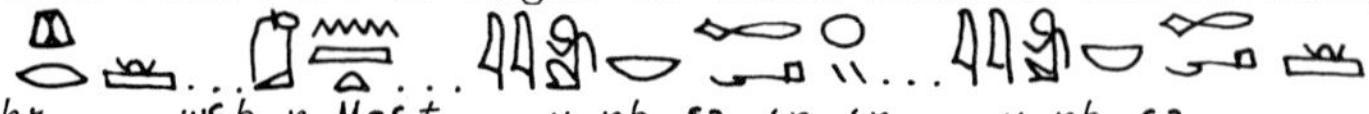

ḥr ... wꜥb n Mꜣꜥt ...y nb ꜥꜣ sp sn ...y nb ꜥꜣ

'...*waᶜb*-priest of Maᶜet, [my?] great lord (twice)... [my?] great lord.'

The following space to the right is blank, and the text may end here. There seems to be no parallel to it in other Abydos texts, but although the representations of this period are similar, the texts do vary.(40) The 'great lord' who is being addressed would be Merymaᶜet, who is also greated as 'our lord(?)' by the mourning women.

Of the register below only a few hieroglyphs remain, written in the opposite direction:

...*y* ... *ḏd.f* ... *n.ỉ* ...

If the *f* refers to Merymaᶜet, the text pertains to a representation of the tomb owner facing right, perhaps shown offering to a divinity like the owner of TT 161 in a similar context. In that case we can probably restore the name of Merymaᶜet, including the two 𓇌 on the fragment and 𓇋𓇋𓂻 before the *n.ỉ* so that the fuller text would be: '[describing the act performed by] the *waᶜb*-priest of Maᶜet, Merymaᶜet. He says, "I have [come] to you..."'.

From the fragment in Florence it is possible to estimate the dimensions of the decoration of this wall, although there is conflicting information as to the size of the fragment. Schiaparelli and Berend both have 45x51cm, whereas in the publication by Brack it has been reduced to 40x42cm. Perhaps the two former include the frame. The height of the register is about 40cm, and on the basis of this, and keeping in mind that the drawing in the Prudhoe MSS is a hand copy, we can estimate the width of the decoration to being about 350cm. The width of the left front wall is about 351cm. With the top and bottom frieze being about 51cm as on the right front wall, we can account for about 211cm of the decoration. The height of the wall was presumably like that of the left front wall, *i.e.* about 216cm, but the ceiling is now destroyed.

Hall, left rear wall

As the left front wall of this tomb had the unexpected subject of a funerary nature, it will be wise to keep an open mind as to the decoration on this rear wall as well. Burton provided a clue as to the motif depicted, supported, with the eye of faith, by evidence on the wall itself.

'At the south end is a curious subject from which one would judge that the deceased man had much to do with canals on his estate... Half the wall is broken away, but 9 escutcheons with names on six remain' (MSS 25639,42), and he refers to his drawing (MSS 25644,83 verso - 84 (one sheet)). Wilkinson drew the same scene in blue and black ink (MSS v.141). The 'south end' could in theory mean the left front wall, which is already accounted for; the south end of the inner room (*i.e.* the left wall), for which we have another solution (see below); the left side wall of the hall; or the left rear wall of the same. In TT 41 this latter wall was chosen for the subject which is not the occupation of the tomb owner, but the Fields of Iaru(Ill. 46).

This vignette to chapter 110 of the Book of the Dead is very similar in appearance to that of the funerary papyrus of Nebseny, except that in the tomb of Merymaꜥet the picture has been reversed.(41) Another close parallel can be seen in TT 57 of Khaꜥemḥēt,(42) from which some of the texts can be restored.

The top register is as follows, from right to left: seated deities, partly destroyed. In P. Nebseny they are 'the great Ennead' being offered to by the deceased. - Merymaꜥet rowing a boat towards three deities. - A man gesturing towards a mummy, and an inscription:

wꜥb n ꜣImn Mrym3ꜥt m3ꜥ ḫrw 'waꜥb-priest of Amūn [*sic*] Merymaꜥet, justified.' Above there is the following legend:

itr ḫ3 pw m 3w.f ḫ3 pw m wsḫ ḥnwt nbt... 'the river a thousand in its length, a thousand in width, mistress of horns, lady of...' - To the left three enclosures called

ḳntḳnt, *ḥtp*, and *wr ꜥ3*. Below a line of

text: *wnn Ḥtp m nb sḫt [m] ṯ3w m(43) fnḏ.f* 'Ḥotep exists as lord of the field [with] breath in his nose.'(44)

Second register: A *bennu*-bird, and the foot and the arm of a man (in P. Nebseny the deceased is shown harvesting behind him), and

Merymaꜥet's name and title. - Three -signs and

three -birds. - Merymaꜥet kneeling before offerings with a legend

šsp snw m sḫty ḥtp n k3.n wꜥb n M3ꜥt Mrym3ꜥt m3ꜥ ḫrw 'Receiving food offerings in the Fields of Offerings to the *k3* of the *waꜥb*-priest of Maꜥet, Merymaꜥet, justi-

fied. - Four enclosures called *ins*, *w3ḥ*, and *nbt t3wy* (the fourth one was left blank).

Third register: Merymaꜥet ploughing with oxen, and

a spell in front of him: ...*r*(45) *ḥḏt itrw ḫ3 m 3w.f n ḏd wsḫ.f n wnt inw nb im.f* 'The spell of the hippopotamus of the river a thousand in its length, unspeakable in its width. There are no fishes whatsoever in it...' TT 57 adds

nn wnt ḥḏf3w nb im.f 'There are no serpents whatsoever in it.'

Fourth register: a person who is, by comparison with P. Nebseny and TT 57, ploughing with oxen. TT 57 has a second man ploughing and the inscription *sk3*, 'ploughing'. But here it is not Merymaꜥet, but

a certain *Nfr*.(46) the inscription along the canal says *3w pt 3w.f* 'the length of the sky, its length'. - To the left, this register joins the one below to make room for an ampty boat. Elsewhere(47) this boat is 'the boat of Rēꜥ when it has crossed the Fields of Iaru.' - Between the fourth and fifth register part of an inscription remains. A text in TT 57 has a more complete version of what appears to be a similar phrase:

A few signs remain of an inscription written in the opposite direction. In TT 57 this is replaced by .

Fifth register: To the left are four kneeling gods, in P. Nebseny designated as 'the great Ennead who are in the Fields of Offerings', in TT 57 as *ḳḳsw*. To the right a basket-shaped area can be made out, which is in P. Nebseny called 'Abode of the city god(?)', in TT 57 *msḫn p3 nỉwt ḳnḳn nbt*... 'abode of the [one of the] city, Ḳenken, mistress...'

Concerning the wall which showed the Fields of Iaru Burton says that 'half the wall is broken away'. In its present condition the base border remains all along the wall. Near the entrance to the inner room the decorated surface is of a curious crumbly texture. Above the border a small patch of pale blue colour remains. No fragments of the Fields of Iaru were found in the tomb, but several fragments of another subject set in a waterscape were recovered, one of which has the same porpus surface as part of the border with the patch of blue above. As there are no surviving Eighteenth dynasty parallels for the subject depicted on the fragments in any other Theban tomb, it remains an open question where the scene would conventionally have been placed. The evidence from this tomb suggests the left rear wall of the hall.

In some Memphite tombs and one Theban tomb of Ramessid date a ceremony on a lake surrounded by flowers is part of the funerary rites.(48) Five fragments collected in the tomb appear to be part of just such a scene (Ills. 56[2a-e],62[1,2]). All five have part of the floral border and the zigzags of water. Two nearly matching fragments depict a boat with a coffin decorated with a floral pattern (or shroud?) supported by a row of men, the in front of them being undoubtedly part of their title *ỉmiw ḫnt*. To the right the *ḏrt wrt* 'older Kite' is represented in her conventional pose. At the stern of the boat a man faces the bank of the lake, with the remains of an inscription above:... ... *n Wsỉr wᶜb n M3ᶜt Mrym3ᶜt m3ᶜ ḫrw* '... to (or 'by') Osiris, *waᶜb*-priest of Maᶜet, Merymaᶜet, justified.'

Somewhere to the right the lake comes to an end, and a third fragment shows that a group of mourners are waiting on the bank. As the remaining inscription ... ... *ỉn ḫri-ḥb* ... .. *wᶜb n M3ᶜt Mry*.... '... by the lector priest... *waᶜb*-priest of Maᶜet, Mery...' again refers to the tomb owner it cannot be linked directly to the inscription on the previous fragment. Apart from the mandrake and poppy being repeated in the border, a third plant, possibly *Cyperus esculentus* L. (49) has been added. The mourners on the bank have been reworked and appear in palimpsest as in the harvest scene (Ill. 62[2]). Here the final layer of plaster is coarser, and so is the drawing which is quite crudely done. In the skirt of one of the men with a stick (a group resembling the 'Nine Friends') a red spot suggested a different design underneath. By scraping away a little of the white paint a face appeared, very similar to the face of the mourning boy to the left. It was not possible to unveil more of the original drawing without destroying the rest. A patch in the lower right corner of the fragment was found bared to the first layer of gypsum, but the decoration beneath could not be identified.

The mourners stand before a white vertical line flanked by two red lines. A similar feature is apparent in a fourth fragment (Ill. 57 [2d]) which represents a corner of the lake with part of a mandrake and hands of mourners painted alternately red and yellow. The hands are too small to belong to the mourners just described (whose legs and feet are red only). If the mandrake in the fragment with the hands is a continuation of the fragment with the boat, the palimpsest mourners belong in a lower register, and the entire lake scene would therefore seem to have taken up a fairly large proportion of the wall, particularly as another register appears below the palimpsest mourners. In the block in Copenhagen and in the scene in TT 222 a similar arrangement with mourners in several registers was chosen, and the lake contained more than one boat.

One last rather pale fragment (Ill. 57 [2e]) appears to belong to this scene. One poppy from the floral border can be made out. Below is, at an angle, what appears to be the top left corner of a coffin. The faint traces above on a pale blue background may be lotus flowers floating on the surface of the lake.

The left rear wall seems thus to have been taken up by representations of riverscapes, or, as Burton put it, 'one would judge that the deceased man had much to do with canals on his estate.' The arrangement of the scenes as suggested here is unusual, but so are the subjects depicted at this time and place. They must have been more or less the first of their kind in the Theban necropolis.(49a).

The remaining walls of the hall

No tomb was complete without a banquet scene. In the tomb of Meryma[c]et the only proof of the existence of such a scene is one tiny fragment of decorated plaster measuring just a few centimeters on either side which shows the foreheads and red unguent cones of three ladies facing left (Ill. 59 [17]). Perhaps they came from the right rear wall which reveals absolutely no clue as to the nature of the decoration. Neither does the left side wall of the hall. On the corresponding right side wall one tiny speck of plaster remains with white and yellow paint, perhaps the limbs of a woman or a goddess. The decoration of these three walls remain conjectural, but one of them probably contained a banquet scene.

Inner room, left wall

The decoration of the inner room of the tomb is thus described by Burton (MSS

> 'In the inner wall chamber are numerous offerings &c, the deceased is seen on the opposite wall, with offering made to him, & led up by two men, with short beards... to Osiris who is seated in the usual way, with [blank] &c in one case with the feathered goddess, who has also a hawk upon her head. Behind him with her arm around him, interceding for deceased, in the other by Anubis in the same manner.'

Some of these subjects belonged on the left wall of the room. Above the base border at the innermost part of the wall a row of ☥ and 𓌀

remain in yellow on black background to a distance of about 54cm from
the rear wall(Ill.60[4]). Osiris is sometimes shown with his throne
resting on a pedestal of a similar design.(50)

The scene showing the deceased led by two men was traced by Hay.
In his MSS there are in fact two identical tracings (29852,256-7, cf.
Ill. 54, and 29853,154-5). The only major difference is that the
former has colour indications added (in French) and preserve a tiny
fraction of the scene adjoining on the left. The figures are moving
to the right and would therefore fit on the left wall approaching
Osiris on his throne. Another scene also traced by Hay (MSS 29852,
250-5, cf. Ill. 53) probably belonged on the same wall. We shall
describe this latter scene first.

The representation of the seated couple is similar in appearance
to the one showing Sennūṯer and Ḥenutsha described above, although the
necklaces differ and the woman holds a mandrake fruit instead of a
lotus flower. The curls at the end of the two wigs are also different.
The man facing them wears a short kilt and a band across his chest
like those worn by priests. The offering table between them is loaded
with loaves of bread, baskets of fruit, a haunch of beef, a bird, and
bunches of grapes. On top of it all is a bunch of lotus flowers with
a poppy (red) inserted.

Above the offering bringer is the title of the scene:

ỉrt ḥtp dỉ nsw wᶜb sp sn n kꜣ n Wsỉr wᶜb n Mꜣᶜt...

'Making an offering which the king gives. Pure! Pure! To the
of Osiris, *waᶜb*-priest of Maᶜet...'
The name was not copied, but there seems to have been room for it.

After the offering list (see below) follow the signs written in
the opposite direction:

*prrt nbt m bꜣḥ [one column lost] n Mꜣᶜt ꜣꜣt Rᶜ [name lost] mꜣᶜ ḫrw
snt.f mrt.f nbt pr [name lost]*
'Everything coming out in front... [the *waᶜb*-priest] of Maᶜet,
daughter of Rēᶜ... justified, (and) his beloved wife, mistress of
the house...'

The offering list includes the following items(51): ~ *mw* 'water';
ḥtꜣ 'ḥtꜣ-bread'; *psn* 'psn-loaves'; *dptỉ* 'dptỉ-loaves';
ỉwr 'meat'; *ꜣšr* 'roasted meat'; *ỉrp* 'wine'; *ḥḳt*
'beer'; *špnt*-jugs (of beer?); *mw* 'water'; (instructions
for the priest); *ỉn bỉt* 'ỉn-jar of honey'; *dšrt* 'dšrt-jar of
water'; *bd* 'natron'; *ỉrp mḥt* 'northern wine'; *ꜣšr* 'roasted
meat'; *wr n ỉwf* 'meat'; *ḥwn* 'rib roast'; *šᶜt* 'šᶜt-cakes';
pꜣt 'pꜣt-loaves'; *mw dšrt* 'dšrt-jars of water'; *snṯr* 'incense'.

The hieroglyphs for the title of the scene and the persons are blue, those of the offerings black, and the measures for the same and the dividing lines are red.

As to the identity of the persons, they must be either Merymaꜥet and his wife, or his parents Sennūṯer and Ḥenutsha. The absence or presence of beard and wig of the man is no pointer: in Ill. 54 Merymaꜥet wears wig and beard, whereas in Ill. 43 he is clean shaven.

The scene as copied by Hay measures 68x88.5cm, and its possible position on the wall will be discussed below.

The next scene showing the deceased being led belongs to the upper part of the wall, for the top border is clearly visible. It shows Merymaꜥet, followed by Sennūfer, his grandfather, and preceded by Sennūṯer, his father, who adjusts his collar and wig. Above them is the following legend in black hieroglyphs:

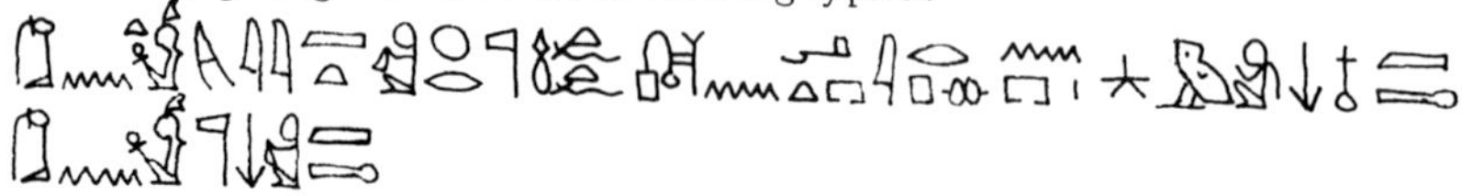

wꜥb n Mꜣꜥt Mrymꜣꜥt mꜣꜥ ḫrw ḫr nṯr ꜥꜣ ỉt ỉt.f sš n ꜥt ỉrp n pr dwꜣ
Snnfr wꜥb n Mꜣꜥt Snnṯr mꜣꜥ ḫrw

'*wꜥb*-priest of Maꜥet, Merymaꜥet, justified with the great god, his paternal grandfather, scribe of the wine cellar of the House of the Morning, Sennūfer, justified, (and) *wꜥb*-priest of Maꜥet, Sennūṯer, justified.'

To the left of Sennūfer, written from right to left, follows a lengthy utterance by Sennūfer to his grandson:

ḏd mdw ỉn sš Snnfr mꜣꜥ ḫrw n sꜣ n sꜣ.f wꜥb n Mꜣꜥt Mrymꜣꜥt mꜣꜥ ḫrw
nḏm ỉn Wnnfr mꜣ.f mtrw.k n(52) wnt sk.k(53) tp tꜣ dỉ.n.f bꜣ.k m-ꜥ(?)(
nṯrwy [sic] ḥr šsp ꜣw(t) m bꜣḥ[.f?] rꜥ nb dỉ.n.f n.k wnḥ(55) n mꜣꜥ ḫrw
m sf n nṯr šsp.k wꜥ sf(?).k ky m tꜣ.f pw (n) wpḳ(56) ỉy[n].k nṯr
ḫn(t).f nn ḫnr n bꜣ.k m mr n.f pr.k r pt [(57)].k sbꜣw hꜣ.n.k r tꜣ
wp(?).k nṯrw m wḏꜥ psḏt nṯrw ꜥꜣt ḥr Tꜣ-wr wꜥb n Mꜣꜥt Mrymꜣꜥt mꜣꜥ ḫrw

'Words to be spoken by the scribe Sennūfer, justified, to his grandson, the *waꜥb*-priest of Maꜥet, Merymaꜥet, justified, ""Sweet!" says Wennūfer when he beholds your righteousness. Your destruction will not occur upon earth. He has placed your *ba* among the gods, receiving oblations before [him] every day, and has given you the garland of justification as a mercy from the god. May you receive one at your ease(?), the other in this land of Peḳer. The god comes to you to ferry (you), without restraint to your *ba*, in accordance with his wish. If you go forth to heaven, you [mingle with] the stars;

if you descend to earth, you judge the gods in the great Ennead of the gods in Abydos. *Waᶜb*-priest of Maᶜet, Merymaᶜet, justified."'

According to Burton, Merymaᶜet is being led to Osiris behind whom stands the goddess of the West with her arm around him. None of the early travellers copied the two divinities. As Merymaᶜet is walking to the right in the picture, Osiris and the goddess of the West must have been immediately to the right, behind Sennūṯer. Then there was another scene which may be taken to be a representation of Merymaᶜet being led by Anubis, perhaps to another depiction of Osiris and the goddess of the West, cf. Burton's description quoted above. Burton also mentions that the 'feathered goddess... is one of the chief [blank] deities' represented in the tomb, therefore there must have been more than one representation of her on the walls. In one of Hay's tracings (MSS 29852,256) the scene adjoining the speech by Sennūfer is just indicated, but hardly more than a single line was copied. It appears to represent the rear outline of a human arm, the height to the shoulder being the same as in the neighbouring scene. The person holds something, possibly a flower. As the person is turned to the left, it suggests that it is a second representation of the goddess of the West whom Merymaᶜet and Anubis are approaching.

The height of this upper register can be measured on Hay's tracings. Excluding the top border it is 33.5cm high. The width of the scene copied is 37.5cm. If one reckons the two scenes to be twice as much as this, or perhaps slightly less if there were no columns of inscriptions in the second scene, the overall width is a minimum of ca. 65cm.

For reasons explained below a third fragment in Florence will be discussed in this place. For stylistical and other reasons it must come from this tomb, and probably from this wall. The provenance is ascertained by the fact that the title of the tomb owner actually remains among the hieroglyphs (Ill. 55).

The fragment (No. 2473) measures about 30x28cm. Like the fragments mentioned above it was wrongly attributed to TT 78. It is mentioned in the catalogues of the collection,(58) and was more recently published in Galvano, *op. cit.*, p. 51, fig. 55. It was acquired by Rosellini, and it shows two squatting women facing left along with two women standing in the same direction. One holds a bowl and a miniature haunch. They are surrounded by an inscription which has a close parallel in Papyrus Nebseny(59) just as the Fields of Iaru were rather similar in this papyrus and the tomb. It is chapter 172 of the Book of the Dead, 'The beginning of the chapter of the praise to be performed in the necropolis'. The first lines of P. Nebseny enumerates the gods who praise the deceased. The beginning appears to be different on the Florence fragment, but from the second column of hieroglyphs and on it follows P. Nebseny rather closely (signs restored in brackets [] when certain):

P. Nebseny ...

Florence

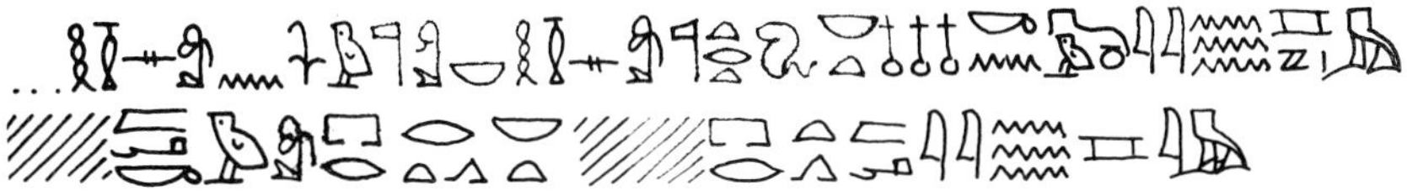

P. Nebseny
Florence
P. Nebseny
Florence
P. Nebseny
Florence
P. Nebseny
Florence
P. Nebseny

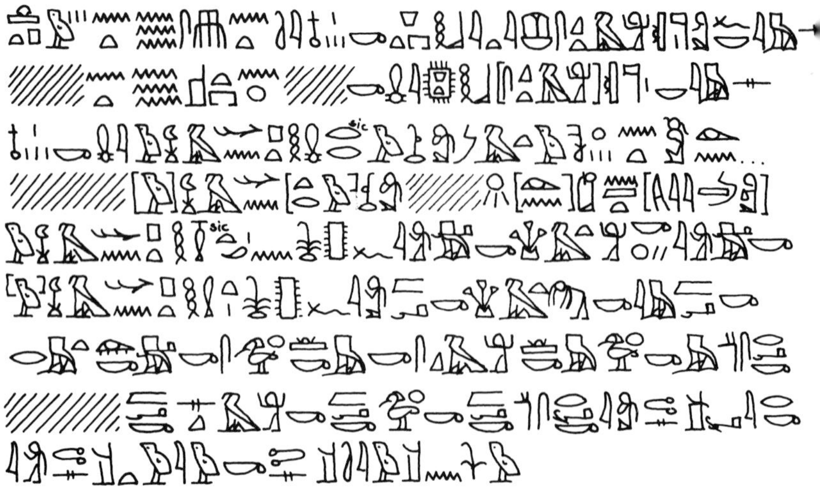

P. Nebseny... *ḥs nṯrt nbt nfrw.k nwy m ḥtpw mỉ nt mw sḫntỉ*
Florence ... *mk wỉ prrt nbt ...prt mꜥy ỉm... nt mw st nḫ...*

P. Nebseny *nfrw.k wsḫt ḥbyt sḳꜣ nṯr.f nb ỉm.s nfrw.k mỉ wḫꜣ n Ptḥ*
Florence *....k mỉ wsḫt ḥb ... nṯr nb ỉm.s ...ḫꜣ n Ptḥ*

P. Nebseny *trw mꜣtw nt Rꜥ ỉr.n sš ḳd n Ptḥ Nbsny*
Florence *..w ḥnmmt ... ...b n Mꜣꜥt*

P. Nebseny *wḫꜣ n Ptḥ ḥst(?) n rsy ỉnb.f ỉ m.k ḥꜣt.k sp sn ỉ m.k rmt.k*
Florence *wḫꜣ n Ptḥ ḥmt n rsy ỉnb.f ỉ m.k ḥꜣt.k ỉ m.k...*

P. Nebseny *m.k sꜣḫ.k m.k sḳꜣ.k m ꜣḫ.k m wsr.k ỉ ṯstw ỉw.k ṯstỉ ṯsw n sw*
Florence *m.k sḳꜣ.k m ꜣḫ.k m.k wsr.k ỉ ṯs ỉr.k ...*

P. Nebseny: 'Every goddess praises him. Your beauty *(nfrw)* is a stream of contentment, like water going forth. Your beauty is like a festival hall where his every god is praised.(60) Your beauty is like a pillar(61) of Ptaḥ, an incense-time of Rēꜥ. The draughtsman of the temple of Ptaḥ, Nebseny has made a pillar of Ptaḥ, a vase(?) of the one south of his wall. Oh, behold, you are being mourned (twice). Oh, behold, you are being lamented. Behold, you are being glorified. Behold, you are being exalted. Behold you are a spirit *(ꜣḫ)*. behold, you are strong. Oh, you who have been raised up, you have been raised up by the rites performed for you, Nebseny.'

Florence: '... Behold, every utterance... utterance is water. Your .. is like a festival hall, where each god is praised... a pillar of Ptaḥ... mankind. The *waꜥb*-priest of Mꜣꜥet [Merymaꜣꜥet has made] a pillar of Ptaḥ, a tentpole of the one south of his wall. Oh, behold, you are being mourned. Oh, behold,... Oh, behold, you are being exalted. Behold, you are a spirit *(ꜣḫ)*. Behold, you are strong. Oh, raise up...'

The height of the register, with the missing hieroglyphs above being restored from P. Nebseny, can be estimated to about 35cm. In TT 55 of Ra̔mosi, where similar figures, but not the text, can be seen,(62) they conclude the actual funerary procession. The dimensions of the Florence fragment excludes this possibility, and also there is just no room for it there, as nothing seems to be missing apart from the final episode showing the mummies before the tomb (Florence No. 2472). The text strongly suggests that we are dealing with event taking place after the burial. The only other scene available from the tomb which seems to be on the same scale is the one showing the tomb owner being conducted to Osiris. As this latter appears to have been positioned on the same wall as the scene with the offering list, there is good reason to believe that all these three scenes belonged here, and, judging from the directions of movement, on the very same wall, the left wall.

Inner room, right wall

The nature of the scenes depicted on this wall is best judged by remains on the wall itself. The wall is chiefly bared to the first layer of mud plaster. Somewhere in the middle chisel marks show that an attempt was made to cut out a piece of about 43x43cm. In the outer corner, near the doorway to the hall, a vertical strip of the second layer of mud plaster remains, including a thin layer of gypsum and its decoration, but also unfortunately the smear of mud plaster applied in the 19th century. It was possible to remove part of this mud smear, and the decoration which appeared underneath shows two registers of priests facing left, each register being about 23cm tall (Ill. 60[5]).

In the MSS of Wilkinson (v.140) a row of priests facing left was drawn (Ill. 46). The priests are accompanied by the following legends:  *sti͗* 'scattering';  *sm* 'sm-priest';  *ḥm nṯr* 'prophet'; 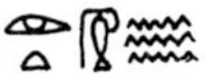 *i͗rt ḳbḥ* 'performing libation';  *ẖry-ḥb* 'lector';  *ḏd mdw ḫft ẖry ḥb* 'words to be recited in front of the lector';  *i͗t nṯr(?)* 'god's father(?)'; 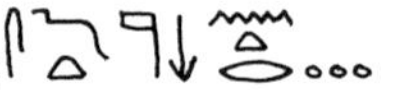 *sḏt snṯr* 'flame (for?) incense'.

An almost identical row of priests, though with slightly different texts, can be seen in the tomb of Ra̔mosi, consecrating the offerings which are specified in an offering list above.(63)

We still need to find room for the subject of the Opening of the Mouth which is briefly referred to by Wilkinson on the same page of his MS. He copied the name and title of Meryma̔et, written from right to left, with the comment: 'on all ye Mummies to which they are performing ye Liturgies'. As the mummy was facing to the right, the scene would fit on the right wall of the inner room, but the rear wall of the same, to the left of the niche or possibly below, is an altrenative possibility.

There is yet another sketch by Wilkinson below the priests (MSS v.140 [upper middle left]), showing a priest (the head is missing)(Ill. 46) kneeling before an offering table with two loaves and a jug, accompanied by 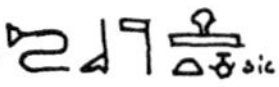 sic *wḏb ḥtp nṯr* 'reverting divine offerings', or perhaps faultily written(64) *kɜb ḥtp nṯr* 'doubling divine offerings'. The figure is turned towards the left and would fit the wall with the Opening of the Mouth ceremonies, which run in the same direction.

A final detail which may pertain to this wall is the note by Wilkinson (MSS v.140 [upper middle right]) saying ' at head &  at foot of the Mummy', suggesting the existence of a scene in which Nephthys and Isis were shown kneeling in the presence of the mummy laid out on a couch.

The niche

In the niche the right part of the rear wall has been cut out, leaving an area ca. 76cm high and 32cm wide bared to the rock. On the left wall only a tiny speck of red and yellow colour remains. The niche itself has an arched roof, the maximum height of the opening being 108cm, its depth 86cm. According to Burton 'the feathered goddess appears also at the end of the chamber in the recess of the statue' (MSS 25639,41 verso), probably the one copied by Wilkinson in MSS v.181 [middle upper](Ill. 60[6]). (65)

Apart from the possibility of scenes of the Opening of the Mouth having decorated the rear wall of the inner room around the niche,(66) there is no evidence to suggest alternative subjects for this wall of the tomb, which was about 220cm wide and about 2m high. Nor is it possible to say what was represented on the two narrow walls on either side of the doorway.

Miscellaneous fragments found in the tomb (Ills. 57-59)

A number of mainly very small fragments of wall-paintings were recovered from the tomb which could not be assigned to any wall in particular. Along with the fragments already mentioned above they were given a consecutive numbering for the present publication as follows:

- 1a-c harvest scene (see above)
- 2a-e funerary lake (see above)
- 3 voyage to Abydos (see above)
- 4 offering bringers with birds and fruit
- 5 inscription mentioning wife
- 6 birds and papyrus column(?) in offerings (Ill. 62[3]), possibly from the same scene as
- 7 fish on a mat, from a bottom register, possibly in the inner room, which had many offering scenes (Ill. 62[4])
- 8 two men from a cooking scene; the pot is black and pink, the stick(?) yellow
- 9a-d inscription in polychrome hieroglyphs, presumably from one and the same inscription; fragment 9d, which comes from the upper part of a scene (inside a kiosque?), refers to 'their hearts'. In tomb inscriptions it is usually a question of the hearts of the gods, who are pleased with the offerings proferred.
- 10a-b hand with a stick, deceptively like the one traced by Hay in Ill. 43, but the hieroglyphs to the left suggests that the two fragments come from a different scene.
- 11 feet of a man, possibly of the figure in 10a-b
- 12 a yellow arm
- 13 head of a man facing a yellow figure; the oblique lines along

the upper edge are red on yellow.
14 yellow hand with a stick = goddess with sceptre?
15 part of a yellow figure
16 knee of a standing man with stick
17 heads of three ladies at a banquet (see above)
18 haunch of an ox and vegetable in offerings
19a-b offering scene in two registers. The top register shows a man facing two yellow pots, the lower register a selection of loaves, meat, fruit and a lettuce. To the right are unidentifiable lines on a large scale.
20 a row of heads in profile, red on a red background and rather difficult to distinguish. They may belong among the mourners at the lake, as the quality of the surface is similar.
21 man with stick, and hieroglyphs in a lower register
22 as 21. the two fragments appear to come from the same wall, which was probably one of those in the inner room with funeral rites.
23 inscription from a top register
24 inscription mentioning a lector priest
25 inscription referring to 'establishing the bones', *i.e.* part of the rites of the Opening of the Mouth.
26 offerings, including a basket
27 head of a man with bouquet
28 head of a man with a papyrus flower. Either of these two heads could belong with
29a-b part of a man's body and a bouquet
30 part of a man
31 part of a running(?) man, and traces of an inscription
32 head of a man
33 part of a man
34 part of a man
35 part of a garden scene. The representation, painted on a double layer of gypsum, is now extremely faded. To the left is a palm tree, to the right a tree with yellow branches and red fruits, possibly meant to be a fig tree. The double layer of gypsum, the quality of the surface, and the fact that the trees appear to be aligned one after the other suggests a connection with the funerary lake, but the fragment may have belonged near the agricultural activities.

For texts from ceiling see p. 124.

Identical horizontal diagonal pattern above:

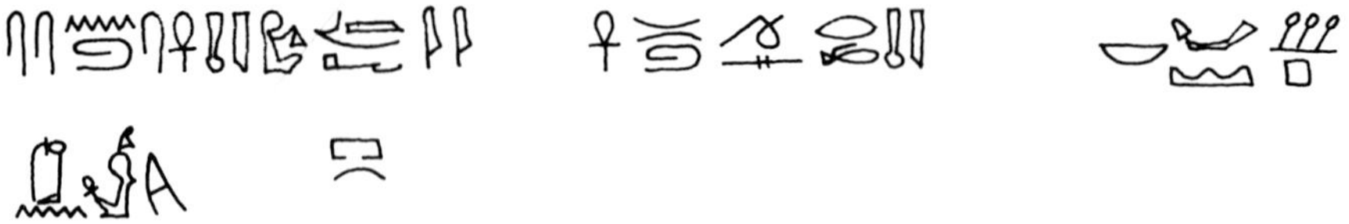

Identical vertical diagonal pattern to the left:

Ceiling texts on fragments found in TT C4

10 Tomb No. C6

The tomb in question was seen by Wilkinson, Champollion, Rosellini and Lepsius(1) who all copied a number of texts, mainly names and titles, and gave very brief descriptions of the scenes to which they pertained. Although the position of the scenes as given by the authors is at times ambiguous, a fairly good idea of the arrangement can be gathered when the indications are considered together and compared with the conventional disposition of the subjects as outlined in chapter 3. The directions of the hieroglyphs, copied in their original direction by Lepsius, give valuable clues to the position and appearance of the scenes. There is no plan of the tomb, and no drawings of the scenes were made,(2) but it is nevertheless possible to gain a more complete picture of the tomb than the one hitherto known.

Apart from the entry in the *Topographical Bibliography* I^2,1 notes were published by Champollion (*Not. descr.* I, pp. 518-9 'Tombeau No. 28') and Lepsius (*Text*, iii, p. 264). Valuable information is to be found in the diary of Lepsius (MSS 340-2).(3) Wilkinson also mentioned the tomb in his note books and copied a few inscriptions (MSS v.121-2 and xvii.H.16 verso [left]), and Rosellini included some names and titles in his diary (MSS 284,G35 verso,37). Names and titles (from Champollion) were included in Helck, *Urk. IV,* 1632-3, cf. *Übersetzung*, pp. 186-7, and *id.*, *Materialien*, pp. 10 and 47.

According to Champollion the wall-paintings were neat ('très soignées'). They were covered by a 'very brilliant varnish'.

The tomb was located in the plain at Sheikh ʿAbd el-Qurna to the east of TT 343 (which in Lepsius' diary is described immediately before our tomb).

<u>The tomb owner and his family</u>

The owner of the tomb was  Ipy, overseer of boats in the mortuary temple of Tuthmosis IV (variants: overseer of boats of Menkheprurēʿ in the temple of Amūn; overseer of the boats of Amūn in the temple of the Lord of the Two Lands, Menkheprurēʿ; overseer of the boats in the temple of Amūn; or simply overseer of the boats of Amūn.(4) His mother was called 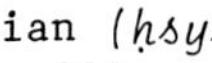 Tuy, and his wife was a songstress *(šmʿyt)* of Amūn and musician *(ḥsyt)* of Ḥatḥor, mistress of ʾIunet (variant according to Champollion: musician *(ḥsyt)* of Mut), Mersger(t).

The couple appears to have had seven children:

1.  Denreg, who was overseer of prophets, first prophet, overseer of the house *(pr)* of Monthu, lord of ʾIuny,(5) (variant: *ḥꜣty-ᶜ* + the above titles). Denreg had a wife called  who was musician *(ḥsyt)* of Ḥatḥor and songstress *(šmᶜyt)* of Amūn.

2.  Piay, first prophet of Menkheprurēᶜ.

3.  Userḥēt, scribe, *waᶜb*-priest.

4.  Merymonthu, scribe.

5.  Tenro, mistress of the house.

6. A 'favourite daughter' whose name was copied by Champollion as  and by Lepsius as . Neither name is known from other sources, and it is possible that the name intended was .(6)

7. Another daughter 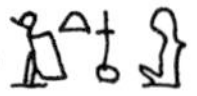 Mutnofre(t).

Ipy is not known from any other monuments.(7) His son Piay is also unknown from other sources. The other son Denreg has an unusual name. A funerary cone(8) of a certain Denreg has been found at Qurnet Muraᶜi, the title of the owner being 'chief *waᶜb*-priest'. A fragment of a sandstone slab with the name of a Denreg now in Philadelphia(9) with part of a hymn to Amūn-Rēᶜ of Karnak appears to be the left door jamb of a tomb. The title on the slab describes the owner as having a position in 'the temple of Nebmaᶜetre ', the mortuary chapel of Amenophis III. The beginning of the title is lost. Ipy clearly functioned under or after(10) Tuthmosis IV, but judging from the title of his son Piay, who was prophet of the king in his mortuary temple,(11) tomb C6 was probably not completed until after the death of Tuthmosis IV. Denreg of the Philadelphia slab could therefore easily have been the same person as Denreg in TT C6. The different titles of prophet of Monthu, *ḥꜣty-ᶜ*, chief *waᶜb*-priest and employment in the temple of Amenophis III may not be totally incompatible. Whether we are dealing with one or several officials called Denreg, the tomb of such a person still remains to be identified. The door jamb suggests that it once existed, unless it was actually part of his father's tomb.

Description of the scenes

In Lepsius MSS 342, last paragraph, the author mentions a scene positioned 'in d. linken Thürlaibung, die sehr zerbrochen',(12), showing a fragment of the hands, body and face of a woman adoring. The accompanying text consisted of an 'adoration formular' and the following signs:

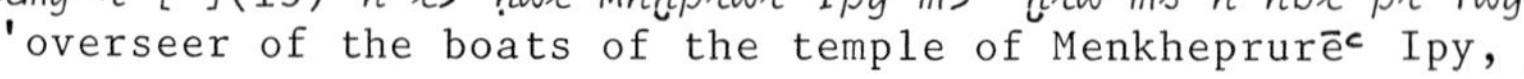

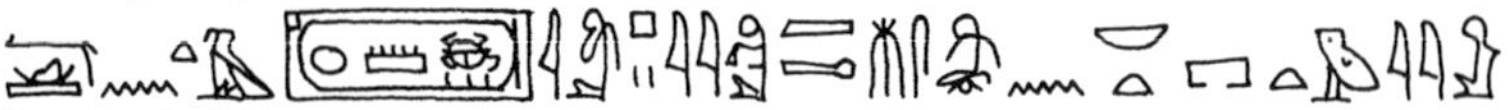

ỉmy-r [ ](13) n tꜣ ḥwt Mnḫprwrᶜ Ỉpy mꜣᶜ ḫrw ms n nbt pr Twy

'overseer of the boats of the temple of Menkheprurēᶜ Ipy, justified, born to the mistress of the house, Tuy.'

The upper part of the three columns of text, to be read from left to right, was missing when Lepsius made his copy, but they are complete in Wilkinson MSS v.121 and Rosellini MSS 284,G37. The persons adoring would have been facing left and situated, as Lepsius says, on the left door jamb. Porter & Moss take the door jamb in question to belong to a doorway between the hall and an inner room, presumably because in Lepsius the description follows after mention of statues in the niche. In between the two entries there is another mentioning boats, which Porter & Moss also interpret as belonging to the inner room. However, there is reason to believe (see below) that the boats may have belonged in the hall, and that when describing the scenes in the tomb, Lepsius worked his way from the left part of the hall to the niche and back to the right part of the hall, finishing with the much destroyed scene on the jamb of the entrance door. A representation of the tomb owner and his wife or mother adoring is very frequently to be found in this place, the god to whom the prayers are addressed being either Rēᶜ-Ḥarakhty or Amūn-Rēᶜ.

The tomb had two chambers: Lepsius speaks of a 'Tiefkammer', Champollion of a 'petite salle longue du fond'. As most tombs of this period were T-shaped, and as the inner room was apparently elongated, and as the scenes described would easily fit into a T-shaped tomb, we shall assume that the tomb was indeed T-shaped. The dimensions of the walls and the size of the tomb remains unknown.

Scenes in the hall

Left front wall(14)

The scene includes the tomb owner and his family offering. There can be no doubt as to the position of the scene. Lepsius says explicitly: 'N(eben) d. Thür nach links geht er [*sc.* Ipy] begleitet v. einer Dame (deren Namen unten von ihr gestanden haben muss, im Ausgebrochenen), welcher noch ein Mann + ein Mädchen folgen - Alle nach der Thür zu Opfer bringend.' Champollion does not mention this scene. As no drawings are available the accompanying inscription is here given as it was copied by Lepsius:

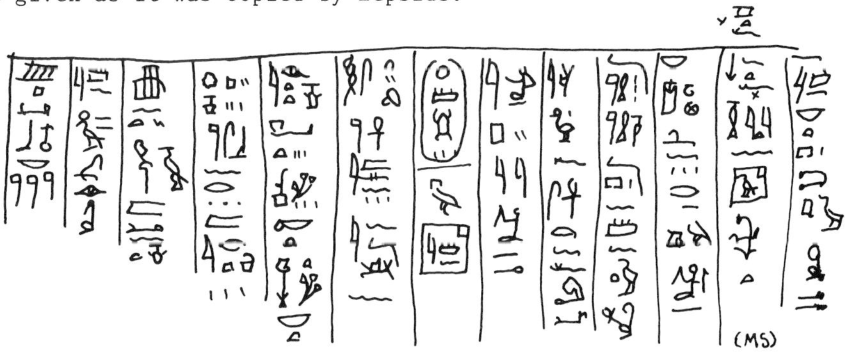

šsp bw nfr nb nṯrw ʾImn Rᶜ-Ḥr3ḫty Wsir ḫnty ʾImntiw m ᶜntiw tpy snṯr bnr m irp irtt ḥnkt rnpt nbt nḏm sty ᶜnḫ nṯr im.sn in imy-r ᶜḥᶜw n Mnḫprwrᶜ m ḥwt ʾImn ʾIpy m3ᶜ ḫrw in s3.f sᶜnḫ rn.f ḥ3ty-ᶜ imy-r ḥmw nṯr ḥm nṯr tpy imy-r pr n Mntw nb ʾIwnw Dnrg m3ᶜ ḫrw snt.f mrt.f ḥsyt n Ḥwt-Ḥr šmᶜyt n ʾImn Ṯpw m3ᶜ(t) ḫrw

'Receive something good, lord of the gods, Amūn,(15) Rēʿ-Ḥorakhty,(16) Osiris, the foremost of the Westerners, consisting of best myrrh and sweet incense, of wine, milk and all sweet-smelling herbs and plants which a god lives on, by the overseer of the boat(s) of Menkheprurēʿ in the temple of Amūn, Ipy. It is his son who makes his name live, the mayor, overseer of prophets, first prophet, overseer of the temple of Monthu, lord of ʾIunu, Denreg. His beloved wife, musician of Ḥatḥor, songstress of Amūn, mistress of the house, Thepu, justified.'(17)

The scene in question belongs to the type showing the deceased offering or libating to a god, not represented, on either side of the entrance doorway, a subject which is part of the rites of the Feast of the Valley. It is almost entirely confined to T-shaped tombs and is particularly frequent in the mid-Eighteenth dynasty. The scene belongs at the upper part of the wall and would have taken up the greater part if not all of its height. Elsewhere Lepsius mentions a person libating, therefore the tomb owner would probably be shown offering on braziers on this wall, rather than libating. He was followed by a woman, presumably his wife, as was habitual after the reign of Tuthmosis III, and by other members of his family. In Lepsius' copy of the inscription the lower line of hieroglyphs is undulating allowing for the heads of the three foremost persons. The name of the wife of the tomb owner is not included in the inscription above but was presuambly written below, between the figures, where the painting was destroyed (*sic* Lepsius).

Following the daughter-in-law were four bald men. Only the names of the last two were left:

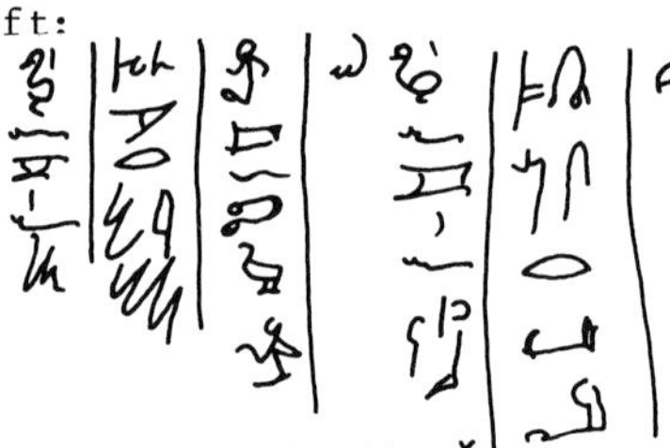
(MS)

s3.f mr.f sš Mrym3ʿt   *s3.f mr.f wʿb sš Wsrḥ3t*

'His beloved son, the scribe Merymonthu. His beloved son, *waʿb*-priest and scribe, Userḥēt.'

We may then take it that one of the anonymous men was Piay, mentioned elsewhere, and that the couple may have had a fifth son whose name remains unknown.

With eight large scale persons in the procession we may assume that there were no more subjects depicted on this wall, except very probably butchers and perhaps more offering bringers in a sub-scene. This may have been destroyed by the tomb Lepsius saw it along with the inscription giving the name of the tomb owner's wife and the adjoining jamb of the entrance door.

Left side wall

The subject depicted on this wall appears to be out of place when compared with other contemporary tombs, but there can be little doubt that the scene described by Porter & Moss as 'deceased before Tuthmosis IV in kiosk' belonged in this part of the tomb. Lepsius positions the scene 'an d. linken Schmalwand'; Champollion refers to the 'paroi à gauche'. As Lepsius places another scene on the 'breiten Hinterwand', the 'Schmalwand' must be the side wall.

According to Lepsius, the inscription accompanying the offering bringer before the king had vanished. Champollion describes him as wearing a panther skin and censing and libating, and he identifies him as 'le 1er fils'. As the inscription was no longer legible, at least when Lepsius saw it, the identification was presumably based on the appearance of the man in question being akin to that of the 'eldest son' in funerary ceremonies.

A representation of the reigning king is almost obligatory in T-shaped tombs of this period. But there are several reasons to believe that the scene mentioned by Champollion and Lepsius was not one of these standard representations. Although there are rare exceptions, representations of the reigning king are to be found on the rear wall of the hall on either side of the doorway leading to the inner room. There are two tombs which depict the king on the right side wall,(18) and our tomb might conceivably be another exception if other facts were not against it.

In representations showing the tomb owner facing his sovereign, he wears the dress and insignia (if any) of his office, not a priestly panther skin, and he is not shown censing and libating. We are told by Champollion that the man in panther skin is standing in front of 'le Pharaon Thoutmosis IVe en socharis assis dans un naos.' The addition 'en socharis', if taken to mean 'with the characteristics of Sokaris', suggests that it was a representation of a king who looked like a god, and the royal element was provided by a cartouche, that of Tuthmosis IV. Taken together with the position of the scene, these details rather suggest that we are dealing with a scene which is totally different from that showing the tomb owner in front of his sovereign of the standard type.

Champollion mentions the presence of a stela in the tomb 'sur la paroi de gauche', but separated from a mention of funerary rites in the inner room by a comma only. A stela has no place on the long walls of an inner room, but belongs on one of the two side walls in the transverse hall, or possibly on the rear wall of the innermost room.(19) The text on the stela as copied by Champollion is as follows:

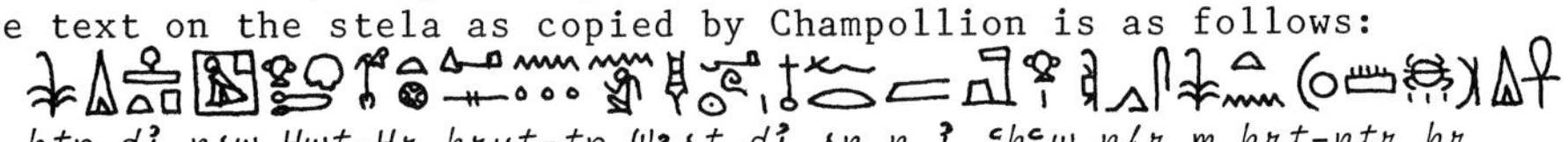

ḥtp dỉ nsw Ḥwt-Ḥr ḥryt-tp Wꜣst dỉ.sn n.ỉ ꜥḥꜥw nfr m ẖrt-nṯr ḥr šms nsw Mnḫprwrꜥ dỉ ꜥnḫ

'An offering which the king gives (to) Ḥatḥor, mistress of Thebes, that they *[sic]* may give me a good lifetime in the necropolis following King Menkheprurēꜥ, given life.'

A representation of the king on a stela occur in one or two Theban tombs.(20) Apart from the ambiguous description by Champollion, all factors point to the stela being on the left side wall of the hall, and to the representation of the king as showing a deceased king represented on it.

Considering the fact that Ipy functioned at the mortuary temple of the king and that his son Piay was first prophet of the king at the time the tomb was inscribed, the date of the tomb as given by Porter & Moss is perhaps to be queried. The identity of the priest who censes to the king cannot be proven beyond doubt, but it was presuambly Piay. He was dressed as a *sm*-priest. From the reign of Amenophis III the first prophets in the mortuary temples changed titles to *sm*-priest of King NN.(21) The garment may have been the same for both.

Below the scene with the king there was another showing the tomb owner and his wife seated. Lepsius copied the name of the latter  *snt.f nbt pr Mrsgrt* 'his wife, mistress of the house, Mersgert'. The hieroglyphs are written in vertical columns from right to left, the couple having thus faced right. They may have been seated within the frames of the stela, as for example in the roughly contemporary TT 69.(22)

Left rear wall

This wall was decorated with a representation of a banquet scene. Lepsius mentions the scene as being on the 'breiten Hinterwand... links v. d. Thür', and Champollion describes it as being on the 'paroi gauche de la porte'. As the front wall is already taken up by the offering scene of the Feast of the Valley, the banquet scene must indeed be on the rear wall. Only one register is described. We may perhaps imagine a number of guests seated above and/or below, but no mention was made of these, nor was it stated whether the wall had suffered any damage, deliberate or accidental.

The description by Lepsius is the most accurate, and judging from the inscriptions he copied, we can restore the one register. At the extreme left ('am Ende') were two bald men each being served wine or beer by a servant. The man to the left was Piay, served by a girl, the other was Denreg, served by a boy. To the right in the same register were the tomb owner and his wife, followed by two children, one of whom was their daughter Tenro. Three girls were shown offering to the couple: Kaia(?), Mutnofret and Tenro again, and they were followed by three musicians playing harp, lute and double pipe. On the basis of the inscriptions copied by Lepsius the general arrangement of the register would have been as follows

Piay girl Denreg boy 3 musicians Kaia Mutnofret Tenro Ipy Mersgert ? Tenro

The inscriptions provide the following details:

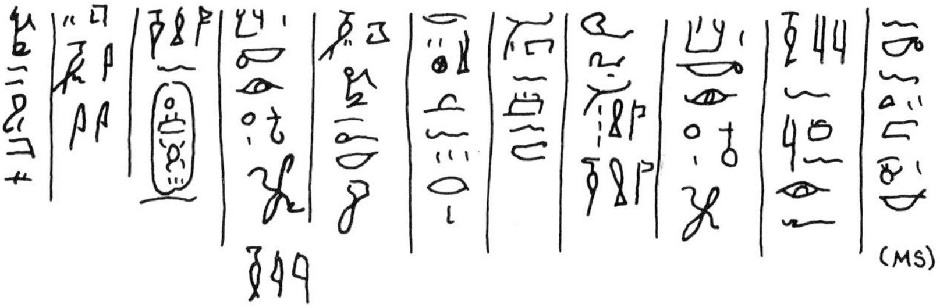
(MS)

ḥꜣty-ʿ ỉmy-r ḥmw-nṯr ḥm nṯr tpy ỉmy-r pr n Mnṯw nb ʾIwny Dnrg mꜣʿ ḫrw nb ỉmꜣḫ (n) kꜣ.k ỉr hrw nfr pꜣ ḥsy ḥm nṯr tpy n Mnḫprwrʿ Pỉꜣy mꜣʿ ḫrw m ... (n) kꜣ.k ỉr hrw nfr pꜣ ḥsy n ʾImn ỉr.f n.k nty m ỉb.k

'The mayor, overseer of prophets, first prophet, overseer of the temple of Monthu, lord of *ʾIwny*,(23), Denreg, justified, lord of veneration. (To) your *ka*! Spend a happy day, you praised one,(24) first prophet of Menkheprurēʿ, Piay, justified in ... (To) your *ka*! Spend a happy day, you praised by Amūn. May he fulfill your wishes!'

Above the wife of the tomb owner:

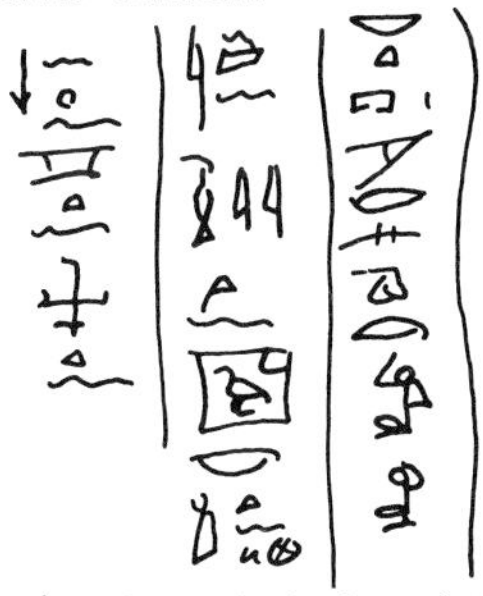
(MS)

snt.f mrt.f šmʿyṯ n ʾImn ḥsyt n Ḥwt-Ḥr nbt ʾIwnt nbt pr Mrsgr(t)

'His beloved wife, songstress of Amūn, musician of Ḥatḥor, mistress of Dendara, mistress of the house, Mersger(t).'

Lepsius did not copy the text of the tomb owner, but an otherwise usidentified inscription copied by Rosellini may supply the missing part. Rosellini drew the signs 'inside' (MSS 284,G37 [middle]):

(MS)

sḫmḫ ỉb r mꜣꜣ bw nfr ỉrt hrw nfr ỉw.k m ḥwt.k n ʾImntt st.k n ḏt wnn.k ỉm.s n kꜣ n ḥsy n nṯr.f n kꜣ n ỉmy-r (&c.)

'Enjoying oneself at seeing something good, spending a pleasant day, being in your house of the West, your seat of eternity. May you exist in it. To the *ka* of the praised one of his god, to the *ka* of the overseer (&c.)'

Above the daughters:

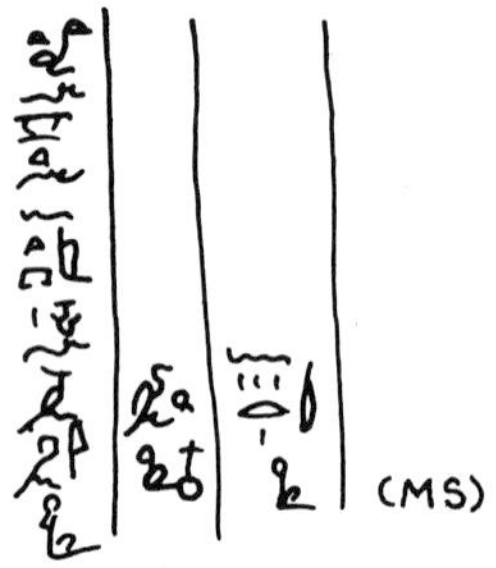

sꜣt.f mrt.f n st-ỉb.f Kꜣỉꜣ(?)(25)... *Mwtnfrt* ... *Tnr*

'His beloved, favourite daughter, Kaia(?)... Mutnofret ... Tenro.'

Tenro occurs again, this time behind her parents, with the following legend: 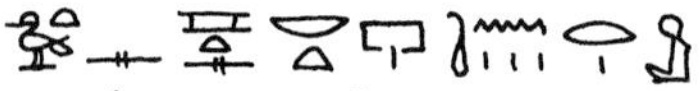 *sꜣt.s mrt.s nbt pr Tnr* 'Her beloved daughter, mistress of the house, Tenro', the hieroglyphs facing left in a vertical column.

The three musicians are described as being 'im vollem Putz' and wearing unguent cones upon their heads. The combination of instruments is very common in the Eighteenth dynasty, cf. for example the famous trio from TT 52 of Nakht.

The three daughters present offerings to their parents, by Champollion specified as 'des bouquets de fleurs'.

Doorway to inner chamber

The lintel of this doorway was in good condition when Champollion and Lepsius saw it, and both copied names and titles from it. It had incised hieroglyphs ('le tout est peint sauf les bandeaux de la porte'). Lepsius copied the inscription as it was 'ueber d. Thür zur Tiefkammer':

(upper left)
(upper right)
(lower left)
(lower right)

ḥtp dỉ nsw ʾImn-Rꜥ nb nst tꜣwy n kꜣ [n] ỉmy-r ꜥḥꜥw m ḥwt ʾImn ʾIpy mꜣꜥ ḫrw
(ḥtp) dỉ nsw Tm nb ʾIwnw n kꜣ n ỉmy-r ꜥḥꜥw n ʾImn ʾIpy mꜣꜥ ḫrw
ḥtp dỉ nsw Wsỉr ḥkꜣ ḏt n kꜣ n sꜣ.f ḥm nṯr tpy Mntw Dnrg mꜣꜥ ḫrw
(ḥtp) dỉ nsw Ptḥ rsy ỉnb.f n kꜣ n sꜣ.f ḥm nṯr tpy n Mnḫprwrꜥ Pỉꜣy mꜣꜥ ḫ

'An offering which the king gives (to) Amūn-Rēᶜ, lord of the thrones of the Two Lands, to the *ka* of the overseer of the boats in the temple of Amūn, Ipy, justified.'
'An offering which the king gives (to) Atum, lord of ʾIunu, to the *ka* of the overseer of the boats of Amūn, Ipy, justified.'
'An offering which the king gives (to) Osiris, ruler of eternity, to the *ka* of his son, first prophet of Monthu, Denreg, justified.'
'An offering which the king gives (to) Ptaḥ-south-of-his-wall, to the *ka* of his son, first prophet of Menkheprurēᶜ, Piay, justified.'

In the second of the titles of Ipy Champollion has a different version:

imy-r ᶜḥᶜw Mnḫprwrᶜ m ḥwt ʾImn

'Overseer of the boats of Menkheprurēᶜ in the temple of Amūn.'

Champollion also adds an inscription pertaining to the wife of the tomb owner:

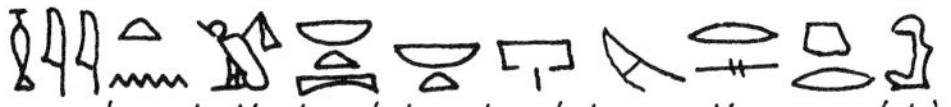

... *ḥsyt Mwt nbt pt nbt pr Mrsger(t)*

'("sa soeur" = his wife) musician of Mut, lady of the sky, mistress of the house, Mersger(t).'

Right part of the hall

Little was recorded in this part of the tomb, and no precise information was given as to the position of the scenes which may possibly be allocated to this half of the hall.

Two subjects are said to be somewhere to the right in the tomb: adoration of Osiris and a representation of the deceased, possibly including boats.

The 'paroi à droite' of Champollion is described immediately before his 'paroi à gauche' which had the representation of Tuthmosis IV, and he then goes back to the inner room once more in his description. Although it is by no means certain, the wall with Osiris could be the right side wall of the hall, as the subject is frequently represented on one of these narrow walls.(24) The god would be facing the entrance of the tomb, *i.e.* in this case right, the deceased facing left.

Lepsius mentions a representation of the tomb owner 'rechts v. d. Thür' after describing the inner part of the tomb and he copied

ỉn ỉmy-r ꜥḥꜥw n 'Imn n tꜣ ḥwt nb tꜣwy Mnḫprwrꜥ dỉ ꜥnḫ Ỉpy
'... by the overseer of the boats of Amūn in the temple of the
Lord of the Two Lands, Menkheprurēꜥ, given life, Ipy.'

Ipy would have been facing left, performing an act which would
have been described by the hieroglyphs preceding the ones copied by
Lepsius. To the right of his copy Lepsius added: 'Die Schiffe, deren
Aufseher er war, waren nicht die heiligen Barken, sondern wohl Last-
barken; sie sehen immer so aus:

It is likely that the inscription on the wall 'to the right of the
door' and the scene showing several boats belonged together. The type
of boat sketched by Lepsius rather looks like the grain barges in TT
A4 (cf. Ill. 18), but it might possibly be one of the boats accompanying the barges taking the deceased and his wife to Abydos. The position
of the Abydos scene is usually shown next to the funeral procession
in the passage of T-shaped tombs, and with very few exceptions it is
therefore placed on the left wall of the passage. The vertical lines
of text above the head of the tomb owner in Abydos scenes usually
give name and title only, not a lengthy inscription followed by *ỉn* 'by'.
Thus the boats mentioned by Lepsius probably do not belong in an
Abydos scene.
   The arrangement of the hieroglyphs as drawn by Lepsius suggests
that the head of Ipy was to the left below, and that he was standing
up. When a person is seated, the inscription is more likely to be
inscribed in front of him. It would seem that the scene in question
would represent Ipy overseeing the boats in his charge, and that the
boats were indeed barges for carrying merchandise, as Lepsius
suggested, and as the plural form indicates - there may have been one
sacred boat in a mortuary temple, but not several.(27) We may therefore
conclude that this scene showing the tomb owner performing his office
was to be found in the hall of the tomb, on the right front or rear
wall.(28)

Scenes in the inner room
   In this little room ('petite salle longue du fond', 'Tiefkammer')
there were, according to Champollion, 'des peintures de famille'.
Above, after describing the inscriptions on the lintel, he mentions
'les cérémonies funéraires, le dueil, l'enterrement'. Wilkinson
(MSS v.121 [near top right]) mentions 'cows drawing boat with mummy'
and gives the title of the tomb owner written from
right to left. Although the funeral procession is usually found on
the left wall of the passage in a T-shaped tomb, the arrangement may
thus have been reversed in this one.

The niche
   Three statues adorned the rear wall of this tomb. Lepsius mentions
the niche and '3 schlecht gearbeitete Statuen', Champollion 'trois
statuettes assises, pleine ronde-bosse', and Rosellini 'tre piccole
statuette'.
   Porter & Moss attribute two inscriptions to these. The inscription
referred to as copied by Lepsius and being on 342 [near top] is,

however, the same as the one they refer to next to the boat (called [middle upper]). Although Champollion re-arranged the signs, his inscription (A) on p. 518 must be the same.

One inscription remains to be identified. It was given by Lepsius, *Text*, iii, 264, but it is not to be found in the MSS:

Wsỉr ỉmy-r ʿḥʿw n tꜣ ḥwt ʾImn Mnḫprwrʿ ʾIpy snt.f mrt.f nbt pr Mrsgrt

'Osiris, overseer of the boats of (the temple of) Amūn (in) the temple of Menkheprurēʿ, Ipy. His beloved wife, mistress of the house, Mersgert.'

An identical inscription is given in Wilkinson MSS v.121 [near top left] as pertaining to a 'man & Lady'. The position of this scene remains unknown.

11 The Tomb of a Scribe and Counter of Grain

Of all the fragments of wall-paintings in museums and other collections eleven pieces in the British Museum are the most outstanding. The queality of the work and the state of preservation are remarkable; they are among the largest fragments removed from a tomb; and as far as can be ascertained they are among those with the longest record outside the tomb from which they were taken.

The eleven fragments considered here are the following:

BM 37976 (recording cattle)
BM 37977 (fowling in canoe)
BM 37978 (recording geese)
BM 37979 (tomb owner inspecting)
BM 37980 (offering bringers)
BM 37981 (banquet)
BM 37982 (horses, mules and measuring crop)
BM 37983 (garden and pool)
BM 37984 (banquet)
BM 37985 (son offering)
BM 37986 (banquet)

The greater part of the fragments are generally taken to come from the same tomb, and it is more than likely that they all belong together The three fragments of banquet scenes are so alike that there can be no doubt of their relationship. The male guests in turn are strongly reminiscent of the tomb owner as represented on BM 37979, and the same title occurs on both. The latter fragment belongs with the recording of cattle and geese, and the title of the tomb owner as well as that of his wife are found on the fowling fragment. For stylistical reasons the fragment with horses must belong with the rest, and this leaves only BM 37985 unaccounted for. A comparison between the jars with herbal stoppers in this fragment and those in BM 37984 shows that they are very similar. The size of the fragment, as well as its context (see below) also point to the fact that it belongs with the rest. It should however be noted that the colours on this fragment are paler and lighter than any of the others.(1) But the fact that ten of the eleven fragments came from the early Salt collection is the strongest link between them. Extracts from letters from Salt, now in the British Museum, dated 5th and 10th October 1821, explicitly refer to these fragments: 'The ten smaller cases contain Egyptian paintings taken from the wall of a Tomb underground, discovered by my man last year.'(2) The eleventh fragment, which was not acquired from the Salt collection, is part of the banquet scene.(3)

The date of the tomb

There can be little doubt that the fragments with which we are dealing date from the reign of Tuthmosis IV or the earlier part of that of Amenophis III.(4) In attempting to identify the fragments with various tombs different dates have been implied (cf. below), and a few points to support the date suggested here will therefore be taken up. Because of the erasure of the name of Amūn in the inscriptions only a date prior to the reign of Amenophis IV is acceptable.(5)

Nowhere is the passing of time more evident than in fashion. This also applied in ancient Egypt, where hair styles,(6) dresses and costume jewellery show changes from reign to reign. The banquet scenes in a tomb are therefore particularly relevant in an attempt to narrow down the date of a tomb.

The method of using a speckled yellow tint for the dresses of the ladies to hip or knee level began sporadically in the reign of Tuthmosis IV(7) and was continued on and off during the dynasty. It has been explained as representing the white garments drenched with unguent,(8) as being a dyed mantle, (9) or as an attempt to show the transparancy of the fabric.(10)

The shape of unguent cones changed through the New Kingdom, the general trend being from small flat ones at the beginning of the dynasty to tall large ones appearing in the reign of Tuthmosis IV and continuing into the Ramessid Period. Some are of a simple cone shape, others have bulky outlines. Some are plain white, others have the top half yellow, others again are yellow or red all over. The cones in some of the BM fragments are unusual in that they have a decoration of horizontal bands or markings across. They are tall, but not very pointed towards the tip of the cone. The upper extremity is yellow. Tall cones, though more pointed than these, appear in TT 69 of Menna(11) which is tentatively dated to the reign of Tuthmosis IV.

An eye-catching feature in the BM banquet scene is the way in which the ladies' wigs have been arranged, a characteristic detail in some of them being the way some strands of hair have been separated from the rest and drawn over the floral diadem across the top of the head. The actual position of the unguent cone in relation to these strands of hair is not quite obvious, but presumably locks or braids of hair were positioned on either side of the cone, not under it (cf. the representation *en face* in BM 37984). A similar arrangement is to be seen in TT 69 of Menna,(12) where the cone was painted first, and the wig apparently altered by having the locks of hair added at the back, beyond the original outline of the wig. In TT 52 of Nakht some of the ladies at the banquet also have the strands of hair draped across the top of the head.(13)

Some of the musicians appear to have made a kind of 'pony tail' out of part of their hair, the rest being left to float over the shoulders,(14) a feature also apparent in the de Benzion fragment with a girl (see below). A similar, though less elaborate hairstyle is shown in TT 69 of Menna,(15) and in TT 38 of Zeserkarēʿsonb.(16) This latter tomb is dated to the reign of Tuthmosis IV.

The treatment of the eyes is very similar to the way eyes were drawn by the artists who painted TT 52 and 69.(17) The eyes are disproportionately large, the eye itself, not just a prolonged cosmetic line, reaching almost to where the wig begins. Also the slant of the eye is similar. The small pouting lips are typical of the mid-Eighteenth dynasty, whereas the tiny rounded chin, and in some cases almost a double chin, are characteristic of the BM fragments.

Remaining within the banquet scene, the choice of musical instruments helps to put a probable *terminus ante quem* to the fragments. The rectangular tambourine was never very common in Egypt except during two well defined periods within the Eighteenth dynasty.(18) They appear in representations and in actual finds in the reign of Tuthmosis III and are used in banquet orchestra in this reign and until that of Tuthmosis IV. In the Amarna Period they appear once moore, but this time in a different context, in the hands of rejoicing women in the streets.

Apart from squatting clappers and singers, female musicians are usually shown standing up. Seated female musicians with instruments are, however, to be seen in a few tombs from the reigns of Amenophis II and Tuthmosis IV.(19) Musicians shown *en face* are rare but appear in a few tombs from the period of Tuthmosis III-Amenophis III.(20)

Judging from the banquet scene alone, there are thus many pointers to a strong similarity to TT 52 of Nakht and TT 69 of Menna,(21) and in particular to a date around the reign of Tuthmosis IV.

The presence of a fishing and fowling scene in the tomb would support a date prior to or just contemporary with the early part of the reign of Amenophis III.(22) The agricultural scene, consisting of the BM fragment and possibly a few others, are with all its details rather close to those found not only in the tombs of Menna and Nakht, but also TT 57 of Khaʿemhēt (which had decoration in relief).(23) This would again point to a date around Tuthmosis IV or just after.

The name of the owner of the BM tomb

The name of the owner of the tomb from which the BM fragments derive does not survive fully intact in any of the inscriptions, whereas there is no doubt about his title and the name of his wife.

The title occurs as follows(21)

BM 37981	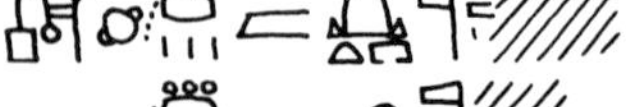	(broken away)
BM 37979		(hacked out)
BM 37977	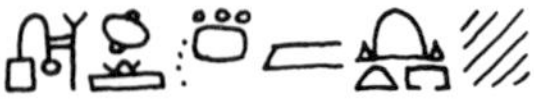	(hacked out)
BM 37976		(hacked out)
BM 37983		(hacked out)

The often small area systematically and neatly hacked out in the inscriptions can only be the word 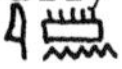 Amūn, obliterated during the Amarna Period in so many other tombs. It was presumably not an act of personal hostility, as in some examples at least the Amūn element was part of the title rather than of the name.

The tomb owner was 'scribe and counter of grain' (or 'scribe of the accounts of grain') 'in the granary of divine [offerings]', a title elsewhere sometimes followed by 'of Amūn',(25) in our tomb occasionally abbreviated to 'scribe and counter of grain of [Amūn]'. In BM 37976 the lower extremity of what could be and a short oblique line of can just be made out (cf. the drawing below).

In the columns of text in BM 37977, the tips of can be distinguished. The preceding column ended with . Unless the rest of the title was written out at great length as *e.g.* '(in the granary) of Amūn and in the granary of the divine offerings',(26) there would appear to be room for another title, depending on the length of the name.

The tomb owner's name is partly visible in BM 37976, where or just possibly is the last sign, followed by a squatting man determinative:

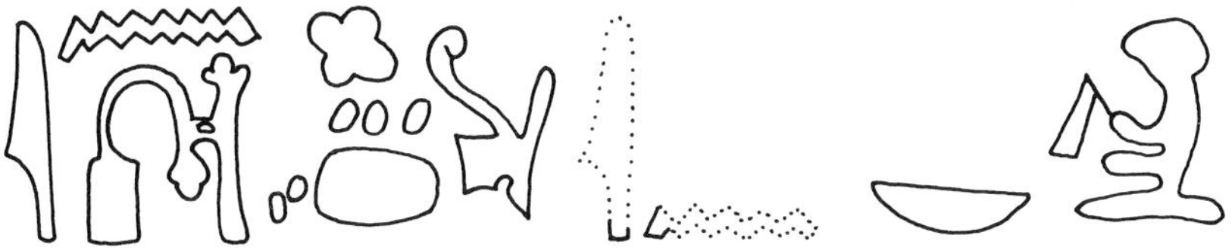

The name most frequently suggested in the literature is Nebamūn. In some of the fragments where the available space can be measured (BM 37977 and 37979, both with large, polychrome hieroglyphs) there is ample room for this name. In BM 37976 (cf. the drawing above) the space is somewhat restricted, but the name could have been written or even . Because of the presence of the an additional is required for the title and would not have been part of the name.

In BM 37983 the atenist chisel does not appear to have touched the area following [ ] of the title. It is possible that the name never followed, and that the sycomore goddess addressed the tomb owner only by his title.(27) The area is very much faded, and it is difficult to distinguish any signs at all.

There remains the possibility that the tomb owner's name was not Nebamūn, but something else. Already Budge suggested Amenemḥab.(28) Apart from the fact that the remaining sign looks more like than there hardly seems to be room for Amenemḥab in BM 37976. A scribe and counter of grain, overseer of the granary of Amūn, called Amenemḥab, occurs on a funerary cone found at Dirā' Abû el-Nagā'.(29) This man had other titles which are not to be found in the BM fragments, and if he is to be identified with the owner of TT A8,(30) his wife had a different name.

Apart from Nebamūn, the choice of name would appear to be limited to alone,(31) Peneb, or another divine name + *nb*, such as Nebrēʿ. But in view of the lack of evidence of any known officials of the relevant date and title to support any such claim, we are inclined to regard Nebamūn as the most likely name for the owner of our tomb. Also, Nebamūn is a very common name.

The name of the tomb owner's wife occurs twice. In BM 37979 it is very clearly written in the last column to the left as 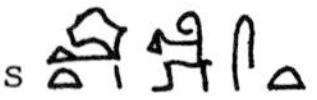 Ḥatshepsut. In the partly preserved vertical column to the right in BM 37977 the following traces can be distinguished 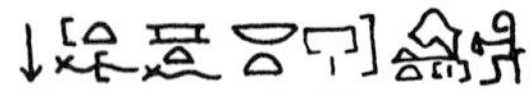 *snt.f [mrt.f nbt pr] Ḥ3tšpst* 'his [beloved] wife [mistress of the house] Ḥatshepsut.(32)

For the son Neṯermosi cf. below, Wall A.

Identifying the BM tomb with a known tomb

Among the known and numbered tombs in the Theban necropolis several were owned by men called Nebamūn with a title similar to the one on the BM fragments. Before its Ramessid usurpation, TT 65 at Sheikh ʿAbd el-Qurna was the tomb of Nebamūn, scribe of the royal accounts(?), overseer of the granary, perhaps of the reign of Ḥatshepsut. The Nebamūn of TT 146 at Draʿ Abû el-Nagaʿ was overseer of the granary of Amūn, scribe and counter of grain and *ṯny* of the god's wife(33) in the reign of Tuthmosis III. The homonymous owner of TT 179 at Khôkha was scribe and counter of grain in the granary of divine offerings of Amūn, and thus carried a title identical to that of our tomb owner, but he functioned in the reign of Ḥatshepsut.(34) The same title was held by Nebamūn, owner of TT 231 at Draʿ Abû el-Nagaʿ, which is also dated to the early Eighteenth dynasty.

In his study of officials of the granary of Amūn Helck attributed the BM fragments to this latter tomb no. 231.(35) Apart from the discrepancy in the date,(36) the names of the wives do not correspond, as the lady of TT 231 was called Nefertere.

The fragments have been tentatively attributed to TT 146,(37) an idea taken up in recent times.(38) Again the date of the tomb(39) and the name of the tomb owner's wife, Suitnub, are at variance.

The remaining possibilities among the known tombs do not qualify either. If the BM tomb was located where we would suggest (cf. below) these two tombs are in the wrong sections of the necropolis. TT 65 was heavily usurped in Ramessid times, and although one of the BM fragments bears an inscription written in a second hand, there is nothing to suggest that the tomb had been effectively taken over by a later occupant. As far as TT 179 is concerned, the date of the tomb and the appearance of its decoration(40) rule out any connection with the BM fragments.

Among the anonymous tombs in the necropolis few would seem to qualify, most being either too small to accommodate the fragments or of a wrong date. The late Eighteenth dynasty TT 152 at Draʿ Abû el-Nagaʿ would provide the missing subjects and should be examined in due course (the few remaining scenes are virtually unpublished). The same applies to the probably contemporary TT 333 also at Draʿ Abû el-Nagaʿ.(41) On the whole it would seem that the original position of the BM fragments was not in any of the numbered tombs.

Reconstructing the BM tomb

No plan of the tomb from which the BM fragments were taken was recorded. The available subjects will therefore be discussed one by one, and their possible position in the tomb considered.

Wall A: The feast of the Valley (Ill. 63)
Available fragment: BM 37985
Bibliography: see *Top. Bibl.* I^{2},2, p. 817

The fragment shows a pile of offerings and a large bouquet carried by an offering bringer (broken off). To the right the legs of the tomb owner remain. The offerings include the usual baskets of figs and grapes, loaves of bread, persea or mandrake fruits and figs arranged on mats, cucumbers, lotus flowers, and the head and haunch of an ox. Underneath the mat on which it all rests are four wine jars on stands draped with wine leaves. The arrangement of the vine leaves is different from that in the banquet scene, but the stoppers made of herbs are very similar. In the top part of the register there is another mat supporting an open vessels with a spiral pattern containing unguent, a lotiform vase, and a plain unguent jar, all of them surmounted by lotus flowers and buds.

The tall bouquet on the left is composed of the conventional papyrus stems with lotus flowers and persea fruits.

The offerings are supplemented by an inscription:

ḫ3 m t ḥnkt ḫ3 m k3w 3pdw ḫ3 m sšrw mnḫt ḫ3 m sntr mrḥt

'1000 loaves and jugs of beer, 1000 oxen and fowl, 1000 pieces of linen and clothing, 1000 bowls of incense and unguent.'(42)

The offering bringer is named as 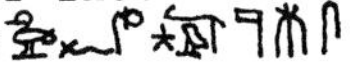 'his son, *wʿb*-priest and overseer of worship (or teaching?), Neṯermosi.'(43)

The hieroglyphs pertaining to the tomb owner on the right are in full colour:

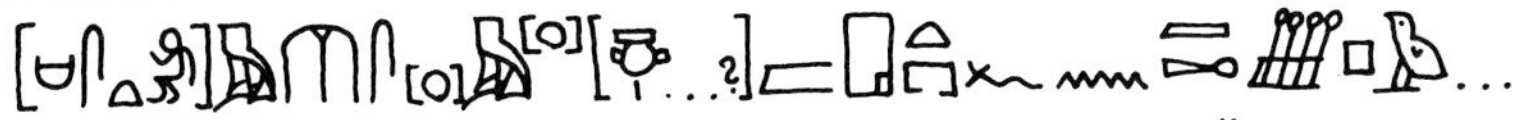

[ḥmst] m sḥ s[ḫ]m[ḫ] ib ... m ḥwt.f n m3ʿ ḫrw šsp w[dnw?] . .

'[Sitting] in the booth, enjoying himself...? in his house of justification; receiving [offerings?]...'

To the left is the beginning of another text, running from right to left:

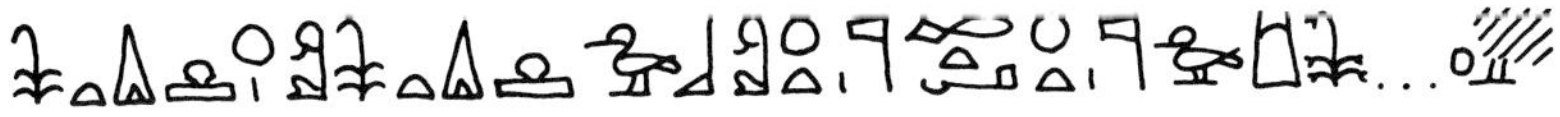

ḥtp di nsw Rʿ ḥtp di nsw Gb psḏt ʿ3t psḏt nḏst itrt šmʿyt ... t ...

'An offering which the king gives (to) Rēʿ, an offering which the king gives (to) Geb and the great Ennead and the little Ennead and the conclave of Upper Egypt ... bread ...'(44)

The large scale of the scene suggests that the occasion depicted was a very special one. The bringing of flowers and 'sitting in the booth ... in the house of justification' point to the scene as being part of a representation of the annual Feast of the Valley, a frequent motif in the hall of Eighteenth dynasty tombs.(45) It was usually linked with the conventional representation of the tomb owner offering or libating to a god, not depicted, on either side of the entrance wall(46) with butchers and/or offering bringers as a sub-scene. Behind the man with flowers would follow the songstresses of the temple of

Amūn with sistra and *menat*, all advancing towards the tomb owner and his wife (cf. Ill. 42 [upper right]). There is no trace of this part of the wall-decoration among our fragments.

Wall B: The banquet (Ill. 64)
Available fragments: BM 37981, BM 37984, BM 37986; Avignon A 51
Bibliography: BM fragments, *Top. Bibl.* I², 2, p. 817 with the following additions: BM 37981, H. Hickmann, *Musikgeschichte in Bildern. Ägypten*, Leipzig 1961, Abb. 30; Lange & Hirmer, *Ägypten* (1978), colour pl. 27 [lower] (called 37984). BM 37984, Lange & Hirmer, *Ägypten* (1978), colour pl. 27 [upper]. BM 37986, (head of female guest) L. Manniche, *Ægyptens Kunst*, Copenhagen 1981, colour ill. 5 and frontispiece; (lower register) R. E. Freed, *Egypt's Golden Age: The Art of Living in the New Kingdom*, Boston 1982, colour fig. 2.
Avignon A 51: *Top. Bibl.* I², 2, p. 814 (Ill. 65).

Although the banquet fragments and BM 37985 (with the son offering) belong together thematically, it is difficult to place them on the very same wall. A tomb owner is usually shown facing his guests, and if linked with the banquet fragments he would be doing just the opposite. It remains a possibility that the two scenes were represented on adjoining walls, the tomb owner being seated to the extreme right of one wall, the guests almost facing him on a wall at right angles to it.

The heights of the two registers of BM 37981 and BM 37984 being 36cm and 30cm on both fragments, the two scenes must have been juxtaposed, the musicians taking up the lower register. To the top right in BM 37984 there remain the feet of the two men who must be restored, followed by a third who is partly visible in the top left of BM 37981. The men wear alternately wigs and unguent cones. To the right in BM 37981 are the feet of two women who must be added (possibly with a third, cf. below) to conclude the register to the right. To the extreme top left in BM 37984 a servant girl must be restored, her hand being all that remains of her.

A harp is strangely lacking in the women's orchestra, but as the large boat-shaped harp conventionally played at banquets had to be played by a standing musician, there was no room for it. Instead an extra lute has been brought in.

The song of the musicians is written above them:

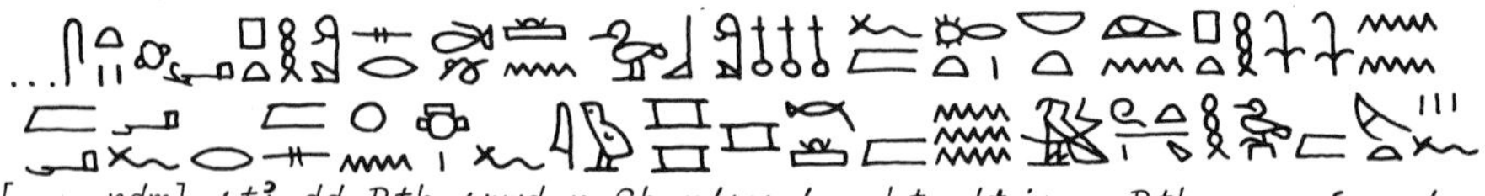

[... nḏm] stỉ dd Ptḥ srwḏ.n Gb nfrw.f m ẖt nbt ỉr.n Ptḥ nn m ˁwy.fy r msḫn(?) ỉb.f ỉw mrw mḥ m mw mꜣwt bˁḥ m mrwt.f

'... [plants of sweet] smell which Ptaḥ has given(?) and Geb has planted. His beauty is in every body. Ptaḥ has done this with his two hands to accommodate(?) his heart. The pools are full of water, the new land is flooded with love of him.'

To the right of the jars there remains an ⊏ at the bottom of a column of hieroglyphs, suggesting that the song continued here.

The text above the second group of musicians appears to be more a speech than a song:

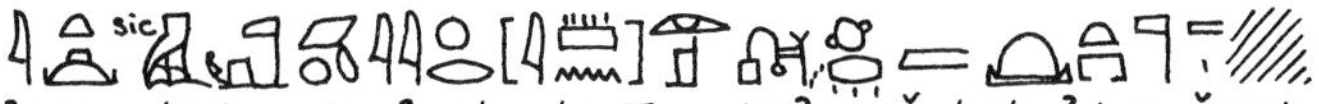

... ỉ3t m ẖrty-nṯr ỉm3ḫy ḫr ʾImn Wsỉr sš ḥsb ỉt m šnwt ḥtp nṯr ...

'... the mound in the necropolis, the venerable one before [Amūn], Osiris the scribe of the accounts of grain in the granary of divine offerings [of Amūn] [name].'

BM 37986 belong to the lower part of a wall, the wide base line being visible, and it would go below the two fragments mentioned above (cf. Ill. 64). In the second register there is room for the Avignon fragment with its seated couple being attended to by a male and a female servant, matching the similar motif in BM 37986. There may have been another similar couple between them.(47)

If space is allowed for another couple here, the two lower registers of the wall are slightly wider than those above. Perhaps another servant was added in the top left of BM 37984, or, more likely, another female guest to the top right of BM 37981. The offering tables in BM 37986 would fittingly conclude the lower registers to the left, another row of male guests of which one member is extant completing the lower register to the right, below the Avignon fragment.

The decorated part of the wall as thus reconstructed measures about 138cm in height and about 2m in width. It is possible that yet another register should be added between the two upper and the two lower registers, or above the upper one. The height of the three upper registers as shown in the preliminary reconstruction equals the height of the scene with the son offering in BM 37985, which most certainly belongs to the upper part of a wall.

Another fragment should be considered here, as it has strong similarities to the BM banquet fragments. But because of the differences and the lack of information about its dimensions, it has not been included in the tentative reconstruction of the wall.

One of the fragments formerly in the de Benzion collection (Ill. 66)(48) shows an offering table, a girl with a bowl of unguent, and the leg of a male servant, both facing right. The group is very similar to the servants and the offering table in BM 37986, but there are a number of differences. First of all the girl wears a curious, transparent rippled garment, which seems to be no more than a shawl draped over her shoulders and with only one corner reaching to the ground.(49) The girl's hair style is more elaborate than that worn by the servant girls in BM 37986 and more like that of the musicians in the other BM fragments. Also she has more than one flower attached to her wig. The lines on the beer and wine jars under the table are diagonal, not horizontal as in BM 37986, and the lines on the slab of calcite of the table are also marked in a different way. On the other hand, the offerings seem to be rather similar.

The size of the de Benzion fragment is nowhere indicated, but judging from the tip of a vertical line framing the space for a hieroglyphic inscription, the fragment is a small one, and about the size of the registers in BM 38986.

The fragment must belong somewhere in our tomb, presumably not on this banquet wall, but perhaps on one of those the decoration of which is not yet accounted for (cf. below).

Wall C: Recording produce (Ill. 67)

Available fragments: BM 37978, BM 37979. Probably from the same wall: BM 37976

Bibliography: *Top. Bibl.* I^2,2, p. 817 with the following additions: BM 37978 (ducks in basket) Manniche, *Ægyptens Kunst*, Ill. 7 (colour); BM 37976, Freed, *op. cit.*, colour fig. 23.

There is good reason to believe that BM 37978 and BM 37979 belong together. The scribe and attendants in BM 37978 would advance towards a figure of the tomb owner facing right, and at a larger scale, filling in the height of the two registers with the birds. BM 37979 suits these requirements, and the connection is supported by the inscriptions on the fragment, mentioning 'revenues', the subject of the other two fragments clearly dealing with recording of produce for taxation.

The top register of BM 37978 is much destroyed. The film of what looks like varnish may have been applied during restoration to keep the flaking pieces in place. To the left are two scribes squatting in front of a sack, facing two attendants. A single hieroglyph remains: . Another attendant facing right keeps the birds in order, the legs of one more being visible on the right. Above the geese a few hieroglyphs can be made out: . To the extreme right are the arms and legs of at least one more attendant.

In the lower register there is to the left a table loaded with produce: cucumbers, grapes, a bunch of reeds(?), lotus flowers, and a cake. Two jars stand below along with a sack which, like the two wooden chests above, would contain the records of the estate. A scribe is reading from a scroll. His speech was apparently never inserted in the columns above his head. Behind him a man guards a stack of wickerwork crates with birds. An inscription above presumably refers to him:

ỉr.k nrỉ sp sn(?) ... ỉw.k ḥr sbỉt ḏꜣmw(?) ... nb

'Take your time, take your time... you will(?) conduct the troops(?)...'(50)

The space behind is divided into two registers, the top one showing three prostrate and three crouching men being addressed by an attendant with a stick: 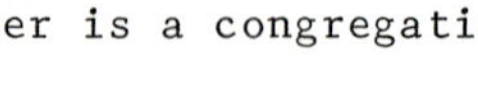 *ḥms n.tn m ỉr mdwt* 'sit (quiet), and do not talk!' More young birds are lined up behind.

In the lower register is a congregation of geese with an attendant in charge. He says:

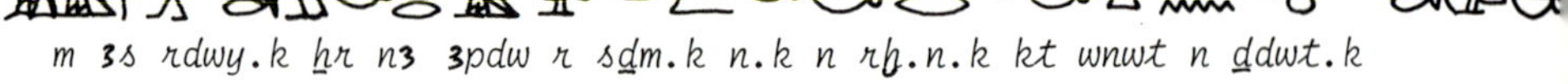

m ꜣs rdwy.k ẖr nꜣ ꜣpdw r sḏm.k n.k n rḫ.n.k kt wnwt n ḏdwt.k

'Do not rush your feet with those birds until you can hear for yourself. You won't find another time for what you have to say.'

To the extreme right in the register another attendant can be seen, followed by four men with their arms to their chests.

Below the upper edge of the fragment there is a horizontal line with faint traces of masses of blue and red above, *i.e.* the remains of a top border. The upper and lower registers measure 24 and 40cm respectively = a total of 64cm.

In BM 37979 the tomb owner is shown seated on a folding stool with a panther skin as a cushion, holding in one hand a sceptre *ʿbꜣ* or *sḫm* and a lettuce (*Lactuca sativa* L.), in the other a long stick. Some hieroglyphs remain above him (shown here with the possible restoration of the text):

In the second column from the right *ʿšꜣw r ḫrp*, possibly with *nbt* to follow in the subsequent column, meaning '... too numerous to manage...' Three signs remain at the bottom of the column. Due to their order and the red colour of O a word like *(m) mnt* 'daily' must be meant.

The following column is quite straightforward: *[n] kꜣ n sš ḥsb it n šnwt* '[to] the *ka* of the scribe and counter of grain in the granary', followed in the next column by a fragment of a sign with thin, red horizontal lines on yellow. This can only be , and compared with the complete sign in BM 37981 there can be no doubt that the full title was 'scribe and counter of grain in the granary of divine offerings of Amūn'. Below in the same column there remain *mꜣʿ ḫrw* 'justified', with a straight horizontal line in red above, undoubtedly of. The space left between *mꜣʿ ḫrw* and *ḥtp nṯr* is too large to contain only the name of the tomb owner, when compared with the area hacked out in other fragments, *e.g.* BM 37979, and 'of Amūn' must be added to the title. This leaves a gap which might possibly accomodate another 'Amūn' as part of the name, but only just so, if we are to allow for to follow.

Below in the last column the name of the wife is clearly visible, although she was not represented: *Ḥꜣtšpst*, presumably preceded by *snt.f mrt.f nbt pr* 'his beloved wife, mistress of the house.'

Above the columns of hieroglyphs a horizontal line with blue and red masses of colour can be made out, clearly the top border line. The height of the register measured from this line to the lower part of the folding stool is 62cm. If joined to the fragment with geese, 2cm would have to be added below the chair as a podium or mat.(51)

Thematically, cattle recording would belong with the presentation of taxes to the tomb owner. It may indeed belong on the same wall as the geese. Unless the cattle are standing on something, the lower register of the fragment appears to be too low to match the corresponding part of the scene with the geese. Another discrepancy is the fact that the colour of the hieroglyphs in the cattle fragment is blue, not black. If the fragment belongs on this wall, it would have to go below the recording of geese.

The upper register shows to the left a standing scribe facing right towards three men with their arms to their chests and a prostrate man. Behind them remain a few signs in two vertical columns:

... n ḥr swhi̓ m ... '... boasting of...'

...w sp n ḏd rmt

A herd of cattle follows to the right.

The lower register shows to the left a man facing left, with two chests and a sack above, and a scribe with a scroll facing right towards an attendant, the cattle, and a man with a rope. To the extreme right are more men with their arms to their chests. The speech of the man with the rope is written in two horizontal bands above:

mi̓ rwi̓.k tw m i̓r mdt m bꜣḥ pꜣ ḥsy bwt.f pw rmt ḥr mdt i̓r.f m mꜣꜥ nn mhy.f ḥr smi̓ nb sš grw mꜣꜥ nn i̓r.f n ḥr n rmt sw rḫ spw nb i̓n sš ḥsb i̓t n ... Nb...

'Come on! Get away! Do not speak in the presence of the praised one. He detests people talking. He does what is right. He will not ignore any complaint. Pass on in quiet and in order. He won't take anyone's side. He knows all the affairs, does the scribe and counter of grain of [Amūn], Neb...'

Wall D: Agriculture (Ill. 68)

Available fragments: BM 37982. Probably also East Berlin 18529-31, 18539, 18540 (Ill. 69-71).

Bibliography: BM 37982, *Top. Bibl.* I^2,2, p. 817; East Berlin 18529-31, 18539, *ibid.*,p. 815; East Berlin 18540, *ibid.*, p. 607.

The BM fragment

There are remains of three registers, but of the upper and lower ones only the edges remain. The central register shows to the left a man swearing an oath at a stela in a corn field, to the right, in two registers, a man with a horse and chariot and, below, two mules and a man sitting in the chariot. A tree completes the register.

The inscription rendering the speech of the man at the stela is as follows:

wꜣḥ pꜣ nṯr ꜥꜣ nty m tꜣ pt iw pꜣ wḏ mty ꜥḥꜥw pꜣy.f ...

'As the great god who is in the sky endures, this stela is correct, standing in its [place].'

In a small fragment adjoining on the left there is a man designated as  *ḥry ḫꜣwy n šnwt* 'chief of the measurers of the granary'. In front of him a head of a ram has been painted in black directly on the mud plaster. A ram was usually attached to the rope used for measuring the fields.

Above the mules a single hieroglyphs remains: 𓄤 *nfr*.

Along the upper line of the fragment, *i.e.* at the bottom of the register above, a few grains of corn are just visible, pertaining to another register depicting agricultural scenes. Grain lying loose on the ground would belong on the threshing ground during winnowing, or to the heap of grain being measured before entering the granary (see below).

The nature of the lower register is more difficult to ascertain. There are traces of ten vertical columns of text with a few blue signs intact. The text ran from left to right:

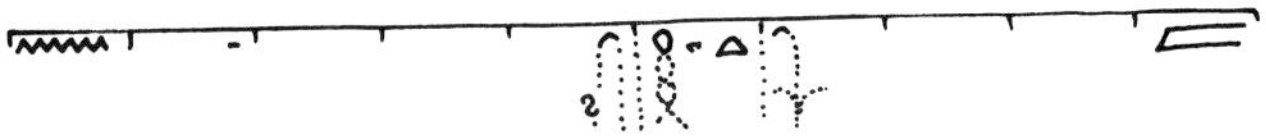

The East Berlin fragments of agricultural scenes

Five fragments in East Berlin appear to be rather similar in style to the BM fragments and possibly to come from the same tomb. They are painted on the same thick layer of mud mixed with straw. As they would provide some of the missing elements of agriculture, a discussion of them would be appropriate in this place.

The fragments in question are

a) East Berlin 18529-31 (Ill. 69): Three small fragments showing the upper part of a man stacking grain, the heads and scoops of three girls winnowing, and a girl with a jar in a corn field, with the leg of a man showing on the left.

b) East Berlin 18539 (Ill. 70): Three men reaping, man asleep under tree, and part of a man with a whip.

c) East Berlin 18540 (Ill. 71): Four men catching quail with a net in a field.(52)

All three fragments were bought by Schäfer at the auction of the Rustafjaell collection on 19th - 21st December 1906. Other painted fragments came up for sale with these, some clearly of a different provenance, a few perhaps not (see below). No provenance was given for the fragments in the lot, but fragment c) above is an exception in that it has an excavation record.

In the season of 1898-99, when the Marquis of Northampton was granted permission to excavate with Spiegelberg and Newberry in the main hill of Draꜥ Abû el-Nagaꜥ and the area to the north east of the hill, the excavators came across a number of New Kingdom private tombs.

Few of these received any detailed mention in the report published in 1908.(53) Because of the unusual subject the scene with the netting of quail gained a place as a vignette to the report, but there is no mention of it in the text.(54) According to Porter & Moss the fragment was found 'projecting from the lower part of a wall' somewhere between TT 14 and 164.(55)

Between the time this fragment was found and drawn and the date of the Rustafjaell auction for which it had been photographed, it suffered considerable damage, a large portion to the right and at the bottom having disappeared.

The indication of a provenance, however approximate, is of particular interest as not a single one of the fragments to be considered with the BM lot can be traced to any place other than the Theban necropolis in general. The question of the possible location of the tomb will be taken up in a separate paragraph below.

It is evident from BM 37982 that the tomb to which it belonged had scenes showing work in the field, a common subject in Eighteenth dynasty tombs. Few such scenes have found their way to museums and other collections.(56) In order to determine the common source for the Rustafjaell agricultural scenes and the BM paintings a comparison will be made between some of the details.

The treatment of the faces in East Berlin 18529-31 with their large, drawn out eyes, compressed lips and chin, and detailed treatment of the hair (though naturally different in style in field hands and farm girls compared to scribes and ladies at a banquet) are not unlike the corresponding features in the BM fragments. The body hair of the man with a fork on East Berlin 18529 is painted with the same attention to detail as the feathering of the geese in BM 37978. The ears of grain in East Berlin 18539 are very similar to those in BM 37982. The hieroglyphs in East Berlin 18539 are drawn in a similar hand as for instance those in BM 37976. Note in particular the long and boldly drawn arm in the hieroglyphs  and . The tree in East Berlin 18539 appears to be rather similar to that of BM 37982, at least in the black and white photographs.

The East Berlin fragments and their context in relation to BM 37982

The position in an agricultural scene of East Berlin 18529-31 and 18539 are not difficult to determine, and the contents of at least one register can be reconstructed on the basis of the available fragments.

The girl in East Berlin 18531 stands in a corn field which has already been harvested. Girls with jars or baskets with provisions are frequently to be found in line with reapers. Judging from the level at which the man's leg behind her is depicted, it can only belong to a man jumping high into the air to force the heads of corn into a basket which would be supported by another man on the left. It is of interest that the jumping man wears a red sandal, an unusual detail to be found also among the quail catchers in East Berlin 18540 and the reapers in 18539.(57)

The larger fragment East Berlin 18539 has to the left three harvesters cutting off the head of corn. It is not possible to say how many figures were interposed between the reapers and the girl in

East Berlin 18531, but they obviously belong in the same register. To the right in 18539 is the sleeping overseer named 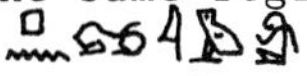 Penriu, and a man with a whip. The latter is only of importance in scenes with oxen, *i.e.* ploughing and threshing. In view of the stationary position of the overseer and the sequence of events in general, threshing seems to be by far the most likely episode to follow. We must therefore add a  -shaped heap of grain with oxen threshing and a man stacking the loosened heads of grain. Ideally suited for the latter character is the man in East Berlin 18529 who is shown standing on an uneven surface, his one leg being raised, with a stick or fork in his hand.

Next to the threshing would follow winnowing, and the three girls in East Berlin 18530 fit in well here. This is usually a symmetrical representation, and we must add another three girls to the right, presumably with a few younger ones in between sweeping away the ears. The carrying off of the threshed grain to the granary does not appear to have been represented in any tombs, the scene passing directly to the measuring process in the granary. This episode would include one or several scribes, labourers with barrels and an overseer seated on top of the heap with a chest for the records at hand. One such detail, including overseer, chest and labourer, can be seen on a fragment sold with the Rustafjaell lot and bought by an English dealer, but the scale of the persons is too large for it to be fitted into a register with the fragments in East Berlin.(58)

As has already been demonstrated, BM 37982 bears evidence of three registers. The top register shows threshed grain lying on the floor. This can only belong to the winnowing or the measuring of grain. In another tomb,(59) swearing by a stela next to a tree concludes a register. As no feet are visible stepping on the grain in the BM fragment, the scene with the stela and horses would probably go below the counting of grain, filling in the extreme right part of the second register from the top.

To the left in the BM fragment is the overseer of measurers of the granary with his coil of rope and ram's head. The sketch of the ram's head was presumably drawn in pharaonic times when the rest of the register, giving a clue to the scene, still existed. We may therefore take it that a line of tax inspectors followed to the left. Measuring the fields is not a very common theme in Theban tombs,(60) but it was used in the period with which we are dealing. In TT 69 of Menna all together eleven tax inspectors, scribes and attendants were included in the procession, whereas in TT 38 of Zeserkaraʿsonb a smaller number was required. On the wall under discussion there is room for a substantial number of participants. The tax inspectors inspected the fields before they were harvested. There is therefore no possibility of transferring the girl of East Berlin 18531 to the attendant in the register showing the measuring of the fields, as she is walking in a field which has already been harvested.

There is no trace of the ploughing and sowing which would certainly have been included in the register below. But to the extreme right, below the register with horses in BM 37982 there is evidence of hieroglyphs in vertical columns. We may perhaps imagine the tomb owner seated here, the hieroglyphs describing what he is supervising.

The scene showing quail catching is difficult to place as no traces of adjoining scenes are left. If we are to take the statement by Porter & Moss that it was found 'projecting from the lower part of a wall' as a reference to the original position of the scene, we may tentatively place it in a lower register. Judging from the size of the registers on the basis of the available fragments, there may not have been more than four registers to this wall, each measuring about 40cm = 160cm + top border and blank area at the bottom.

When reconstructed as suggested above, the wall measures about 250cm or more in width, depending on the number of harvesters and scribes represented.

There is another fragment in East Berlin, no. 18532, which may belong in this tomb and on this wall (Ill. 72). It is listed in the *Top. Bibl.* I^2,2, p. 817, and is also mentioned in J. Broekhuis, *De Godin Renenwetet*, Assen 1971, pp. 16 and 61. The fragment appears to have been acquired from the Rustafjaell collection, although it is not immediately identifiable with any of the fragments in the sales catalogues (many of which were not illustrated).

The painting shows a black shrine on a stand with cornice and an imitation door. The inscription above identifies the occupant as 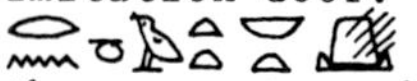 'Renenwetet, mistress of the granary'. Next to it there are two ring stands with spoutless *nmst*-jars and a large bouquet of lotus flowers and buds. To the left the top corner of the cornice of another stand can just be made out. All the items appear to be placed on a much larger stand of which the top edge of the cornice is just visible. A vertical line almost cuts off the  on the right. In the top left corner another short vertical line can be seen (a hieroglyph?).

The painting is executed with the same free-flowing and expert hand which is so characteristic of the fragments in the British Museum, and the originality of the treatment of the subject, concealing the goddess within her shrine, would seem to match the spirit of the decoration of this tomb.

Renenwetet, mistress of the granary, is represented in TT 38,(61) but this time sitting in a basket. The tomb owner is shown offering to her on the feast of Renenwetet.(62) In a register above there was once a corresponding figure of Amūn-Rēᶜ, now hacked out. Amūn is not frequently depicted in Theban private tombs, although reference to him is abundant. Perhaps the neighbouring divinity in the East Berlin fragment was a similar figure.(63)

Representations of Renenwetet are often found in vintage scenes, below fishing and fowling. But as mistress of the granary she may in this case belong on the wall with the agricultural scenes, as in TT 38.

Wall E: Fishing and fowling (Ills. 73, 74, 75)

Available fragments: a) BM 37977; b), c) two fragments formerly in the de Benzion collection.

Bibliography: BM 37977, *Top. Bibl.* I^2,2, p. 817; de Benzion b), *ibid.*, p. 820; Keimer in *BIE* 34, 1953, fig. 180, p. 407; *de Benzion Sale Cat.* 1947, no. 89; de Benzion c), *Top. Bibl.*, *loc. cit.*; Keimer, *op. cit.* fig. 146, p. 338; *de Benzion Sale Cat.* 1947, no. 90.

There can be little doubt that the two small fragments formerly in the de Benzion collection belong with the larger fragment in the British Museum. The style and technique is very similar, but minor differences reveal that the two halves of the scene may have been executed by two different hands, or else that the artist did not draw right and left profiles absolutely alike. In the face of the tomb owner in fragments a) and b) the lips are drawn differently: in fragment a) the upper and lower line of the lips meet at the corner of the mouth, whereas in fragment b) they do not. The nostrils are differently marked, and so is the curve of the chin. The differences in the necklaces, wigs and bunches of flowers are not unusual and only contribute to the lively and individual character of Egyptian art at its best. In TT 69 of Menna, for example, the necklaces of the two corresponding figures differ, and so do the wigs in TT 52 of Nakht.

Failing indications of the measurements in fragments b) and c), the adjustment of the three pieces has been made by first joining b) and c). Part of the leg of the tomb owner is extant in c), and the whole figure can easily be reconstructed. The distance from the top border to the water line was then measured on b)+c) and the scale adjusted to match the identical distance in a), the two extremities of the harpoon in a) and b) being joined together. The water line in a) is not strictly horizontal, but appears to rise slightly towards the centre. On restoring the length of the boat in b)+c) and the partly preserved column of text to the right in a), and on the basis of the available measurements for a), the resulting total width of the scene can be estimated to about 170cm. The lower part of the stretch of water being destroyed, the height of the register remains approximate, but it was probably around 85cm.

The scene belonged to the top part of the wall, the lower part of the top border being visible on b). Above there would be a frieze taking up 10 or 20cm. Very few Theban tombs are too low to accomodate a standing person of medium height. If we assume that the total height of the wall was a minimum of 175cm, some 80cm of the decoration remains unaccounted for. About 20cm at the bottom would be undecorated and have a border of red and perhaps yellow, or it would have the 'palace facade' as in TT C4, cf. above. For the possible subject of the missing register see below.

The inscriptions on the fragments are as follows:

sḫmḫ ỉb m33 ḫw nfr ỉrt Sḫt m k3t Sḫt ỉn ḥsy n [nbt hb] ỉn sš ḥsb ỉt [m šnwt ʾImn m pr ʾImn Nb... m3ʿ ḫrw] snt.f [mrt.f nbt pr] Ḥ3tšpst

'Amusing himself, looking at good things and the deeds of the god of the trap, the works of Sekhet, by the one praised by the mistress of hunting, by the scribe and counter of grain [in the granary of Amūn in the temple of Amūn, Neb..., justified,] (and) his [beloved] wife, [mistress of the house], Ḥatshepsut.'(64)

The hieroglyphs are polychrome, large and bold. Inserted between the two figures in black ink is the following repetitive inscription:

a) fowling 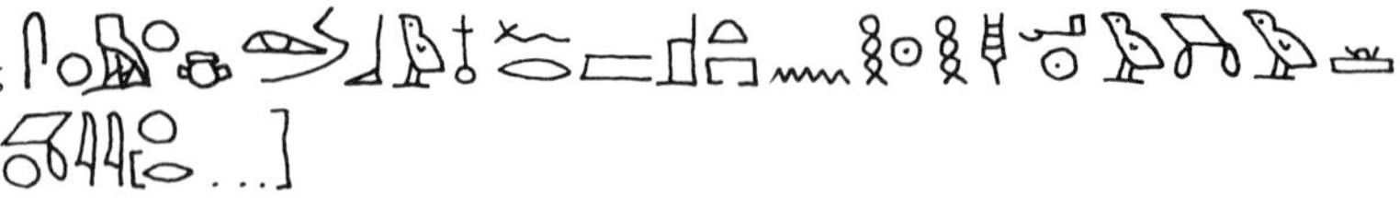

sḫmḫ ib mȝȝ bw nfr m st nḥḥ ꜥḥꜥw ȝw nn ḫȝ ib imȝḫy ḫr...
'Amusing himself, looking at good things in the place of eternity for a long lifetime, without a wish in the world: the honoured(65) one...'

b) spearing fish (signs in brackets restored from TT 165)

[ḫns sšw hbhb sḫmḫ ib stt mḥyt] m pḥw in mry Sḫt smȝy n [nbt hb in...]
'[Transversing the marshes travelling, amusing oneself spearing fish] in the pools by the one beloved of Sekhet, companion of [the mistress of hunting, by... (name and title)].'

c)next to the boy are scribbled a few hieroglyphs which look like

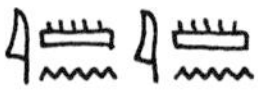.(66)

Fishing and fowling occur from the beginning of the Eighteenth dynasty to the beginning of the reign of Amenophis III. The scene is to be found in the majority of T-shaped tombs, most frequently on the right rear wall of the hall, but occasionally on one of the front or side walls, or on one of the walls of the passage. The motif often has as a sub-scene either a row of offering bringers or a representation of vintage.

By comparison with other tombs, BM 37983 showing a garden pool may belong on the same wall as fishing and fowling, and the fragment will be discussed here.
Bibliography: *Top. Bibl.* I^2,2, p. 817; Freed, *op. cit.*, colour fig. 9.
The fragment shows a rectangular pool surrounded by a variety of trees and shrubs: date palm, dom palm, sycomore fig, a 'typical', unidentifiable tree, a bushy vine and a prolific mandrake. Along the muddy banks of the pool grow papyrus, poppy and other plants less easy to identify. The pool itself is full of *Nymphaea* lotus, fish and ducks. In the top right corner the goddess of the sycomore appears from her tree with food and drink which would have been received by the deceased couple seated to the right (now broken away). A few blue hieroglyphs in vertical columns remain below:

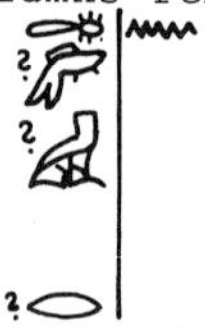

In the top left corner is the speech of the sycomore goddess written from right to left in vertical columns. Although no goddess is represented in the tree next to the signs, the words may be thought

of as coming from the tree, and perhaps being directed towards another representation of the tomb owner and his wife, once seated to the left and, judging from the size of the signs, at a large scale. The faint blue hieroglyphs are as follows:

ḏd mdw ỉn nht ... n.k(?) š pn sš ḥsb ỉt ...

'Spoken by the sycomore goddess ... to you(?) this pool, O scribe and counter of grain of ...'

A similar scene is to be found in the roughly contemporary TT 63 of Sebkḥotep where two goddesses deliver their speech above the pool, the tomb owner and his wife being shown at a small scale matching that of the goddess.(67)

The lake may have been positioned on the top half of the wall as in other tombs. In the top left corner of the fragment there are faint traces of black and red which would appear to belong in a top border. In the contemporary TT 63 the lake follows to the left of the fishing and fowling scene, on the right wall of the passage. This wall would be the longest available wall for this subject in a T-shaped tomb, the opposite, left wall being almost invariably taken up by the funeral procession and the voyage to Abydos (traces of which appear to be absent from this tomb, but the subjects must have been represented).

The fact that faint traces of paint along the left edge of the lake fragment suggest a continuation of the scene emphasizes the need of a long wall to accomodate the subjects. The traces consist of a pale blue area with irregular, diagonal lines in white or pale yellow. The blue area is very slightly curved, expanding towards the middle and almost touching the trees projecting on the left side of the lake. Regardless of their colour, the diagonal lines at uneven intervals are reminiscent of a plant wound round a column. Adjacent to a lake a vineyard is sometimes represented with vines growing up against green papyriform columns. The columns are usually smaller than this one, which would take up the height of the register up to the level of the upper edge of the lake, if, as seems probable, the speech of the sycomore goddess continued towards the left. With a column of this size the scene would extend a fair amount to the left. The length of the wall when including both the fishing and fowling as well as the lake is about 250cm, to which must be added the architectural elements on the left.

Other fragments from the tomb

A. Offering bringers BM 37980 (Ill. 76)

Bibliography: *Top. Bibl.* I^2,2, p. 816.

Offering bringers are often difficult to place in a tomb, as they would occur almost anywhere, following the tomb owner when offering or libating, advancing towards the tomb owner in a sub-scene to agriculture, in connection with fishing and fowling, or just walking towards the inner part of the tomb.

BM 37980 shows five persons facing right, carrying sheafs of grain, a gazelle, two hares, and something on a yoke. The hares are reminiscent of those brought by attendants following the tomb owner when hunting in the desert.(68) Hunting scenes were much favoured in the reigns of Tuthmosis III and Amenophis II, but they seem to have gone out of fashion with the reign of Tuthmosis IV,(69) and as the sheafs of grain suggest, the context of the BM fragment would appear to be different.

The offering bringers belong in a lower register. The pale blue line, which can only be a base line, is visible at the lower edge of the fragment, just as in one of the banquet fragments (BM 37986). It is possible that they belong below the agricultural scenes, or, if the tomb owner was represented on the other side of the entrance doorway, in a subscene on the right front wall.

B. Crouching man with offerings East Berlin 18528 (Ill. 77)
Bibliography: *Top. Bibl.* I^{2},2, p. 815.

This fragment in East Berlin, acquired with the Rustafjaell lot, ought to be considered in this place, as it shows some similarities to the fragments under discussion. It represents a crouching man, facing right, before a basket of food and three jars of beer and wine. The man is named as 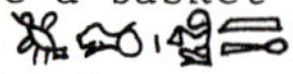 'Paru, justified'. Above the basket is written  . To the extreme right are traces of a standing man; only his toe and part of his garment is visible. The remaining hieroglyphs, written in a vertical column from right to left, mention 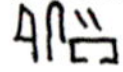 *is* 'the tomb'. Above Paru there remains a mat, and behind him a vertical line appears to conclude the scene.

Paru wears an unguent cone and a white band around his head, possibly as a sign of mourning.(70) The food in the basket, including two unusual items: a  -shaped cake and a napkin, are presumably funerary offerings, attractively decorated with sprigs of some herb.

On the basis of the available photographs the following points would appear to bear a significant resemblance to some of the fragments in question. The twigs in the basket are reminiscent of the solitary twig shown on the tree in East Berlin 18539, and the hieroglyphs, notably the  may have been drawn by the same hand, although two different determinatives have been chosen for the names. The rendering of the loaves of bread and the yellow substance in the little basket is little at variance with the corresponding items on BM 37986.

In the publication by the Berlin Museum the fragment has been dated to the Ramessid Period. Judging from a close parallel to the scene in TT 69 of Menna a slightly earlier date would seem to suit it equally well. In the tomb of Menna(71) the arrangement of the crouching man with head band, collar, cone and lotus flower, the jars and the basket of food is very similar (although reversed). Facing the crouching figure there is a standing man, corresponding to the man whose foot appears on the fragment. The register above has members of Menna's family seated on chairs which are placed on mats. On the fragment such a mat is just visible along the upper edge. In the tomb of Menna the topic of the scene is devoted to offerings being presented to the tomb owner and his family, and it is to be found on the right rear wall of the hall. As the scene is reversed on the fragment in East Berlin, one might thus expect it to be on the left rear wall, if there was to be any consistency. The height of the fragment is 24cm. With a mat below a few centimeters would have to be added to give the full height of the register.

Reconstructing the tomb

On the basis of the available fragments and the portions of the tomb which can safely be reconstructed, it would seem that the tomb from which they came was a T-shaped tomb. This is particularly evident from the size of the fishing and fowling scene *cum* lake which, when juxtaposed, would take up 250cm + a portion to allow for a vineyard or a building with a column. This scene required a long wall such as the wall of a passage (on the reconstructed plan below called [F]).

The subject of 'Wall A', the Feast of the Valley, possibly including an offering next to the entrance doorway, would conventionally be situated on one of the two front walls of the hall, in this case the left front wall. In order to make the banquet scene ('Wall B') relate to the Feast of the Valley, it should be placed on the left side wall of the hall, being ca. 2m wide. The agricultural scenes ('Wall D') is estimated to being ca. 250cm wide. We would tentatively place it on the right rear wall, with the geese and cattle ('Wall C') on the opposite right front wall. If the transverse hall was symmetrical, it would thus be about 5m in width + the width of the doorway.

As to the left rear wall there is some reason to believe that the subject depicted was offerings. It is possible that the offering bringers with hares also came from here. They walk in the same direction as the crouching man with offerings. A similar arrangement is apparent in TT 69 of Menna. The wall will here be called [E].

The right side wall may have had a representation of a stela, with scenes of offerings flanking it. The de Benzion fragment with the girl in a rippled garment cannot at present be positioned in the tomb.

One subject was never omitted from an Eighteenth dynasty tomb: the funeral procession. This subject would fit the left wall of a passage, in this case opposite the fishing and fowling scene as in TT 52 of Nakht. Perhaps the voyage to Abydos was represented in a lower register, and the rites before the mummy further back on the same wall, here called [G].

No statues of suitable date with the proper title and the name suggested here can at present be traced. Perhaps this centre piece is to be found among the many anonymous statues of the Eighteenth dynasty, or it could have been a rock cut statue still awaiting discovery under the sand.

The following sketch indicates the position of the scenes as suggested above, but it must be emphasized that due to lack of precise information about the appearance of the tomb, the reconstruction is conjectural.

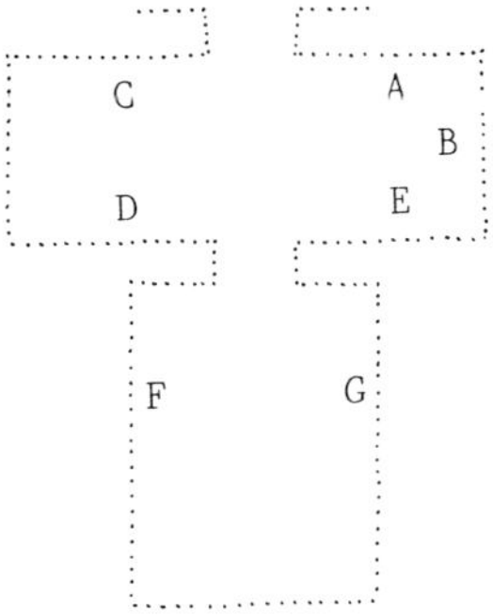

The history of the BM fragments and those related to them

Ten out of the eleven fragments now in the British Museum arrived in England in 1821,(72) and with the rest of Salt's 'first' collection they were acquired by the museum. BM 37981, however, was bought by Waddington and Hanbury in Egypt in 1821 and was presented to the museum by Sir Henry Ellis on 9th November 1833.(73) Two of the fragments, BM 37977 and BM 37984, were drawn for the Bankes MSS in 1821, when they had already been cut out, but apparently before they were mounted in frames.(74)

The letter mentioned above, p. 136, by Salt supports the evidence for the arrival of the fragments late in 1821, but the reference to the pieces being found by 'my man' (= Giovanni d'Athanasi) 'last year' is slightly puzzling. This, when taken literally, would mean during the year 1820, at which time the first collection was already on its way north, collecting and packing having begun as early as 1817-18: The following sequence of events can be reconstructed:

Oct. 1817- Jan. 1818	Salt in Upper Egypt with the Belmores, Beechey, Bankes, Linant and others.(75) Belzoni and d'Athanasi are charged with getting the 'first' collection to Alexandria.(76) During this season d'Athanasi began to work for Salt.
Oct. 1818- Jan. 1819	Salt in Upper Egypt with Bankes, Beechey, Ricci and Linant, already building up his 'second' collection, later to be sold to the king of France.(77)
Feb. 1820	The 'first' collection has arrived in Alexandria.(78)
Nov. 1820	The 'first' collection is shipped from Alexandria.(79)

Objects were presumably added to the collection as they were found, and the tomb could have been discovered any time between 1817 and 1819.

As the fragments were removed at such an early date and the tomb stripped of its decoration, it is hardly surprising that it was not mentioned in detail by any of the early travellers, who worked in the other tombs included in this study. Salt himself does not appear to make a particular reference to them in print, although they may be included in his general allusion to the topics depicted in the Theban tombs.(80)

The few early travellers who copied selected scenes from the fragments may have done so when they had already entered the collections of the museum. Wilkinson, who copied a few of the scenes, left for Egypt in 1821 and did not return to England for twelve years. He must therefore have had access to the fragments before he departed, or, more likely, he copied them after his return in 1833.(81) Champollion, or maybe his editor, claims to have copied the musicians and dancers *in the tomb*. This was clearly not possible, as he only arrived in Egypt in 1828. But he did go to London in the spring of 1824(82) and would thus have had a chance to make a drawing in the museum. It is puzzling, however, that both the publication by Champollion and that of Rosellini have the drawings of the BM fragments immediately after scenes from Beni Ḥasan and that Champollion says that it was from 'Beni Hasan el Qadim'.(83) In the drawings, the musician to the left is slightly more complete than in the fragment in its present state, and the feet of the dancers are intact, but this may well be a retoration by the draughtsman and is no proof that the scene was copied *in situ*. In

Rosellini's publication the musicians have been coloured, but otherwise the two publications are very similar. A possible link between the drawings in these two works and the paintings seen by Bankes would be Linant de Bellefonds, who worked for all parties concerned. Linant appears to have met Bankes in 1818,(84) and it is possible that he was responsible for the drawings published by Champollion and Rosellini and that they were based on paintings he had seen long before the Franco-Tuscan expedition set foot in Egypt.

The fragments in the de Benzion collection

The present whereabouts of these fragments are unknown. They were sold from the collection in Cairo in 1947. They had by then been seen and photographed by Keimer, who published them in 1953. There is no information available as to how de Benzion acquired them, nor can the original Keimer photos be traced.

The Avignon fragment

This fragment was acquired by the Musée Calvet from the sale of the Sallier collection in Aix-en-Provence in 1833.(85) Sallier had died in 1831. The fragment may have been one of the 'beaux tableaux' seen by Cherubini in the Sallier collection in 1828.(86) It is thought that the objects collected by Sallier chiefly derived from the Anastasi collection.(87) Anastasi in turn employed Piccinini as his agent in Upper Egypt. This latter appears to have been most active after 1820,(88) by which time out tomb had already been opened and cut to pieces.

The East Berlin fragments

These pieces were acquired by Schäfer from the Rustafjaell collection sold at Sotheby's in London on 19th - 20th December 1906. Rustafjaell collected antiquities in Egypt by the beginning of the century. It is not known how he acquired the fragments, but one of them, no. 18540, had been excavated by the Marquis of Northampton at Draᶜ Abû el-Nagaᶜ in 1898-99.

The location of the tomb

As demonstrated above it has not proved possible to identify the tomb from which the BM fragments and related pieces derive with any known tomb. If we accept that the East Berlin fragments belong with those in the British Museum, this is hardly surprising, as one of the former was found in a position which would appear to be the original one. The fragment was found between TT 14 and 165 where no known and numbered tomb is located. The distance between these two tombs is no more than a couple of dozen paces on the slope of the hill. The area in question was searched and partly cleared by the present writer in March 1985, but the finds proved to have no bearing on the location of the BM tomb, although some possibilities for its location were proven to be out of the question. Further clearance of the site may one day give the final clue to the original position of what must once have been one of the most magnificent tombs in the necropolis.(89)

12 The 'Bankes' Tomb

The tomb described in the following pages has not previously been recognized as a separate tomb, but it is quite clear from the scattered descriptions by the early travellers that the tomb existed, and that it is not identical with any of the tombs known at the present day nor with any of the others visited by the early travellers. As substantial fragments of the tomb survive in the Bankes collection at Kingston Lacy, the tomb is here named after this collector, the name and the title of the original owner remaining unknown. Most of the fragments are included in the bibliography of Porter & Moss but without provenance,(1) and the publication of some of them by Nina de Garis Davies implies that they were not related, although they are all given an Eighteenth dynasty date.(2) Porter & Moss assign the date of the Nineteenth dynasty to one of the fragments.(3)

In the works of the early travellers there are rarely any records of any specific tomb being dismantled. But regarding the Bankes fragments there is indeed some mention of the proceedings prior to the shipment of the pieces and their arrival in England in 1821.(4) In 1830 Bankes published an account in English of the life of his interpretor, Giovanni Finati, an Italian who rendered his assistance to many of the Europeans travelling in Egypt in those days.(5) Here and there Bankes inserted his own comments as footnotes. On pp. 342-3 of volume II of the account Finati refers to the fragments in question:

> 'At Thebes he [*sc.* Bankes] was successful in detaching the stucco from one of the most interesting and best preserved of the better tombs, so as to be enabled to send several groups to England, and especially a large one of musicians, with harps and other instruments, as fresh as when first painted.'

To this Bankes added the following footnote:

> 'This group is mentioned by Belzoni and is additionally remarkable for having been painted in the reign of one of the earliest sovereigns of that dynasty, whose succession is given on the tablet of Abydos- his name and effigy being represented several times in

the paintings of this tomb.'

Tracing this reference back to Belzoni in the narrative of the latter we find the following brief statement (there can be little doubt that this is the one alluded to by Bankes, as it is the only mention of musicians in wall-decorations of a private tomb):

> 'The same day [*sc.* 13th October 1817] we [*sc.* Belzoni and three anonymous travellers(6)] visited another mummy-pit, which I had opened six months before. The construction is somewhat similar to what I have just described,(7) a portico and a subterraneous cavity where the mummies are. Here the paintings are beautiful, not only for their preservation, but for the novelty of their figures. There are two harps, one with nine strings, and the other with fourteen, and several other strange representations: in particular six dancing girls, with fifes, tambourine, pipes of reeds, guitars &c.'(8)

A great number of travellers passed through Thebes that autumn. Some left detailed descriptions of what they saw, while the records of others are of little use in the present study. The letters of two Englishmen are particularly interesting in that the travellers were keen observers, yet not involved in the personal conflicts or national strifes which took place over the finds in the necropolis. C. L. Irby and J. Mangles, commanders in the royal navy, who had been most active in digging out the temple at Abu Simbel with Belzoni during that summer when the local work force failed him, did extensive sightseeing at Thebes during the few days they spent there on their way back to Cairo. Their letters home were later published in the form of a diary.(9) On the 17th August 1817 they spent all day visiting the private tombs at Qurna, Belzoni himself and Beechey, secretary to Salt, being their expert guides. The later part of the day was spent as follows:

> 'We now went to inspect a newly discovered tomb, that well recompensed us for the trouble. Having crawled in by a small hole barely sufficient for the body to be squeezed trhough, we entered a small sepulchral antechamber adjoining to a tomb filled with mummies. From the finished style of the decorations of this chamber, we concluded that it must have been the tomb of some noble family; the paintings are all in fresco, and so wonderfully well preserved, that not the least scratch or stain is visible; the pure white ground of the wall not being tinged with yellow. Amongst the groups we noticed an interesting troop of six female musicians, dressed in white robes reaching down to their ankles; over this they have a sort of black, loose woollen net hanging over their shoulders, and reaching down to their waist. Their hair is jet black, plaited in ringlets, reaching down from the outer part of the eyelids all round the head, and has, at first sight, the appearance of a veil. They are walking in procession and playing at the same time: the leader has a harp with fourteen strings; then comes a girl with a guitar, which is not unlike that now in use; then one with a lute, handsomely shaped; after which comes another girl clapping her hands, apparently keeping time; then another with a sort of double pipe: this instrument is played on like a clarionet, and is long and

slender; both the tubes are of equal length. The procession closes with a female beating on a tambourine, which is this shape: .The gestures of these musicians, with their uplifted eyes, would lead one to suppose they were playing some impassioned air. The preservation of this painting is astonishing, the colours being perfectly fresh, and no part whatever in the least defaced. What would not the French(10) have given for such a specimen to put in their splendid work? There is nothing throughout Egypt to be compared to it. In this apartment there are figures of two male harpers; both are squatted down, and playing on smaller instruments than that just described, having only nine strings each: one is playing alone, the other is accompanied by a man playing on a guitar. These last-mentioned musicians are bare-headed, and have bare feet; they are apparently elderly men. There are many other groups. The sacred Bull (Apis) is here most magnificently ornamented, and is a handsomer animal than it generally is. The ceiling of the apartment is divided into four compartments, each of which is painted with a different device. Adjoining the chamber, and connected by means of a small well, is a tomb filled with mummies, amongst which are the fragments of a mummy-case, richly painted and glazed. Some of the bodies are covered with canvas, over which is a coat of plaster painted. We found concealed in the envelope of the corpses some of the small ornaments of earthenware, called Nilometers(11)' (pp. 45-6).

There can be no doubt that Irby and Mangles described the orchestra of female musicians now in the Bankes collection, apart from the fact that the 'handsomely shaped lute' is in actual fact a lyre and the 'guitar' is a lute. The number of strings in the harp agrees with that given by Belzoni (fourteen). One of the male harpists with bald head and playing a smaller harp with nine strings is probably the other published fragment in the Bankes collection, whereas the other harpist and his lute-playing companion appear on an unpublished fragmen in the collection.

Another visitor to Thebes in the autumn of 1817 left not only a description but also a drawing of one of the scenes in a tomb which is undoubtedly our tomb. Colonel J. Straton (cf. note (6)) was present at Thebes at one of the animated arguments which took place between Salt and Belzoni.(12) This happened some time during or after the month of November, as Salt only arrived in upper Egypt around this time Straton left a description of the tombs at Qurna,(13) and he was one of the travellers taken round the necropolis by Belzoni on 13th October that year. The drawing given by Straton shows a female orchestra which corresponds to the description by Irby and Mangles and to the painting in the Bankes collection, the only major difference being that the clapper and the oboe player are reversed. The rectangular tambourine which occurs in the scene is not a frequently depicted instrument, and the scene does not belong in any of the known tombs.

As Straton's description adds important new elements to the decoration of the tomb, it will be quoted *in toto*.

'In the cavern where the dancing girls are painted on the walls, the first figure, on entering, is a male harper sitting, as is still the practise in these countries, with his legs across: his head is shaved; and the harp has nine strings. Then follows the group of dancing girls represented in Plate X (Ill. 82). The upper part of the dress is red, and resembles hair; the lower part is white and transparent, without any folds. On a pannel above, in the same room, there is a row of five female guests seated, some on camp stools, others on chairs with four legs. Each of these females holds a lotus flower in the right hand, turned towards the nose, and the left hand rests on the knee. In the pannel under the dancers, is another row of seated females; the hair is matted, thickened, and made wig-like, with grease or oil, exactly as the Nubians of the present day wear their hair.

On the adjoining wall is seated a female, having on her knee a young boy, his face turned towards her, holding the crook in his right hand, and the sacred Tor(14) in his left, with a figure of the Scarabaeus suspended from his neck, like the Bulla worn by the Roman youth of distinction. From the attributes, it is probably meant to represent Isis and Orus.

On another wall are two harpers cross legged. One of the harps has seven, and the other fourteen strings... A mummy-pit adjoins the chambers, containing several mummies in a tolerable state of preservation, but none of them were in cases. They were all in linen, which was wrapped round in vast quantities; this linen had a border and fringe, and was, as well as the thread, in perfect preservation.'

On the basis of the information given by these early travellers and the existing fragments it is possible to gain a good idea of the appearance of this hitherto unknown tomb.

The date of the tomb

The style of the paintings and the subjects depicted point to a date around the middle of the Eighteenth dynasty. The rectangular tambourine in the female orchestra is a reliable criterion for dating, as this instrument only occurs in this context during a limited period, namely in the reigns of Tuthmosis III, Amenophis II and Tuthmosis IV.(15)

Bankes mentions that a king was represented and/or named several times in the tomb, and that the name in question occurred on the Abydos tablet which he himself had found and copied.(16) The relevant kings, apart from Amosis, Amenophis I and III and Ḥaremḥab, who must be excluded for stylistical reasons, are Tuthmosis II and III, Amenophis II and Tuthmosis IV. As very few tombs have any mention of Tuthmosis II, the choice appears to stand between the remaining three, Ḥatshepsut being omitted on the Abydos tablet. Representations of the sovereign are frequent during all three reigns, but as Bankes specifically refers to 'one of the earliest sovereigns of that dynasty', Tuthmosis III seems the most likely candidate. For reasons explained below, Amenophis II is the second alternative.

The decoration of the tomb

According to Belzoni the tomb had a 'portico and subterraneous cavity where the mummies are', *i.e.* a decorated chamber and a shaft. He compared it to the tomb he described immediately before which had two decorated chambers. Straton also mentions 'chambers' and a mummy pit. As two of the subjects depicted on the walls are very frequent on the walls of T-shaped tombs, it remains a possibility that our tomb conformed to this pattern. But Irby and Mangles mention just one room ('a small sepulchral antechamber adjoining to a tomb filled with mummies'). As it is difficult to fit in a representation of the sovereign in a tomb which is not T-shaped, it is possible that the tomb lacked the long passage and that the adjoining two rooms, in any case of modest proportions, would be described as one.

The scenes depicted were the following:

1) representation(s) of the sovereign (referred to by Bankes)
2) nurse with young king (referred to by Straton)
3) the tomb owner offering on braziers (fragment in the Bankes collection)
4) banquet (two fragments in the Bankes collection; drawings by Bankes and Straton; references by Bankes, Finati, Belzoni, Irby and Mangles, Straton)
5) musicians on another wall (fragment in the Bankes collection; references by Irby and Mangles, and Straton)
6) an 'Apis' bull (mentioned by Irby and Mangles)

The scenes will be discussed separately.

1) Representation(s) of the reigning king

This subject occurs frequently on one or both rear walls of the transverse hall of a T-shaped tomb, being arranged symmetrically at the doorway to the inner room(s). The remark by Bankes presumably refers to a representation of this type.(17) We may therefore imagine one or two large scale representations of the king, Tuthmosis III or Amenophis II, in this place, with the tomb owner facing him, possibly with scenes relating to his particular duties on the remaining part of one of the walls. The name and occupation of the tomb owner being unknown, the nature of this scene cannot be determined.

2) Nurse with young king

Straton's mention of a scene showing a woman nursing a prince does not exclude the presence of the one or two conventional scenes of the sovereign. In fact most tombs with nursing scenes include a representation of the king, although it is not always obvious of the reigning king is the same as the young prince being nursed, or whether the prince is his son.(18)

The existence of a nursing scene in the tomb suggests that either the tomb owner's wife or his mother had held the post of nurse to the king's eldest son. Among the infants in question at a period compatible with the date of the tomb are Tuthmosis III, Amenophis II and Tuthmosis IV. Being biographical the subject is not very frequent in the tombs, as a very limited number of women would have held the office of nurse to the future king.

In order to establish the sequence of royal nurses in the period concerned a list has been drawn up(19) (see the following page). It is assumed here that nurses who were wives of tomb owners were either nurses to the king of the following reign or to the king in whose reign the tomb was decorated, and that mothers of tomb owners were nurses to the king who was contemporary with the tomb owner, their son.

infant concerned	name of nurse	title	source	date
Tuthmosis III	Taiunet	royal nurse	mother of TT 86	Tuthmosis III
"	Neferiꜥoḥ	chief nurse	mother of TT 39	"
"	Ipu	chief nurse	mother of CG 23034	"
Amenophis II(?)	unknown	chief nurse of the Lord of the Two Lands	mother of TT 98	Tuthmosis III - Amenophis II(?)
"	Baky	"	wife of TT 85	Tuthmosis III - Amenophis II
Amenophis II	Ḥunay	"	mother of TT 84 and TT 95	Amenophis II
"	Amenemopet	royal nurse	mother of TT 93	"
"	Ḥenuttawy	royal nurse	mother of Kaemimen	"
Amenophis II or Tuthmosis IV	Neit	chief nurse of the Lord of the Two Lands	wife of TT 88	"
"	Sentnay	chief nurse	wife of TT 96	"
"	Sentnefert	royal nurse	wife of TT 96	"
Tuthmosis IV	Nefertwaḥ	nurse of the king's son Men-kheprurēꜥ	wife of TT 350	"
	Nebtkabeny	chief nurse	CG 34117	"

A nurse of a named future king, or a 'nurse of the Lord of the Two Lands' would be nurse to the future king himself, the chief royal nurse and 'royal nurse' perhaps including his sisters and/or brothers in their care. 'Royal nurse' may also be interpreted as 'king's nurse' and this taken to refer to one child only.

Among these nurses, the husbands of two(20) are not accounted for. One is Amenemopet, who was nurse to Amenophis II and represented in the tomb of her son.(21). The other is Ḥenuttawy, whose son is known from several Theban monuments, although no tomb of his has as yet been discovered.(22) As his name has been found on several funerary cones, he was obviously the owner of a tomb in the necropolis. Kaemimen was fourth prophet of Amūn and second prophet of Amūn in the mortuary temple of Tuthmosis III, Ḥenketꜥankh, and he had also been a *ẖrd n kꜣp*, a title deignating the children of high officials brought up with the royal children.

It is tempting to identify Kaemimen with the owner of the Bankes tomb. It would account for the frequent mention of the name of 'one of the earliest sovereigns of that dynasty',(23) as the royal name would be part of the tomb owner's titles, although we may then have to assume that the representation of the reigning king would accordingly depict Amenophis II instead of Tuthmosis III, who would have departed, if the tomb was decorated after the tomb owner has become his mortuary priest.(24)

With the exception of the owners of the tombs at Deir el-Medîna and some of the viziers of the Eighteenth dynasty it is not very often that a family relationship can be established between tomb owners in the Theban necropolis.(25) Albeit an argument *ex silentio* it may suggest that the person depicted as a royal nurse in the Bankes tomb was the mother of Kaemimen, depicted in the tomb of her son, and that she and her husband had no elaborate tomb of their own. As to the other possible candidates among the nurses, there is no tangible evidence pointing to their having had a tomb of their own, the tombs of their sons being mostly known already.(26) If the Bankes fragments can be attributed to a lost tomb of Kaemimen, it should be reconsidered whether any of the two known statues of Kaemimen stem from the tomb. In his study of the statues (pp. 10-11) de Buck takes the Louvre statue to have been a votive statue set up in Ḥenketʿankh, and the Leiden statue to have been a similar monument, probably in the temple of Amūn at Karnak. These assumptions are based on the mention of offerings of the relevant deities to be passed on to Kaemimen and his family. On the Louvre group the name of Amūn has been hacked out, whereas on the Leiden statue it was left intact.

The Louvre statue group(27) was apparently set up by the son of Kaemimen, who made the name of his parents 'live' in this way, probably, as de Buck suggests, by placing it in the mortuary temple of Tuthmosis III, where it did not escape the chisel of the followers of the Aten.

The Leiden statue, of which the upper half is missing, was also, according to de Buck, a votive temple statue, probably at Karnak, as Amūn of Karnak is the chief deity mentioned in the inscriptions. De Buck was unable to trace the modern history of the statue beyond the owner from whom the museum acquired it, and her father, the artist Lion Cachet, who presumably bought it. But the statue was actually seen by Lepsius in a house opposite TT 32 at Khôkha.(28) It is highly unlikely that the statue should have been ferried across the river, and it remains a possibility that, in spite of the god invoked being Amūn of Karnak, it came from the tomb itself. After all, Amūn of Karnak played a major part in the annual feast in the necropolis. If the statue stood in the tomb, it would explain why the inscriptions were left intact. It does not provide an answer to when and why the top part of the statue was cut off. Perhaps it was done by the local inhabitants for easier handling and sale of the more atractive top half.

After this excursus on the possible identity of the owner of the Bankes tomb the remaining scenes will be discussed.

3) The tomb owner offering on braziers (Ill. 78)
Measurements: h 53.5cm, w 68cm
Bibliography: *Top. Bibl.* I^2,2 p. 820; Davies, *Eg. Tomb Paintings*, pl. 2 (29)

The scene showing the tomb owner facing right and offering on braziers is part of the scene featuring the Feast of the Valley, a common theme in early and mid-Eighteenth dynasty tombs. The scene in the Bankes collection would be positioned on the right front wall of the hall, possibly with another similar scene on the other side of the entrance doorway.

The tomb owner offers loaves of bread, fowl and a piece of meat(?). He wears a wig elaborately rendered in drops of liquid plaster painted black (now a greyish black),(30) and a semitranslucent garment. Some hieroglyphs pertaining to the scene remain at the lower extremity of the vertical columns of text: or ... ..., and below an with a thin red line in front is visible. The grafitto of the serpent is a later addition, showing that the tomb was accessible some time after the burial.

Below such scenes of offering would be a sub-scene with butchers and/or offering bringers, and next to it a banquet scene. The fragments described below may well belong on the same wall.

4) Banquet
a) harpist (Ill. 79)
Measurements: h 56.5cm, w 37cm
Bibliography: *Top. Bibl.* I^2,2, p. 820;
(1895), pl. 8 [48] ; Davies, *Eg. Tomb Paintings*, pl. 6.

The fragment shows a squatting male harper playing a ladle-shaped harp with nine strings and nine pegs, and decorated with a female head.(31) The upper end of the suspension rod appears to be shaped like a falcon's head, an unusual feature. It is tied to the main body of the harp with lashings. The harpist is represented with his eye intact.(32) His mouth is open to indicate that he is singing. The right (lower) hand plucks the third string. The fingers of the left hand are twisted around the same string. The columns intended for the harpist's song were left blank.

The fragment belongs on the top part of the wall, as the polychrome border shows. The upper border consists of poppy petals and mandrake fruits. Superimposed on the top half of the border there is another consisting of inverted lotus flowers and bunches of grapes.(33) The upper edge appears to have been skillfully restored when the fragment was framed.

To the left of the harpist a vertical line indicates the end of this section of the scene. But the top border continues, so this was by no means the end of the wall. A few fragments of painting survive from the register below. It shows the top part of a man facing left (black mass of hair and a tiny speck of red indicating the colour of male skin). Behind him a lotus flower is being held by another person, and a bunch of lotus flowers rests on a pile of offerings(?). For the context of this scene cf. below.

b) female orchestra (Ills. 81 and 82)
Measurements: h 54cm, w 137cm
Bibliography: *Top. Bibl.* I^2,2, p. 820; Straton, *op. cit.* with pl. 10 (excluding servant and offerings); Bankes MSS.ii.A 7 (five musicians); Davies, *Eg. Tomb Paintings*, pl. 5 (excluding three musicians)

Some red sketch lines remain above the shoulders of the servant and among the offerings. The eyes and eyebrows of the figures have been touched up in modern times. The painting is now in a very fragile condition and has apparently suffered a great deal from being exposed to European living conditions.

The orchestra includes six musicians, all drawn by Straton and referred to by Belzoni and Irby and Mangles. The musicians are preceded by a male servant with a shallow yellow bowl in one hand and two minute white jars in the other. He is advancing towards a heap of offerings including loaves of bread, onions, a cucumber, fowl, meat, baskets and bunches of grapes, a mat with some unidentifiable objects, and flowers. These items rest on an offering table reaching down to the base line of the register below. Beyond it, and at a larger scale, was presumably a representation of the tomb owner and his wife, facing right and receiving the offerings and the music.

Irby and Mangles mention a 'black, loose woollen net hanging over their shoulders', the garment being referred to by Straton as '... red, and resembles hair'. Davies on the other hand says that 'the scene has the appearance of damage resulting from the effect of smoke.' When Irby and Mangles saw it, it was in prime condition: '... the paintings are... so wonderfully well preserved that not the least stain or scratch is visible; the pure white ground of the wall not being even tinged with yellow'. The area of painting taken up by the 'black net' (or 'red hair'; the strokes of the brush are indeed reminiscent of fur) corresponds to the area stained yellow on garments of mid and late Eighteenth dynasty date.(34) Although yellow ochre usually wears well, it is possible that some change has taken place where this coat of paint was applied. It is, however, difficult to understand how Irby and Mangles could have seen it as black. Perhaps the reference is not to the stained part of the garments at all, but to the wigs, which are indeed black and may resemble net.

The bodies of the women have the conventional yellow colour. The dresses from hip level are white and transparent over the limbs. All the girls except the harpist wear a hip belt underneath the garment. The wigs are black with many individual strands of curly hair, decorated with a floral diadem and a lotus flower. The ear-rings are very large and disc-shaped, the necklaces of different designs.

The harp has at least twelve strings and at least eight black pegs alternating with seven red ones. The soundbox of the instrument is polychrome with ringlets and lotus flowers. The musician plucks the third string with her left (upper) hand, her right forefinger and thumb touching the fifth string. The lute is of the very elongated, long-necked type, played with a plectrum attached to the instrument with a string. The lyre is an asymmetrical lyre with a trapezoidal soundbox. The left hand of the musician is spread out to deaden the sound of all strings but one, the other hand is not visible. The instrument appears to have nine strings. The double oboe has tubes of equal length, and the rectangular tambourine is of the usual type with concave sides, being held in one hand and beaten with the other. A dark vertical line behind the player concludes the scene.

Of the register above enough remains to determine the nature of the scene. It shows another register of guests at the banquet, but only the feet are left. A standing servant girl faces five men on folding chairs and straight stools. The mat does not extend beyond the fifth man, thus suggesting the end of the register.

Even less remains of the register below the musicians. To the right are the heads of two male servants facing left, on a smaller scale than the guests. To the left are the upper parts of three black wigs with yellow unguent cones. To the left of these three guests were two(?) vertical columns of text, including a 𓄤. A portion is then missing, but below the large offering table in the register above there is an unidentifiable yellow area.

According to Straton the scene had at least three registers: a) five seated females; b) dancing girls and orchestra; c) row of seated female. The lower row of guests, of which only the cones are visible, may well be females, but in the top register the body colour of the participants is definitely red, and the guests must therefore be men. On the same wall was the harpist ('the first register on entering'). The scene was thus positioned on one of the front walls of the hall, where the Feast of the Valley is usually to be found. As the harpist turns in the opposite direction of that of the female orchestra, he was probably shown accompanying the tomb owner in the offering scene described above, facing right towards the entrance doorway. The height of the register with the musicians is 39cm; the height of the register with the harpist is 39.5cm. The figure of the tomb owner when complete was about 130cm. The distribution of the scenes on the wall was probably roughly as follows:

[tomb owner and wife receiving offerings]	five male guests servant + orchestra female guests	harpist	tomb owner offering	ENTRANCE
(sub-scene)				

5) musicians on another wall (Ill. 80)
Measurements: h 43cm, w 50cm
Bibliography: none

This scene is not to be confused with the banquet scene just described. Straton explicitly says that it was 'on another wall'. The sources agree that two squatting harpers are represented in the tomb. According to Irby and Mangles the instruments had nine strings each, whereas Straton counted seven and fourteen. One of these harps was not joined by other instruments, whereas the other was accompanied by a 'guitar', by which Irby and Mangles would mean a lute.

One of the fragments in the Bankes collection, not previously published, shows a squatting harpist and a standing lutist. The height of the register in which the musicians perform is 31cm. Both face left and wear white underkilts, a pink vest and a long white tunic. A previous sketch in red is visible behind the lutist. The eyes of both men have been retouched in modern times. The lute is the same very elongated instrument as that played in the girls' orchestra and is also played with a plectrum. The harp was also sketched differently before the final drawing. The instrument has nine strings and nine black, triangular pegs. The circular decoration on the soundbox is in red and green, and a lotus flower ornates the extremity. The stand has the habitual Isis knot. The shape of the head decorating the tip of the instrument is difficult to determine. The harpist plucks the fourth string with his left (lower) hand, while the right hand plucks the sixth string.

Behind the lutist a light blue vertical line suggests the end of the scene. In front of the harpist a sketched line in red indicates a column intended for an inscription.

The fragment belonged on the top part of a wall, a polychrome border being visible, possibly with a floral border above. In a register below the musicians there are traces of a mass of green (papyrus?), with a faint red vertical line to the right.

The combination of lute and harp with no other instruments, except perhaps voices, is not found elsewhere in the Eighteenth dynasty,(35) but the scene is perhaps to be compared with the one in TT 343 (temp. Tuthmosis III) where the lute and harp are joined by a flute-player and clappers in another register.(36) The context of this scene features the tomb owner receiving offerings, with parents and guests being present.

6) An 'Apis' bull

In the tomb Irby and Mangles saw a representation of 'the sacred bull (Apis)' more impressive than any other bull they had seen. The Apis being chiefly a Memphite god, its presence in a Theban tomb would be most unusual, although it does occur once in a Saite tomb (TT 33). As the bull in question was 'magnificently ornamented' it can hardly have been one in a herd of cattle being counted before the tomb owner, nor perhaps even an offering bull such as the handsome specimen depicted in TT 101.(37) A bull and seven cows of divine nature occur in a few tombs of the early Eighteenth dynasty (TT 71, 82, 353), all in a funerary context and represented either in the burial chamber or the innermost part of the tomb.

In the above-mentioned TT 101 there is another splendid bull, depicted back to back with a representation of Amenophis II receiving gifts. The scene is a rare one,(38) but it may be the best parallel to the bull depicted in the Bankes tomb.

The scenes described above can be positioned in the tomb as in the sketch on the following page, the placement of the sovereign and the tomb owner being almost certain. The banquet scene followed behind the offering, and the woman nursing the royal infant was on an adjoining wall.

The position of the harpist and lutist remains uncertain, but in TT 93 a girl lutist, a harpist and clappers appear to perform to the young king on the lap of the nurse.

No tomb was complete without representations of the funeral procession, but the early travellers left no records of this subject, nor are there any other fragments in the Bankes collection showing such episodes.

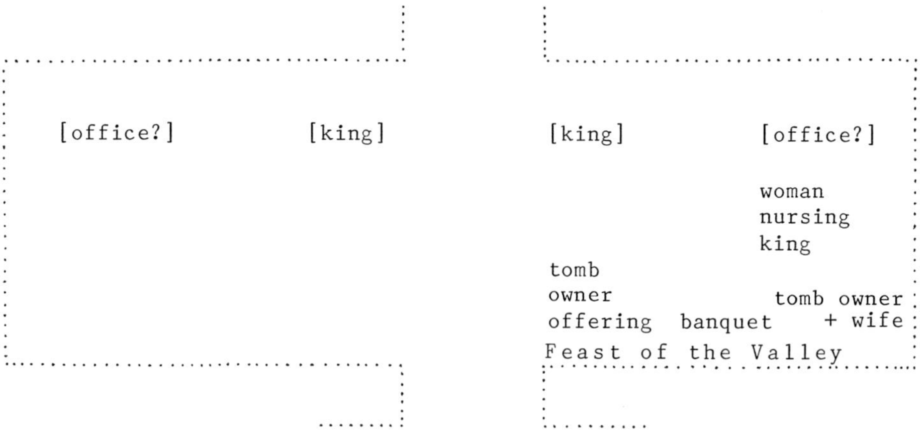
[office?]
[king]
[king]
[office?]
woman nursing king
tomb owner offering
banquet
tomb owner + wife
Feast of the Valley

Appendix I: Fragments of Painted Decoration from Known Tombs

During the course of the the investigations for the main part of this work a great many fragments of painted tombs were studied for possible identification with a 'lost' tomb. Though many remain anonymous it was thought appropriate to include a list of these as well of the fragments which can be attributed to tombs already known.

TT 15 TETIKY  king's son, mayor in the Southern City
Early Dyn. XVIII.

The tomb was excavated by Carter and Carnavon during the years 1907-11. A brief report with photographs was published,(1) and later Davies drew the wall-decoration.(2)

In 1977 a painted fragment from the tomb came up for sale:
Seated man → and shoulder of another →. *Christie's ... Antiquities and Primitive Art ... Dec. 5, 1977*, no. 79, pl. xiii.
In situ: Carnavon & Carter, *op. cit.*, pl. iii.

TT 38 ZESERKARA^{c} SONB 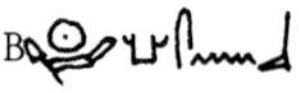 scribe, counter of grain in the granary of divine offerings of Amūn.
Temp. Tuthmosis IV.

The tomb was opened by Hay. He left his autograph on one of the walls, and copied substantial parts of the decoration. It was cleared in the 1880's and published by Scheil in 1894.(3) At that time it was in a far better condition than when Davies began copying it in 1908. His drawings were published by his wife more than half a century later.(4)

In 1946 Fakhry published a list of tombs from which pieces had been cut during the years 1937-42.(5) Two fragments from TT 38 were located by Fakhry as having been sold to a dealer in Cairo:

1) Servant girl →. Fakhry, *op. cit.*, pl. VII [left]. This fragment was later reproduced in B. de Rachewiltz, *Egyptian Art*, London 1960, fig. 63.
   In situ: Fakhry, *op. cit.*, fig. 7 = Davies, *op. cit.*, pl. VI.
2) Upper part of a female guest. Fakhry, *op. cit.*, pl. VII [right].
   In situ: as 1)

A third fragment from the tomb was not traced by Fakhry:

3) Two female guests ←, now in the Israel Museum, Jerusalem,

Inv. no. 69.71.231. *Israel Museum News*, 8, 1970 (back cover); E. Brunner Traut, *Die alten Ägypter*, Stuttgart 1976, colour pl. II (without provenance).
In situ: as 1)

More fragments than these have been cut from the walls of the tomb, notably the heads of two of the musicians,(6) but their present whereabouts remain unknown.

TT 40 AMENḤOTP, called ḤUY, viceroy of Kush, governor of the South Lands.
Temp. Amenophis IV - Tutʿankhamūn.

The tomb was discovered by Wilkinson some time before 1828, and it was later visited and copied by Champollion, Hay, Nestor l'Hôte and Lepsius among others. Especially the drawings of the latter two are important as part of the decoration was destroyed when Davies began his work there in 1925(?).(7) The tomb had been inhabited and was only cleared by the end of the century.

One fragment, bought at Cassira (a dealer in London) in 1958, has been identfied:

Head of an Asian with tribute. Brussels 8024. Werbrouck in *BMRAH* 4e série, 30 année, 1958, pp. 102-4; Mekhitarian in *Serapis* 6 (1982), p. 89, fig. 6.
In situ: Davies, *op. cit.*, pl. 18 (from drawing by Lepsius).

Another tiny fragment (in two pieces) should be considered here, although a final identfication is hampered by the very fragmentary state of the piece as well as of the wall:

University Museum, Philadelphia L 55-229/230 (lent by the Pennsylvania Museum of Art in 1935), showing the nose, lips and hand (one piece) and part of the arm and dress (the second piece) of an Asian(?). The hand and nose are red, whereas the arm appears to be yellow, but this may be the sleeve of the garment. The rest of the cloth is blue with large black dots surrounded by six small light dots. Like the decoration from TT 40 it is painted on mud plaster mixed with straw. A first hand inspection of the original coloured drawing by Lepsius may reveal whether the fragment does indeed stem from TT 40.(8)

TT 52 NAKHT scribe, astronomer of Amūn.
Temp. Tuthmosis IV(?)

The tomb was cleared by Grébaut in 1889 and appears then to have been recently found. Drawings were made by Maspero and Boussac during the following decade, but nothing was recorded that was not included in the final publication bu Davies. Davies made his copies of the wall-paintings in the season 1908-09.(9) At that time one of the walls was somewhat destroyed: 'A part has been lost by the falling of the stucco surface'.(10) The wall in question(11) included the banquet scene, of which two registers of female guests had been damaged.

A small fragment, now in four pieces (Ill. 85) on loan to The Brooklyn Museum (L70.1-4) since 1970, showing the upper part of two female guests, very probably once belonged to the banquet scene in the tomb of Nakht. Details in the fragment, such as the eyes, the combination of the two characteristic necklaces, the lotus diadems and lotus buds, as well as the garments and the way in which the locks of hair are arranged over the earrings are strikingly similar.

In the relevant plate of Davies' publication(12) the lower part of all the female guests is extant, and there is only one place where out two banqueting ladies would fit in: to the extreme left in the top register, where the three feet would belong to two women (not three, as the two lines of the legs show).(13)

TT 54 ḤUY, sculptor of Amūn.
Temp. Tuthmosis IV to Amenophis III(?).
Usurped by KENRO, *waᶜb*-priest, head of the magazine of Khons, early Dyn. XIX.

The tomb was discovered by Daressy but first mentioned in print by Mond, who cleared it in the spring of 1903.(14) Most of the scenes have since been photographed by the Oriental Instutute, Chicago, and the inscriptions were copied by Sethe.(15) Some details from the tomb have been published.(16)

The tomb was partly usurped in Ramessid times, leaving two walls of the original decoration of the Eighteenth dynasty intact: the funerary scenes, and the stela with surrounding scenes. Part of the former is destroyed or has been cut out. One fragment, purchased in Cairo in 1920, has recently been identified by Silverman:
Men and oxen from funerary procession,(17) Oriental Institute 11047.
Silverman in *Serapis* 6, 1982, pp. 125-33.

TT 63 SEBKḤOTP mayor of the Southern Lake and the Lake of Sobk.
Temp. Tuthmosis IV.

No complete publication has ever been undertaken of this tomb of which several fragments are in museums. A number of fragments which had fallen from the walls have been restored to their original positions, while others are still lying on the ground.

The tomb was known to the members of Lepsius' expedition. It was later photographed by the Egyptian expedition of the Metropolitan Museum of Art, and others have published selected details from this once beautiful tomb.

Most of the fragments were detached or collected from the tomb in the previous century. Many are in the *Topographical Bibliography* under TT 63 and these will therefore be only briefly dealt with here.

1) Two offering bringers. Metropolitan Museum of Art 30.2.1.(18)
Hayes, *Sceptre*, II, fig. 85; Russman in *BMMA*, Winter 1983-84, p. 28, no. 27 (with colour fig.), cf. p. 56.
Until 1930 the fragment was in a private collection in England.
2) Two offering bringers. British Museum 919. Porter & Moss do not give an exact position for this fragment in the tomb, but by comparison with 1), and the wall in its present state as published by Hermann,(19) there can be no doubt that BM 919 belongs to the right of the stela, giving the middle register and parts of the upper and lower registers, where the fragment in New York has the corresponding lower register with parts of the middle register and the sub-scene.
The fragment was acquired in 1869 from H. Danby Seymour.

3) Syrians with tribute in two registers, British Museum 37991.(20)

4) Nubians and Syrians in two registers. Florence 7608.(21)

5) Nubians with tribute in a top register. British Museum 922.(22)
The fragment was acquired in 1869 (as 2)).

6) Syrians with tribute and horses. British Museum 37987.
This fragment was not recognized by Porter & Moss as having come from TT 63.(23). It was acquired by the museum in 1852 from J. W. Wild, who was a member of Lepsius' expedition, and who visited the tomb and drew some sketches in it.(24) The style of the fragment is very similar to the above mentioned, and it would fit in somewhere to the right of BM 37991. On the fragment there remains part of the register above showing four yellow and two red feet.
The fragment is published in G. Cornfeld (ed.), *Adam to Daniel*, New York 1961, fig. pl. 337.

7) Bead workshop. British Museum 920.(25)
The position of this fragment was not given by Porter & Moss. But it must belong on the right front wall of the hall,(26) above right in relation to the granary, where two men, vases and rows of beads still remain (cf. also MMA Photo 2758).
The fragment was acquired in 1869 (as 2)).

8) Syrian vase. In a private collection.(27) J. Leclant (ed.) *L'Empire des Conquerants*, Paris 1978, fig. 72 (colour).
In situ: MMA Photo 2763 (lower row of three vases).

TT 66 ḤEPU , vizier.
Temp. Tuthmosis IV.

The tomb was known at the beginning of the century, and it was photographed by Wreszinski, later also by members of the Egyptian expedition of the Metropolitan Museum of Art, and by Schott. By then it was already in a very ruined state, some of the damage having been done in ancient times. Nina de Garis Davies drew the remaining wall-paintings before World War II, the better ones among them being published in 1963.(28) According to Fakhry,(29) pieces were cut out during 1937-42. An impression of the present condition og the tomb can be gathered from a photograph taken by me in 1970 showing the remains of the banquet orchestra.(30)

A fragment from the wall with the scenes of the funerary ritual(31) showing the upper part of a priest and the hand of another behind him has appeared on the art market: *Ägyptische Kunst. Münzen und Medaillen*. Basel, Auktion 49, 27 june 1974, no. 32 with fig. (without provenance). *In situ:* Davies, *op. cit.*, pl. xi [lower left].

Other fragments appear to have been cut out of this tomb as Fakhry noticed.

TT 78 ḤAREMḤAB 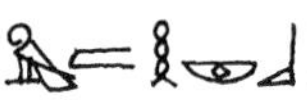, royal scribe, scribe of recruits.
Temp. Tuthmosis III to Amenophis III.

The tomb was well-known to the early travellers many of whom copied the scenes. Part of the decoration has since been destroyed. It was published by Bouriant in 1894,(32) cleared by Newberry in 1901, and restored by Mond and the Metropolitan Museum of Art in the years 1911-16. It has recently been published in full by A. and A. Brack.(33)

The tomb suffered deliberate destruction in ancient times, the owner, his wife and sometimes also other persons being mutilated completely or in part. Hieroglyphs written in blue or green appear to have been washed off with a sponge in order to re-use the pigment. A number of very small unidentifiable fragments were found when the tomb was studied in the 1970's. A larger fragment has been in Florence(34) since the time of Rosellini:

Two men dragging a boat. Museo Archeologico no. 2470. Berend, *Principaux monuments*, pp. 3-6; Wreszinski, *Atlas*, i,250; Brack, *op. cit.*, pl. 74a.
In situ: Wilkinson, *Manners and Customs*,iii.37 (no. 333) = ed. Birch, ii. 102 (No. 361).

According to information obtained from the Egyptian Antiquities Organization January 1984, some fragments were recently cut from the tomb, but most of them were retrieved and replaced on the walls.

TT 87 MINNAKHT overseer of the granaries of Upper and Lower Egypt, overseer of horses of the Lord of the Two Lands, royal scribe.
Temp. Tuthmosis III.

Hay and Lepsius were among the early travellers who knew this tomb. It was briefly published by Virey in 1891,(35) and photographed by Mond in 1914-16.(36) Some of the walls were already destroyed or had been left unfinished, while others were in good condition.

The wall with the funerary ceremonies(37) was photographed by Swaan in recent times,(38) and shows the paintings virtually intact. But since then the wall has suffered considerable damage, and a number of fragments have appeared on the art market.

1) Three men → carrying a chest. *Fine Antiquities from the Collections of the Late Joseph Müller of Solothurn, Switzerland. Christie's, London, 14th June 1978*, no. 394, pl. 87; *Apollo*, vol. 107, no. 196, June 1978, p. 60 (advertising the above sale); *Important Classical, Western, Asiatic & Egyptian Antiquities, Christie's, New York, 25th January 1979*, no. 176. (All without giving the provenance).
In situ: Mond Photo 17038, cf. *GM* 50, 1981, figs. pp. 8 and 10.
2) Man → with two vases and lotus flowers. *Christie's, London (op. cit.)*, no. 395, pl. 88; *Christie's, New York (op. cit.)*, no. 177. (Without provenance).
In situ: Mond Photo, cf. *GM* 50, 1981, fig. p. 10 [lower, centre], and Nims, *op. cit.*, fig. 60.

The butchers in the top register and other pieces have also been removed and are now with dealers. In January 1984 the wall was found to be almost completely cut to pieces with only a few patches of decoration left.

TT 93 ḲENAMŪN , chief steward of the king.
Temp. Amenophis II.

The tomb was copied by Davies in 1914-15 and thereafter, but it had already been entered by the early travellers (Hay, Wilkinson, Champollion, Lepsius and Prisse) neither of whom copied any of the scenes which were missing when Davies began. According to the latter(40) 'the few robberies from the walls were made before Hay's day, and none of the pieces removed seems to be extant'. When Mond cleared the tomb in 1903 no fragments were recorded as having fallen from the walls.

Since Davies' publication some fragments have found their way to the art market. Other fragments, removed from a tomb towards the end of the previous century, must also be considered in connection with this tomb.

The fragments which can easily be identified with the corresponding scenes in Davies' publication are the following:

1) Papyrus thicket. The fragment appears in G. Cornfeld (ed.), *Adam to Daniel*, New York 1961, fig. p. 133.
   In situ: Davies, *Ḳen-Amūn*, ii, pl. LI,A.
2) Head of an attendant →. Along with the following two fragments this one came up for sale at Christie's in 1975: *Christie's, Important Antiquities* &c., July 16, 1975, no. 147, pl. 12 [upper]. This and the following fragments are now in Los Angeles.
   In situ: Davies, *Ḳen-Amūn*, i, pl. LII [lower right].
3) Heads and shoulders of two male guests ←. *Christie's* no. 148, pl. 12 [lower].
   In situ: Davies, *Ḳen-Amūn*, i, pl. LII [second row from the top].
4) Upper part of a man with arrow→. *Christie's*, no. 149, pl. 13.
   In situ: Davies, *Ḳen-Amūn*, i, pls. LII-LIII.

All these fragments come from the same wall (right wall of passage). No provenance was suggested in the sale catalogue.

One of the main characteristics of the tomb of Ḳenamūn is the yellow colour used for the background. In the Eighteenth dynasty this is extremely rare (except for the few tombs of this date at Deir el-Medîna).(41) The decoration was executed with the utmost care and with exceptional attention to detail (for example in the now very fragmentary hunting scene). But the way in which the plaster has fallen off and bared the first layer of brown mud plaster with the red lines of the grids is also characteristic of this tomb. A number of fragments now in the Staatliche Kunstsammlungen in Dresden show exactly the same features, and it is tempting to suggest the tomb of Ḳenamūn as their place of origin. The fragments were bought in Luxor by Herr R. Dietz of Dresden in 1885 and were given to the museum in 1911.

5) No. 757a (Ill. 84). Eight fragments mounted together: [a] male guest →at a banquet, with the hand and foot of another →, and the elbow of a third→; [b] arms and legs of a standing man ← with two tall bouquets and two birds; [c] head and shoulder of a similar man ←; [d] upper part of a lady ←, presumably from a banquet scene. The base line of an upper register is visible along the edge of the fragment; [e] - [g] three fragments of the zigzag pattern of a ceiling; [h] a small fragment with remains of polychrome hieroglyphs
   The fragments are mentioned in *Ägyptische Altertümer aus der Skulpturensammlung, Dresden. Staatliche Kunstsammlungen Dresden. Ausstellung im Albertinum Mai 1977*
6) No. 757b (Ill. 85). Two fragments, undoubtedly belonging together, showing the heads of a man ← and a woman ←. Remains of hieroglyphs above: ...  .
   Bibliography as 5).

7) No. 757 c(Ill. 86). Upper part of a seated couple. Remains of hieroglyphs above:
Bibliography as above, with colour pl. Also in J. Pijoan, *Summa Artis*[2], Madrid 1945, III, p. 460, fig. 614.

TT 93 has suffered in particular where banquet scenes were depicted, and there are hardly any large scale representations of Ḳenamūn and his wife. A possible position for no. 757a [a] and [d], and nos. 757b and c would be somewhere in the left part of the hall where male guests →, seated on straight-legged stools were once shown.(42)

The dress of the lady with one shoulder bare is also shown in TT 93,(43) and the technique of emphasizing the eyelid by a thin line (the 'banana line' of modern cosmetics) as on no. 757b has also been used for the lutist in the tomb.(44)

In no. 757c the wig is rendered in black on a greyish-blue background. This type of wig has been studied by Mackay who recorded it in four Theban tombs.(45) This was presumably a way of rendering in paint an effect elsewhere achieved by the artist using small drops of gypsum,(46) giving a relief effect to a wall which was otherwise only painted.

The men's necklaces are very elaborate, and the one on no. 757b rather similar to one shown in TT 38. The arm band of the woman, set just below the elbow, also has a parallel in this tomb.(47).

Although some hieroglyphs remain above the couple in the two fragments they are not very helpful in identifying the persons. The before *mꜥ3 ḫrw* would appear to belong to the name of the man, except that the signs face in the wrong direction. But no tomb owner of the Eighteenth dynasty had a name with *n* as the last letter (there was always a determinative to follow, or the Amūn element was written first). The hieroglyphs could, however, be part of a phrase incorporating an expression such as 'the house of justification &c.',(48) followed by *in* 'by' and then the name, except that again the *m3ꜥ ḫrw* (but not the name) would be reversed.

TT 108 NEBSENY , first prophet of Onuris.
Temp. Tuthmosis IV(?)

The tomb was photographed by the Metropolitan Museum of Art and by Wreszinski, and a few of the scenes have been published by various scholars.

In 1896, before any work had been done in the tomb, one fragment of the wall-decoration was presented to the museum in Berlin by Dr. Carl Schmidt:

Head of the tomb owner with bouquet. Berlin 13616. mentioned in *Ausf. Verz.*, p. 156. Photograph in the Griffith Institute Archives, photo 42A.(49)

TT 130 MAY harbour-master in the Southern City.
Temp. Tuthmosis III(?)

The tomb was published by Scheil in 1894, but with hardly any drawings.(50) A few details were photographed by Schott or drawn by Baud and Davies, but it is almost impossible to gain an impression of this tomb on the basis of these works. Nevertheless M. Werbrouck was able to identify one fragment now in Brussels:

Six male mourners and two men carrying a chest. Brussels E 7962. Werbrouck in *CdE* 34, 1959, pp. 203-7 with fig.; Mekhitarian in *Serapis* 6, 1982, p. 88, fig. 5. The scene is part of the funeral procession, which is one of the comparatively few which moves from right to left, and therefore was placed in the right part of the tomb.(51)

TT 161 NAKHT  bearer of the floral offerings of Amūn.
Temp. Amenophis III(?)

When the early travellers visited this tomb, they found it in prime condition. Hay made superb water colours of most of the scenes,(52) and certain details of texts and pictures were copied by Cailliaud, Champollion, Rosellini, Prisse and Lepsius. The tomb has never been completely published.

In 1910 three fragments of the wall-decoration were acquired from a dealer in Cairo by the Ny Calsberg Glyptotek in Copenhagen. Their provenance was ascertained by van de Walle in 1965.(53)

1) ÆIN 1074. Man ⟵ offering before shrine. O. Koefoed-Petersen, *Catalogue des bas-reliefs et peintures égyptiens*, Copenhagen 1956, no. 67; van de Walle, *op. cit.*, p. 40, fig. 6.
In situ: ibid., fig. 5 [top right].(54)
2) ÆIN 1076. Upper part of a woman ⟵ adoring. Koefoed-Petersen, *op. cit.*, no. 68; van de Walle, *op. cit.*, pp. 37 and 40, fig. 4.
In situ: ibid., fig. 5 [top centre].(55)
3) ÆIN 1075. Man ⟶ with bouquet. Koefoed-Petersen, *op. cit.*, no. 66; van de Walle, *op. cit.*, pp. 35-7, fig. 2.
In situ: ibid., fig. 38.(56)

A fourth fragment is now in the Musée Rodin in Paris:

4) Prince Aḥmosi Sapair. Vandersleyen, 'L'identité d'Ahmes Sapair', *SAK* 10, 1983, pl. XVII [lower].

The tomb suffered damage during the years 1937-42,(57) but other fragments have not been located. In January 1984 many pieces were indeed found to be missing.

TT 162 ḲENAMŪN  mayor in the Southern City, overseer of the granary of Amūn.
Temp. Tuthmosis IV(?).(58)

The tomb is now inaccessible, having been reburied after its clearance in 1922. Davies copied some of what remained on the walls on the basis of photographs published by Daressy in 1895.(59). These drawings were published by Nina de Garis Davies in 1963.(60)

Since its discovery towards the end of the previous century the plaster has fallen from the walls, and pieces were stripped off for sale. Colour facsimiles of some of the fragments collected by Davies from the debris are now in the Metropolitan Museum of Art, cf. Davies, *op. cit.*, pp. 17-8, pl. xx.

TT 172 MENTIYWY 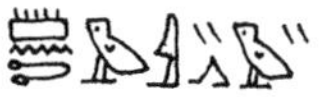 royal butler, child of the nursery.
Temp. Tuthmosis III - Amenophis II(?)

The tomb was known to some of the early travellers (Wilkinson and Lepsius), and it was thoroughly photographed by the Metropolitan Museum of Art. Until now only selected scenes have been published.

Some time before any photographs were taken pieces were cut from the walls. Two of them at least came to the Rustafjaell collection and are now in the Fitzwilliam Museum, Cambridge, having been presented to the museum by A. G. W. Murray.(61)

1) Upper part of a man → with quiver and bow case. E 83.1913 (Ill. 87) *Sotheby Sale Cat. [Rustafjaell], Dec. 9-10 1907,* no. 160 [b].
   For a photograph of the wall(62) with the fragment removed cf. MMA Photo 3082 [lower].
   The height of the lower register is 42cm. The size of a companion figure, measured from where the hand touches the skull to the waist line is 15.4cm. The dimensions of the Fitzwilliam fragment are h 26cm, w 18cm. The gesture of hand to head is repeated by several other figures on the same wall. There can be little doubt that the figure once belonged to the right of the four persons with chariots and similar equipment in the lower left corner of the left wall of the passage.
2) The goddess of the West ← seated. E 84.1913. (Ill. 88).

   For a photograph of the wall(63) with the fragment removed cf. MMA Photo 3079.
   The fragment undoubtedly belongs in the lower register, below the corresponding figures of Anubis and Osiris. The thrones are similar, so is the vertical red line behind the figures. The scepter of the divinities and the hieroglyphic inscription (mentioning adoration of the goddess of the Western desert) are equally faded. The dimensions of the fragment including part of the thick red base line is h 39cm, w 25cm. The height of the lower register in the tomb is 38.5cm.

A number of other pieces have been cut from the walls of the passage it is possible that these also ended up in the Rustafjaell collection; but due to the fact that their present whereabouts are unknown and that they were not illustrated in the sale catalogues an identification is at present impossible.

TT 181 NEBAMŪN  head sculptor of the Lord of the Two Lands
IPUKY 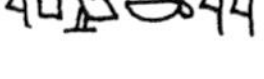 sculptor of the Lord of the Two Lands
Temp. Amenophis III - IV.

This tomb was one of those which suffered irreparable damage in the years 1937-42, as Fakhry's photograph shows.(64) Most of the fragments located so far appear to have entered the various museum collections in the 1960's and 1970's. By means of the publication by Davies from 1925(65) it would be easy to identify the fragments if and when they can be found. The tomb saw its first publication in 1894,(66) but it seems to have been unknown to the early travellers. Having been discovered in 1891(?), it was re-excavated in 1910-11, and fragments fallen from the walls replaced.

1) Upper part of Nebamūn offering at the Feast of the Valley. *Schimme Collection 1974,* no. 196; *Von Troja bis Amarna* (1978), no. 216 with colour pl.
   In situ: Davies, *op. cit.*, pl. v.
2) Upper part of Thepu, mother of Nebamūn, following her son at the Feast of the Valley. Brooklyn 65.197. *Égypte éternelle.*

Chef-d'oeuvres du Brooklyn Museum. Palais des Beaux Arts de Bruxelles 9 December 1976 - 20 February 1977, no. 40 with colour pl.; R. S. Bianchi, *Egyptian Treasures from the Collections of The Brooklyn Museum*, New York 1978, no. 8 with colour pl.
In situ: as 1).

3) Man with flowers, bird and incense(?) cone. Kestner Museum, Hanover, Inv. 1962,72. I Woldering, *Kestner-Museum 1889-1964*, no. 20 (without provenance).
In situ: as 1).
4) Five banqueting ladies and a servant girl. William Rockhill Nelson Gallery, Kansas City, no. 64-3. Museum slide (without provenance).
In situ: as 1).
5) Upper part of seated couple. Kestner Museum, Hanover, Inv. 1962,71. Woldering, *op. cit.*, no. 19.
In situ: as 1).

All the fragments 1) - 5) stem from the same wall.(67).

6) Two offering bringers. Royal Ontario Museum, Toronto. *Rotunda* I, no. 1, 1968, p. 22; R. L. Leprohon, *The World of Tutankhamon*, Toronto 1979, fig. on p. 15.
In situ: Davies, *op. cit.*, pl. VI [right, lower register].
7) Head of Thepu, mother of Nebamūn. In a private collection in Switzerland. Mekhitarian in *CdE* 30, 1955,pp. 318-22 and fig. 26.
In situ: Davies, *op. cit.*, pl. v.(68)
8) Upper part of a priest with scroll and another with a vase. *Schimmel Collection 1974*, No. 195; *Von Troja bis Amarna*, No. 215 (without provenance).
In situ: Davies, *op. cit.*,pls. xxiv-xxvi.(69)
9) Group of female mourners. Museum of Fine Arts, Boston, No. 68.555.
In situ: Davies, *op. cit.*, pl. xix.(70)
10) Head of Queen Aḥmosi Nefertere. Kestner Museum, Hanover, Inv. 1962,70. Woldering, *op. cit.*, no. 21; *Osiris, Kreuz und Halbmond*, Mainz am Rhein 1984, p. 79 (No. 65) with colour pl. and provenance. Cf. also Manniche in *AO* 40, 1979, p. 12, n. 4.
In situ: Davies, *op. cit.*, pl. ix.(71)
11) Upper part of a lady and shoulder of a man. Kestner Museum, Hanover, Inv. 1962,69. Woldering, *op. cit.*, no. 18.
In situ: Davies, *op. cit.*, pl. xxvii.(72)

TT 226 ḤEKARESHU  royal scribe, god's father, overseer of the royal nurses.
Temp. Amenophis III.

The identity of the owner of this tomb was established by Labib Habachi.(73) The tomb was almost completely destroyed when it was discovered in 1913, but numerous fragments were retrieved from the debris and the remains published by Davies.(74)

A scene with four children on the lap of the tomb owner was removed from a pillar and remounted by Mackay, but its present whereabouts has not been established. Other fragments are now in museums.

1) A large fragment (assembled by Nina and Norman de Garis Davies from numerous small pieces) showing Amenophis III seated in a kiosk. Luxor Museum, J. 134. *The Luxor Museum of Ancient*

Egyptian Art. Catalogue, Cairo 1979, No. 101 with pl. and colour pl. vii.

2) Three fragments of the ceiling. Metropolitan Museum of Art, 13.180.23/24/25. Unpublished.

TT 338 MAY 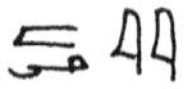 outline-draughtsman of Amūn.
Late Dyn. XVIII.

The exterior of this tomb must have been known in the early part of the previous century, for a lucarne-stela from the now destroyed pyramid was acquired by Bankes, and another stela from the tomb has been in the Turin museum for a century.(75)

The chapel was discovered by Schiaparelli in 1905. The following year the entire decoration was taken down and arranged in a facsimile chapel in the Turin Museum (Suppl. 7886).

To the references listed in the *Top. Bibl.* can now be added the following: E. Scamuzzi, *Egyptian Art in the Egyptian Museum of Turin*, New York 1965, pls. l-lii; M. Tosi, *La Cappella di Maia* (Quaderno n. 4 del Museo Egizio di Torino), Turin 1972; *id.*, *Une stirpe di pittori a Tebe* (Quaderno ... n. 7), Turin 1972, pl. II.

Cf. also the fragment listed below as no. 37.

Appendix II: The Turin Tomb

In the Museo Egizio in Turin there is a substantial number of smaller fragments of wall-decorations of Theban tombs. Some have a provenance, others do not. Among the latter, twelve fragments can be demonstrated to come from the same tomb, although the tomb in question cannot as yet be identified. The fragments were acquired by Schiaparelli in Egypt during the season 1900-1901.(1) As exhibited in the museum, they are not assembled, but fragments related by subject are kept together. The topics depicted are as follows:

1) Scenes from a laundry. Three fragments, Suppl. 1344, cf. *Top. Bibl.* I^2,2, p. 820; *Museo egizio ... Guida* [1965], p. 27.
2) Harvesting. Four fragments, Suppl. 1342, cf. references above.
3) Part of a banquet orchestra. Three fragments, Suppl. 1341, cf. references above.
4) Heads and shoulders of a man and a woman. One fragment, Suppl. 1348. This fragment was omitted by Porter & Moss.
5) Stewards supervising jars with siphons. One fragment, Suppl. 1343, cf. references as under 1) - 3).

All the fragments are reproduced in our Ills. 89-90.

1) The three fragments clearly belong together, although at present(2) they are incorrectly joined. The smallest and the largest piece are to be joined at the laundryman's vat. The remaining fragment joins to the left, the squatting female and the woman with the basket providing the link.

2) The four fragments of harvesters can be joined more accurately than at present. A small piece, showing the abdominal regions of the woman with a child to the right, is now missing, but was there when the museum photographs were taken.

The link between 1) and 2) is suggested by the vertical red and blue lines at the extreme right of the registers. Also the head and hand at the extreme left of 1) joins the body of the woman to the left in 2).

3) The three fragments of the banquet orchestra can be joined by means of the strings of the harp and the body of the dancing girl.

Behind the harpist, the red and blue lines when joined to the similar feature of the harvest scene indicate the position of the musicians as being above the harvesters and the laundrymen. The foot of the dancing girl and the feet of the harpist are just visible at the upper edge of 2). On the basis of the measurements provided by the museum, the height of this register can be estimated at about 44cm.

4) The dimensions of the register from which the man and the woman came can be restored to approximately the height of the register with the musicians. As the couple face to the right, there is some reason to believe that they belonged somewhere to the left in the register, probably with an offering table and other persons (musicians, and/or girl pouring drink or the like) in between.

5) The men with the jars bear such a close resemblance to the persons in 1) and 2) that they must belong in the same tomb. The fragment was positioned at the top part of the wall, as the top border of mandrake fruits and red flowers indicate.(3) In many tombs a representation of the tomb owner and his wife, with a large text above, face standing figures the height of the couple when seated, with two registers of persons at a smaller scale behind.(4) At the lower edge of the fragment a red vertical line is visible, possibly joining one of the dividing lines between the (empty) columns for hieroglyphs above the musicians. If the stand and jars conclude the register on the right, the projecting fragment of the lower register would fit in exactly where a corner has disappeared at the upper right edge of the fragment with the lutist.

The height of the wall as so far reconstructed amounts to about 108cm: register with musicians about 44cm, registers with harvesting and laundrymen about 20cm each, men with jars about 24cm. To this must be added a lower register just visible in 1), which, with an empty space along the lower part of the wall and a few centimetres added at the top,would bring the wall to about the height of man.

We are thus in the rare position of having almost the entire height of a wall consisting of twelve fragments. The musicians are drawn with an expert hand, whereas the servants and working people are rendered with a free sketchy line betraying the novelty of the scenes. Washing and/or dyeing(?) is only represented twice in Theban tombs,(5) one, TT 254, from the end of the Eighteenth dynasty, after the Amarna Period,(6) the other, TT 217, from the reign of Ramesses II.(7) In the latter, white lengths of cloth are plunged into or lifted out of vats on the river bank and stretched out in the sun, and no cloth of any other colour is to be seen. In our tomb the cloth is both red and white, and tightly wrung almost in the likeness of the hieroglyph . The lines visible on both colours may suggest folds in the cloth, unless the material depicted is not the woven cloth but the thread to be taken to a weaver's workshop. The girl on the left carries an object in her hand which may either be a piece of very crumpled cloth with a fringe (similar to the one the laundryman to the right is lifting from the vat), or a bundle of yarn held together with a string (the colours here are red lines on white). Weavers' workshops are rarely represented in Theban tombs,(8) but one of the scenes may give a clue to the proceedings in our fragment. In TT 133 (temp. Ramesses II) the weavers of the Ramesseum are represented in a lower register. Above are shown some of the activities prior to weaving. Several women are bringing material which looks very much like fleece or wool,(9) and it is also reminiscent of the material held by the girl to the left in the fragment.(10) In TT 133 it is yellow, and Davies and Gardiner suggested that it might be unbleached linen, as opposed to the white material used by the weavers in the workshop. The yellow colours in the Turin fragments are sometimes close to red (for example in the complexions of the musicians and the wife of the tomb owner), and it may be that the 'red cloth' in the laundry scene is in fact the unbleached strands of coarsely spun linen thread, and that the white material is the threads after bleaching. In support of this interpretation is the observation that the red material is being handed to the squatting woman, and white material is being carried away. It would also elucidate an obscure point in the washing scene in TT 217: why should the laundrymen use vats for washing the linen when the river is adjacent (even today the fellahîn take their laundry to be washed in the river). In this tomb as well it must be the process of bleaching which is represented.(11)

In view of the nature of this representation one should perhaps reconsider the harvesting scene above. Although some of the baskets used are similar to those usually containing grain, it is just possible that the harvesting of a different crop is represented here. The man to the extreme left pours something from a container into the woman's large sack. It appears to be coloured red, but it is difficult to identify. Theoretically the contents could be one of the several kinds of plants used for dyeing, although dyeing on a large scale does not appear to have taken place in Egypt.(12)

The servants with the siphons are also an unusual subject in the Theban tombs, though not unique. It occurs in two Ramessid tombs, TT 13(13) and TT 113.(14) Siphons were also used at el-Amarna,(15), and a well-known ostrakon from Deir el-Medîna shows an animal drinking through one.(16) In the latter instance the tube is bent like in our fragment and obviously only used for drinking. In TT 113 it is a siphon tube used to transfer liquid from one jar to another.(17) When using a siphon any residue in the wine or beer would be left undisturbed at the bottom of the jar.

In the *Topographical Bibliography* the servants with the siphons and the laundrymen were dated to the Nineteenth dynasty, but the harvesters and musicians to the Eighteenth dynasty. Although the unusual features in the Turin tomb appear to be mainly paralelled in Ramessid tombs, the banquet orchestra is a typically Eighteenth dynasty orchestra,(18) and, unless it was directly copied from an earlier tomb for an archaizing effect, it could hardly belong in any other period. The lute appears to be of the rare type with concave sides, first found in the late Eighteenth dynasty.(19) The garment worn by some of the harvesters appears to be a leather kilt with the characteristic solid 'patch' at the back which is seen during the Eighteenth dynasty, but no later than the Memphite tomb of Ḥaremḥab.(20) In order to arrive at a more precise date for the tomb the pre-Amarna character of the musician' faces and gestures should be balanced against the features which do not seem to occur until after this date: siphons, washing/dyeing scenes, the unusual shape of the lute. Although the style of the fragments is rather different from that seen in TT 254, which is more obviously influenced by Amarna art,(21) I would be inclined to suggest that the Turin tomb is roughly contemporary and dates from the end of the Eighteenth dynasty.

If the Turin tomb contained a weaving scene it is possible that this reflected the profession of the tomb owner. Only three tombs at Thebes belong to weavers or inspectors of weavers: TT 45 (temp. Ramesses II?); TT 133 (temp. Ramesses II); and TT 246 (Eighteenth dynasty). The title of the latter owner is derived from a funerary cone.(22) Another stamp in the *Corpus* (no. 334) suggests that one more weaving inspector, called 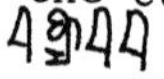 Iy, once had a tomb in the necropolis, but a proof of a connection between this man and the Turin tomb is as yet lacking.

Appendix III: Painted Fragments of Unknown Provenance

Ideally this chapter should not exist. But the 82 fragments listed here which have not been identified must be compared to the number which have been placed in a context, for the greater part certain, in a few cases conjectural. About 76 fragments of the Eighteenth dynasty in museums, private collections or with dealers have been identified, some 57 of them by me for the present work. This means that nearly half the fragments known to me have been related to their place of origin. No doubt many among the remaining fragments will one day have a similar fortune.

In the following section, fragments from unidentified tombs have been classified according to subject, but with a flexible margin envisaged for each group. Fragments being what they are, the context is often far from certain. There are three main categories: 'banquet scenes'; 'offering bringers'; and 'funerary scenes'. There are two specific groups: 'agriculture' and 'crafts'; and a small section for fragments which do not fit into any of the above mentioned, either because they differ, or because information concerning their appearance is lacking.

The fragments included under 'banquet scenes' may in actual fact be part of offering scenes with the tomb owner and his wife receiving offerings; but any fragment which shows either the tomb owner or others in a festive outfit, with necklace, unguent cone, or flowers has been included here. In 'funerary scenes' persons with their hands raised in adoration have been included, as the deity to whom praise is given is usually connected with the funerary cult.

Within each category, fragments with obvious similarities, like for example similar types of wigs, are grouped together. Cross-references are made to fragments in other groups which may share similar characteristics (similar technique of painting, or identical surface wear).

'Banquet scenes'

Fragments showing women with a wig ending in long, separate curls

1) East Berlin, Ägyptisches Museum No. 15003; h 43cm, w 63cm. *Top. Bibl.* I², p. 814; S. Wenig, *The Woman in Egyptian Art*, Leipzig 1969, pl. 37 (colour); museum slide.

A servant girl → offering a bowl to four women ← seated on low chairs, holding lotus flowers and buds. On bluish background. Fragments of an upper register with a mat and a lower register remain. A very similar group of servant girl and ladies can be seen in TT 80,(1) 85,(2) and 22,(3) although in the latter the ladies squat on mats,

2) Frankfurt am Main, Museum alter Plastik, IN 717; h 60cm, w 46cm. *Ägyptische Kunst im Liebighaus, Museum alter Plastik,* Frankfurt 1981 cat. no. 15; *Städtische Galerie* 1909, p. 42, no. 246; *ibid.*, 1910, p. 47, no. 246; *ibid.*, 1915, no. 246; *ibid.*, 1930, p. 89, no. 717.
The fragment (painted limestone) shows a woman → seated on a low chair next to a person on a much larger scale of whom only the legs are visible. The catalogue suggests that the large person is also a woman. A similar difference in scale occurs in other tombs, though not between persons of the same sex.(4). The fragment was acquired in 1909 along with fragment no. 28. Both may come from the same tomb.

3) Turin, Museo Egizio, Suppl. 1345; h 38cm. (Ill. 91)
This unpublished fragment shows the upper part of a woman with a lotus flower on her forehead. Acquired by Schiaparelli in Egypt in 1900-1901.
Cf. fragments nos. 14 and 15, and also nos. 35 and 51 for a possible common provenance.

Fragments showing women with wigs ending in short, separate curls

4) Bruxelles, Musées royaux du Cinquantenaire, E 2815; h 34cm, w 25cm. *Top. Bibl.* I^2,2, p. 815; Mekhitarian in *Serapis* 6, 1982, p. 88, fig. 2.
The painting on mud plaster with white stucco shows the upper part of a seated woman ← and the wig of the man ← next to her, and a border line behind her. The inscription  gives part of the man's title as *iry ˁt* 'guardian of the room'. The following column of text appears to have been hacked out, as if it once contained the name of Amūn. None of the guardians of a room known to have had a tomb at Thebes seems to have had a name of which Amūn was a part,(5) though Amūn was part of the title of two of them.(6) In addition, a man named Ḳen, who was 'guardian of the room of Amūn' is also known to have a connection with Thebes.(7) The tombs of these persons have not been located.
The fragment was bought by Capart at Nahman's in Cairo in 1909.

5) Formerly in the Rustafjaell collection(8) (bought by Llewellyn). *Sotheby Sale Cat.* Dec. 19-21 1906, no. 395 [c], with fig. pl. VIII. Head of a woman ←.

6) East Berlin, Ägyptisches Museum No. 18533 (Ill. 92).
Top. Bibl., I^2,2, p. 815.
This unpublished fragment, at present framed with another discussed above in chapter 11, shows a lady → with a lotus

flower on her forehead and in her hand. The lower part of the wig is missing, but it was presumably similar to the one in the fragment mentioned above. The surface of the painting is rather worn. The size and shape of the eye suggest a date around the reign of Tuthmosis IV or later.

Fragments showing women with tripartite wigs

7) East Berlin, Ägyptisches Museum No. 18527 (formerly the Rustafjaell collection) (Ill. 93); h 26cm, w 26cm.
Top. Bibl. I^2,2, p. 815; *Ägyptisches Museum 1823-1973*, fig. 16.
The painting on mud plaster shows two squatting ladies ←, the wig of a third ←, and the knees and elbow of a fourth ←. They have flat unguent cones and large lotus flowers. The surface of the fragment with straw mixed with the mud eaten by ants is rather similar to some other fragments offered at the same Rustafjaell sale (cf. nos. 29 and 30).

8) Formerly in the Rustafjaell collection; h 38cm, w 51cm.
Sotheby Sale Cat., Jan. 20-24, 1913, No. 591 (with pl.).
The painting depicts a woman ← with her arms around the shoulders of a man ←, presumably both seated, with remains of hieroglyphs above and in front. They seem to give part of the names and titles, but in spite of this an identification with a known tomb has not proved possible. The remaining signs are:

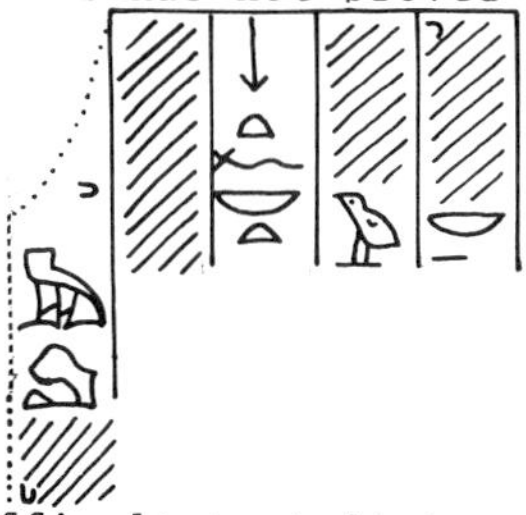

... *m ḥ3t* ... ... *snt.f nb[t pr]*
...*w* ... *nb(?)*

It is difficult to tell from the photo whether the damage to the inscription is accidental or deliberate. The *m ḥ3t* would appear to be part of the tomb owner's title rather than of his name, as more signs follow (and no tomb of an Amenemḥat seems to have been the original place for the fragment). A feasible title would be *rmn m ḥ3t* (usually preceded by *wʿb*).(9) If the name included that of Amūn (hacked out?) one candidate would be a man called Amenḥotp, son of the owner of TT 87,(10) though it is doubtful whether the fragment can be dated as late as to the son of a person who functioned in the reign of Tuthmosis III.
The wife's name, neatly preceded by 'his wife, the mistress [of the house]' includes the letter *w*. Possible women's names ending in *w* are 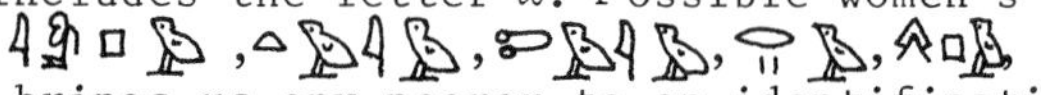 but neither of these brings us any nearer to an identification. As more signs, including a *nb* follow after the *w*, the name may have been a longer, composite one, ending in *nb.s* or the like.

9) Frankfurt am Main, Museum alter Plastik, IN 1650; h 37cm, w 34cm.
Ägyptische Kunst im Liebighaus, Museum alter Plastik, No. 14.
The fragment which has been in the collection for a long time

('Alter Bestand') has been put together from numerous small pieces and has been restored in several places. It shows a man ⟶ and wife ⟶ seated. They have no cones nor flowers. The man holds a kerchief in his hand. In front of his face an remains of the inscription. The man's face with the short, square beard is reminiscent of a painting in Turin (cf. below no. 14).

Fragments with square stools

10) Formerly in the de Benzion collection.(11)
Top. Bibl. I^2,2, p. 820.
Two fragments of a scene, joined in one frame, showing a female servant ⟶ handing a bowl to two male guests ⟵; a male servant ⟶ adjusting the necklace of a male guest ⟵; (on the second fragment) a male servant ⟶ putting an unguent cone on the head of one male guest ⟵ with another looking on. The men sit on stools of a characteristic, though not unique shape. They have been described by Davies and Gardiner,(12) who compared the stools in TT 82 to stools in TT 59, 84 and 88. Apart from being represented on a few more fragments (cf. below) they also occur in TT 22;(13) 63;(14) 87;(15) 155;(16) 200;(17) 261;(18) and 279.(19) The chairs are represented in the round in TT 349.(20) In TT 24 the similarly shaped stools are without the markings.(21 But none of the fragments with similar chairs seem to stem from any of these tombs.(22)

11) Bruxelles, Musées royaux du Cinquantenaire, E 2877; h 32cm, w 30cm.
Top. Bibl. I^2,2, p. 815; Leca, *La médicine égyptienne* &c., fig.10(
P. Ghalioungui, *The House of Life: Magic and Medical Science*, Amsterdam 1973, pl. 7; Darby *et al.*, *Food* II, fig. 14.3; Mekhitarian in *Serapis* 6, 1982, p. 87, fig. 1.
The fragment was bought by Capart at Nahman's in Cairo in 1909. The background is blue, pointing to a date around Tuthmosis III. For the stools cf. the remarks under fragment no. 10. The painting shows two male guests ⟵ and the legs of a third ⟵ and a woman ⟵ embracing a man ⟵ (who is mostly destroyed). The columns for inscriptions were left empty. One of the men, who is shown vomiting, has parallels in a number of other tombs.(23)

12) Hanover, Kestner Museum, Inv. no. 1960,9; h 34cm, w 54cm.
I. Woldering, *Kestner-Museum 1889-1964*, no. 18; *id.*, *Meisterwerke der Kestner-Museum zu Hannover*, 1961, colour pl. I.
Five male guests ⟵ with lotus flowers, seated on square stools like those discussed under fragment no. 10. These have no markings.

Other fragments possibly from banquet scenes

13) New York, The Brooklyn Museum, no. 32.1600.(Ill. 94)
This unpublished fragment shows the upper part of a man wearing a garment which covers one arm. He holds a very large lotus flower. His wife, now almost completely destroyed, had her arm around his shoulder. The background is bluish.

14) Turin, Museo Egizio, Suppl. 1346 and 1347; h 30cm and 23cm. (Ill. 95).
An unpublished fragment showing the face of a man ⟶ with a square beard, and another similar fragment, both acquired by Schiaparelli in Egypt in 1900-1901. Cf. fragments nos. 3 and 15.

15) Turin, Museo Egizio, Suppl. 1349(24) (Ill. 96).
Another unpublished fragment showing a bald man ⟵ (pink skull) with a necklace. This fragment, as well as no. 14 and no. 3, all in Turin, may come from the same tomb. Acquired by Schiaparelli in Egypt 1900-1901.

16) Hildesheim, Pelizaeus-Museum, No. 1027; h 16cm.
H. Kayser, *Das Pelizäus-Museum in Hildesheim*, Hamburg 1966, pp. 27ff.; *id., Die altägyptischen Altertümer im Roemer-Pelizaeus-Museum,* Hildesheim 1973, p. 64, pl. 5; *Echnaton-Nofretete-Tutanchamun*, Hildesheim 15 July - 26 Sept. 1976, no. 76.
The top part of three ladies ⟶ at a banquet, the one in the middle showing a mandrake fruit to her companion. The very tall unguent cones point to a date late in the Eighteenth dynasty. The scene has a close parallel in a detail copied by Wilkinson, except that the fruit is here a lotus flower.(25)

17) Hildesheim, Pelizaeus-Museum, No. 1028; h 25cm.
Bibliography as above, except that the exhibition catalogue no. is 77. Three men ⟶ at a banquet, overlapping approaching to layering. To the left a polychrome border marking the end of the register. The fragment no doubt belongs with no. 16. Both were given to the museum in 1907.

18) Luzern, Sammlung Kofler-Truniger, Inv. No. K 416; h 16cm, w 13.5cm.
Le Don du Nil. Art égyptien dans les collections suisses, Bales 1978, cat. no. 199.
The small fragment shows a servant girl bent over, very much like those in TT 38,(26) 45,(27) and 108.(28)

19) Formerly Rustafjaell collection; 35.5cm x 25.5cm.
Sotheby Sale Cat. Jan. 20-24, 1913, no. 598[a].
A man and a woman seated before a table of offerings. Bright colouring.

20) Formerly Rustafjaell collection.
Sotheby Sale Cat. Dec. 9-10, 1907, no. 156.
A large fragment with the head of a woman wearing a large black wig and necklace. The flesh painted red. Finely preserved. Thus the sale catalogue. Although women's complexion is not usually depicted as red, some yellow colours have changed as an effect of varnishing to look as if they were a deep orange.

The following four fragments, formerly in the de Benzion collection, may also be part of banquet scenes. The sale catalogue is too brief to be certain, but it does say that they are all of the Eighteenth dynasty.

21) *Benzion Sale Catalogue*, no. 79: 'girl'.

22) *Ibid.*, no. 82: 'man and woman'.

23) *Ibid.*, no. 84: 'woman'.

24) *Ibid.*, no. 87: 'woman'.

The next fragments are difficult to place. They may and they may not belong in a 'banquet scene'.

25) Formerly Rustafjaell collection.
Sotheby Sale Cat. Dec. 9-10, 1907, no. 162[b].
'Figure of a man'.

26) Formerly Rustafjaell collection; 35.5cm x 45.5cm.
Sotheby Sale Cat. Jan. 20-24, 1913, no. 593[b].
Head and shoulders of a large figure←, with an inscription.

27) Formerly Rustafjaell collection; 11.5cm x 11.5cm.
Sotheby Sale Cat. Jan. 20-24, 1913, no. 585[d].
Head and shoulders of a man, with well preserved colouring.

Offering bringers

Fragments showing figures of men

28) Frankfurt am Main, Museum alter Plastik IN 718; h 54cm, w 35cm.
Ägyptische Kunst im Liebighaus, Museum alter Plastik, cat. no. 16; *Städtische Galerie* 1909, p. 42, no. 247; *ibid.*, p. 47, no. 247; *ibid.*, 1915, no. 247; *ibid.*, 1930, p. 89, no. 718.
The fragment (limestone with painting on a layer of stucco) shows a man← with a tray of loaves and onions, and two garlands of flowers hanging from it. Two columns for hieroglyphs show traces of blue, and red sketched lines, with the words for bread and beer still legible (*sic* the catalogue).
The fragment may stem from the same tomb as fragment no. 2. Both are on limestone, and were bought together in 1909. This one has been restored, particularly in the face. The entire surface was varnished leaving a yellowish hue.

29) East Berlin, Ägyptisches Museum, No. 18547 (formerly Rustafjaell collection); w 13cm.(Ill. 97)
Sotheby Sale Cat. Dec. 19-21, 1906, no. 399[c], pl. VIII,13 [upper left].
Upper part of a man ← carrying in his left hand a basket of fruit(?) and a bunch of onions(?). Surface wear as fragment no. 7. It comes from the same scene as fragment no. 30.

30) East Berlin, Ägyptisches Museum, No. 18549 (formerly Rustafjaell collection); w 10.5cm. (Ill. 98).
Sotheby Sale Cat. Dec. 19-21, 1906, no. 399[c], pl. VIII,13 [top right].
Head of a man←, very similar to fragment no. 29 and undoubtedly from the same scene.

31) Formerly Rustafjaell collection.
Sotheby Sale Cat. dec. 9-10, 1907, no. 160[a].
Man holding a table of offerings.

32) Sold at Galerie Günther Puhze, Freiburg.
Kunst der Antike. Galerie Günther Puhze, Freiburg. Katalog 1981, no. 318.
Painting on mud mixed with straw, with a thin layer of stucco. Slightly restored, showing the upper part of a man ⟶ with a large square object. It is possible that this piece should be classified under 'funerary scenes' if the object in question is, for example, a canopic chest, but an identification is difficult.
The catalogue dates the fragment to the Nineteenth dynasty. An Eighteenth dynasty date would fit equally well, or better.

Fragments showing figures of women

33) Sold at Galerie Günther Puhze, Freiburg
Op. cit., no. 319.
Painting on stucco showing a woman ⟶ walking along holding a rope in one hand (undoubtedly attached to a calf or a gazelle at the other end) and a tray of offerings in the other. More offerings are piled up on the ground before her. For a similar motif cf. among others TT 82.(29)
The catalogue dates the fragment to the Nineteenth dynasty. The Eighteenth seems more appropriate. The painting is rather crudely executed.

34) Formerly Rustafjaell collection; 29cm x 20.5cm.
Sotheby Sale Cat. Jan. 20-24, 1913, no. 583[a].
The fragment shows the upper part of a woman with a libatory vase and three lotus stalks. For a similar motif cf. for example TT 69.(30)

35) Turin, Museo Egizio, Suppl. 1349.(31) (Ill. 99).
An unpublished fragment showing the head and shoulder of a man with a yoke, and a large papyrus flower in front of him. Acquired by Schiaparelli in Egypt in 1900-1901.

36) Turin, Museo Egizio, Suppl. 7885 (Ill. 100)
Another unpublished fragment showing the head of a man ⟵ with a branch. The face is reminiscent of those in TT 338 of Maya, now in the same museum (cf. above, p. 179). It comes from the Schiaparelli excavations at Deir el-Medîna 1905, and perhaps from this tomb where certain figures, also facing left, are missing.(32)

37) Formerly Rustafjaell collection; 25.5cm x 18cm.
Sotheby Sale Cat. Jan. 20-24, 1913, no. 599A[b].
A fragment showing a man carrying a small table on which rests a large vulture headdress? (the question mark is in the catalogue).

38) Formerly Rustafjaell collection; 58.5cm x 28cm.
Sotheby Sale Cat. Jan. 20-24, 1913, no. 592[a].

A fragment with a figure of a man bearing an offering of two large feathers on his left hand.
This person may belong in the funerary scenes below, as the description may fit one of the conventional figures in the scenes of the Opening of the Mouth.(33) On the other hand, he may be part of a tribute bringing scene, as for example in TT 78.(34)

Funerary scenes

Scenes showing the funeral procession

39) Formerly Rustafjaell collection.
Sotheby Sale Cat. Jan. 20-24, 1913, no. 599A[a]; 31.5cm x 31.5cm.
Figures of three men holding a long rope. Judging from this caption in the catalogue, the fragment may have been part of a field measuring scene. But as a number of pieces from this sale come from funerary scenes, and possibly the very same one, it is more likely that the men on this fragment followed the oxen dragging the coffin to the tomb.

40) Formerly Rustafjaell collection; 45.5cm x 51cm.
Sotheby Sale Cat. Jan. 20-24, 1913, no. 593[a].
A procession of figures →, and remains of an inscription.

41) Formerly Rustafjaell collection; 43cm x 24cm.
Sotheby Sale Cat. Jan. 20-24, 1913, no. 597[b].
Men walking to the right. Possibly connected with the previous scene?

42) Formerly Rustafjaell collection; about 21.5cm x 14cm.
Sotheby Sale Cat. Jan. 20-24, 1913, no. 599[b].
Upper parts of three men →. Possibly connected with the two previous fragments?

43) Formerly Rustafjaell collection; 48cm x 38cm.
Sotheby Sale Cat. Jan. 20-24, 1913, no. 599.
Fragment showing a man supporting a mummy, with a woman seated on the ground in mourning. Remains of inscriptions. A conventional scene known from numerous tombs.

Scenes with boats (35)

These boats belong either in the funerary procession itself, or in scenes, usually on the same wall, showing the pilgrimage to Abydos.

44) Brussels, Musées royaux du Cinquantenaire E 2380; h 38cm, w 75cm.
Mekhitarian in *Serapis* 6, 1982, p. 88, fig. 2.
The fragment (painting on stucco and with light background, bought in Cairo in 1905) shows an unusually complete scene with two boats mooring in front of two funerary booths. The style of the painting is very much like that of the Eighteenth dynasty part of TT 54 of which a large fragment is in Chicago, cf. above, p. 171. It would be tempting to place the Brussels

fragment in a lower register on the very same wall, but there is hardly room for it there, as traces on the wall itself suggests the presence of a boat just where the vertical line to the right in the Brussels fragment indicates the end of (part of) the register.
A few hieroglyphs remain on the fragment:

... *[ỉmỉ] wrt [r Imntt] ḥr [ḥꜣt]* ...
'... starboard to the West, in front of...'

45) Brussels, Musées royaux du Cinquantenaire E 6120 (B.48); h 22.5cm, w 10.5cm.
B. van de Walle, *La collection égyptienne*, 1980, no. B.48; Mekhitarian in *Serapis* 6, 1982, p. 88, fig. 4.
The fragment came to the museum in 1924 from the Hagemans collection. The background colour is blue. A man ↶ is shown standing under the rigging of a barge, turning backwards with his hand outstretched. He is wearing sandals, and has a stick in his hand to measure the depth of the water.(36) Although the scene is here classified among the funerary scenes, it is just conceivable that it belongs with more secular subjects (cf. TT A4 of Wensu with a similar cargo, Ill. 18).

46) East Berlin, Ägyptisches Museum No. 18535 (formerly Rustafjaell collection); h 11 cm. (Ill. 101)
Sotheby Sale Cat. Dec. 19-21, 1906, no. 399[a], pl. VIII,10 [lower left].
The tiny fragment shows two men ⇆ →, presumably aboard a funerary barge carrying the coffin.(37).

47) Formerly Rustafjaell collection; 68.5cm x 25.5cm.
Sotheby Sale Cat. Jan. 20-24, 1913, no. 587.
A boat with four rowers and three draped figures. 'Interesting and in very fair condition'.

48) A private collection. 21.3cm x 20.3cm.
Sotheby Sale Cat, Dec. 4, 1978, no. 108.
Man in a boat ← 'painted in red and white slip'. The painting is said to be on sandstone. Either this is a mistake, or the fragment can only be part of a jamb or lintel, if it came from a tomb at all.

49) East Berlin, Ägyptisches Museum No. 18537 (formerly Rustafjaell collection); h 10.5cm (Ill. 102)
Sotheby Sale Cat. Dec. 19-21, 1906, no. 399[a], pl. VIII,10 [middle right].
This tiny fragment shows a man ← squatting in front of a vertical line. As he sits on a horizontal line, he cannot be a hieroglyph. Similar figures are often seen on a small boat in the funerary procession.

Fragments showing scenes of purification

Men making libation

50) Birmingham, Museum & Art Gallery (formerly Rustafjaell collection); h. 18.5cm, w 21.7cm. (Ill. 103)
Sotheby Sale Cat. Dec. 19-21, 1906, no. 395[a], pl. VIII,1.
The fragment shows the upper part of a man ⟶ with a large *ḥs*-vase. He wears a necklace. The mud plaster is worn in the same way as nos. 7, 29, 30, 107. The background is now greyish.

51) Turin, Museo Egizio, Suppl. 1349.(38) (Ill. 104)
This unpublished fragment shows the upper part of a man ⟵ with a *ḥs*-vase, standing in front of a vertical line. He is most probably part of an Opening of the Mouth scene.(39). The fragment was acquired by Schiaparelli in Egypt 1900-1901.

52) Formerly in Rustafjaell collection; 42cm x 28cm.
Sotheby Sale Cat. Jan. 20-24, 1913, no. 588[a].
Three men making libations.

Fragments showing funerary deities

53) Formerly Rustafjaell collection; 50.5cm x 30.5cm.
Sotheby Sale Cat. Jan. 20-24, 1913, no. 594.
The upper part of a figure of Anubis ⟶, with unusually well preserved colouring.

54) Formerly Rustafjaell collection.
Sotheby Sale Cat. Dec. 19-21, 1907, no. 162[a].
A seated figure of Anubis.

55) Formerly Rustafjaell collection.
Sotheby Sale Cat. Dec. 19-21, 1907, no. 158.
A funeral boat with two figures of Anubis beneath a canopy.

56) Formerly Rustafjaell collection; 23cm x 18cm.
Sotheby Sale Cat. Jan. 20-24, 1913, no. 598[c].
A figure of a jackal lying upon a bier. With bright colouring.

57) Formerly Rustafjaell collection.
Sotheby Sale Cat. Dec. 19-21, 1907, no. 161.
Three fragments (in two frames), all with figures (one the god Amūn-Rēʿ).

58) Bristol, Museum & Art Gallery, H 4639 (formerly Rustafjaell collection); h 50cm, w 31.5cm. (Ill. 105)
Sotheby Sale Cat. Jan. 20-24, 1913, no. 596[c].
Upper part of the goddess of the West ⟶ with red dress and head-band, and on yellow background.(40)

59) Formerly Rustafjaell collection; 46cm x 23cm.
Sotheby Sale Cat. Jan. 20-24, 1913, no. 590[b].
Fragment showing the upper part of a figure of Isis. *Sic* the catalogue. She may in fact be Ḥatḥor or the Western goddess as 58).

60) Formerly Rustafjaell collection; 38cm x 38cm.
Sotheby Sale Cat. Jan. 20-24, 1913, no. 588[b].
A scene with a figure of the hawk-headed Rēʿ.

61) Formerly Rustafjaell collection; 24cm x 19cm.
Sotheby Sale Cat. Jan. 20-24, 1913, no. 585.
Fragment with a figure of 'a mummied Apis Bull', with well preserved colouring.
For the subject of Apis bulls in Theban tombs, cf. above under the 'Bankes' tomb.

62) East Berlin, Ägyptisches Museum No. 18534 (formerly the Rustafjaell collection); h 18cm.
Top. Bibl. I^2,2, p. 815; *Sotheby Sale Cat.* Dec. 19-21, 1906, no. 399[b], pl. VIII,10 [top left]; Wenig, *The Woman in Egyptian Art*, pl. 36 (colour); *Gudar och Menniskor*, Gothenburg 1973, cat. no. 212, pl. 4; *Det eviga Egypten. Aegyptus aeterna*, Helsinki 1973, cat. no. 83, with colour fig. 4; Tran Tam Tinh, *Isis lactans*, 1973, p. 27.
This fragment has been described as representing a woman → suckling a prince ←. But the branches behind suggest that it is the tree goddess suckling the tomb owner. Scenes with the tree goddess begin to appear in the reign of Tuthmosis IV, and the fragment can hardly be much later that this date.

63) Formerly Rustafjaell collection; 20.5cm x 15.5cm.
Sotheby Sale Cat. Jan. 20-24, 1913, no. 583[c].
A fragment with a seated mummified figure of a god, with well preserved colouring.

64) Formerly Rustafjaell collection; 21.5cm x 45.5cm.
Sotheby Sale Cat. Jan. 20-24, 1913, no. 590[c].
A fragment with two figures of seated gods.

65) Formerly Rustafjaell collection; [b] 20.5cm x 11.5cm; [c] 13cm x 10.5cm.
Sotheby Sale Cat. Jan. 20-24, 1913, no. 585[b], [c].
Fragments with seated mummiform figures of men, with well preserved colouring. These figures may be similar to our fragment no. 49.

Various funerary scenes

66) East Berlin, Ägyptisches Museum No. 18553 (formerly the Rustafjaell collection); h 16cm, w 34cm. (Ill. 106)
Sotheby Sale at. Dec. 19-21, 1906, no. 399[b], pl. VIII,11
A detail of the Fields of Iaru with the names of three pools

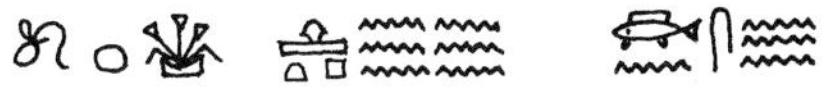

67) East Berlin, Ägyptisches Museum No. 18551 (formerly the Rustafjaell collection); h 18cm. (Ill. 107)
Sotheby Sale Cat. Dec. 19-21, 1906, no. 399[c], pl. VIII,13 [lower left].
A fragment showing three women →, overlapping, with feathers

on their heads and clappers in their hands. The surface appears similar to that described under fragment no.7.

68) Formerly Rustafjaell collection; 23cm x 15.5cm.
Sotheby Sale Cat. Jan. 20-24, 1913, no. 583[b].
Fragment with the upper part of a woman with her hands raised in adoration. Well preserved colouring.

69) Formerly the Rustafjaell collection; 45.5cm x 33cm.
Sotheby Sale Cat. Jan. 20-24, 1913, no. 592[b].
The painting represents two bearded figures walking to the left.

70) Formerly Rustafjaell collection; 30.5cm x 43cm.
Sotheby Sale Cat. Jan. 20-24, 1913, no. 597[a].
The fragment shows two men, one with a mattock and with a brazier at his feet; the other opening or closing a large door. The two men may be part of the funeral procession.

71) Moscow, Pushkin Museum of Fine Arts I.1.a; h 20.5cm, w 12.5cm.
S. Hodjash & O. Berlev, *The Egyptian Reliefs and Stelae in the Pushkin Museum of fine Arts*,
The fragment of mud plaster shows a person ← before a shrine. Above there is a green line and a yellow mass of colour. An inscription ascertains the provenance of the fragment as coming from a funerary scene:

... *dỉ.k pr.ỉ ʿḳ.ỉ m ẖrt-nṯr mỉ* ...

'... may you cause me to come and go in the necropolis as...'

Until 1906 the fragment was in the Bakhruslin collection; from 1906 to 1918 in the Rumiantsev Museum; and from 1918 to 1924 in the Museum-and-Institute of the Classical orient.

Agricultural and related scenes

72) Formerly Rustafjaell collection (sold to Ready).
Sotheby Sale Cat. Dec. 19-21, 1906, no. 401, pl. VIII,15.
The fragment shows a sitting man ← and another ← at a lower level. A box with a scribe's palette is inserted above, next to blank columns for hieroglyphs.
This must be part of a harvest scene with the inspector sitting on top of a pile of grain, cf. a similar detail in TT 69.(42) The fragment appears too large to be fitted into a register with the other agricultural fragments in Berlin, related to the fragments in the British Museum (cf. above, p. 148).

73) Bristol, Museum & Art Gallery, H 4637; 37cm x 41cm. (Ill. 108)
Sotheby Sale Cat. Jan. 20-24, 1913, no. 596[a]; L. V. Grinsell, *Guide Catalogue to the Collections from Ancient Egypt*, 1972, pp. 48-9.
A fragment of mud plaster with grey background showing corn being winnowed. The piece, which is rather fragmentary, was acquired by the museum in 1938.

74) Formerly Benzion collection.
Benzion Sale Cat. no. 85.
The fragment shows 'a harvest woman'.

75) Hanover, Kestner-Museum Inv. nr. 1961,4; h 19cm; w 45cm.
I. Woldering, *Kestner-Museum 1889-1964*, no. 17; *id.*, *The Arts of Egypt*, 1967, fig. 62 on p. 129 (detail), and cat. no. 50.
The scene is part of rural activities, showing to the right two men →← plucking fowl; in the centre a boy← about to place a cleaned bird in a jar; and to the left the beginning of a bird counting scene←.
The chairs have been discussed above under no.10.

76) New York, Metropolitan Museum of Art 06.1332.1 (Ill. 109)
Hayes, *Sceptre* II, pp. 166-7.
The fragment shows the back of a man, presumably engaged in plucking fowl in a shelter, and another carrying geese on a yoke. It was acquired by the museum in 1906.
The chairs are are of the same type as those in the preceding fragment, but the markings are different.

Crafts

77) East Berlin, Ägyptisches Museum No. 23731; h 15cm, w 11cm.
Top. Bibl. I^2,2, p. 815; museum slide; *Das Altertum* 8, 1962, fig. on p. 193; Shimanova, *Iskusstvo Drevnego Egipta*, pl. 118; Vilimkova, *Starověky Egypt*, fig. 104; W. Müller in *Schätze der Weltkultur*, 1980, fig. on p. 39 [lower]; *Det eviga Egypten. Aegyptus aeterna*, Helsinki 1973, cat. no. 381 with fig. 35;

A fragment with two carpenters, possibly engaged in boat building.

Other scenes

78) Copenhagen, Ny Carlsberg Glyptotek IN 2581 a,b (ÆIN 1145 and 1146); w of a ca. 37cm; h of b ca. 31.5cm (Ill. 110)
The two fragments are said to have been acquired from Petrie's excavations in 1910. Although Petrie worked at Thebes a few years earlier, there is no record in the publications of these fragments. Each one shows a hand holding the tail of a leopard's skin. Priests wearing panthers' skins normally hold them by a hind leg, not by the tail. As the animal cannot be a live one, the fragment probably belongs in a tribute bearing context.

79) Formerly Rustafjaell collection.
Sotheby Sale Cat. Dec. 19-21, 1907, no. 163[a].
Two crouching figures.

80) Sold in Basel; h 26cm, w 16cm.
Ägyptische Kunst. Münzen und Medaillen A. G. Basel. Auktion 49, June 27, 1974, no. 34.
A bunch of two lotus buds and a flower on white stucco. The

few irregular lines along two edges of the fragment give no clue as to the context. The piece was sold with a fragment from TT 66 (cf. above).

81) East Berlin, Ägyptisches Museum No. 18538 (formerly Rustafjaell collection); w 7.8cm.
Sotheby Sale Cat. Dec. 19-21, 1906, no. 399[a], pl. VIII,10 [lower right].
A tiny fragment with hieroglyphs (? possibly a  on the right).

82) Moscow, Pushkin Museum of Fine Arts, I.1.a. 7155; 18cm x 14.5cm.
S. Hodjash & O. Berlev, *op. cit.* , no. 51 (wrongly attributed to the tomb of Tuthmosis III).
This fragment of limestone shows the lower part of a royal inscription, with part of a sketched blue crown + uraeus below.
The inscription is as follows: 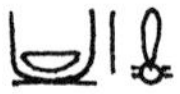
the  being blue, the  red.
As the fragment can under no circumstances come from any of the royal tombs whose owner have a name incorporating  or , the fragment must either be a very large ostrakon or part of a private tomb, presumably showing the reigning king on the left side of the entrance doorway from the hall to the passage, or similar (cf. above, chapter III).
The fragment was in the A. Prakhov collection from 1881 to 1939.

(1) Gauthier found about 300 cones of a certain Sebkmosi (TT 275 - Ramessid: *BIFAO* 16, 1919, p. 174). Mond found 267 cones of Ḳen-amūn (TT 93 - Eighteenth dynasty: *ASAE* 5, 1904, p. 98 n. 3).

(2) Surprisingly few objects which may have served as 'matrix' have been found. One such may be the limestone cone, 'gravé en creux', found by Chassinat (*BIFAO* 7, 1910, p. 161 (XX), cf. *BIFAO* 12, 1916, p. 131). Daressy, *Recueil*, p. 270 mentions a frog-shaped schist seal which might have served the purpose. Davies thought that a wooden matrix had been employed; this would account for the irregularity of the circle and for the fact that none has apparently survived (Davies & Macadam, *Corpus*, p. vi).

(3) Borchardt with Königsberger and Ricke, 'Friesziegel in Grabbauten', *ZÄS* 70, 1934, pp. 25-35. Borchardt refers to a similar practise in ancient Mesopotamia of using pottery cones in brick buildings (p. 34).

(4) 'The Egyptian Expedition 1925-27', *BMMA*, Sect. 2, Feb. 1928, pp. 6-7, figs. 4 and 5. Detached cones are shown in fig. 1. Winlock found more uninscribed cones in the courts of the Eleventh dynasty tombs in the area.

(5) Cf. Borchardt, *op. cit.*, figs. 4 and 7.

(6) *Notice descriptive des monuments égyptiens du Musée Charles X*, Paris 1827, p, 164.

(7) '... imbedded in the building, and stretching very nearly its entire length, were two rows of clay cones impressed with a hieroglyphic subject on ends turned to the light'. There were altogether 90 cones.

(8) A. H. Rhind, *Thebes, Its Tombs and their Tenants*, London 1862, pp. 136-8. At this early date Rhind had grasped the point more accurately than most of the subsequent writers. - The cone depicted by Rhind is that of Userḥēt (TT 47), but Rhind himself describes how the cones he took as a sample from the row *in situ* was packed with others. On arrival in England the labels had rubbed off. The statement in the *Topographical Bibliography* I^2,1, p. 87 that this was the tomb in which he saw the cones *in situ* should perhaps be taken with some caution.

(9) A. Mariette, *Notice des principaux monuments de Boulaq*, Cairo 1874, pp. 185-6.

(10) G. Maspero, *Guide du visiteur au Musée de Boulaq*, Cairo 1883, p. 138.

(11) B. Bruyère, *Fouilles de Deir el-Médineh (1926)*, Cairo 1927, pp. 53-4.

(12) Quoted by Heyler in *Kêmi* 15, 1959, p. 80.

(13) Daressy, *Recueil*, p. 270.

(14) Winlock, *op. cit.*, p. 7.

(15) N. de G. Davies, *The Tombs of two Sculptors at Thebes*, New York 1925, p. 45 n. 3.

(16) *Lexikon der Ägyptologie* II, cols. 857-9. The article announced for *ZÄS* 104 never appeared in this journal.

(17) Daressy, *Recueil*, p. 270.

(18) *Ibid.* Cf. also Northampton, Spiegelberg and Newberry, *The Theban Necropolis*, p. 35.

(19) Darressy, *loc. cit.*

(20) Cf. L. Manniche, 'Body colours of gods and men on jewellery and related objects from the tomb of Tutankhamun', *AO* 43, 1982, pp. 5-12.

(21) The hieroglyph 𓏏 is usually interpreted as representing a loaf of bread (cf. K. Sethe, 'Die altägyptischen Ausdrücke für rechts und links', *Nachrichten KGWG*, Phil.-Hist. Klasse, Berlin 1923, pp. 218-20), although some have seen in it a drill cap (W. M. F. Petrie, *Medum*, London 1892, p. 32), a semi-circle (H. Sottas & E. Drioton, *Introduction à l'étude des hiéroglyphes*, Paris 1922, p. 157) or a 'geometrical figure' (G. Möller, *Hieratische Palaographie* I, Leipzig 1909 (Y 575)). The conventional blue, though sometimes black or green, colour of the object has not been queried in relation to its interpretation as a loaf of bread.
(22) Only Daressy, *Recueil*, no. 53.
(23) Cones from the tomb of Ḳenamūn (TT 93), cf. p. 6.
(24) Cones from the tomb of Merymaᶜet at Qurna *(sic)* found near TT 325 at Deir el-Medîna, cf. Bruyère, *Fouilles (1926)*, p. 57. Twenty-two cones from TT 48 at Khôkha were found by Gauthier at Qurnet Muraᶜi, cf. *BIFAO* 16, 1919, p. 173.
(25) Cones of Amenemopet, cf. Gauthier in *BIFAO* 16, 1919, p. 177.
(26) TT 91, 116, 119, 129, 143, 147, 152, 167, 171, 175, 225, 227, 229, 262, 333, 334, 348, 350, 354, 376, 393, 396, 402, A9, A25, C5, C15. TT 226 has now been shown to belong to Ḥekareshu (L. Habachi in *Festschrift Schott*, Wiesbaden 1967, pp. 61-70).
(27) TT 114, 115, 136, 153, 180, 269, 309, 352, 370, 377, 378, 394, 395, 399, A14, A26.
(28) For other factors influencing the evaluation of the number of lost tombs cf. p. 8.
(29) Arnold in *MDAIAK* 28, 1972, pp. 19-21, cf. fig. 3. This is the only royal person who seems to have possessed funerary cones.
(30) Davies & Macadam, *Corpus*, no. 121. This person named Amenḥotp was not the king's real son, cf. A. H. Gardiner, *Egypt of the Pharaohs*, Oxford 1961, p. 178, but it does give a date for the cone.
(31) Daressy, *Recueil*, no. 230; Davies & Macadam, *Corpus*, nos. 21, 517-8.
(32) Daressy, *Recueil*,nos. 17-8; Davies & Macadam, *Corpus*, nos. 84, 88.
(33) Davies & Macadam, *Corpus*, no. 558.
(34) Daressy, *Corpus*, no. 16; Davies & Macadam, *Corpus*, no. 120.
(35) Davies & Macadam, *Corpus*, nos. 538-9.
(36) Daressy, *Recueil*, nos. 68, 178; Davies & Macadam, *Corpus*, no. 367.
(37) Daressy, *Recueil*, no. 45; Davies & Macadam,*Corpus*, no. 73.
(38) Davies & Macadam,*Corpus*, nos. 441, 544.
(39) Daressy, *Recueil*, no. 272?; Davies & Macadam, *Corpus*, no. 311.
(40) Daressy, *Recueil*, no. 36; Davies & Macadam, *Corpus*, no. 103.
(41) Daressy, *Recueil*, no. 15 (wrongly giving Bakt for Bak); Davies & Macadam, *Corpus*, nos. 85-6, cf. N. de G. Davies, *Five Theban Tombs*, London 1913, p. 27.
(42) Daressy, *Recueil*, no. 171 (wrongly giving the name as Pederēᶜ instead of Penrēᶜ); Davies & Macadam, *Corpus*, no. 438.
(43) Gauthier in *BIFAO* 16, 1919, pp. 166-7 referring to a statue group published by Wiedemann.
(44) Daressy, *Recueil*, nos. 132-3; Davies & Macadam, *Corpus*, no. 31.
(45) Davies & Macadam, *Corpus*, no. 140. The title is lost, but the name being rare it remains likely that the cone came from this tomb. The only other funerary cone that can in any way be placed around the Amarna Period is the cone of a scribe called Pa-iten

(Daressy, *Recueil*, no. 561, cf. R. Hari, *Repertoire onomastique amarnien. Aegyptiaca Helvetica* 4, 1976, no. 80).

(46) Daressy, *Recueil*, no. 113; Davies & Macadam, *Corpus*, nos. 169-170, 441. Cf. Gauthier in *BIFAO* 16, 1919, pp. 167-9.

(47) Daressy, *Recueil*, no. 289; Davies & Macadam, *Corpus*, no. 291.

(48) Daressy, *Recueil*, p. 270; Bruyère, *Fouilles (1923-1924)*, p. 101.

(49) Cf. Borchardt, *op. cit.*

(50) Daressy, *Recueil*, no. 205.

(51) Davies & Macadam, *Corpus*, no. 529.

(52) Daressy, *Recueil*, no. 231.

(53) Daressy, *Recueil*, no. 246; Davies & Macadam, *Corpus*, no. 501.

(54) Davies & Macadam, *Corpus*, no. 471.

(55) Daressy, *Recueil*, no. 228; Davies & Macadam, *Corpus*, no. 524.

(56) Daressy, *Recueil*, nos. 12 and 165; Davies & Macadam, *Corpus*, nos. 532 and 554, possibly also no. 204. Cf. also Gauthier in *BIFAO* 6, 1908, p. 125 for the suggested date of the tomb.

(57) Davies & Macadam, *Corpus*, nos. 25-6, 225.

(58) *E.g.* Davies & Macadam, *Corpus*, nos. 409-11, 418-20, 449, 460-1, 471-3, 485-6, 604. Cf also no. 3, cone of Raᶜmosi, treasurer of Taharqa.

(59) *ibid.*, nos. 444-5 from TT 27 (temp. Apries and Amasis); nos. 450-1 from TT 36 (temp. Psammetikhos I); no. 391 from TT 197 (temp. Psammetikhos II); nos. 329, 385 and 602 from TT 389 (Saite).

(60) Cf. chapter 2.

(61) Daressy in *ASAE* 26, 1926, pp. 18ff.

(62) R. Mond & O. H. Myers, *Cemeteries of Armant*, London 1937, I, pl. 22.6 [top].

(63) Arnold in *MDAIAK* 23, 1968, p. 35, n. 2, referring to unpublished cones.

(64) Daressy in *ASAE* 26, 1926, p. 19.

(65) G. Steindorff, *Anîba*, Glückstadt/Hamburg/New York 1937, II, pp. 161, 187.

(66) von Bissing in *AO* 5, 1927, p. 171.

(67) Sayce in *ASAE* 6, 1905, pp. 163-4.

(68) Steindorff, *op. cit.*, pp. 242-5.

(69) *Ibid.*, pp. 61, 187.

(70) Daressy, *Recueil*, no. 293. This cone gives the title of ᶜAnu as *ỉdnw n sȝ nsw*...whereas the cones from ᶜAnība have *šms n ḥm.f*. The name is not known from other sources, and the name of the wife is identical on the two sets of cones.

(71) Davies seems to have suggested that the tomb should be at Khôkha, cf. Steindorff, *op. cit.*, p. 187.

(72) Davies & Macadam, *Corpus*, no. 555. The cone is one of those copied by Macadam, and no mention is made of its provenance or whereabouts.

(73) For ᶜ*gn* cf. A. H. Gardiner, *Ancient Egyptian Onomastica*, Oxford 1947, II, pp. 12*-14*.

(74) Davies & Macadam, *Corpus*, no. 187.

(75) *Ibid.*, nos. 431-2.

(76) Glanville in *ZÄS* 66, 1930, pp. 108-9.

(77) *ASAE* 5, 1904, p. 98 with n. 3.

(78) Davies & Macadam, *Corpus*, no. 497.

(79) *Ibid.*, nos. 122 and 345. Armant is an alternative possibility.

(80) Daressy, *Recueil*, nos. 172, 221-2; Davies & Macadam, *Corpus*,

nos. 446-7 and 514. A cone identical to the latter was found by Petrie in TT A2: W. M. F. Petrie, *Qurneh*, London 1909, pl. 31,13, p. 10 (called Senmut).

(81) Daressy, *Recueil*, no. 232; Davies & Macadam, *Corpus*, no. 534.

(82) Davies & Macadam, *Corpus*, no. 511.

(83) Daressy, *Recueil*, no. 88.

(84) Davies & Macadam, *Corpus*, no. 429; *ibid.*, nos. 90 and 493. Cf. *ibid.*no. 89 from TT 89, and Daressy, *Recueil*, no. 249 from TT 123.

(85) Daressy, *Recueil*, no. 10; Davies & Macadam, *Corpus*, no. 15; cf. also *ibid.*, no. 491.

(86) Daressy, *Recueil*, no. 8; Davies & Macadam, *Corpus*, no. 8; cf. also *ibid.*, no. 494.

(87) Davies & Macadam, *Corpus*, no. 435.

(88) TT A19 also belonged to a *ḥ3ty-ᶜ* of Thinis, cf. pp. 52-3.

(89) Cf. chapter 2.

(90) Cf. chapter 2.

(91) Cf. n. 24 above.

(92) Bruyère, *Fouilles (1923-1924)*, pp. 101-2, 104 [7]; *Fouilles (1926)*, pp. 53-4; cf. a wooden fragment with the name of Smen *ibid.*, p. 54 [16], fig. 47 [E]. A fragment of a stela has 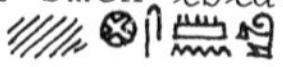 (p. 54 n. 1, fig. 46).

(93) A cone was found in pit no. 1090. Two cones were found by Gauthier, cf. *BIFAO* 16, 1919, p. 186 (called Smensa).

(94) Bruyère, *Fouilles (1926)*,p. 55 n. 1, cf. p. 54.

(95) *Recueil*, no. 49.

(96) *Corpus*, no. 74.

(97) Apart from being connected with Deir el-Medîna the name Smen is known at Draᶜ Abû el-Nagaᶜ (cartonnage fragment, cf. *Top. Bibl.* I^2,2, p. 608) and from a statue set up in the temple of Amenophis I and Aḥmosi Nefertere (*Top. Bibl.* II^2, p. 422). This latter person was 'brewer of Amūn'.

(98) Cf. n. 24 above.

(99) Bruyère, *Fouilles (1926)*, p. 54 [17].

(100) Bruyère, *Fouilles (1923-1924)*, pp. 7-16.

(101) Bruyère, *Fouilles (1930)*, pl. 32. In a model of the two tombs in the Museo Egizio in Turin the cones are also omitted.

(102) Bruyère, *Fouilles (1923-1924)*, p. 101.

(103) Mond in *ASAE* 5, 1904, p. 97 n. 1, and p. 98 n. 3.

(104) TT 122 (Qurna), 181 (Khôkha), 291, 329 and 339 (Deir el-Medîna).

(105) TT 45, 54, 58, 65, 68, 70, 77, 84, 112, 127, 152, 190, 257, 284, 337, 346 and 348.

(106) TT 61/131; 71/353; 80/104; 84/95; 86/112; 7/212/250; 299/359; 4/337; and possibly 340/354. The tombs numbered 215 and 265 are in fact one tomb.

(107) In the *Top. Bibl.* I^2,1 wives are not named as joint tomb owners. An inexplicable exception has been made for TT C3.

(108) Daressy, *Recueil*, nos. 5 and 20; Davies & Macadam, *Corpus*, no. 360.

(109) Davies & Macadam, *Corpus*, no. 75; cf. *ibid.*, no. 323.

(110) Davies & Macadam, *Corpus*, no. 52; cf. *ibid.*,no. 303.

(111) Davies & Macadam, *Corpus*, no. 340.

(112) Davies & Macadam, *Corpus*, no. 312.

(113) Davies & Macadam, *Corpus*, no. 295; cf. *ibid.*, no. 416; Daressy, *Recueil*, no. 200.

(114) The titles on the cones reflect a wide spectrum of Egyptian

society and include high ranking officials (high-priests, mayors, treasurers and so on) whom one would most certainly have expected to possess a tomb.

(115) The number of tombs thus arrived at may affect the calculations of the population of Thebes in the New Kingdom. The population of all Egypt is discussed by K. W. Butzer, *Early Hydraulic Civilization in Egypt*, Chicago/London 1976, cf. in particular p. 92 and Table 2, and Table 4 for the basis of an estimate for Thebes West.

(116) Rhind who was the only person in modern times to have seen inscribed funerary cones *in situ* (cf. notes 7-8 above) does not mention whether all the cones he saw were identical.

(117) For an estimate of the population and number of tombs in the Old Kingdom one may compare J. Baines & C. Eyre, 'Four notes on literacy', *GM* 61, 1983, pp. 66ff. with a reference to the Theban tombs of the Eighteenth dynasty on p. 68.

Chapter 2 Notes

(1) The dates employed in the tables have been calculated on the basis of the system used in the *Topographical Bibliography*, *i.e.* for monuments of private persons the reign(s) during which the person is estimated to have functioned. The dates in the Tables may thus cover a wider span of years than the time employed to carry out the wall-decoration. I am indebted to E. Dziobek for providing me with a copy of his dissertation *Die Ikonografie der Personendarstellungen in Thebanischen Privatgräbern der 18. Dynastie* (Heidelberg 1980, unpublished) which to a large extent deals with problems of dating. - Apparent 'exceptions' noted in the Tables may not have been so in actuality, when one considers how much has been lost. A scene unique to us by accident of survival may in fact have been more common. This should always be kept in mind when trying to classify any documentation from ancient Egypt.

(2) Bruyère, *Rapport (1922-1923)*, p. 58; *Rapport (1926)*, fig. 1, p. 8; *Rapport (1929)*, fig. 4, p. 19; fig. 54, p. 111; *Rapport (1934-1935)*, pt. 3, fig. 10, pp. 37-8; *Rapport (1935-1940)*. pt. 1, fig. 48, pp. 15-6 and 93.

(3) C. M. Firth, *The Archaeological Survey of Nubia. Report for 1910-11*, Cairo 1927, colour pls. 31-4, cf. pp. 236-7. The decoration is painted on mud plaster over a coating of lime wash, the walls being of mud brick.

(4) Now in the Egyptian Museum, Cairo, JE 38574-5, cf. K. Lange & M. Hirmer, *Ägypten*, Munich 1978, colour pl. XVII.

(5) A. Lucas, *Ancient Egyptian Materials and Industries*[4], Oxford 1962, pp. 52, 55, 56.

(6) Cf. *ibid.*, pp. 54-5. Limestone temples of the New Kingdom include a temple of Amenophis I at Karnak and his mortuary temple on the west bank; the temple of Tuthmosis III north east of the Ramesseum; the temple of Amenophis II between the latter and the Ramesseum (most of these now being destroyed); the temple of the Aten at el-Amarna (see below); the temples of Sethos I and Ramesses II at Abydos; and the temple of Merneptaḥ between the Ramesseum

and Medinet Habu, largely built of blocks from the mortuary temple of Amenophis III.

(7) For example TT 39. Cf. also G. Steindorff & W. Wolf, *Die thebanische Gräberwelt*, Glückstadt/Hamburg 1936, pp. 65-6.

(8) Cf. the block published in Manniche, *Anc. Eg. Musical Instruments*, p. 33, fig. 40.

(9) For an index of temple scenes in the Theban area cf. *Top. Bibl.* II². - One of the voices from the past suggests just how incomplete a picture we are left with today. In 1818-19 E. de Montule travelled in Egypt and provided a description of the 'palace of Memnon', *i.e.* the Ramesseum and the vaulted brick store-rooms behind; de Montule dug to the base of one of the walls and found 'upon a white sand, hieroglyphic designs executed in red, one of which I copied, being similar to what are frequently found upon the temples.' The accompanying drawing shows a man wringing the neck of a bird, with a plant in front. (E. de Montule, *Travels in Egypt during 1818 and 1819*, London 1821, pp. 42-3). The walls of the brick buildings behind the brick buildings behind the Ramesseum, including the vaulted rooms, still preserve large portions of plaster with a thin wash of stucco. But no design is visible. Judging from de Montule's drawing the design would be similar to that found in tombs, cf. for example TT 103: N. de G. Davies, *Five Theban Tombs*, London 1913, pl. 32 [lower right].

(10) Cf. Wegner in *MDAIAK* 4, 1933, pp. 55-8 and chapter 3.

(11) The 'official' gods represented in private tombs being adored by the king include Rēᶜ-Ḥarakhti (TT 4, 192 (twice)), Ptaḥ (TT 10) Ḥatḥor (TT 10, 192), Atum (TT 23,192), Amen-Rēᶜ (TT 48), Maᶜet (TT 4, 192), and the Aten (TT 55 and *passim* at el-Amarna). The Ḥatḥor cow, worshipped in the temple at Deir el-Baḥri, is shown worshipped by the king in TT 10.

(12) The gods of the Underworld (TT 192) and Osiris (TT 255). - An interesting unprovenanced block is published in A. Radwan, 'Ein Relief der Nachamarnazeit', *Orientalia* 43, fasc. 3-4, 1974, pp. 393-7. Radwan is doubtful whether the block comes from a private or royal monument, but is inclined to prefer a temple, as Sobk-Rēᶜ, represented on the block, rarely has a funerary role. The presence of the fan-bearer behind the king, however, would perhaps rather point to a private tomb.

(13) Now in the Louvre E 13461 bis, cf. C. Boreux, *Antiquités Égyptiennes*, I, Paris 1932, pp. 134-6.

(14) *Top. Bibl.* II², p. 358, cf. Chicago Oriental Institute photos 7282-3. The statues witness the Feast of the Valley.

(15) *Medinet Habu* IV, pls. 213-4. The statues take part in the festival of Min.

(16) *Ibid.*, pl. 203. The scene was copied from the aforementioned in the Ramesseum and also celebrates the festival of Min.

(17) *Top. Bibl.* I²,1, p. 464, index 3 (c).

(18) There is an exception in TT 65 where Ramesses IX is represented censing and libating to twelve statues of deceased kings in kiosks, cf. Lepsius, *Denkmäler* III, 235. In this case the scene is painted and can thus not be mistaken for a scene from a temple.

(19) Apart from Amenophis I and Aḥmosi Nefertere the following deceased members of the royal family are represented in some

Ramessid tombs: king Montuḥotp-Nebḥepetrēʿ(TT 2, 31, 277); queen Aḥḥotp (TT A18); princess Merytamūn (TT 2,4); Tuthmosis I (TT 51); Tuthmosis III (TT 153); Tuthmosis IV (TT 7); Amenophis III and queen Teye (TT 277 (twice)); Sethos I (TT 10 (presumably twice)); unnamed kings and queens are shown in the Ramessid tombs nos. 41, 266, and 284. In the Eighteenth dynasty there is a representation of Aḥmosi, Ḥenut-tameḥ and queen Inḥapi in TT 53 (temp. Tuthmosis III), a scene with Tuthmosis III in TT 89 (temp. Amenophis III) and another with Tuthmosis III on one side of a doorway and Amenophis I and prince Aḥmose-Sapair on the other in TT 161 (temp. Amenophis III). For evidence from Saqqâra see below.

(20) For the iconography of Amenophis I see Černý in *BIFAO* 27, 1927, pp. 159-203, and for Aḥmosi Nefertere Manniche in *AO* 40, 1979, pp. 11-19.

(21) TT 192 showing Amenophis IV libating to Amenophis III and Teye, cf. *The Tomb of Kheruef*, Chicago 1980, pls. 11 and 13.

(22) Mut (temple of Sethos I at Qurna, *Top. Bibl.* II², p. 410, showing Ramesses II as a boy, cf. Lepsius, *Denkmäler* III, 150 [b]); Isis (temple of Khonsu at Karnak, *Top. Bibl.* II², p. 236, with young Ramesses IV); Ḥatḥor (temple of Sethos I at Qurna, *ibid.*, p. 410, showing Sethos I as a boy, cf. Lepsius, *Denkmäler* III, 131 [f]). Cf. also a scene in the temple of Karnak, *Top. Bibl.* II², p. 105 with Ḥatshepsut, and another *ibid.*, p. 117 with Tuthmosis III.

(23) TT 85 (twice; temp. Tuthmosis III-Amenophis III); TT 93 (temp. Amenophis II); TT 350 (temp. Tuthmosis IV). Cf also the 'Bankes tomb' below.

(24) TT 48 and 57, showing Amenophis III being suckled by Termuthis. The two representations in TT 73 of a goddess nursing a royal child (Ḥatshepsut) depict statues and are thus not to be considered as wall-decoration proper. The child sits on the lap of the goddess (T. Säve-Söderbergh, *Four Eighteenth Dynasty Tombs*, Oxford 1957, pls. 1 and 2) and the pose of the group would have resembled a group like the one depicted in C. Aldred, *Akhenaten and Nefertiti*, New York 1973, fig. 54.

(25) TT 64 (twice); TT 109; TT 226 (with four royal children); princesses on the lap of their nurse occur in TT 63 and 78, and a scene showing the wife of the tomb owner nursing, but not suckling, the young king occurs in TT 85 and 93. Cf also TT A11 discussed below.

(26) Cf. Wegner, *op. cit.*, pp. 58-64. For foreigners in a totally different context cf. p. 21.

(27) Wegner, *op. cit.*,pp. 64-6.

(28) Sistra (*passim*); round tambourine (way station of Ramesses III and the High Gate at Medînet Habu); barrel-shaped drum (Deir el-Baḥri, Luxor temple, Medînet Habu, and the temple of Khonsu at Karnak); trumpets (Deir el-Baḥri, Luxor temple, shrine of Ḥaremḥab at Gebel es-Silsila, Abu Simbel and Medînet Habu); harp ('Chapelle rouge' of Ḥatshepsut at Karnak (twice) and Medînet Habu (among offerings)). The instruments depicted in the High Gate belong to secular music, *i.e.* palace music performed by the princesses on a large boat-shaped harp, lute (being tuned), and lyre (the instruments were not identified in the publication).

(29) W. Wolf, *Das schöne Fest von Opet*, Leipzig 1931, pl. II,2.

(30) An exception is TT 65 from the reign of Ramesses IX with a drummer (Manniche, *Anc. Eg. Musical Instruments*, fig. 6). Cf. also a representation in TT A16.

(31) *E.g.* a carefully dressed limestone block from the tomb of Ay, Egyptian Museum, Cairo 10/11/26/11; limestone slab from the Royal Tomb, G. T. Martin, *The Royal Tomb at El-Amarna* I, London 1974, pp. 91-3, pl. 54, cf. also nos. 403-4, and, for gypsum plaster reliefs, pp. 99-103; another fragment from the tomb of Ay, University College London 409, J. Samson, *Amarna. City of Akhenaten and Nefertiti*, Warminster 1978, fig. 29, cf. other fragments *ibid.*, figs. 28 and 30. A large fragment in Florence is in Wreszinski, *Atlas* I, pl. 395.

(32) Cf. Löhr in *SAK* 2, 1975, pp. 170-87, and a forthcoming work by J. Berlandini, *La nécropole Memphite du Nouvel Empire.*

(33) In terms of art the 'Amarna Period' includes the first years of the reign of Amenophis IV before the move to el-Amarna, as represented in the Theban chapels for the Aten and the tombs of Raᶜmose (TT 55) and Parennūfer (TT 188), and ending with the decoration of the tomb of Tutᶜankhamūn.

(34) G. Roeder, *Amarna-Reliefs aus Hermopolis*, Hildesheim 1969; J. Cooney, *Amarna Reliefs from Hermopolis in American Collections*, New York 1965.

(35) R. W. Smith & D. B. Redford (ed.), *The Akhenaten Temple Project*, Warminster 1976; Sauneron & Saᶜad in *Kêmi* 19, 1969, pp. 137-78; 21, 1971, pp. 145-50.

(36) For the existence of a separate temple to the Aten at Luxor cf. Smith & Redford, *op. cit.*, pp. 48-9. Characteristically the sandstone blocks from this site have a strong pink colour, and are usually very friable. Cf. also n. 38.

(37) For the Aten temple at Medâmûd cf. Smith & Redford, *op. cit.*, p. 49, and for the name of the building, p. 62 [§5]. The blocks found, now untraceable(?), were published by F. Bisson de La Roque, *Rapport sur les fouilles de Médamoud 1926, 1927, 1929-32*, cf. in particular the 1932 volume by R. Cottevieille-Giraudet. The blocks used at this site were yellowish, rarely red sandstone. Cf. also the following note.

(38) The existence of a temple for the Aten at Memphis as well as other buildings elsewhere apart from those at Karnak and el-Amarna is disputed by some scholars (Assmann in *LdÄ* I, 1973, col. 527 with n.29 and col. 547, n.4, and, concerning Medâmûd, M. Doresse in *Orientalia* 24, 1955, p. 114, n. 3). Others maintain that these buildings existed: H. Bonnet, *Reallexikon der ägyptischen Religionsgeschichte*, Berlin 1952.1971, pp. 69-70; Tawfik in Smith & Redford, *op. cit.*, p. 62 [§7]; Löhr, *op. cit.*, pp. 139-87. For the blocks found at Memphis itself cf. Petrie in R. Engelbach, *Riqqeh and Memphis VI*, London 1915, p. 32, pl. 54, and for the name of the temple *Royal Society of Literature*, 2nd Series, Vol. 9, 1870, p. 192, pl. 2, cf. *ZÄS* 55, 1918, p. 20, n.1. Cf. also *Top. Bibl.* III^2, pp. 839, 844, 850, 862, 872.

(39) Heliopolis: L. Habachi in *Festschrift Ricke (Beiträge zur ägyptischen Bauforschung und Altertumskunde*, Heft 12, Wiesbaden 1971), pp. 35-45, especially the limestone blocks in figs. 17-8, re-used in Islamic monuments. Cf. also Bakry in *CdÉ* 47, 1972, pp. 55-67, especially fig. 4 on p. 60; and Löhr in *GM* 11, 1974

pp. 33-8. These blocks may have come from Memphis and not from Heliopolis, but inscriptional evidence (Habachi, *op. cit.*, fig. 16, cf. *LdÄ* I, col. 547, n.4) suggests the existence of a temple at Heliopolis; cf. also Habachi, *op. cit.*, pp. 41-4 for the possible provenance of Cairo stela no. 34175. It may be pointed out here that there is also some evidence of Akhenaten's activities in connection with the Serapeum, cf. A. Mariette, *Le Serapéum de Memphis*, Paris 1882, pp. 131ff. Blocks of *talatât* type have been seen by J. D. Ray built into the corridors of the Serapeum. - Athribis: Fairman in *JEA* 46, 1960, pp. 80-2 (big limestone block), and *LdÄ* I, col. 536, n.30. - Armant: R. Mond & H. W. Fairman, *The Bucheum* III, London 1934, pl. 55 (no. 56) and R. Mond & O. H. Myers, *The Bucheum* I, London 1934, pp. 15 and 24, cf. III, p. 51, § 56. M. Doresse, *op. cit.*, p. 129 places the building from which these blocks came at Thebes. - Lahûn: *Top. Bibl.* IV, p. 112, cf. W. Stevenson Smith, *The Art and Architecture of Ancient Egypt*, Hammondsworth 1958, pl. 125 c; *MDAIAK* 20, 1965, pp. 79-81.

(40) Larger fragments with decoration in Amarna style are not infrequent, *e.g.* Cairo 26/6/28/8 (calcite), Aldred, *op. cit.*, fig. 31; Cairo 30/10/26/2 (*ibid.*, fig. 33); large fragments from Karnak: *Kêmi* 20, 1970, pp. 87-8, and *MDAIAK* 22, 1967, pl. 23 c-d. Cf. also the large block with an offering list of Amenophis IV found with the *talatât* in the IXth pylon at Karnak: Saᶜad & Manniche in *JEA* 57, 1971, pp. 70-2, and the block from Athribis, *supra*, n.39. Larger than *talatât* are also the boundary stelae, Aldred, *op. cit.*, nos. 8 and 28.

(41) For this term cf. Sauneron & Saᶜad in *Kêmi* 19, 1969, p. 143, n.1, and Smith & Redford, *op. cit.*, p. 1. Strictly speaking only the Karnak blocks should be referred to as *talatât*, as this seems to be a local term or at least one applied to blocks of sandstone only. The references by two Egyptian Egyptologists seem to imply this: Habachi, *op. cit.*, p. 45 calls the limestone Heliopolis blocks 'blocks cut in the shape of *talatâts*', and Bakry, *op. cit.*, p. 61 refers to the Memphis limestone blocks as 'blocks of the so-called 'talatat' type'; on p. 63, however, a block is referred to as 'fragment of talatat'. This latter is made of sandstone, like the Karnak blocks. - For the size of the Hermopolis blocks cf. Roeder, *op. cit.*, pp. 9-10.

(42) Sometimes there is decoration on both sides (Smith & Redford, *op. cit.*, pp. 30-1; Roeder, *op. cit.*, pp. 11-2); on three sides (Smith & Redford, *op. cit.*,, p. 31; Roeder, *op. cit.*, p. 13), or on the two short sides (Smith & Redford, *op. cit.*,, p. 31).

(43) Roeder, *op. cit.*, p. 6. One exception in sandstone was noted by Holthoer in the filling of the northern pylon of the temple of Thoth, cf. *Studia Orientalia* 43, fasc. 5, 1972, pp. 3-4.

(44) Doresse, *op. cit.*, pp. 121-2 (nos 1-2), cf. p. 128 ('C') lists a building of limestone at Karnak. The Fitzwilliam Museum block is illustrated in Aldred, *op. cit.*, no. 11. For the provenance of this block cf. also n.49 below.

(44) For possible painted decoration on the exterior surfaces of the Karnak and Luxor chapels cf. Smith & Redford, *op. cit.*, p. 54.

(45) Cf. my previous remarks in *CdÉ* 53, 1978, p. 13 n.1.

(47) Roeder, *op. cit.*, chapter VI; Smith & Redford, *op. cit.*, pp. 5-18.

(48) Cooney, *op. cit.*,(list of contents); Redford in *JARCE* 10, 1973, pp. 90-1; Sauneron & Sa^{c}ad in *Kêmi* 19, 1969, p. 156 n.3.

(49) The block in the Fitzwilliam Museum, Cambridge, mentioned above, n.44 shows the king (twice) during the ceremony of the *ḥb-sd*. Apart from the intriguing fact that it is a limestone block, it is identical in style and subject matter to similar Karnak blocks. The block may come from an otherwise unknown monument at Karnak or may have been part of one of the temples in the north, such as the Memphis temple, as suggested by Aldred, *op. cit.*,p. 97. Or the block may simply have found its way into the sandstone building at Karnak accidentally, or it may have been used deliberately by the craftsmen, *e.g.* a limestone rather than a sandstone block might have been regarded as a more suitable medium for carving this scene. All reliefs were ultimately painted, and a difference in stone would not be apparent. Cf. the presence of a single sandstone block at Hermopolis above, n.43.

(50) G. T. Martin, *The Royal Tomb at El-Amarna*, vol. II (forthcoming).

(51) The evidence includes not only wall-decoration, but also painted plaster pavements, as the technique used for this was similar to that used on the walls. Not included are tiles such as those found at Malqata, el-Amarna and the Delta.

(52) As for instance the splendid pavement found by Petrie (W. M. F. Petrie, *Tell el-Amarna*,London 1894, pl. 2 and details in colour pls. 3-4, cf. pp. 12-4). The pavement was partly destroyed by local inhabitants, then removed to the Egyptian Museum, Cairo.

(53) There is nothing left of any New Kingdom wall-decoration at Gurob, but that such existed is suggested by a Middle Kingdom example from 'Kahun': W. M. F. Petrie, *Illahun, Kahun and Gurob*, London 1891, p. 7, pl. 16,5-6. The decoration of the houses of the priests at the sacred lake at Karnak consisted of slabs of relief not unlike the lintels in tombs, cf. Sa^{c}ad in *Kêmi* 21, 1971, pp. 217ff.

(54) H. Frankfort, *The Mural Painting of El-Amarneh*, London 1929, pp. 1, cf. Bruyère, *Rapport (1934-1935)*, pp. 40ff., and Davies in *JEA* 7, 1921, pp. 1-7.

(55) Petrie, *Tell el-Amarna*,pl. 5 (colour).

(56) *Ibid.*, pl. 2.

(57) Frankfort in *JEA* 13, 1927, pl. 45 (2,3).

(58) Kemp in *JEA* 65, 1979, pp. 48-50, fig. 2.

(59) R. de P. Tytus, *A Preliminary Report on the Re-Excavation of the Palace of Amenophis III*, New York 1903, pp. 20-1; *ASAE* 4, 1903, p. 166 and 170 with pls.

(60) Tytus, *op. cit.*, p. 16, figs. 6-7; Kemp, *op. cit.*, pp. 47-8, fig. 1

(61) Tytus, *op. cit.*, fig. 17, cf. Frankfort, *op. cit.*, pl. 13 (called el-Amarna); Tytus, *op. cit.*, p. 15.

(62) *Ibid.*, pp. 20-1.

(63) Bruyère, *Rapport (1934-1935)*, p. 255, fig. 131; p. 257, fig. 133; p. 259, fig. 136; p. 330, fig. 202; cf. also p. 305.

(64) Bruyère in *BIFAO* 22, 1923, pp. 121-33, fig. 5, cf. Brunner-Traut in *MIO* 3, 1955, pp. 14-6 and Abb. 5, and Kemp, *op. cit.*,pp. 52-3. Cf. also a woman 'à sa toilette', *Rapport (1934-1935)*, p. 311, fig. 182.

(65) Vandier d'Abbadie in *RdÉ* 3, 1938, pp. 27-35, pl. 3.

(66) Bruyère, *Rapport (1934-1935)*, p. 286, fig. 157. For the symbolic significance of the duck in boating scenes cf. A. Hermann, *Alt-*

ägyptische Liebesdichtung, Wiesbaden 1959, p. 163 and *id.* in *RAC*, 436 ('Ente').

(67) Bruyère, *Rapport (1934-1935)*, fig. 192.

(68) Cf. E. Hornung, *Altägyptische Unterweltsbücher*, Zurich/Munich 1971.

(69) The sketched decoration was intentional and final, as opposed to preliminary sketches in *e.g.* the royal tomb of Ḥaremḥab, where the decoration was left unfinished.

(70) Although the Book of the Cow does not appear on the walls of royal tombs until the reign of Sethos I, a precursor occurs on one of the golden shrines from the tomb of Tutʿankhamūn.

(71) Ramesses III is represented in the tombs of his sons in the Valley of the Queens; Ay performs the funeral ceremonies in the tomb of Tutʿankhamūn.

(72) Most royal tombs have now been published to the extent at least that it is possible to identify fragments when comparing them with drawings or photos of the walls. Sometimes the photos show blank areas where pieces have been cut out deliberately. This is the case with the publication of the tomb of Amenophis III, as seen in photos taken by the end of the 19th century. In the subsequent publication in *MDAIAK* 17, 1961, pls. 23, 24 and 27 five king's heads have been cut out in neat squares, three turned towards the left, two towards the right. The accompanying comment by Hornung, pp. 116-7 says 'Grabräuber haben übriges getan, indem sie zu einem nicht näher bestimmbaren Zeitpunkt an vielen Stellen des Grabes den Kopf oder das Gesicht des Königs quadratisch herausschnitten... Es ist möglich, dass einer dieser herausgeschnittenen Stücke inzwischen den Weg in öffentlichen oder privaten Sammlungen genfunden haben.' It is indeed possible to trace most of these fragments. In that Champollion actually drew one of these heads, it is not entirely unexpected to find three of the pieces in the Louvre. One of them is mentioned in the *Top. Bibl.* I^2,2, p. 549; two are pointed out by Boreux, *op. cit.* II, p. 415, n.1, but without giving the provenance. For two of the heads the Louvre cards tentatively place the provenance as 'de la tombe d'Amenophis III?' (this information was kindly obtained for me by T. Holm-Rasmussen in 1978). When comparing these three fragments with the plates in *MDAIAK* there is no doubt that the heads belong to this tomb, no. E 13100 (facing right) on the pillar, pl. 27 (2); no. N 521B on the right part of the right wall above the shaft, pl. 23 (2); and no. N 521A on the left part of the same wall, pl. 23 (1). The missing fragments, fitting the left wall of the shaft (pl. 24 (1)) and a pillar (pl. 27 (1)) would show the king wearing the *nemes* headdress, looking right and left respectively. Cf. also a 'recent photograph' in J. Romer, *The Valley of the Kings*, London 1984, p. 124, and the following colour slides in the *UNI-DIA* series: 35241 (*MDAIAK*, pl. 23 (1)); 35242 (= pl. 23 (2)); 35236 (= pl. 24 (1)); 35237 (= pl. 24 (2)); 35258 (= pl. 27 (1)); 35260 (= pl. 27 (2)). For N 521 *(sic)* cf. also M. Kanawati in *GM* 51, 1981, p. 103, n.30.

(73) It is interesting that the only mortuary temple in which are represented the Fields of Iaru is the mortuary temple of the same king at Medînet Habu.

(74) Piankoff in *MDAIAK* 16, 1958, pp. 246-7, pl. 21.

(75) This detail occurs in the tombs of Sethos I and II, Merneptah and Ramesses III.

(76) Cf. for example TT 39: N. de G. Davies, *The Tomb of Puyemrê at Thebes*, New York 1932-33, I, frontispiece (colour).

(77) For the subjects depicted at Thebes one may compare the enumeration of details in Abdul-Qader Muhammed, *The Development of the Funerary Beliefs and Practices Displayed in the Private Tombs of the New Kingdom at Thebes*, Cairo 1966, and, for the Eighteenth dynasty, Wegner, *op. cit.*, pp. 55-92. For a summary of the scenes at Saqqara cf. Kitchen in *Festschrift Edel* (ed. M. Görg & E. Pusch), Bamberg 1979, pp. 272-84, especially pp. 275ff.

(78) *Top. Bibl.* I^2,1, especially the index of scenes.

(79) N. de G. Davies, *The Rock Tombs at El-Amarna* I-VI, London 1903-8.

(80) *Top. Bibl.* III^2,2.

(81) Other New Kingdom tombs have been found at the following provincial sites: Zâwiet el-Mayitîn (*ZÄS* 62, 1927, p. 75); Deir Durunka (Asyût) (*ASAE* 16, 1916, pp. 90-3, cf. Karig in *ZÄS* 95, 1968, pp. 27-34); Deir Rifa (*Top. Bibl.* V, pp. 1-3); Naga el-Mashâikh (A. Mariette, *Monuments divers recueillis en Égypte et en Nubie*, Paris 1872, pl. 78); Abydos (E. R. Ayrton, C. T. Curelly & A. E. D. Weigall, *Abydos* III, London 1904, pls. 26-8, p. 65; *Top. Bibl.* V, p. 74); Rizeiqât (*ibid.*, p. 161); Kôm el-Ahmar (*ibid.*, pp. 198-9; W. Wreszinski, *Bericht uber die photographische Expedition von Kairo bis Wadi Halfa*, Halle 1927, pl. 44); Qasr Ibrim (Champollion, *Not. descr.*, I, pp. 79-86.) The tomb of Usersatet, viceroy of Kush in the reign of Amenophis II, was visited by the early travellers (Hay, Burton, Wilkinson, Champollion, Rosellini, Lepsius and others). Apart from the representation of the king and various deities the scenes include the king receiving an emblem from Ḥatḥor and tribute being brought to the king. The tomb of Setau (temp. Ramesses II) was seen by Bankes and Champollion; in it there was a scene showing the deceased before the king. The tomb of Nehi (temp. Tuthmosis III) has a tribute scene. Nehi appears to have been buried in TT D1 at Thebes. For references to the three tombs at Qasr Ibrim cf. *Top. Bibl.* VII, pp. 92-3. No travellers after Breasted seem to have taken much interest in these tombs; ʿAnîba (G. Steindorff, *Aniba* II, Glückstadt/Hamburg/New York 1937, pls. 101-4). The rock tomb of Pennē I was visited by Hay, who copied some reliefs, and by other early travellers. The scenes include the weighing of the heart, opening of the mouth, adoration of the Ḥatḥor cow in the mountain and a statue of Ramesses VI in a shrine. For a reference to pieces stolen from this tomb cf. Haykal and Abu-Bakr, *Tombeau de Pennout à Aniba*, Cairo (n.d.), p. 3; Tôshka East (three tombs described by Nestor l'Hôte, cf. *Top. Bibl.* VII, p. 95, with no details of the decoration); the Bahrîya oasis (C. C. van Siclen, *Wall Scenes from the Tomb of Amenhotep (Huy) Governor of Bahria Oasis*, San Antonio 1981). The reliefs include the preparation of wine, measuring and storing grain, and a banquet, all traditional Eighteenth dynasty subjects. Van Siclen dates the tomb to the beginning of the Ramessid period.
From sites outside Egypt there is a curious example of Egyptianizing decoration: a painted slab of stone allegedly from the tomb of an Egyptian official in Syria, executed by a Phoenician artist, cf. *The Art of Ancient Egypt. A Series of Photographic Plates*

Representing Objects from the Exhibition of the Art of Egypt at the Burlington Fine Arts Club in the Summer of 1895, pl. 7 (no. 47). The slab was then in the Kennard collection.

(82) The existence of a New Kingdom necropolis at Giza is doubtful, cf. Málek in *JEA* 67, 1981, pp. 156-7. For the comparison between tombs at Thebes and Memphis cf. also my remarks in *GM* 71, 1984, pp. 39 and 40.

(83) Cf. Wegner, *op. cit.*, pp. 55-8.

(84) G. T. Martin, *The Memphite Tomb of Ḥoremḥeb, Commander-in-Chief of Tutᶜankhamun* (forthcoming).

(85) Berlandini in *BIFAO* 76, 1976, pp. 46ff. (a representation of Menkauḥor (Fifth dynasty) dating from the reigns of Tutᶜankhamūn/Ḥaremḥab).

(86) Ankhesenamūn in the tomb of Ḥaremḥab (at least twice), cf. n.84.

(87) J. J. Tylor & F. Ll. Griffith, *The Tomb of Paheri at el Kab*, London 1894, pls. 4 and 10.

(88) At el-Kâb there is a representation of the deceased fishing and fowling, dating from the reign of Sobkḥotp III(?). Other early scenes may have existed at Thebes.

(89) TT 51, 157, 158, 324 (Ramessid). A precursor is in TT 93 (temp. Amenophis II).

(90) Fishing and fowling scenes with the deceased as the main character are not to be taken at their face value. They have nothing to do with the sporting activities of the tomb owner during his life time, but in a symbolic way they express the idea of re-birth, cf. Desroches-Noblecourt in *Kêmi* 13, 1954, pp. 33-42.

(91) Davies, *El Amarna* III, pl. 8 (tomb of Ḥuya).

(92) A block in Leicester, cf. *Top. Bibl.* III^2, p. 758.

(93) Banquet scenes, agriculture, vintage, festivals, arts and crafts.

(94) At el-Amarna the god in question is either the Aten or the king. The gods to whom offerings or prayers are presented do not seem to vary much at the different sites. The tree-goddess, who embodies either Ḥatḥor or Nut, is frequently represented at Thebes, mainly in the Ramessid tombs, but there are a few examples from Saqqâra (Hanover, Kestner Museum no. 2933; Cairo JdE 52542 (Ramessid), and one from ᶜAnîba (Steindorff, *Aniba* II, p. 214)). Termuthis, the snake goddess presiding over vintage scenes, is only known at Thebes.

(95) The tomb of Tia at Saqqâra, to be published by G. T. Martin.

(96) Borchardt found only one example in the Theban tombs (TT 44), cf. *ZÄS* 64, 1929, pp. 12-3.

(97) Davies, *El Amarna* III, pls. 22-4, cf. pp. 16-7.

(98) On the cutting and preparation of Theban tombs cf. Mackay in *JEA* 4, 1921, pp. 154-68. Some tombs have both relief and painting.

(99) Parts of the tombs of Ḥuya and Aḥmes have (preliminary?) decoration in painting, cf. Davies, *El Amarna* III, pp. 5, 27, 28, 29.

(100) It is possible that those yet to be excavated may have painted decoration. Some of the buildings just visible seem to be of the free-standing mud brick type, like some of the chapels at Deir el-Medîna (private communication by G. T. Martin).

(101) Notably the tombs at el-Kâb. In the tomb of Paḥeri, some of the scenes are indistinguishable from a Theban tomb, see chapter 5.

(102) For recent publications of Memphite tombs cf. G. A. Gaballa, *The Memphite Tomb Chapel of Mose*, Warminster 1977; E. Graefe, 'Das Grab des Schatzhausvorstehers und Bauleiters Maya in Saqqara', *MDAIAK*

31, 1975, pp. 187-222, cf. also *id.* in *GM* 16, 1975, pp. 9-15, and *MDAIAK* 33, 1977, pp. 31-3, as well as *Porticus. The Journal of the Memorial Art Gallery of the University of Rochester* 4, 1981, pp. 1-8; J. Berlandini, 'Varia Memphitica', *BIFAO* 76, 1976, pp. 304-16 (tomb of Imeneminet, chief of craftsmen), *BIFAO* 77, 1977, pp. 29-44 (the tombs of Pay, chief of the harem, and the general Kasa); C. Zivie in *BIFAO* 75, 1975, pp. 285-310 (the tomb of Ptaḫ-may) and *BIFAO* 76, 1976, pp. 17-36 (the tomb of the chief of the royal carpenters Khaᶜemwaset), both said to be at Giza, but cf. above, n. 82. Cf. also forthcoming works by G. T. Martin.

(103) Tombs with painted decoration from periods prior to the New Kingdom are by no means rare and have been found at the following sites: Gîza and Saqqâra (OK); Dahshûr (OK); el-Riqqeh (MK); Maidûm (OK); el-Lahûn (MK); el-Hawawîsh (OK); Beni Ḥassan (MM); el-Bersheh (MK); Sheikh Said (OK); Deir el-Gebrawi South (OK); Meir (OK-MK); Gebelein (OK); el-Miᶜalla (First Intermediate Period); el-Kâb (Dyn. XVII); Asswân (MK). Tombs with painted decoration later than the New Kingdom, of which there are several, are not considered in this study. The point intended here is that there was apparantly nothing in convention nor geographical circumstances that would have prevented the decoration from being executed in painting.

(104) Lady Cecil in *ASAE* 4, 1903, pp. 60-4. The subjects depicted include funerary ceremonies (mourning women in front of the mummy, stela and pyramid tomb in mountain; weighing of the heart; adoration of the Ḥatḥor cow in mountain). The pillars have decoration suitable for a royal tomb: large scale representations of the deceased and a god. This design is unheard of in any other private tomb, but it is a standard motif in royal tombs.

(105) *Top. Bibl.* VII, pp. 38-9, cf. Hermann in *MDAIAK* 6, 1935, pp. 11ff. This tomb was visited by Hay in the 1820s, cf. Hay MSS 28845,125. The tomb, with its paintings on mud plaster, is attributed to dynasties XIX-XX by Porter & Moss. Fakhry in *ASAE* 35, 1935, p. 57 dates it to the end of the Eighteenth or the beginning of the Nineteenth dynasty. He compares it with the tomb of Kakemet at Asswân, and appears to date this latter tomb to the reign of Amenophis III. The scenes depicted at Nagaᶜ Bogaᶜ are those common to the Nineteenth dynasty Theban tombs: funeral processions with the mummy on a boat, opening of the mouth, weighing of the heart, the deceased before gates and gods (Osiris, Isis, the Ḥatḥor cow in mountain and others). An unusual detail is the deceased offering four calves to Atum. The four calves normally belong in the temple decoration. Judging from the subjects depicted a Nineteenth dynasty date seems plausible.

(106) *Top. Bibl.*VII, pp. 78-9, cf. Steindorff, *Aniba* II, pl. 27. The paintings on mud plaster 2.5cm thick include the weighing of the heart, funeral rites, Ḥatḥor cow in mountain, and a tree-goddess scene, dated to the Nineteenth or Twentieth dynasty. - Whether the tomb mentioned in *Top. Bibl.* VII, p. 80 quoting Somers Clarke MSS FE,4,5 was also a painted tomb is not known. The scenes showing ploughing, men bringing tribute, and cooking(?) point to an Eighteenth dynasty date for this tomb.

(1) Cf. chapter 2.
(2) As regards the architectural design, many of the subjects depicted, the occupations of the tomb owners, as well as the style and technique employed.
(3) A. Hermann, *Die Stelen der thebanischen Felsgräber der 18. Dynastie*, Glückstadt/Hamburg/New York 1940.
(4) For this subject see Ali Radwan, *Die Darstellungen des regierenden Königs und seiner Familienangehörigen in den Privatgräbern der 18. Dynastie*, Berlin 1969, and Wegner in *MDAIAK* 4, 1940, p. 55.
(5) TT 92 (temp. Amenophis II), a tomb with a square hall in front of the transverse hall, depicts the king to the right of the doorway leading to the transverse hall; TT 239 (temp. Tuthmosis IV-Amenophis III?) shows the king to the left of the doorway, but the tomb lacks the passage leading to the inner room. Finally TT 89 (temp. Amenophis III), with only one room, shows the king against the niche on the rear wall.
(6) It is noteworthy that among the few Thebans who prepared more than one tomb for themselves during their lifetime, one did not include a representation of the king in either of his tombs. The owner of the two T-shaped tombs TT 80 and 104 was overseer of the treasury and thus a high ranking official who might well have depicted his sovereign when virtually every contemporary did so. The owners of TT 61/131, 86/112 and 84/95 represented the king in one of their tombs, whereas the owner of TT 71/353 (temp. Ḥatshepsut) apparently did not (but the T-shaped tomb TT 71 was left unfinished, and the other had only one room.)
(7) TT 11, 22, 45, (48), 50, 52, 53, 72, 82, 101, 121, 147, 241, 345.
(8) Cf. also Wegner, *op. cit.*, pp. 64-5.
(9) For representations of the individual foreigners bringing tribute, see Wegner, *op. cit.*, pp. 58-64.
(10) Cf. below n.12.
(11) Or on a pillar in the hall (TT 67).
(12) Except TT 38 where the measuring of fields is depicted on the left side wall alone. But it is a question whether this scene does really depict the tomb owner's occupation, or whether it is a more general representation of agricultural activities.
(13) Two tombs which have a transverse hall yet are not T-shaped conform to this (TT 39, 109). So does in a way TT 92, which has the scene in the first of the two halls.
(14) Cf. Schott, *Das schöne Fest*, pp. 12ff.
(15) In TT 125 (temp. Ḥatshepsut) there is on the left jamb of the entrance doorway a scene showing the tomb owner 'pouring myrrh over offerings'. It is as yet unpublished (but cf. MMA Photo T 3491), but it may be the only time the subject is shown elsewhere.
(16) In these tombs (TT 89, 92, 109, 161, 165, 225, 229, 295) it is shown very close to the entrance doorway.
(17) In the T-shaped TT 251 only the butchers are now extant. Their presence suggests that this tomb may also have contained a representation of the tomb owner offering.
(18) Cf. Wegner, *op. cit.*, pp. 74-7, and for the hippopotamus scene T. Säve-Söderbergh, 'On Egyptian representations of hippopotamus hunting &c.', *Horae Soederblomianae* III, 1953. For the symbolic significance of the fishing and fowling cf. C. Desroches-Noblecourt in *Kêmi* 13, 1954, pp. 33-42.

(19) TT 24, 39, 81, 85, 89, 109, 165, 318.
(20) Also in the non T-shaped TT 39, 81, 85.
(21) In the tombs which are not T-shaped the scene was depicted on the right rear or front wall of the hall, if the tomb had more than one room. In one tomb (TT 85) the hippopotamus was placed on the left rear wall of a transverse hall separated from the fishing and fowling which was on the right side wall of the same room.
(22) Also in the non T-shaped TT 24, 39, 165, 318.
(23) Cf. Wegner, *op. cit.*, pp. 79-80. Wegner prefers a rather more narrow date for the occurrence of the scene, but his dating of the tombs seems to be slightly different from the one used here, and his list is incomplete.
(24) In TT 12, 24, 39, 81, 109, all showing the tomb owner hunting on foot.
(25) In the non T-shaped tombs the scene is shown in the hall, preferably in the right part of the tomb.
(26) Probably inspired by the 'sporting tradition' prevailing at this time, cf. W. Decker, *Die physische Leistung Pharaos*, Cologne 1971.
(27) For the style of the scenes cf. Wegner, *op. cit.*, pp. 67-8.
(28) TT 15, 24, 59, 81, 144, 175, 176, 254, 255, 260, 318, 334, 349.
(29) For the scene in this tomb cf. above, n.12.
(30) In the index of agricultural scenes in the *Topographical Bibliography* I^2,1, p. 466 (15a) TT 131 and 297 were not included, presumably because they were thought to depict the tomb owner's occupation and not work in the fields. The scenes in TT 188 and 333 were, however, taken to belong with these. The scene in the non T-shaped TT 39 also seems to belong with the rendering of the tomb owner's profession. He was second prophet of Amūn, and the agricultural scene belongs with the inspection of temple workshops.
(31) The agricultural activities obviously did take place in real life, but the point intended here is that it was not necessarily on the estate of the tomb owner in whose tomb they were depicted.
(32) In the non T-shaped tombs it is shown three times on the right wall of a passage, four times in the right and five times in the left part of tombs with only one chamber.
(33) Not 'very frequently' as Wegner puts it, cf. *op. cit.*, p. 69.
(34) TT 15, 39, 49, 81, 92, 165. the scene is placed on the right rear wall of the hall in TT 81 and 92, and on a right wall in the remaining tombs, except in the early TT 15, which has it in a shrine separated from the only other room in the tomb by a court-yard.
(35) Few scenes are left in this tomb. The occurrence of the vintage may perhaps suggest a date prior to the reign of Amenophis III.
(36) The proximity of the two scenes has been expleined by referring to the fact that they took place in similar environments, more specifically the Delta (T. Säve-Söderbergh, *Four Eighteenth Dynasty Tombs*, Oxford 1957, p. 17). This association is understandable, but perhaps a less realistic view should be taken considering the symbolic significance of the fishing and fowling scene, cf. n.18 above. Besides, vine would grow in most places in Egypt.
(37) For this subject cf. J. Settgast, *Untersuchungen zur altägyptischen Bestattungsdarstellungen* (ADAIK III), Glückstadt/Hamburg/New York 196.
(38) TT 318 seems to be the only tomb which does not allow for this subject.

(39) TT 12, 15, 24, 39, 49, 85, 89, 96B, 122, 144, 161, 175, 176, 179, 254, 255 and 260.
(40) This tomb also includes a representation of the funeral procession in the subterranean burial chamber called TT 96B.
(41) In the T-shaped TT 139 they are facing left, being depicted on the right side wall of the hall. Among the non T-shaped tombs TT 39 has the scene on a right wall of the shrine with the figures facing left; TT 49 has the scene dispersed on the two front walls of the hall, facing right. In TT 161, depicted on the right wall, the procession heads to the left. TT 122 with the scene on a right wall in a side room is unpublished. TT 130 has the procession in a similar position, cf. the fragment published by Werbrouck in *CdE* 34, 1959, pp. 203-7.
(42) Also in the non T-shaped TT 24, 39, 89, 161, 175, 176, 260.
(43) Cf. Settgast, *op. cit.*, pp. 112-4.
(44) TT 39, 89, 96B, 161, 165, 175, 176, 243, 260.
(45) Cf. a representation in the burial chamber of the same tomb (TT 96B).
(46) In the non T-shaped tombs it is six times represented on a left wall, once (TT 161) on the right wall. In TT 39 it is positioned above the inner doorway to one of the chapels.
(47) Cf. E. Otto, *Das altägyptische Mundöffnungsritual*, Wiesbaden 1960.
(48) TT 24, 89, 122, 144, 161, 165, 260, 295. The scene is mostly depicted on the rear or left wall.
(49) Cf. Hermann, *op. cit.*, pp. 78-84.

Chapter 4 Notes

(1) TT A27, a New Kingdom tomb belonging to Say, royal scribe of the altar of the Lord of the Two Lands; TT A28, tomb of Nakht(?) of the Twentieth dynasty.
(2) For tomb B4 see recently Manniche, 'A lost tomb re-allocated', *GM* 71, 1984, pp. 37-45 and a forthcoming publication by J. Assmann of TT 41, with a contribution by the present writer.
(3) For a recent biography of Hay, mentioning many other early travellers see S. Tillett, *Egypt Itself*, London 1984.
(4) For the date of TT A17 cf. *Top. Bibl.* I^2,2, Addenda, p. xxiv, and for a fragment described by Hay, now in Copenhagen, Manniche, 'The provenance of a wall-painting in the Ny Carlsberg Glyptotek, Copenhagen', *GM* 58, 1982, pp. 49-51. Hay's tracings of TT A15-17 are of a superb quality and will be published in a future study.
(5) The two drawings in Hay MSS 29822,30-40, showing two men with birds, walking to the right, and a kneeling man, cannot be fitted into any of the known scenes as suggested by Porter & Moss, who add them to the fishing and fowling scene. The kneeling man very probably belong in TT A4 which is described in the following pages of the Hay MSS (see below).
(6) Hay MSS 29822,43-4 does not omit the hyena, as quoted by Porter & Moss, but includes it.
(7) Keimer, *op. cit.*, p. 59.
(8) G. d'Athanasi, *A Brief Account of the Researches and Discoveries in Upper Egypt, Made under the Direction of Henry Salt Esq.*, London 1836, pp. 105-8.

(9) In the Appendix to his *Oasis de Thèbes*, listing the items in his collection, Cailliaud refers to another painted fragment, no. 478, also from a Theban private tomb, though perhaps not this one.
(10) *Antiquités* ii, pl. 44 [7] showing a man carrying two honey pots.
(11) Hay MSS 29824,19 verso.
(12) Cf. the reference under TT A4 below, chapter 5, n. 55.
(13) Hay, *loc. cit.*
(14) Hay MSS 29824,20.
(15) Keimer was misled by the information in the first edition.
(16) Hay MSS 29824,19 verso-20.
(17) Cf. chapter 3.
(18) Cf. chapter 3.
(19) This scene was separated from the rest when the MSS were mounted, and it now appears under the heading of 'The 7th Tomb' (TT 106).
(20) Cf. chapter 3.
(21) *op. cit.*, p. 106.
(22) MSS 29824,20.
(23) Cf. chapter 3.
(24) Inscriptions copied directly from the MSS (*i.e.* not in my own hand) are marked '(MS)'.
(25) *Loc. cit.*
(26) *Loc. cit.*
(27) For *ꜣIn(r)ty*, Gebelein cf. Kees in *ZÄS* 60, 1925, pp. 14-5 and *ZÄS* 71, 1935, p. 151; Sethe in *ZÄS* 47, 1910, pp. 44ff. 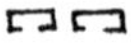 for 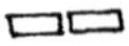 seems to occur only in Lepsius' copy of the inscription in the tomb. On the statue group the wife has a slightly different name and title: 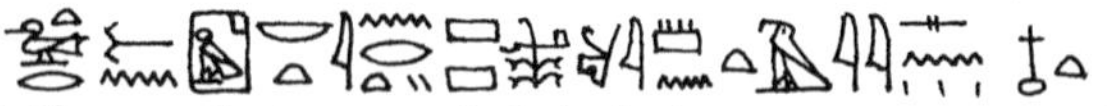 'chief of the harim of Ḥatḥor, mistress of Gebelein, songstress of Amūn, Taysen-nefert'. Ḥatḥor of Gebelein is also mentioned in the *ḥtp dỉ nsw*-formula on the statue. For Gebelein cf. further Reich in *Mizraim* 1, 1933, pp. 68ff.
(28) Cf. also the head published in D. Wildung, *Fünf Jahre. Neuerwerbungen der Staatlichen Sammlung Ägyptischer Kunst München 1976-1980*, Munich 198 , pp. 22-3.
(29) Cf. Manniche, 'The complexion of Queen Ahmosi Nefertere', *AO* 40, 1979, pp. 11ff.
(30) A representation on a lintel in TT 57 (temp. Amenophis III).
(31) Cf. the index of private names in I^{2},2, and recently J.-L. Chappaz, *Les figurines funéraires égyptiennes du Musée d'Art et d'Histoire et de quelques collections privées*, Geneva 1984, pp. 26-7, esp. n.5.
(32) Cf. Ranke, *Personennamen* I, p. 346 (1).
(33) Cf. the forthcoming publication by G. T. Martin.
(34) On the statue the  was copied as .
(35) Cf. Helck, *Zur Verwaltung*, pp. 526-7.
(36) *BIFAO* 7, 1910, p. 157.
(37) Adoration of Amenophis II is represented in TT 101 and 256, and in TT 200, where the king is shown with Tuthmosis III. Perhaps the conventional representation of the sovereign is meant?
(38) Helck, *Zur Verwaltung*, p. 510 (5).
(39) *Loc. cit.*
(40) A Minmosi of the reign of Tuthmosis III is well known from other sources (cf. Kees, *Priestertum*, pp. 33-5 and addenda p. 9). On a statue from Karnak he was represented as a child alongside two

sons of Amenophis II whose teacher he was (*sic* Kees). But this person is probably too early to be identical with the baby in TT A11.

(41) Champollion's hieroglyph looks more like 'the Elder', but his comments show that he meany it to be. *Sic* also Ranke, *Personennamen* I, p. 240 (15).

(42) For this lamp cf. Davies in *JEA* 10, 1924, pp. 9-14.

(43) Photographed by Schott, and by me in 1984. The children are at a larger scale than those of TT A11.

(44) TT 63, 85, 93 and 350, cf. also the discussion below under the 'Bankes Tomb'.

(45) In Hay's MS there is below these figures a rough sketch of another(?) woman with a child, and at the bottom of the page is scribbled 'the other... the king'.

(46) Rather than the mother, whose titles were copied.

(47) Apart from scenes with the tree-goddess.

(48) Cf. Davies, *loc. cit.* Already Hay suggested that these objects were lamps 'for incense or for fire'.

(49) In *Top. Bibl.* I^2,1 TT 176 is described as belonging to [Amen]userḥēt. But 'Amūn' belongs to the title of the owner who was *sḏm ꜥš n ꜣImn* 'servant of Amūn' (checked *in situ* by me in 1972).

(50) For this translation cf. Faulkner in *JEA* 42, 1956, p. 33, n.29.

(51) *Materialien*, p. 170.

(52) Davies, *Ken-Amun*, pl. 38.

(53) *Serapis* 5, 1979, pp. 17-20. For the priests of Onuris cf. Kees, *Priestertum*, p. 53, with a reference to this tomb in n.7.

(54) Davies & Macadam, *Corpus*, no. 482.

(55) Cf. *British Museum. A Guide to the Egyptian Galleries (Sculpture)*, London 1909, p. 12, no. 902.

(56) For some reason Porter & Moss also suggest 'Nakht'.

(57) Cf. C. Vandersleyen, *Les guerres d'Amosis*, Brussels 1971, p. 227 for the different writings of the name of this king.

(58) Buttons were not known in ancient Egypt. The garments were presumably tied with a string at the neck.

(59) The instruments are mentioned in Manniche, *Anc. Eg. Musical Instruments*, pp. 29 and 56.

(60) By Porter & Moss described as 'castanets'. The head of the girl was traced by Hay, cf. our Ill. 8a.

(61) Manniche, *op. cit.*, p. 49.

(62) *Sic* also Porter & Moss.

(63) This instrument, frequently represented in the Old kingdom, never occurs in the banquet orchestras of the New Kingdom. In TT 343 from the reign of Tuthmosis III a flutist precedes three men clapping their hands. In TT 192 (temp. Amenophis III-IV) a *nây* played by a girl accompanies a song during the *sed*-festival. Cf. Manniche, *op. cit.*,pp. 15-6.

(64) Giovanni d'Athanasi's house was just above TT 52 of Nakht.

(65) For this title cf. below under TT A4.

(66) An almost identical inscription is in Rosellini MSS 284,G 48 verso, except that Rosellini has for in the title of the tomb owner. 'Amūn' seems to have been hacked out.

(67) This MS, catalogued as 'various papers', contains a complete record of wind and temperatures during Hay's visits to Egypt, as well as a diary for the period 30th April 1830 - 15th July 1833.

(68) Cf. below, p. 137 for this garment.
(69) It is unusual that the name of the grandfather is omitted. Perhaps  is for  (cf. a similar name in Ranke, *Personennamen* I, p. 1 (5)).
(70) This composite name is not in Ranke. Hepu may be a separate person but there would hardly be room for him in this scene.
(71) *Materialien*, p. 41.
(72) E. Pusch, *Das Senet-Brettspiel im alten Ägypten*, Munich 1979, I, p. 147 [Da.44].
(73) J. Vercoutter, *L'Égypte et le monde égéen préhellenique*, Cairo 1956, docs. nos. 395 and 418.
(74) *Ibid.*, no. 492.
(75) MSS 29858,258-9 (15th - 16th April 1832).
(76) Restored from TT 82: Davies & Gardiner, *Amenemḥēt*, p. 28, pl. 1.
(77) For 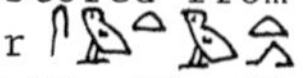.
(78) TT 39, 53, 81, 82, 85 (possibly temp. Amenophis II), 123, 125 (temp. Ḥatshepsut), 155, 164, 342. For the subject cf. T. Säve-Söderbergh, 'On Egyptian representations of hippopotamus hunting [&c.]', *Horae Soederbloemianae* III, 1953, pp. 5-12. The text is reproduced on p. 10.
(79) For a discussion of whether this Neferweben, who is elsewhere called '*waᶜb*-priest of Amūn' and who was father of the vizier Rekhmirēᶜ, was identical with a vizier Neferweben who left monument in the north, see Helck, *Zur Verwaltung*, p. 294; cf. also pp. 296 and 438 (7).

Chapter 5 Notes

(1) A paper on this tomb was read at the Third International Congress of Egyptology in Toronto, September 1982, and an abstract (in Danish) appeared as a newspaper essay in *Kristeligt Dagblad* of 23.11 1982, reproducing our Ill. 15; reprinted in *Papyrus*, No. 3, 1982, pp. 2-7. Cf. also another article in Danish, 'Kornskriveren Wensu's grav i Theben' in *Carlsbergfondet, Frederiksborgmuseet, Ny Carlsbergfondet Årsskrift 1985*, pp. 39-45. The illustration on p. 41 = our Ill. 22; p. 42 [left] = Ill. 37; p. 42 [right] = Ill. 38; p. 43 = Ill. 15; p. 44 [upper left] = Ill. 33; p. 44 [upper right] = Ill. 21; p. 44 [lower] = right part of Ill. 17; and the illustration on p. 45 reproduces in colour the original page of Hay MSS 29853,131 = Ill. 36.
(2) Giovanni d'Athanasi.
(3) Cf. also Rosellini MSS 284,G 62: 'Tomba che fu ben dipinta, ma non vi resta più niente.'
(4) *Sic* Burton. This presumably means that the figures filled out more than one register.
(5) In the *Top. Bibl.* the name is given as 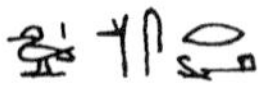 whereas in actua fact only  remained on the wall when Hay copied it. Cf. however below for the identity of this person (who did not hold the title of 'counter of grain' as Porter & Moss suggest).
(6) Already Rosellini (MSS 284,G 62) gave the name of the deceased as 'the scribe Wensu'. His note is on the same page as a reference to TT 19, suggesting that the two tombs were not far removed from each other.

(7) According to a letter from J. L. de Cenival there are other minor fragments of wall-paintings in the Louvre which may come from this tomb. Photographs were not available.

(8) The agricultural scenes and the offering bringers, the latter called 'une sorte de marché public'.

(9) J. F. Champollion, *Notice descriptive des monuments égyptiens du Musée Charles X,* Paris 1827, p. 99.

(10) For mention of this sale in the correspondance of Salt and Champollion with others cf. J. J. Halls, *The Life and Correspondance of Henry Salt*, London 1834, II, pp. 251, 252, 260, 262, 264; and H. Hartleben, *Lettres de Champollion le Jeune*, Paris 1909, pp. 239-40, and in various letters until p. 284, when the sale was accomplished.

(11) Salt had sent his first lot of antiquities from Upper Egypt in January 1818. This lot was eventually acquired by the British Museum. A third lot, collected between 1824 and 1827, was sold by public auction in 1835, Salt having died in 1827.

(12) Halls, *op. cit.*, p. 185.

(13) W. Hamilton, *Remarks on Several Parts of Turkey. Part I. Aegyptiaca or some Account of the Antient and Modern State of Egypt, as Obtained in the Years 1801, 1802,* London 1809. The private tombs are described on pp. 161-7. - As early as 1737 R. Pococke drew plans of two tombs which enable us to identify the tombs he saw with those now numbered 33 and 37.

(14) Cf. Burton MSS 25639,40: 'An interesting example of an Egyptian house & courtyard remain in part though mutilated also in order to get off some of the subject above.'

(15) MSS v.109 [middle left], re-drawn for *Manners and Customs* ii,122 (no. 111) = ed. Birch, i, 361 (no. 131), and reproduced in G. Maspero, *L'Archéologie égyptienne*, Paris 1887, fig. 17; 1907, fig. 18. Fig. 275 in Perrot & Chipiez, *Histoire de l'Art* is presumably also based on Wilkinson's copy, although the balcony on the left is omitted.

(16) Hay indicates that the square objects are white. They cannot therefore be copper ingots which often have the same shape, but are coloured red.

(17) The only other example of such a loop on a tambourine occurs in TT 273, cf. Manniche, *Anc. Eg. Musical Instruments* fig. 21 and p.6.

(18) Burton calls it a courtyard, cf. n.14 above and a comment next to the drawing: 'line of bottom of building on opposite side of court'.

(19) A whole row of houses is not known from other representations. For the type of house in question cf. N. de G. Davies, 'The town house in ancient Egypt' in *Metropolitan Museum Studies* I, pt. 2, May 1929, pp. 233-54.

(20) According to Hay the contents are yellow and red. Burton says that the basket has 'red ground with greyish coloured lines of meshes passing over the hoops &c.'

(21) There is a faint horizontal line before the cartouche framing this word = . For a similar feature cf. The inscription quoted p.56

(22) For the presence of women in market scenes cf. Herodotus II,35 and the comment in A. B. Lloyd, *Herodotus, Book II, Commentary 1-98*, Leiden 1976, p. 147.

(23) The red sacks are shaped like those containing *dôm* nuts, as depicted with monkeys on certain ostraka (cf. J. Vandier d'Abbadie,

Catalogue des ostracas figurés de Deir el Médineh, Cairo 1937, nos. 2274-9), and they undoubtedly contain the sycomore figs referred to in the text. For a representation of heaped sacks cf. N. de G. Davies, *The Tomb of Ḥuy, Viceroy of Nubia in the Reign of Tutankhamun*, London 1926, pl. XVIII.

(24) In MSS v.130 [upper left] Wilkinson gives a sketch of the woman turning her head, the man with the sack, and the scribe, as well as the inscription mentioning Pakedu. Next to it is a line written in hieratic:  [or ]  *ḥry mḏȝw ʾIrw* 'chief of the Medjay, Iru'. The writing appears to be of the Twentieth dynasty. I am indebted to Mr. S. Quirke for his comments on this graffito.

(25) For this word cf. Meeks, *AL* I, 77.2222 and the fundamental article by Keimer, *AO* 6, 1929, pp. 288-304, cf. *id.* in *Ancient Egypt*, 1928, pp. 65-6.

(26) Hay left an empty space between 'granary' and 'Siuser'. Judging from other sources (see below) the tomb was accessible during the Amarna Period, the name of Amūn being erased. Presumably 'in the temple of Amūn' is to be restored.

(27) There is no surviving representation of Wensu in this scene. On the other hand there is no first hand evidence that the mayor usurped the tomb. It is possible that Wensu had him depicted out of reverence, or because it was part of his daily duties to report to the mayor. A mayor of Thebes is depicted in TT 82, the owner of which was also scribe and counter of grain.

(28) Cf. W. C. Hayes in *Cambridge Ancient History*[3], vol. II, pt. 1, 1973, pp. 384-5.

(29) For the word *ỉnw* cf. *ibid.*, pp. 385-6, and the recent discussion by Müller-Wollerman in *GM* 66, 1983, pp. 81-93 and Boochs in *GM* 71, 1984, pp. 61-6. For some remarks on the trade business in the New Kingdom one may consult the chapter 'Handel' in W. Helck, *Wirtschaftsgeschichte des alten Ägypten* (*Handbuch der Orientalistik* I,5 , Leiden/Cologne 1975, pp. 259-67, and *id.* in *LdÄ*, vol. II, fasc. 6, cols. 943-7. It seems that free trade was only slowly emerging during the Eighteenth dynasty. Market scenes are rarely represented in Theban tombs, the one most frequently referred to being TT 162. The earliest example is from the Eleventh dynasty (TT 366), then follow TT 143 (temp. Tuthmosis III-Amenophis II?), TT 54 (Tuthmosis IV-Amenophis III), TT 57 and 89 (Amenophis III), and TT 217 (Ramesses II). In three of these tombs (57, 162, 217) the market is set up on the quay to served incoming ships. For an Old Kingdom parallel cf. A. M. Moussa & H. Altenmüller, *Das Grab des Niankhkhnum und Khnumhotep*, Mainz am Rhein 1977, pl. 24, cf. pp. 79-85. See also remarks on markets by Janssen in *BO* 40, No. 3-4, May-July 1983, cols. 278 and 282.

(30) For the date of the tomb cf. below.

(31) On food and ointment given to workmen cf. R. Caminos, *Late Egyptian Miscellanies*, London 1954, p. 312 with refs.

(32) There would presumably be more than one register, the lower ones on a wall being often more like sub-scenes, cf. Tylor & Griffith, *Paheri*, pls. III and IV.

(33) Hamilton, *op. cit.*, p. 164.

(34) Tylor & Griffith, *op. cit.*, pl. IV.

(35) Among the fragments now in museums there is one which shows plucking fowl and storing it in earthenware pots: Kestner Museum Inv. No. 1961,4. Although certain details such as the chairs are similar to those on a fragment considered in connection with the banquet scene (see below) the figures do not appear to have been drawn by the same hand as the paintings of TT A 4. The same applies to a fragment in the Metropolitan Museum of Art, New York, no. 06.1332.1 showing a man carrying birds and the back of a man undoubtedly engaged in plucking fowl in a shelter (cf. Ill. 109).

(36) There is hardly any difficulty in matching the three fragments to the left, joining the ploughman to the plough and the people pulling flax, who are replicas of figures in the tomb of Paḥeri. The little fragment with three men with a measuring rope must join the two men carrying the other end of the rope. A slight problem arises when joining the large fragment to the right. as put together in the Louvre, space has been allowed for two more ploughs with oxen. But unless the doorway was very much narrower than estimated above, or the tomb was more asymmetrical than Hay's plan suggests, there is hardly room for two ploughs. It is just possible to squeeze in the second span of oxen, and one may perhaps assume that the plough they pulled is the one temporarily drawn by the men. In the tomb of Paḥeri there are only two sets of ploughs with oxen, plus the plough drawn by men.

(37) Apart from being reversed the boats in the tomb of Paḥeri lack the decorative birds on the steering oars.

(38) But the three registers have been displaced to one side or the other so that on the Louvre fragments the figures are not directly above or below the corresponding figures in the tomb of Paḥeri.

(39) Paḥeri has *rnpt* 'year'.

(40) There are at least five more columns of hieroglyphs to follow. On the available photograph the following signs can be made out: 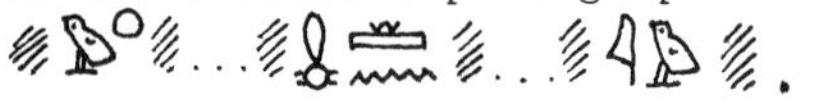 . There appears to be no parallel to this text in the tomb of Paḥeri.

(41) Cf. n. 36 above.

(42) The first sign is illegible, and so are the signs following .

(43) Cf. B. van de Walle, *La chapelle funéraire de Neferirtnef*, Brussels 1978, p. 54 n. 170.

(44) Cf. Meeks, *AL*, II, 78.1877.

(45) *WB* V.138.1 'Böswilligkeiten'. Griffith translates 'meanness'.

(46) Paḥeri omits *nw ḥtp nṯr*.

(47) Cf. A. H. Gardiner, *Egyptian Grammar*^{3}, Oxford 1957, 491,2 (last example).

(48) Hamilton, *op. cit.*, pp. 163-4. For scenes with bulls on tomb walls cf. A. B. Lloyd, 'Strabo and the Memphite Tauromachy' in *Hommages à Maarten J. Vermaseren*, II, Leiden 1978, pp. 621-2.

(49) Tylor & Griffith, *Paheri*, pl. III [lower left].

(50) Cf. however below, p. 78.

(51) *BIE* 34, 1953, fig. 164.

(52) It has not been possible to trace any fragments of the fishing and fowling scene to a museum collection. Only five such fragments are known to me, three of which belong to a tomb to

be discussed below, the fourth to TT A 5, and the fifth to TT 93.

(53) *Calotropis procera* Ait., a common desert shrub, cf. V. Täckholm, *Students' Flora of Egypt*², Cairo 1974, pp. 413, 414 and colour fig. 31.

(54) Hamilton, *op. cit.*, p. 164.

(55) Painted fragments of hunting scenes are exceedingly scarce in museums and other collections. If the 'hunting scene fragment' in the Michaelidis collection in Cairo, mentioned in *Top. Bibl.* I², 2, p. 820 is a painted fragment, it may perhaps belong in this tomb.

(56) Davies, *Rekh-mi-rē*, pls. LXXIX-LXXXIV, LXXXVII-XCIII.

(57) Beginning from the bottom. Hay apparently used this numbering of registers, but he drew the two lower registers together so that his '1st' register is in actual fact the second from below, and his '2nd' register the lower one (he explicitly says so). Hay's '3rd' register is in any case the one in the middle, his '4th' and '5th' registers being also reckoned from below, as became clear during the reconstruction. The Burton MSS do not specify where the groups described and drawn are to be found. - The registers are here described from left to right.

(58) Hay: 'Some are white with red spots others black spots'.

(59) The right part of this, including two figures, was apparently destroyed.

(60) Wilkinson MS v.130 scribbled 'young doms?' next to the trees. The colours in his minute drawing are blue, red, and green.

(61) Burton drew the palm trees (red trunks, yellow branches, he noted), the two other trees, the row of little pots (red) on a stand(?) (green with blue lines), the four chapels of which he says two are open, two shut, and the figure of Osiris with 'b' (probably = blue) face and hands, white crown and garment, yellow flail.

(62) MS 29824,18: 'The third line is as follows, but much is broken away'.

(63) According to Hay the shrine was green.

(64) Burton drew the three men in a boat (green), the hawk and two of the shrines beyond (MS 25638,50). In Hay's sketch the four shrines on the right are drawn on a larger scale below the others. The text says: '8 sanctuaries, these last have figures in them.' The six shrines on the right in the reconstruction are taken from Paḥeri, while the two on the left are as Burton drew them.

(65) Davies, *Rekh-mi-rē*ʿ, pl. XC.

(66) Cf. a similar member of the procession *ibid.*, pl. LXXXIII.

(67) A drawing of this man is in Hay MS 29822,36 [right].

(68) For the mysterious *tekenu* see H. Bonnet, *Reallexikon der ägyptischen Religionsgeschichte*, Berlin/New York 1952.1971, pp. 774-6.

(69) Burton, who also drew the *ḫbt*-dancers and what was left of the coffin on the sledge (MSS 25638,49) indicates that the inscriptions were in black.

(70) The figures were drawn by Hay in MSS 29822,36. Traces of hieroglyphs denoting the 'younger kite' remain.

(71) Hay says that 'the rest is drawn with the dancing men of the line below'.

(72) Cf. a similar arrangement in Rekhmirēʿ, Davies, *op. cit.*, pl. LXXXII.

(73) These offerings and apparently others in the part of the wall to the right of the five registers described above are referred to by Burton in MSS 25639,40: 'The goose & calf are seen repeatedly cut up as offering & we have the head (calves), lotus & [blank] & fruit & cakes lies by it - onions, figs, grapes.'

(74) 'Tyger' meaning of course 'panther'.

(75) Tylor & Griffith, *Paheri*, pl. V [lower right].

(76) According to Burton the mummy was white, the face light brown, and the beard blue, the garments of the priest white. Above was the title 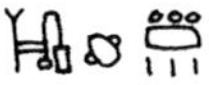 *sš ḥsb it* 'scribe and counter of grain'.

(77) At the level of the bottom of the middle register Hay wrote: 'this space measures 2 feet 6 inches', but it is not quite obvious which space is meant.

(78) Tylor & Griffith, *Paheri*, pl. VI, adjoining the banquet scene. For the monkey cf. J. Vandier d'Abbadie, 'Les singes familiers dans l'ancienne Égypte', *RdÉ* 18, 1966, fig. 27.3.

(79) The stripes are omitted in my tracing of the wig.

(80) For details concerning the Opening of the Mouth cf. E. Otto, *Das ägyptische Mundöffnungsritual* I-II, Wiesbaden 1960. The numbers in brackets <> following the descriptions of the scenes in the tomb of Wensu correspond to the number given to the scene in Otto's study, based on representations in the tomb of Rekhmirēꜥ. For an attempt of interpreting the rites cf. R. Bjerre Finnestad, 'The meaning and purpose of *Opening the Mouth* in mortuary contexts', *Numen*, Vol. 25, fasc. 2, 1978, pp. 118-34.

(81) *Šdp*, *Štpt* or *Šrpt* was the ancient name for Wâdi Natrûn, where the natron came from.

(82) Rekhmirēꜥ has the wakening of the *sm*-priest in this place <9> <10>.

(83) Presumably 'with the little finger' to be restored.

(84) The pellets in the bowl may be grapes. In the tomb of Rekhmirēꜥ <38> they have a similar shape, but are described as *ìȝrrt* 'grapes'.

(85) *Sic* the text, but he is without the panther skin. The final names of the characters should correspond to the figures in the scenes, but this is not always observed very clearly.

(86) Cf. W. Barta, *Die altägyptische Opferliste von der Frühzeit bis zur griechisch-römischen Epoche* (*MÄS* 3), Munich 1963, pp. 111, 120-1.

(87) The context and meaning of the remaining hieroglyphs ? is not obvious.

(88) Cf. Hermann, *Stelen* (chapter 3, note 3).

(89) No. D.51: C. Leemans, *Monumens égyptiens du Musée d'antiquités des Pays-Bas*, Leiden 1842, pp. 100-1; plate vol. IIe partie, 1846, pl. 13 [lower]. I am indebted to M. J. Raven and J. van Dijk for providing photographs and checking the inscriptions of this statue.

(90) Probably 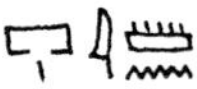 *pr ʾImn* 'of the temple of Amūn'.

(91) There is a group of signs between *ʾImn* and *di.f*, including two horizontal lines. Below *ʾImn* there is another horizontal line.

(92) Presuambly 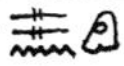 *ssn* (*WB* IV.277). The mention of myrrh and incense is interesting in view of the sweet-smelling products of the market scene.

(93) The word *ʾImn* escaped erasure on this part of the statue.
(94) Hacked out. An adjective is called for here.
(95) For the word *nis* in solar hymns cf. J. Assmann, *Liturgische Lieder an den Sonnengott*, Berlin 1969, pp. 194-5.
(96) For this sale see also H. D. Schneider (ed.), *Rijksmuseum van Oudheden*, Leiden 1981, p. 46.
(97) Cf. Halls, *op. cit.*, pp. 231-2. At the time Mrs Salt gave birth to her second daughter and died in childbirth, the wife of Dr Cimba who was attending her caught the plague. Eventually all the members of his family caught the disease, and Mrs Cimba was the only one to survive (cf. W. R. Dawson & E. Uphill, *Who was Who in Egyptology*, London 1972, p. 64).
(98) Vandier, *Guide*, 1970, pp. 30-1 (A 54).
(99) CGC 42132: G. Legrain, *Statues et statuettes de rois et de particuliers*, I, pp. 84-5. Cf. also *Top. Bibl.*, II², p. 284.
(100) No funerary cones of our Wensu seem to have survived. In Daressy, *Recueil*, no. 62 belongs to a man named 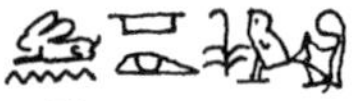 also called Ḏḥoutemḥeb, scribe of the city, vizier. The name may be read *Wnirsw*, and he would appear to be a different individual.
(101) Another possible Theban connection with the tomb of Paheri has been observed by Bothmer in the catalogue of the Luxor Museum. No. 91 is a stela of a certain Irhatsen adoring Amenophis I, the latter having, according to Bothmer, the features of Amenophis II The only other occurence of the name Irhatsen seems to be in the tomb of Paheri designating a man in an offering scene. Bothmer suggests that this could be one and the same person, and that he had at some time migrated to Thebes from el-Kâb. (I am indebted to J. D. Ray for drawing my attention to this reference).
(102) Nina de G. Davies, *Scenes*, pl. 6, cf. pp. 6-7; Davies, *Two Officials*, pl. 5.
(103) A. Mekhitarian, *Egyptian Painting*, Geneva/Paris/New York 1954, p. 80; *id.* in *CdE* 31, 1956, pp. 238 ff.
(104) Identical figures are marked with grey in our Ills. 20 and 28.
(105) Cf. the ostrakon in *MMA Bulletin*, Spring 1979, fig. 21. TT 93 of Ḳenamūn shows examples of a grid being drawn over the finished paintings.
(106) For the presumed existence of books on art in ancient Egypt cf. H. Schäfer, *Principles of Egyptian Art*, Oxford 1974, pp. 62-3.
(107) The kind of ostracon one would have to look for would perhaps be like the one reproduced in A. Page, *Ancient Egyptian Figured Ostraca*, Warminster 1983, no. 47 depicting three registers of the decoration of a wall. The ostracon in question probably illustrated the reverse process, *i.e.* a copy from wall to ostracon. Cf. also the ostracon Cairo 36407 with a perfect sample of ceiling decoration in full colour, as well as another one (exhibited in case 16 of the Museum) showing four registers of decoration similar to that of the wall of a tomb.
(108) S. Schott, *Die Schrift der verborgenen Kammer in den Königsgraber der 18. Dynastie*, Göttingen 1958.
(109) How the pictures of the grain barges became reversed remains a mystery. It is also a strange coincidence (but explicable if the artist used a 'pattern book') that there is in TT 146 a replica, also reversed, of the unusual scene with the swine in

the field of the tomb of Paḥeri, according to Hamilton also to be found in the tomb of Wensu.

(110) If the drawing was done by Dupuy, the French artist who worked for Hay on his second expedition, this error in drawing birds was repeated elsewhere, cf. Tillett, *op. cit.*, p. 61.

(111) K. Sethe, *Urkunden der 18. Dynastie*, III, Leipzig 1906, pp. 1039-41.

Chapter 6 Notes

(1) Lepsius, *Denkmäler, Text*, iii, p. 239. Lepsius' tomb no. 5, belonging to Parennūfer, First prophet of Amūn, has not been identified and is absent in the *Top. Bibl.* Lepsius recorded the name of Parennūfer on a stamped brick (now in Berlin, no. 1553), and made no mention of any decorated chambers. Parennūfer may be identical with the divine father of Amūn of the same name represented in TT 50 (temp. Ḥaremḥab) belonging to a colleague of his (for the identity of First Prophets and Divine Fathers cf. Gardiner, *Onomastica* I, *47ff.) For the group of tombs in question Lepsius refers to Section V of his plan of the necropolis (*Denkmäler* I,73) = the main hill of Draᶜ Abû el-Nagaᶜ.

(2) *BIFAO* 6, 1908, pp. 124-5.

(3) Daressy, *Recueil*, no. 165; Davies & Macadam, *Corpus*, no. 396. Twenty-nine more cones with horizontal text were found by Gauthier, but some had the variant title *sš ḥsb kȝw ȝpdw n ʾImn*= Davies & Macadam, *Corpus*, no. 397 (cf. Gauthier, *loc. cit.*).

(4) Daressy, *Recueil*, no. 12; Davies & Macadam, *Corpus*, no. 14.

(5) Hayes, *Scepter* II, p. 166 appears less certain. One cone is said to be in the Metropolitan Museum of Art.

(6) Hayes, *loc. cit.*

(7) Gauthier, *op. cit.*, p. 139 [B].

(8) Hayes, *op. cit.*, II, fig. 91.

(9) By Hayes called 'Senu', by Porter & Moss 'Seshu (or Seniu)'.

(10) *Op. cit.*, p. 138.

(11) *ibid.*, p. 140.

(12) *Naissance de l'Écriture* [Exhibition Catalogue Paris 1982], p. 140.

(13) For this name cf. the following page.

(14) Daressy, *Recueil*, no. 165 = Davies & Macadam, *Corpus*, no. 396.

(15) According to a letter from E. Leospo of 16.4.83 a 'third' stela, mentioned in Lieblein, *Dictionnaire* as no. 17 is the same as no. 157 due to a duplication of museum numbers. The stelae are due to be published by the Museum and photographs have therefore not been included in this place.

(16) Maspero in *RT* 4, 1883, pp. 127-8 (No. 153); A. Fabretti, F. Rossi & R. V. Lanzone, *Regio Museo di Torino. Antichità egizie* I, Turin 1882, No. 1639; Lieblein, *Dictionnaire*, No. 75.

(17) Maspero, *op. cit.* (No. 157); Fabretti, Rossi & Lanzone, *op. cit.*, No. 1638; Lieblein, *Dictionnaire*, No. 2048. Helck takes the owner of this stela to be identical with the owner of the cones, Davies & Macadam, *Corpus*, nos. 14 and 396-7, but does not relate him to TT A 6 (*Materialien* p. 32).

(18) Cf. Ranke, *Personennamen* I, p. 97 (12).

(19) *Ibid.* p. 96 (14).

(20) *Ibid.*, p. 97 (13) One could guess that the last syllable was *-ma (cf. Coptic ⲘⲀ 'place' and the corresponding *bw* in Middle Egyptian (I owe this observation to J. D. Ray)).

Chapter 7 Notes

(1) I am indebted to Prof. Dr. J. Osing for deciphering the hand of Lepsius in his notebook, and to the Griffith Institute, Oxford for making the MS available to me.
(2) Possibly misread for 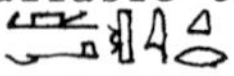 *wᶜ ỉkr?*
(3) For the word *ỉnw*, cf. above under TT A4.
(4) Porter & Moss interpret the notes by Lepsius as 'texts of wife and man offering, near door, on a stela (?)' and do not mention the mummies.
(5) The spare  may be a re-writing of Lepsius. A coffin and a mummy cloth of a certain Iuy, and re-used canopic jars of a Sen-sonb, divine adoratress of Amūn, were found in the same tomb at Sheikh ᶜAbd el-Qurna (*Top. Bibl.*, I^2, p. 677). The connection may be coincidental, although these items have also been dated to the Eighteenth dynasty. Maybe that *ẖry-ḥb ᵓInwy* 'the lector priest Inuy' was what was meant?

Chapter 8 Notes

(1) *Topographical Survey of Thebes*, London 1830.
(2) The career of Simut has been studied by Aldred in *JNES* 18, 1959, pp. 113-6. Cf. also Varille in *ASAE* 40, pp. 642ff; Hayes in *JNES* 10, 1951, pp. 237-8; and G. Lefèvre, *Histoire des grands prêtres d'Amon de Karnak*, Paris 1929, p. 24 (whose nos. 1 and 9 are the same person, cf. Hayes, *op. cit.*, p. 238, n. 464), and p. 62.
(3) Champollion copied 2, whereas Wilkinson twice gives 3 (according to Aldred, *op. cit.*, p. 115 this was probably a mistake).
(4) For the title 'god's father' cf. Gardiner, *Onomastica* I, *47ff. For *ḥry sštꜣ* cf. H. Gauthier, *Le personel du dieu Min*, Paris 1931 p. 27, although little is known about this title/epithet. Elsewhere (*e.g.* relating to a contemporary of Simut, Lefèvre, *op. cit.* p. 240) *ḥry sštꜣ* is followed by *m tꜣwy dwꜣt* 'in the Two Lands (and in) the Netherworld'. If  is not a misreading for , this may be what is meant here, the following columns of text being destroyed.
(5) The *Ḥwt-sr* appears to have been a building in Heliopolis (cf. Gauthier, *Dictionnaire* IV,127). But there was a Theban equivalent cf. Caminos, *LEM*, P. Lansing 13b,2, and Kitchen, *RI* II, 293.5; 600.6.11; 603.4, all referring to Ramesses II. Cf. the remarks by Yoyotte in *Kêmi* 11, 1950, p. 53, note a.
(6) Newberry, *Funerary Statuettes*, nos. 46539 and 47632. Cf. also Petrie, *Shabtis*, pl. 18.
(7) Newberry, *op. cit.*, no. 46558.
(8) *Top. Bibl.*, I^2,2, p. 785; Borchardt, *Statuen* IV,60; Helck, *Urk. IV* No. 733 + *Übersetzung*. The statue showing Simut and his wife seated is of unknown provenance, but cf. below.

(9) For the title cf. Kees, *Priestertum*, pp. 20-1, and *ZÄS* 85, 1960, pp. 45ff. Hayes (*op. cit.*, p. 238) suggests that Simut was related to Amenophis III (p. 46, no. 9 and p. 49 refer to Simut). *Wʿb m ḥꜣt* and *rmn* refer to the duties of the priests when carrying the boat of the god and other sacred objects, *sꜣ nsw* being an honorific title bestowed on them, not (as Hayes suggested) a family relationship to the king.

(10) Lepsius, *Denkmäler* III, pl. 84b. Simut is one in a row carrying a palm branch.

(11) Hayes, *op. cit.*, pp. 237-8, fig. 36D, 39,2; *Top. Bibl.* I^{2},2, p. 779. A stela was found near these jambs and a lintel, but there is no definite proof of it having anything to do with Simut.

(12) Helck, *Urk. IV*, 1886,9.

(13) *Top. Bibl.* II^{2}, p. 261; Borchardt, *Statuen* III, 161; Helck, *Urk. IV*, 733 + *Übersetzung*. This is one of two battered statues found in the temple of Mut, cf. M. Benson & G. Gourlay, *The Temple of Mut in Asher*, London 1899, pp. 347-8 (XXII = Cairo 932, and XXIII).

(14) For the implications of this title cf. D. Nord in *Serapis* 2, 1970, pp. 1-16 and R. Drenkhahn in *SAK* 4, 1976, pp. 59-67.

(15) An epithet of a priest, cf. Gardiner, *Onomastica* I, *43.

(16) Cf. below, pp. 98-9.

(17) For the reading of this title cf. the suggestion by Helck, *Urk. IV*, 1950.12 and the comment by Kees in *ZÄS* 85, 1960, p. 48 n. 1, who thinks that this reading  for ) is erratic. The signs copied here are those copied by Borchardt, with  to be read .

(18) Aldred, *op. cit.*, suggests that this was the scene with tribute, which we place on another wall, cf. below.

(19) Both Wilkinson and Champollion have  for .

(20) For this name cf. Ranke, *Personennamen*, p. 328 (8), for the New Kingdom referring to a Gurob papyrus in addition to the present example.

(21) TT 78 (temp. Tuthmosis III-Amenophis III), 91 (temp. Tuthmosis IV-Amenophis III), 89 (temp. Amenophis III), and a tomb to be discussed in a subsequent chapter.

(22) The missing signs can easily be restored from other sources, in this case TT 165, Davies, *Five Theban Tombs*, pl. 39.

(23) *Sic* Wilkinson. Presumably 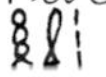 is meant, cf. n. 27

(24) The 'fen goddess'.

(25) Cf. above, n. 4. It is tempting to restore *ḥry-ḥb ḥry-tp*. For this title which effectively meant 'magician' see J. Vergote, *Joseph en Egypte*, Louvain 1959, pp. 66ff.

(26) Cf. above, n. 5.

(27) Ointment was often distributed as part of the pay to workmen, cf. Caminos, *LEM*, p. 312, and the remarks above under TT A4, p. 67.

(28) Cf. above, n. 3.

(29) *Ibid.*

(30) Wilkinson says explicitly that the Shemsnūfer carrying the grapes was carrying them 'on a table'. The Shemsnūfer in the vintage scene holds them in his hand.

(31) The first sign of the name is indistinct. In Wilkinson's MS the hieroglyphs go below the base line, presumably written at a larger scale to make them more legible.

(32) It is possible that Simut also held the title of *wʿb*-priest of Mut, although the title was not recorded elsewhere. After all

he did set up two statues of himself and his wife in the temple of Mut.

(33) G. d'Athanasi, *op. cit.*, chapter 4, n. 8, pp. 108-9. In the tomb d'Athanasi found a mummy covering of a lady, with gilded hieroglyphs and figures, apparently of a later date than that of the decoration of the tomb (no. 1126 of the Salt sale catalogue). It has not been possible to identify any fragments of the tomb paintings with those acquired by early travellers.

(34) Contrary to Aldred, cf. above. Surely Champollion would have distinguished between the 'sons and servants' he mentions, and anonymous tribute bringers.

(35) For this term cf. chapter 5, n. 29.

(36) For a representation of a wine cellar in the oasis of Bahriya cf. C. C. van Siclen III, *Wall Scenes from the Tomb of Amenhotep (Huy), Governor of Bahriya Oasis*, San Antonio 1981, pl. I, cf. pp. 8-9.

(37) Helck, *Urk. IV*, 1950.s (*Übersetzung*) translates: 'der den Tempel betritt, ungehindert im heiligen Gemach'.

(38) Cf. Borchardt, *Statuen* IV, pp. 60-1.

Chapter 9 Notes

(1) Yanni (Giovanni d'Athanasi) had a house near TT 52 of Nakht. A paper on this tomb was read at the Fourth International Congress of Egyptology in Munich, August 1985.

(1a) The drawings in the Prudhoe MSS were made by Major Felix.

(2) For the 'House of the Morning' cf. Blackman in *JEA* 5, 1918, pp. 148-65.

(3) Daressy, *Recueil*, no. 9; Davies & Macadam, *Corpus*, no. 11. The cone copied for these publications was one of the very few cones found at Deir el-Medîna, where it was obviously out of context (cf. chapter 1, pp. 7-8, and Bruyère, *Rapport (1926)*, p. 57.)

(4) *Not. descr.*, p. 825.

(5) The personal pronouns in inscriptions accompanying representations on tomb walls often appear to refer to the nearest person. Cf. for example the inscriptions in the contemporary TT 161, to be published by the present writer in *JEA* 1986. One of the daughters is called 'his daughter' or 'her daughter', depending on the position of the inscriptions (inscr. nos. 11 and 23). These pronouns should be interpreted with some caution.

(6) *Wsm* is a rare name. The only other occurrence seems to be in the Old Kingdom, cf. Ranke, *Personennamen* I, p. 84.14.

(7) Yet in the scene showing the Fields of Iaru, the name of Amūn *(sic)* in the title of Merymaᶜet seems to be left intact. Cf. also the text in our Ill. 43.

(8) Varille, *Karnak* I, pl. 45, p. 27 (Inv. 1722). The stela was partly mutilated during the Amarna Period, but the picture and texts of Merymaᶜet were spared.

(9) Only Merymaᶜet, his father Sennūter, and his son Pewaḥ (cf. Helck, *Materialien*, pp. 65-6); possibly also the son of the owner of TT A13, cf. above.

(10) One was the son of User, the vizier, who was prophet of Amūn

at Deir el-Baḥri (Davies & Macadam, *Corpus*, no. 1, and Davies & Gardiner, *Amenemhet*, pp. 32 and 33). Another was the owner of TT 403, a steward of Maᶜet in Thebes *(sic)* and scribe of the naos. A third was chief lector of Tuthmosis I (*Top. Bibl.* I^2,2, p. 795). A double statue the present location of which is now unknown is interesting as it may show our Merymaᶜet and his mother (*ibid.*, p. 610 = Philadelphia photo 40083).

(11) *RdÉ* 30, 1978, p. 16.

(12) J. J. Janssen, *Commodity Prices from the Ramessid Period*, Leiden 1975, p. 186.

(13) Words designating such a state were discussed by the late Ramadân Saᶜad in an as yet unpublished thesis *Les martelages de la XVIIIe dynastie à Karnak* (Lyon 1972).

(14) J. Assmann, *Sonnenhymnen in Thebanischen Gräbern*, Mainz am Rhein 1983, text 141.

(15) I am indebted to the Griffith Institute for providing first xerox copies, later photographs of the relevant pages of the MSS.

(16) The colours were noted (in French) on the tracings in the Hay MSS.

(17) It rather looks as if the woman was seated at a lower level and as if the feet of Merymaᶜet were resting on a low stool. According to the sketch in the Prudhoe MSS, the lower part of the scene appears to have suffered some damage, and the drawing by Rosellini is probably to be taken as imaginary restoration.

(18) Schäfer, *Principles*, pp. 177ff.

(19) MMA Photo T 836.

(20) Hay MSS 29852, 258-64. For the inscription cf. Rosellini MSS 285, G 40.

(21) The *mn* had been erased(?). The following signs are apparently incorrectly disposed. Perhaps *nsw nṯrw* is meant?

(22) The first *n* may just conceivably be an  reading *sn* 'they'.

(23) The loop of the basket is missing, reading *nb* instead of *k*?

(24) The inscription in the booth in the register below may also have undergone some changes, as the distribution of signs giving the name and titles of the wife is somewhat peculiar. Perhaps the parentage of Merymaᶜet was added later (by Wesem?), and the woman's name removed from the top left vertical column to the horizontal line below.

(25)  for .

(26) Rosellini, *Breve notizia*, pp. 50ff. (no. 51); Migliarini, *Indication succinte*, p. 58; Berend, *Principaux monuments*, pp. 3-4; Schiaparelli, *Museo archeologico*, pp. 317-20.

(27) A. & A. Brack, *Das Grab des Haremheb*, Mainz 1980, pp. 72-3.

(28) The sense of the three remaining signs is dubious.

(29) Davies, *Rekh-mi-rēᶜ*, p. 80.

(30) *Top. Bibl.* II^2, pp. 11-13.

(31) Helck, *Materialien*, pp. 65-6.

(32) Berend has 73x42cm. Either this is a mistake, or part has now been lost.

(33) Cf. TT A4, discussed above.

(34) Maᶜet is omitted in the Prudhoe MSS, perhaps by mistake, unless one 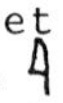 is .

(35) In the sketch in the Prudhoe MSS, the *prw nfr* as well as the right extremity of the register above was drawn below for lack

of space, but an x and an o mark where they join. The building was reproduced in Perrot & Chipiez, *Histoire de l'art*, fig. 278, presumably on the basis of Wilkinson's drawing. In the Prudhoe MSS a small structure surmounts the building. Cf. also n. 67 below.

(36) Rosellini, *loc. cit.*; Migliarini, *op. cit.*,p. 58; Berend,*op. cit.*, pp. 4-5; Schiaparelli, *op. cit.*,pp. 317-20; Brack, *op. cit.*,pp. 72-3.

(37) Davies, *Two Officials*, p. 17, n.3; Brovarski in *JEA* 63, 1977, p. 178.

(38) Shelters with two papyriform columns, though not in the middle but at either side, are depicted on Brussels E.2380, cf. Mekhitarian in *Serapis* 6, 1982, p. 88 with fig. 3.

(39) Above the sketch Wilkinson wrote: 'Qu! reading ye Acts of ye deceased? No. How could he be heard amidst ye cries of ye Women!'

(40) *LdÄ* I. cols. 45-6. For parallels to the representation in TT C4 one may compare TT 139 and 161, although they are not very close.

(41) G. Kolpatchy, *Livre des morts des anciens égyptiens*,Paris 1954, p. 187. I am indebted to Dr G. T. Martin for making his file on Fields of Iaru scenes available to me.
The scene from this tomb is mentioned by Mohammed Saleh, *Das Totenbuch in den thebanischen Beamtengräbern des Neuen Reiches*, Mainz am Rhein 1984, pp. 58-61. In the index of this work (p. 101) the tomb is correctly dated to the reign of Amenophis III, but in the text it is grouped with Ramessid tombs, only four tombs of the Eighteenth dynasty (TT 57, 120, 353 and B2) reproducing the Fields of Iaru. In his publication Dr Saleh does not mention the rediscovery of the tomb. The position of the scene, on his schematic plan on p. 61 given as on the right wall of the transverse hall of a T-shaped tomb, is in the text (p. 60) referred to as 'rechts?', apparently based on the information available from the *Top. Bibl.* and not on a personal observation on location.

(42) MMA Photo T 844.

(43) Wilkinson(?) copied  for .

(44) For an identical phrase cf. T. G. Allen, *The Egyptian Book of the Dead Documents*,Chicago 1960, pl. 31.

(45) Both Wilkinson and Burton copied the sign as .

(46) Cf. the presence of a man called Panūfer in the scene with the mummies.

(47) R. Lepsius,*Das Totenbuch der Ägypter* , Leipzig 1842, pl. 41.

(48) Cf. in particular a relief in the Ny Carlsberg Glyptotek, ÆIN 38 to be published in facsimile by G. T. Martin. The closest parallel for Thebes can be seen in TT 222 from the reigns of Ramesses III-IV. For a reference to lakes in funerary ceremonies cf. B. Geissler-Löhr, *Die heiligen Seen ägyptischer Tempel*, Hildesheim 1983, p. 437.

(49) For the identification of this plant cf. Keimer in *Revue de l'Égypte ancienne*,1, 1927, p. 183 and 2, 1929, p. 210.

(49a) TT 353 of Senmut has a small representation of the Fields of Iaru in the burial chamber.

(50) TT 8: *Mém. Miss.* LXXIII, 1 partie, pl. VIII (Wennūfer).

(51) Cf. above under TT A4.

(52) ~~~ for ...; *n wnt* for *nn wn*.
(53) *sk* has boat determinative from *Sktt*.
(54) Possibly in sense of 'accompanying'. *m-m* would be better.
(55) *WB* I.323, cf. Davies, *Two Sculptors*, pl. 6.
(56) ⲞⲨⲠⲰⲔⲈ= *w-pḳr*.
(57) Traces suit *3bẖ*, but a preposition is needed.
(58) Rosellini, *loc. cit.*; Migliarini, *op. cit.*, p. 58; Berend, *op. cit.*, p. 5; Schiaparelli, *op. cit.*, pp. 317-20; Brack, *op. cit.*, pp. 72-3.
(59) E. Naville, *Das aegyptische Totenbuch des XVIII. bis XX. Dynastie*, Berlin 1886, pl. 193. This Chapter is not illustrated in any other Theban tomb, cf. the reference quoted above, n. 41.
(60) For the architectural meaning of *wsḫt ḥbyt* cf. P. Spencer, *The Egyptian Temple. A Lexicographical Study*, London 1884, pp. 80ff. The author takes the word to designate the forecourt of the temple where the public was admitted.
(61) *Ibid.*, pp. 243ff, in particular the reference to 'Ptah who is upon the column' on pp. 244-5.
(62) Davies, *Ramose*, pl. 24.
(63) *Ibid.*, pl. 20. For a rather similar, but reversed representation cf. also Davies, *Rekh-mi-rēʿ*, pl. 91. I am indebted to W. Murnane for pointing out another parallel in the Eighteenth dynasty temple at Medinet Habu, cf. OI Photos 3047 and 7557, to be published by the Oriental Institute.
(64) Inserted above the inscription Wilkinson copied once more and added 'perhaps thus' (the stem of the flower is longer, perhaps including the foot of the which may then be another sign).
(65) Wilkinson's accompanying text says 'Niche at end fig of West standing Lady + at either side of niche within are man and lady of Tb'. Below he gives an inscription which is very nearly identical to the one pertaining to the anonymous couple which we have just assigned to the left wall of the inner room, except that the scene, showing 'Lady + Man of Tb seated' and the upper part of a priest is reversed. Wilkinson's 'niche' may perhaps be interpreted as including the entire 'inner room', and the inscription he copied may thus be placed on the right wall, in the exact position where we expected to find such a scene (cf. above). Wilkinson's 'niche at end' may thus correspond to our 'niche' and the goddess of the West be depicted at its rear wall.
(66) For a similar arrangement cf. Hermann, *Stelen*, pl. I (d) (TT 260).
(67) Wilkinson gives a more detailed drawing of three of the bringers of funerary equipment in the second register from the top (MSS v.181 [lower right], carrying a chest, two shrines and two vases. Above the figures is written 
šmt mḥ rdwy.k w3ḥ.k n.k '... going. Hurry up, store for you...'

Chapter 10 Notes

(1) According to Wilkinson MSS v.121 [near top left] it was a 'tomb opened by Ahmet below us.' Lepsius worked there on 26 November 1844.
(2) Hay and Burton, who were among the most diligent copyists,

did not work in this tomb.
(3) I am indebted to Prof. Dr. J. Osing for deciphering the hand of Lepsius in the diary, and to the Griffith Institute for making the MS available to me.
(4) For the abbreviations of these titles cf. Helck, *Materialien*, p. 10.
(5) Lepsius, *Text* iii, p. 264 copied whereas his notebook MS 342 has . Presumably *ꜣIwny*, Armant, is meant, cf. Helck, *Materialien*, p. 160 (Denreg is here called *Dlg*).
(6) Ranke, *Personennamen* I, p. 341 (17).
(7) Daressy, *Recueil* identifies the owner of cone no. 194 with the owner of TT C6, although the title on the cone is 'overseer of the garden *ḫnty-š*)'. For the location of this cone cf. *BIFAO* 16, 1919, pp. 175-6. Helck, *Materialien*, p. 113 does not relate the *ỉmy-r ḫnty-š* to the owner of TT C6. For Ipy and Denreg cf. also Kees, *Priestertum*, pp. 60. 72.
(8) Davies & Macadam, *Corpus*, no. 45.
(9) University Museum No. 39-12-5, acquired from a dealer in Cairo in 1939. The slab and the relevant information were kindly made available to me by the staff of the museum in August 1982. The slab measures 39.7cm (width) x 22.9cm.
(10) Depending on whether the staff was appointed while the king was alive.
(11) Cf. Helck, *Materialien*, p. 98, who makes Piay a contemporary of Tuthmosis IV.
(12) Cf. Rosellini MSS 284,G 37: 'Entrando è rotta ma resta un bell'avanzo di scultura colla figura del morto'.
(13) There are several options for reading the word . For the title Gardiner suggests *ꜥḥꜥw* (*Egyptian Grammar*, p. 498 (P1)). If one excludes the possibility that the boats were sacred barks (*wỉꜣ*) and take into consideration the function of any other vessel attached to a mortuary temple, as well as the appearance of the boat in Lepsius' minute sketch (see below) compared with the boats represented in TT A4, a grain barge is by far the most likely interpretation of in this particular instance. In P. Sallier IV verso 9.3 the word used for such a barge is *ḳr* (alternate possibility *mnš* (Caminos, *LEM*, p. 356 and pp. 19 and 403). For the general title *ꜥḥꜥw* is perhaps preferable.
(14) Porter & Moss place it on the 'entrance wall, right of doorway'.
(15) For a similar way of addressing Amūn cf. an inscription in the contemporary tomb no. 147, Schott, *Das schöne Fest*, p. 105 (54).
(16) According to Schott, *op. cit.*, p. 13 the roles of Amūn and Rēꜥ-Horakhty are quite distinct until the reign of Amenophis III. In our tomb the two deities, as well as Osiris, are recipients of offerings on equal terms.
(17) The text was also copied by Rosellini MSS 284, G 35 verso (including the missing *ṯ*).
(18) TT 256 (temp. Amenophis II) and 43 (temp. Tuthmosis III - Amenophis II).
(19) Cf. Hermann, *Stelen*, chapter 4.
(20) *Ibid.*, pp. 39-40 (TT 42 and 96A).
(21) Helck, *Materialien*, p. 80.
(22) Hermann, *op. cit.*, pl. 6a.

(23) Cf. above, n.5.
(24) For this expression cf. Quagebeur in *OrLovPer* 8, 1977, pp. 129-43, suggesting a saint-like state of the deceased.
(25) For this name cf. above, p. 126.
(26) Hermann, *op. cit.*,pp. 86-8, cf. pls. 10 c,d and 11 a,b. Mention of this scene was omitted by Porter & Moss.
(27) For the role of merchant boats in temples cf. Kemp in P. Ucko, R. Tringham & G. W. Dimbleby (ed.), *Man, Settlement and Urbanism*, London 1972, pp. 658 and 660.
(28) Porter & Moss place this scene in the inner room 'entrance wall, right of doorway (probably)'.

Chapter 11

(1) One and the same tomb sometimes shows different colouring on different walls; cf. for example the contemporary TT 175, where the right wall is painted in almost transparent colours, whereas the left wall has rich and heavy colours.
(2) I am indebted to Dr I. E. S. Edwards and Dr M. L. Bierbrier for bringing this letter to my attention.
(3) The history of the fragments will be outlined in a separate paragraph.
(4) *Sic* also Nina de G. Davies and A. H. Gardiner, *Ancient Egyptian Painting*, London 1936, iii, p. 125.
(5) C. Aldred, *Egyptian Art*, London 1980, p. 176, fig. 141 dates the banquet scene to the first years of the reign of Amenophis IV. This dating appears to be based on the representation of 'left and right feet'. S. Wenig, *The Woman in Egyptian Art*, Berlin 1969, pp. 48-9 dates it to the reigns of Amenophis III-IV. On the basis of the dresses, J. R. Harris, *Egyptian Art*, London 1966, p. 37 implies a date just prior to the Amarna Period.
(6) Cf. J. L. Haynes, 'The Development of Women's Hairstyles in Dynasty Eighteen' in *SSEA Journal*, Vol. VIII, No. 1, Dec. 1977, pp. 18-24. The author appears to date the BM fragments to the reigns of Amenophis III-IV, following Wenig. If given a slightly earlier date, the hair style would fit Haynes' criteria even better.
(7) As for example in TT 77.
(8) Wreszinski, *Atlas*, I,39b.
(9) Davies, *Nakht*, p. 56, n. 2.
(10) *Sic* possibly also Harris, *Egyptian Art*, p. 37 (to pl. 21).
(11) Mekhitarian, *Egyptian Painting*, p. 94.
(12) K. Lange, *Altägyptische Lebensbilder*, Berlin 1952, Abb. 55.
(13) Davies, *Nakht*, pls. 16 and 24.
(14) Differing from the so-called tripartite wig popular during the earlier part of the dynasty in that the section of hair at the back includes less hair than either of the ones at the sides.
(15) Mekhitarian, *Egyptian Painting*, p. 92.
(16) *Ibid.*, p. 69. Some alteration in the wig seems to have taken place.
(17) Davies, *Nakht*, frontispiece; Mekhitarian, *Egyptian Painting*, p. 94.
(18) Manniche, *Anc. Eg. Musical Instruments*, pp. 5-6.
(19) TT 56 (temp. Amenophis II), 75, 90, 101 (temp. Tuthmosis IV).

(20) TT 78, 90, 175(?), 249.
(21) Hence also TT 139 of Pairi, cf. Mekhitarian in *CdE* 61, 1956, pp. 238ff. This tomb is dated by the cartouches of Amenophis III on the lintel. Mekhitarian believes that the decoration of the tomb was a pastiche of that of TT 69 of Menna. For a comparison between the BM tomb and TT 69 cf. A. P. Kozloff, 'A Study of the Painters of the Tomb of Menna, No. 69' in *Acts 1st ICE*, pp. 395-402, esp. pp. 401-2.
(22) Cf. chapter 3.
(23) Cf. Wegner in *MDAIAK* 4, 1933, pp. 68-9.
(24) Possibly also in BM 37978, vertical text, where a remains and preceding signs have been hacked out. There is no determinative. - In BM 37979 the hieroglyph is rather similar to *(3ḫt)*, but the two vertical lines at the sides are narrower, and the rounded area is clearly not a sun disc, but a heap of grain with red speckles.
(25) The owners of TT 38, 82, 179, 317, cf. Helck, *Materialien*, p. 35.
(26) As the owner of TT 253, cf. Helck, *loc. cit.*
(27) As in some banquet scenes, cf. Schott, *Das schöne Fest*, p. 83.
(28) *Wall Decorations of Egyptian Tombs*, London 1914, pp. 10-2. A different name from Nebamūn was also hinted by Kozloff in *ARCE Newsletter*, No. 95 (Fall 1975-Winter 1976), p. 8.
(29) *BIFAO* 7, 1910, p. 157 (V).
(30) Cf. above, pp. 22ff.
(31) A man called is known in a Theban context, cf. *Top. Bibl.* I^2,2, p. 608. Although the evidence was found in a part of the necropolis which is of particular interest in relation to the possible location of the BM fragments (see below), there is no proof that this man was the official named on the fragments.
(32) The top left corner of a square, blue sign (?) remains.
(33) Cf. *WB* V.372.9-10.
(34) Cf. also Davies & Macadam, *Corpus*, no. 558.
(35) *Materialien*, p. 35. No supporting argument was given, but both BM 37976 and Davies & Macadam, *Corpus*, nos 66 and 318 were taken to belong to TT 231.
(36) Only a stela in the hall appears to have survived. The name of Amūn was not erased (cf. Schott photo 8650).
(37) *Top. Bibl.* I^2,2, p. 817.
(38) H. W. Müller in J. Leclant (ed.), *L'Empire des Conquerants. L'Égypte au Nouvel Empire (1560-1070)*, Paris 1978, figs. 66 and 7
(39) The owner was very probably the same as the one of the reign of Tuthmosis III mentioned in P. Abbott, cf. Northampton & Spiegelberg, *The Theban Necropolis*, p. 15.
(40) Cf. for example *MDAIAK* 4, 1933, pl. 6 [a] for the banquet scene in this tomb.
(41) Cf. the tracing by Davies in *GM* 65, 1983, fig. p. 57.
(42) For the conventional use of precisely these items cf. Schott, *Das schöne Fest*, p. 72.
(43) Three funerary cones mention a Neṯermosi (Davies & Macadam, *Corpu* nos. 62, 67 and 71), the two latter presumably belonging to the same man. He was 'scribe of the accounts of Amūn' (no. 71), and 'scribe of the accounts of grain, guardian of the chamber of Amūn' (no. 67), and 'scribe of the offering table of the Lord of the Two Lands' (no. 62). The owner of cones nos. 67 and 71

similar in style and arrangement of the signs, may be our Netermosi. His wife was called Mutnofret. - The title  occurs on nos 393-4 of the *Corpus*.

(44) Cf. Schott, *Das schöne Fest*, p. 124 (inscr. no. 121).

(45) Cf. *ibid.*, *passim* and the remarks and illustration in connection with TT C4 above.

(46) Cf. chapter 3.

(47) The measurements of the fragment as obtained from Musée Calvet in Avignon are h 40cm, w 32cm, but the fragment is obviously wider than it is high. It has also been so ruthlessly restored that only a close first hand inspection of it can yield the exact measurements. The height of the suggested, corresponding register in BM 37986 is 36cm. (The Avignon fragment was seen by me in 1978).

(48) *Top. Bibl.* I^2,2, p. 820; Keimer in *BIE* 34, fig. 148, pp. 365-7; J. Omlin, *Der Papyrus 55001 und seine satirisch-erotischen Zeichnungen und Inschriften*, Turin 1973, pl. 25c.

(49) Rippled shawls were known in Eighteenth dynasty tombs until the reign of Amenophis II, usually worn by the tomb owner or sometimes the king, but once by dancing girls and the wife of the tomb owner (TT 179, cf. n. 40 above). For rippled garments cf. Mackay in *JEA* 10, 1924, pp. 41-3.

(50) Cf. above n. 24 for the last sign.

(51) As for instance the mat in TT 69 of Menna, where the tomb owner is seated on a folding chair behind an offering table next to agricultural scenes.

(52) Porter & Moss date this fragment to the Ramessid Period. This seems unlikely. A subsequent publication in *Ägyptisches Museum 1823-1973* has '15th cent. B.C.'.

(53) Northampton & Spiegelberg, *The Theban Necropolis*.

(54) For the subject depicted cf. L. Klebs, *Die Reliefs und Malereien des Neuen Reiches* III, Heidelberg 1934, pp. 83-4.

(55) The source from which the authors drew their information remains unknown. There is no mention of the fragment among the very brief entries in the Spiegelberg Fundjournal now in the Griffith Institute.

(56) Other fragments with agricultural scenes are those in the Louvre from TT A4; another in the Rustafjaell collection; one in the de Benzion collection; and a group of fragments in Turin, for all of which cf. the appendices below.

(57) A very similar jumping man in TT 57 is also shown wearing sandals (carved in relief, cf. Wreszinski, *Atlas*, i,189), and a fragment found in TT C4, cf. above.

(58) Cf. *Sotheby Sale Cat.*, Dec. 19-21 1906, pl. 8 (no. 15).

(59) TT 38, cf. Davies, *Scenes*, pl. 2.

(60) Cf. Wegner, *op. cit.*,p. 67, quoting TT 38, 69, 75 and 86 from the reign of Tuthmosis IV, TT 57 from that of Amenophis III, and TT 297 (early Eighteenth dynasty).

(61) Davies, *Scenes*, pl. 2.

(62) Cf. Schott in H. H. Nelson & U. Hölscher, *Work in Western Thebes 1931-33*, Chicago 1934, p. 88.

(63) One fragment formerly in the Rustafjaell collection is said to represent Amūn-Rēᶜ (*Sotheby Sale Cat.*, Dec. 9-10 1907, no. 161), but as long as the whereabouts of the fragment are unknown, no identification can be made.

(64) For a similar text cf. TT A24 above.
(65) Cf. also Capart in *CdE* 19, 1944, pp. 192-3.
(66) Possibly for 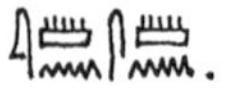. A limestone figure of a man of this name (with  added) was found by Northampton & Spiegelberg at Dra^{c} Abû el-Naga^{c} (*Theban Necropolis*, p. 8 [12]).
(67) This scene miraculously survives on the wall in this much destroyed tomb (cf. Wreszinski, *Atlas*, i,222).
(68) Cf. for example TT 276 (MMA Photo T 2644).
(69) Cf. chapter 3.
(70) Cf. the courtiers represented in the tomb of Tut^{c}ankhamūn.
(71) *GM* 65, 1983, fig. p. 61 (print of a photo taken by Mond).
(72) Davies, *Eg. Tomb Paintings*, p. 6, n.1.
(73) I am indebted to Dr M. L. Bierbrier for answering my queries about the BM fragments.
(74) I am grateful to Mr A. Mitchell of the National Trust for providing me with xerox copies of the relevant pages of the Bankes MSS.
(75) A description of the visit by the Belmores is given in R. Richardson, *Travels along the Mediterranean and Parts Adjacent in Company with the Earl of Belmore during the Years 1816-17-18*, London 1822. The beginning of Vol. II deals with the early part of 1818 and the party's stay at Thebes. The antiquities acquired by 'the Greek' (= d'Athanasi) for Belmore are mentioned (p. 2), and there is some discussion of private tombs, though they were virtually unexplored (p. 78).
(76) Halls, *op. cit.* above under chapter 5, n.10, ii, pp. 45-6.
(77) See above chapter 5 (TT A4).
(78) Halls, *op. cit.*, ii, p. 153.
(79) *Ibid.*, p. 178.
(80) *Ibid.*, pp. 117-8; 143-5.
(81) The first edition of his *Manners and Customs* came out in 1837.
(82) Hartleben, *op. cit. supra*, chapter 5, n.10, i, p. 499.
(83) There is hardly any possibility of the tomb being located at Beni Hasan, cf. chapter 2, and the letter by Salt referred to above pp. 137 and 156. Champollion and Rosellini co-operated so closely during their expedition to Egypt that it is by no means surprising to find duplicate drawings in their publications. the error is repreated by Perrot & Chipiez, *Histoire de l'Art*, pp. 793-4, who reproduce the drawing by Champollion with the comment that 'on ne voit pas que la peinture thebaine soit en avance sur celle de Beni-Hassan'. Indeed not. (A similar mistake was made in a guide book published some thirty years later, W. H. Davenport Adams, *The Valley of the Nile. Its Tombs, Temples and Monuments*, London 1867. In the chapter dealing with Thebes, there is no mention of any private tombs. These have apparently been transferred to the section of Beni Hasan where, on p. 82, the drawing of the brick makers from TT 100 of Rekh-mirē^{c} is also wrongly attributed. The book appears to be based on secondary sources, notably a book by H. Martinaeu who does indeed describe the Theban tombs, but perhaps without clarific-ation.)
(84) Letter from Salt 22 May 1819, cf. Halls, *op. cit.*, pp. 133 and 135.

(85) Personal communication from the chief curator of the museum, G. de Loÿe.
(86) Letter from Aix, dated 23.7 1828, quoted in Hartleben, *op. cit.*, ii, p. 10.
(87) Dawson in *JEA* 35, 1949, p. 160.
(88) Dawson & Uphill, *Who Was Who*, p. 232.
(89) For work carried out by the present writer at the site cf. a forthcoming volume of *ASAE*.

Chapter 12 Notes

(1) *Top. Bibl.* I^2,2, p. 820.
(2) *Eg. Tomb Paintings*, pls. 2, 5 and 6. In the accompanying text to pl. 2 it is said that 'whether the piece has been cut out from an existing tomb chapel or whether all except this fragment has perished we cannot tell'. From Finati's account (see below) it is obvious that 'several groups' were cut out. There is nothing incompatible about the date and style of the painted fragments in the Bankes collection, and we may take it that they come from the same tomb, a fact amply substantiated by the references given by the early travellers.
(3) The harpist, cf. Davies, *op. cit.*,pl. 6.
(4) This date is quoted by Davies, *op. cit.*, pl. 6. Cf. also p. 155 above. The BM fragments arrived onboard the same ship.
(5) W. J. Bankes (ed.), *Life and Adventures of Giovanni Finati* I-III, London 1830.
(6) *I.e.* a small tomb with 'two rooms painted all over', and a shaft with mummies.
(7) G. Belzoni, *Narrative of the Operations and Recent Discoveries within the Pyramids, Temples, Tombs and Excavations, in Egypt and Nubia* I-II, London 1820, p. 356. The three anonymous travellers are probably those mentioned by Finati, *op. cit.* II, pp. 217ff.: Col. Straton, Capt. Bennet and Mr Fuller.
(8) C. L. Irby & J. Mangles, *Travels in Egypt and Nubia, Syria and the Holy Land*, London 1844.
(9) The authors presumably refer to the members of the expedition of Napoleon, who hardly included any material from private tombs at thebes in their publication, although they had access to TT A5 among others.
(10) The only likely 'earthenware ornaments' on the mummies would seem to be ushabti figures, possibly called Nilometers because of their resemblance to the fogurines thrown into the Nile during the ceremony of opening the canals in the previous century (I owe this suggestion to Dr G. T. Martin). But perhaps they were amulets wrapped up in the bandages.
(11) Halls, *op. cit.*, II, p. 45.
(12) 'Account of the Sepulchral Caverns of Egypt', *The Edinburgh Philosophical Journal* 3, 1820, pp. 345-8.
(13) Possibly an ☥.
(14) Manniche, *Anc. Eg. Musical instruments*, p. 5.
(15) Bankes' own copy was used as a frontispiece to H. Salt, *Essay on Dr. Young's and M. Champollion's Phonetic System of Hieroglyphics, with some additional Discoveries*, &c., London 1825.

(16) In theory the royal name could refer to a deified king, but representations of for example Amenophis I in this capacity only appear during the reign of Amenophis III. The royal name may also be part of the tomb owner's title, cf. below.

(17) The closest parallels showing a woman nursing a prince are: TT 85 (temp. Tuthmosis III-Amenophis II: wife nursing an unnamed prince); TT 93 (temp. Amenophis II: mother nursing Amenophis II); TT 63 (temp. Tuthmosis IV: wife nursing a princess). With the exception of TT 350, which appears to be unfinished, all of these tombs include a representation of the sovereign on one or both sides of the doorway to the inner chamber(s).

(18) I am indebted to Dr R. G. Robins for providing me with a list of royal nurses of the Eighteenth dynasty. The suggestions as to which infants were in their care as well as any other conclusions expressed here are my own. For other (anonymous) nurses to royal(?) children one may compare TT A11.

(19) Nor is the husband of Ipu of CG 24034, but the couple would seem to be rather too early to be seriously considered in this context.

(20) His name does not occur in TT 93 of Ḳenamūn, his son (or at least the son of his wife), nor is it included in the funerary cones and on a headless statue found in the temple of Mut (Cairo Museum 935).

(21) M. Werbrouck, 'Cones funéraires de Kaemimen', *CdÉ* 33, 1958, pp. 223-6, also referring to the statue in a private collection, now Leiden F 1962/81 and another in the Louvre, 10.443. The author mentions that the cones in question are of a kind frequently found in the northern part of the necropolis (Assâsîf and Draᶜ Abû el-Nagaᶜ). For the statues cf. A. de Buck in *Jaarbericht, Ex Oriente Lux* 15, pp. 5-11, pls. 1-2.

(22) In terms of years the reign of Tuthmosis III falls in the middle of the Eighteenth dynasty. On the basis of the Abydos list, Tuthmosis III is the fourth out of eight rulers mentioned.

(23) It has not been established with any certainty at which point the staff of the mortuary temples was appointed, cf. the remarks under TT C6 above.

(24) In Shrine no. 11 at Gebel es-Silsila there is a rock cut statue of a royal nurse, also called Ḥenuttawy (R. Caminos & T. G. H. James, *Gebel Es-Silsileh* I, pl. 25). The shrine was cut in the reign of Amenophis II. The possible family relationship between this Ḥenuttawy and the other persons who were represented in the rock cut statues next to her has not been established. One was Usersatet, viceroy of Amenophis II, another represented his mother. Usersatet left a statue at Thebes, but no tomb of his has as yet been discovered.

(25) Militating against the attractive identification with the tomb of Kaemimen there is one fact: the ornament worn by the young king. According to Straton he wore a 'scarab' around his neck. This was presumably part of a pectoral such as that shown on the chest of the young king Tuthmosis IV represented on the lap of his tutor in TT 64 (*JEA* 14, 1928, pl. 12). The scarab being part of most royal names of the Eighteenth dynasty it may have been worn by other royal children, not just Tuthmosis IV, but evidence is lacking.

(26) This group was taken by Helck, *Materialien*, p. 95 to belong to Kaemḥeribsen, who was owner of TT 98 and had titles rather similar to those of Kaemimen (he was second prophet of Amūn, but not necessarily in Ḥenketᶜankh. The daughter was songstress of ᶜAkheprurēᶜ). The names of Kaemimen and his wife, Merytrēᶜ, who was songstress of Amūn, were mutilated when the name of Amūn was persecuted, but only along the front of the statue group. On the sides they were left intact.

(27) MSS 289 [top], cf. also *Top. Bibl.* I², 2, p. 627.

(28) All the Bankes fragments are at present undergoing restoration at the Canterbury Cathedral Wallpaintings Workshop. I am grateful to Mr D. Windfield of the National Trust and to Miss D. L. Langslow of the Wallpaintings Workshop for making the paintings accessible to me (May 1983).

(29) Cf. E. Mackay, 'On the various methods of representing hair in the wall-paintings of the Theban tombs', *JEA* 5, 1918, pp. 114-5.

(30) For the instrument cf. Manniche, *Anc. Eg. Musical Instruments*, pp. 46-50.

(31) For a discussion of blind and intact eyes cf. L. Manniche, 'Symbolic Blindness', *CdÉ* 53, 1978, pp. 13-21.

(32) There is a very similar double border above the funeral procession in TT 151, temp. Tuthmosis IV (unpublished).

(33) Cf. remarks above, p. 136 under the BM fragments.

(34) In TT 65 (temp. Ramesses IX) a harpist and a lutist perform at a sacred procession.

(35) H. Guksch, *Das Grab des Benja, gen. Paheqamen*, Mainz 1978, pl. 13. The long flute (*nây*) does not belong in the banquet orchestras of the New Kingdom, cf. a representation in TT A22 above.

(36) Davies & Gardiner, *Egyptian Paintings* I, pl. 34.

(37) N. de G. Davies in *BMMA* Nov. 1935, pp. 53-4 with fig. 8: 'Doubtless the rarity of this representation of bull worship will be diminished before long by the discovery of parallels.' It should be mentioned here that one of the fragments formerly in the Rustafjaell collection allegedly represented a 'mummied Apis bull' (*Sotheby Sale Cat.* Jan. 20-24 1913, no. 585 [a]).

Appendix I Notes

(1) Lord Carnarvon & H. Carter, *Five Years' Exploration at Thebes*, London 1912.

(2) *JEA* 11, 1925, pp. 10-18.

(3) V. Scheil, 'Le tombeau de Ratᶜeserkasenb' in *Mém. Miss.* v [2], pp. 571-9.

(4) Davies, *Scenes*.

(5) *ASAE* 46, 1946, pp. 31-33.

(6) Cf. Davies, *op. cit.*, n. 1 on p. 7. For the publication the heads were restored on the basis of Hay's drawings. The term 'cut out in recent years' must refer to the time when Norman de Garis Davies copied the tomb.

(7) Nina de Garis Davies & A. H. Gardiner, *The Tomb of Huy, Viceroy of Nubia in the Reign of Tutankhamūn*.

(8) The fragment was seen by me in August 1982. Its maximum height is 16.3cm.

(9) Davies, *Nakht*.
(10) *Ibid*., p. 55.
(11) *Top. Bibl.* I^2,1, p. 100 (3).
(12) *Ibid*., pl. xv.
(13) The height of the figures in this register is from shoulder leve to the baseline 16.5cm.
(14) *ASAE* 5, 1904, p. 103.
(15) Cf. the article by Silverman quoted below, especially his n. 18.
(16) To the references quoted by Porter & Moss may be added M. Abdul-Qader Muhammed, *Funerary Beliefs*, pls. 16, 38, 43 and 52.
(17) *Top. Bibl.* I^2,1, p. 104 (2).
(18) *Ibid*., pp. 125-6 (3).
(19) Hermann, *Stelen*, pl. 4 [a].
(20) *Top. Bibl.* I^2,1, p. 126 (9).
(21) *Ibid*.
(22) *Ibid*.
(23) *Top. Bibl.* I^2,2, p. 818
(24) I am indebted to Dr M. L. Bierbrier and to Dr A. J. Spencer for providing information from the records of the museum.
(25) *Top. Bibl.* I^2,1, p. 126 [bottom].
(26) *Ibid*., p. 126 (7).
(27) *Ibid*., p. 126 (9).
(28) Davies, *Scenes*, pp. 9-13.
(29) *ASAE* 46, 1946, p. 32.
(30) *Anc. Eg. Musical Instruments*, fig. 7.
(31) *Top. Bibl.* I^2,1, p. 132 (7).
(32) U. Bouriant, 'Tombeau de Harmhabi' in *Mém. Miss.* v,2, pp. 413-34.
(34) A. & A. Haremhab, *Das Grab des Haremhab*, Mainz 1980, cf. also a review article by the present writer in *WZKM* (forthcoming).
(35) Two or three of the fragments in Florence, quoted by Porter & Moss under TT 78, and shown by Brack not to stem from this tomb, have now been assigned to TT C4, cf. above.
(36) P. Virey, 'Tombeau de Khem-nekht' in *Mém. Miss.* v,2, pp. 314-21.
(37) Photos 17000-17151, now in the Griffith Institute.
(38) *Top. Bibl.* I^2,1, p. 179 (8).
(39) In C. F. Nims, *Thebes of the Pharaohs*, London 1965.
(40) Davies, *Ḳen-Amūn*.
(41) TT 21 has yellow background, and so does the passage of TT 79.
(42) Davies, *Ḳen-Amūn* i, p. 44.
(43) *Ibid*. ii, pls. IX A and X A.
(44) *Ibid*. ii, pl. X A.
(45) 'On the various methods of representing hair in the wall-painting of the Theban tombs', *JEA* 5, 1918, pp. 113-6. The four tombs which had the wig rendered by means of black lines on greyish blue were TT 16, 147, 181 and 255. Six tombs (TT 38, 43, 55, 56, 64 and 93) were found to have red or brown with the strands or curls painted in black. The wig of the owner of TT 38 (cf. Davies *Scenes*, pl. V) is indeed exceedingly similar to the one in our fragment, except that the colour is different, and there is a slight difference in the curve at the back. Mackay does not specify which of the figures in TT 93 he studied.
(46) Cf. the similar feature in the 'Bankes' tomb, described above.
(47) Davies, *Scenes*, pl. VI.
(48) Cf. above under the BM tomb.

(49) The fragment is listed under the tomb in *Top. Bibl.* I^2,1, p. 226.
(50) 'Le tombeau de Mai' in *Mém. Miss.* v,2, pp. 541-53.
(51) (9) III in the *Top. Bibl.*
(52) A model of the tomb made by M. Baud based on Hay's drawings is now in the Musées royaux du Cinquantenaire, cf. M. Werbrouck & B. van de Walle, *La tombe de Nakht, Notice sommaire*, Brussels 1929. A number of Hay's original tracings, re-drawn by the present writer, will appear in *JEA* 72, 1986.
(53) 'Identification de trois fragments peints de la tombe du jardinier Nakht (tombe thébaine no. 161)', *CdÉ* 40, 1965, pp. 34-45.
(54) *Top. Bibl.* I^2,1, p. 274 (5).
(55) *Ibid.*, p. 275 (6).
(56) *Ibid.*, p. 275 (7).
(57) Fakhry in *ASAE* 46, 1946, p. 32.
(58) In the *Top. Bibl.*I^2,1 the tomb is dated to the Eighteenth dynasty as in Davies' publication. But in view of the similarity with TT 69 of Menna and TT 52 of Nakht (for example in the painting of a couple on pl. XX [lower left]) and TT 38 (the servant girl *ibid.*, [lower right]) one should be able to narrow down the date to around the reign of Tuthmosis IV or perhaps slightly earlier. The occurrence of the title *ḫrd n kȝp* in the tomb would support such a date. Previous attempts at dating the tomb include Hatshepsut (Helck, *Zur Verwaltung*, p. 525); Amenophis II (Säve-Söderbergh, *Four Eighteenth Dynasty Tombs*, p. 25, n. 5); and Amenophis III (Davies & Faulkner in *JEA* 33, 1947, p. 40).
(59) *RA* 3 Sér., 27, 1895, pls. XIV-XV.
(60) Davies, *Scenes*.
(61) A third fragment in the Fitzwilliam Museum appears to be a fake (cf. *Sotheby Sale Cat.* Jan. 20-24 1913, no. 583 [a]).
(62) *Top. Bibl.* I^2,1, p. 280 (5) [lower register].
(63) *Ibid.*,p. 280 (6) [lower register].
(64) *ASAE* 46, 1946, pl. VI, cf. p. 32. Cf. also Mekhitarian, 'La déprédation des tombes thébaines', *CdÉ* 30, 1955, pp. 318ff.
(65) Davies, *Two Sculptors*.
(66) J. V. Scheil, 'Le tombeau des graveurs' in *Mém. Miss.* v,2, pp. 555-69.
(67) *Top. Bibl.* I^2,1, p. 286 (2).
(68) *Ibid.*, p. 287 (3).
(69) *Ibid.*, p. 287 (4).
(70) *Ibid.*, p. 287 (5).
(71) *Ibid.*, p. 288 (6).
(72) *Ibid.*, pp. 288-9 (9).
(73) *Festschrift Schott*, Wiesbaden, 1968, pp. 61-70; cf. also P. J. Frandsen in *AO* 37, 1976, pp. 5ff.
(74) N. de G. Davies, *The Tombs of Menkheperrasonb* &c., pp. 35-40.
(75) Cf. the references under this tomb in *Top. Bibl.* I^2,1.

Appendix II Notes

(1) Letter of 18/11 1981 from Dr E Leospo of the Turin Museum. The fragments have no excavation record and were presumably collected from the debris of a tomb rather than bought on the market.

(2) The fragments were seen by me in April 1980.

(3) For mandrake fruits in a top border cf. a similar feature in the 'Bankes' tomb.

(4) *E.g.* in TT 38, Davies, *Scenes*, pl. VI.

(5) Outside Thebes it is shown in a tomb at Beni Ḥasan, cf. Newberry, *Beni Hasan* I, pl. 29 [top left]. In a drawing by Wilkinson, *Manne and Customs* (ed. Birch) II, No. 396, the washing boards are virtually identical with those shown in TT 217 (for the latter cf. also n. 12 below).

(6) This tomb is unpublished except for a few details, but Davies made tracings of almost all the walls. These documents are now in the Griffith Institute. The scene also appears in MMA Photo T 314(and OI Photo 2964, and it was seen by me in January 1984. The activities take place in front of the house of the tomb owner and spreads over two registers. In the upper register, a great number of kilts(?) are hung on a string to dry. They appear to have a pattern of red and pink stripes. Three men are shown attending shallow bowls on a fire-place(?) or carrying them. Below, men and women are occupied with bowl similar to those above and those in the Turin fragments. Bundles of pinkish yellow cloth(?) are laid out above. It would seem that dyeing may be represented here A totally different interpretation of this lower register was proposed by Dr N. Strudwick at the Fourth International Congress of Egyptology in Munich, August 1985. Dr. Strudwick, who plans to publish this tomb on the basis of the tracings by Davies, prefers to see a baking scene in this place.

(7) N. de G. Davies, *Two Ramesside Tombs*, New York 1927, pl. 27. For a representation in colour of part of the scene cf. Nims, *Thebes*, fig. 74.

(8) TT 49, 103, 104, 133, 279 (Eleventh dynasty to Saite Period).

(9) N. de G. Davies & A. H. Gardiner, *Seven Private Tombs at Ḳurnah*, New York 1948, pl. 35, cf. pp. 49-50. It is generally believed that wool was not much in use for garments in ancient Egypt. This is based on a statement in Herodotus (II,81) that wool was considered unclean (cf. A. B. Lloyd, *Herodotus Book II Commentary 1-98*, Leiden 1976, pp. 342-3). However, woollen garmen seem to have been in use among the workmen at Deir el-Medîna, cf. Janssen, *Commodity Prices*, pp. 443-4. Dyed wool has been found at el-Amarna and Illahûn.

(10) Cf. also a representation at Beni Hasan where Lepsius' copy is particularly suggestive (*Denkmäler* II,126). The roves (coarsely spun fibres) are lying in a heap on the floor next to the girl spinning.

(11) The same remark may apply to a representation of Middle Kingdom date allegedly showing men dyeing and wringing cloth (TT 36 of Sarenput at Asswan, cf. *Top. Bibl.*V, p. 239 (13)). The men appear to plunge cloth into a tall vat. - The Egyptians were famous for their fine linen, and white seems to have been the favourite colour for this material. The reason for this may be a purely practical one, in that linen fibres do not accept dye easily, and not without the use of a mordant. One of the sources which the Egyptians probably used for bleaching their linen may have been alum (cf. J. R. Harris, *Lexicographical Studies in Ancient Egyptian Minerals*, Berlin 1961, pp. 185ff.) The word 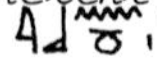 *ibnw*

'alum' is found in the New Kingdom, although in a different context, but Pliny mentions that alum was used for bleaching wool. He also described its use as a mordant in Egypt (*Natural History* 35:42). I am indebted to J. R. Harris for his comments on this scene, agreeing with my own.

(12) Cf. E. Riefstahl, *Patterned Textiles in Pharaonic Egypt*, The Brooklyn Museum 1944. For patterned textiles the linen thread would have to be bleached before weaving, whereas for plain white garments the bleaching could be carried out afterwards (as in TT 217?). For a representation of the dyeing process one would expect cauldrons to be depicted, cf. the description by Pliny quoted above. To the very left in the Turin fragment the heel of a kneeling or prostrate person can just be made out. A figure which would fill the very limited space available would be someone like the man shown in TT 217 blowing at a cauldron supporting a pot of carpenter's glue (Davies, *Two Ramesside Tombs*, pl. 36). Although the evidence is very slender, it may suggest that dyeing was also represented on this wall. - In TT 217 one of the vats rests on a support with a sloping surface. Davies interpreted it as a baker's grinding stone borrowed from the kitchen (*op. cit.*, p. 54). Wreszinski, *Atlas* i,57 and Klebs, *Reliefs... Neuen Reiches* pp. 180-1 prefer to regard it as a fireplace with hot ashes to heat the water. A similarly shaped object can be seen next to the weavers in Tt 104 (MMA Photo T 1683).

(13) Unpublished, cf. Schott Photos 4931 or 4933.

(14) A beautiful facsimile in colour was made of this scene by Hay (MSS 29822,121), but only a small sketch made by Wilkinson has been published (*Manners and Customs* (ed. Birch), II, No. 433). In TT 217 a jar with a siphon stands in a shelter in the market (Davies, *Two Ramesside Tombs*, colour pl. 30).

(15) Stela Berlin 14122, cf. *ZÄS* 36, 1898, p. 129 with fig; the angular joining piece of a siphon was also found, cf. *JEA* 12, 1926, pp. 22-3.

(16) Ostracon formerly in Munich (destroyed during World War II), cf. E. Brunner-Traut, *Die alten Ägypter*, Stuttgart 1976, fig. 43.

(17) For the use of siphons cf. W. Helck, *Das Bier im alten Ägypten*, Berlin 1971, pp. 74-5. Cf. also Klebs, *op. cit.*, pp. 58-60. The author refers to the scene in Turin. In addition to the instances of tubes already mentioned, 'soft' tubes can be seen among funerary gifts in TT 79. Siphon tubes are used by present day home brewers when bottling beer.

(18) Particularly reminiscent of the orchestras in TT 38 and 75.

(19) Cf. Manniche, *Anc. Eg. Musical Instruments*, pp. 77-8. To the references given there should be added the possibility of a representation in TT 40 of Huy. Davies' copy (*Huy*, pl. 7) shows the usual type of lute, but the earlier copy by Hay (*ibid.*, pl. 5) suggests that the lute had concave sides.

(20) I owe this observation to J. R. Harris.

(21) Cf. for example the musicians published by me, *op. cit.*, fig. 18.

(22) Davies & Macadam, *Corpus*, no. 229. The tomb is a very small one, and only fragments of the decoration on two walls are preserved. As it is also unpublished, inspection of the remains *in situ* is necessary in order to determine if this was the original position of the fragments in Turin. Only the title 'scribe'

is extant on the jambs, but as the unusual name of the wife  Sitmenḥit occurs on both the jambs and on the cone, an identification with the owner of the cone is fairly certain. In January 1984 the tomb was inaccessible, being filled almost to the brim with rubble. Fragments are known to have been removed from this tomb at the beginning of the present century. cf. A. H. Gardiner & A. E. P. Weigall, *A Topographical Catalogue of the Private Tombs at Thebes*, London 1913, p. 9.

Appendix III Notes

(1) Hay MSS 29824,83 (sketch).

(2) *Top. Bibl.* I², 1, p. 174 (28) II.

(3) Wreszinski, *Atlas*, i,271.

(4) For example TT 78, 139 and C4.

(5) Cf. Davies & Macadam, *Corpus*, nos. 37, 67, 91, 152, 388, 459 and 487.

(6) *Ibid.*, nos. 91 and 487 *iry ʿt n ʾImn.*

(7) Hay MSS 29816,186 (a vase seen at Yanni's); 187 (another vase with a similar inscription seen at Piccinini's).

(8) The Rustafjaell collection, sold at Sotheby's in 1906, 1907 and 1913 included a very large number of fragments of painted tombs, most of them quite small (the catalogue for a sale in New York, Anderson Galleries, Nov. 29 - Dec. 1 1915 was not available for consultation). In a marked 1906 catalogue it appears that some were bought by Schäfer for the museum in Berlin, others by dealers Ready and Llewellyn. Some fragments eventually ended up in the Wellcome collection. This latter was distributed among various musums in England, but with no record of which pieces went where. Others were bought by private individuals and were later presented to provincial museums. In the *Sotheby Sale Catalogue* only a few of the fragments are illustrated, and, with one exception, at a very small scale. On the basis of the catalogue entries alone it is exceedingly difficult to identify the remaining, unillustrated fragments listed there with paintings in museums, and it is equally complicated to attribute them to any specific tomb. Nevertheless in some instances it has proved possible.

(9) For this title see note 9 on p. 227.

(10) *JEA* 18, 1932, pp. 55-6 (palette of *sš nsw ḥry ḫ3w rmn m ḥ3t*), cf. *ZÄS* 85, 1960, p. 47, n. 11 with correct reading.

(11) The de Benzion collection was sold on 20 March 1947. The catalogue (*Succession de feu M. Moïse Levy de Benzion*) is without illustrations and so brief as to be virtually useless for the present purposes. Three fragments, photographed and published by Keimer, can be linked with the fragments in the British Museum. They are quite small and may have been left over in the tomb after the large pieces were cut out during the second decade of the previous century and found much later (as possibly the fragments in Berlin), and it does not necessarily indicate that the de Benzion collection was very ancient. The present fragment cannot be identified with any of the entries in the sale catalogue.

(12) *Amenemhet*, p. 64 (to pls. XV-XVI). The stools in this tomb are yellow, the upper third being white. In TT 59 they are green below and white above. In TT 84 they are white with red lines, and in TT 88 yellow and white.
(13) MMA Photo T 3007 (fowl pluckers sit on these stools).
(14) MMA Photo T 2782 (banquet scene, yellow stools with white upper edges).
(15) Unpublished (yellow chair without markings in banquet scene).
(16) Säve-Söderbergh, *Four Eighteenth Dynasty Tombs*, pl. X, no. 10.
(17) MMA Photo T 3147 (fowl pluckers and fish mongers).
(18) Mekhitarian, *Egyptian Painting*, p. 19 (rope makers on yellow stools).
(19) Unpublished (two kinds of white and yellow stools in banquet).
(20) MMA Photo T 1524 (red at base, yellow above).
(21) Unpublished (red base, yellow above).
(22) Cf. the reference under TT A4 above.
(23) TT 38, 49, 53, 332 and 396. A woman in a similar state occurs in TT A5 (cf. above). Bowls under chairs available for similar emergencies are shown in TT 84 and 181.
(24) Seven fragments in Turin have this number, cf. our nos. 35 and 51.
(25) *Manners and Customs* (ed. Birch 1878), No. 296.
(26) Mekhitarian, *Egyptian Painting*, fig. p. 67.
(27) Wreszinski, *Atlas*, i,28 A.
(28) Mekhitarian. *op. cit.*, fig. p. 64 (but here the girl is not naked).
(29) Davies & Gardiner, *Amenemhet*, pl. XIX.
(30) *GM* 65, 1983, fig. p. 60.
(31) Seven fragments have this no., cf. nos. 15 and 51.
(32) Cf. M. Tosi,*La cappella di Maia*, Turin 1972, figs. on pp. 24-5 and 29.
(33) Cf. Otto, *Mundöffnungsritual*, scene 39.
(34) Mekhitarian, *Egyptian Painting*, fig. p. 104.
(35) A fragment in Bristol, City Museum H 4638, formerly in the Rustafjaell collection (*Sotheby Sale Cat.*, Jan 20-24 1913, no. 596 [b] was found to be of dubious authenticity.
(36) Cf. for example TT 69, Mekhitarian, *Egyptian Painting*,fig. pp. 80-1.
(37) A similar group, but with the figures in reverse position in TT 56 (*ibid.*, fig. p. 27).
(38) Seven fragments have this no., cf. nos 15 and 35.
(39) Otto, *Mundöffnungsritual*, scene 69B.

LIST OF WORKS ABBREVIATED IN THE TEXT

Acts, First International Congress of Egyptology, Cairo, October 2-10, 1976 (ed. W. F. Reineke), Berlin 1979.
Ausführliche Verzeichnis der aegyptischen Altertümer und Gipsabgüsse Königliche Museen zu Berlin, Berlin 1899.
W. B. Berend, *Principaux monuments du Musée égyptien de Florence,* Paris 1882
L. Borchardt, *Statuen und Statuetten von Könige und Privatleuten im Museum von Kairo,* Cairo 1911-36.
B. Bruyère, *Rapport sur les fouilles de Deir el Médineh,* Cairo 1924-53.
F. Cailliaud, *Recherches sur les arts et métiers* [&c], Paris 1831.
F. Cailliaud, *Voyage à Méroé* [&c.] *dans les années 1819, 1820, 1821 et 1822,* Paris 1826.
J. F. Champollion, *Monuments d'Égypte et de la Nubie. Notices descriptives,* Paris 1844-79.
G. Daressy, *Recueil de cônes funéraires (Mém. Miss.* 8,2*)*, Paris 1893.
Nina de G. Davies, *Egyptian Tomb Paintings,* London 1958.
Nina de G. Davies, *Scenes from some Theban Tombs,* London 1963.
Nina de G. Davies & A. H. Gardiner, *The Tomb of Amenemhet,* London 1915.
Norman de G. Davies, *The Tomb of Ḳen-Amūn at Thebes,* New York 1930.
Norman de G. Davies, *The Tomb of Nakht at Thebes,* New York 1917.
Norman de G. Davies, *The Tomb of Rekh-mi-rē at Thebes,* New York 1953.
Norman de G. Davies, *The Tomb of the Vizier Ramose,* New York 1941.
Norman de G. Davies, *The Tombs of Two Officials of Tuthmosis the Fourth,* London 1923.
Norman de G. Davies, *The Tombs of Two Sculptors at Thebes*, New York 1925.
Norman de G. Davies & F. L. Macadam, *A Corpus of Inscribed Egyptian Funerary Cones,* Oxford 1957.
A. H. Gardiner, *Ancient Egyptian Onomastica,* Oxford 1968.
H. Gauthier, *Dictionnaire des noms géographiques* [&c.], Cairo 1925-31.
W. C. Hayes, *The Scepter of Egypt,* New York 1953-59.
W. Helck, *Materialien zur Wirtschaftgeschichte des Neuen Reiches,* Wiesbaden 1960-69.
W. Helck, *Urkunden der 18. Dynastie: Historische Inschriften Tuthmosis' III und Amenophis II,* Vol. IV, Berlin 1955.
W. Helck, *Zur Verwaltung des Mittleren und Neuen Reiches,* Leiden 1958.
H. Kees, *Das Priestertum im ägyptischen Staat vom Neuen Reich bis zur Spätzeit,* Leiden 1953.
K. A. Kitchen, *Ramesside Inscriptions Historical and Biographical,* Oxford 1975 - .
K. Lange & M. Hirmer, *Ägypten. Architektur Plastik Malerei in drei Jahrtausenden,* Munich 1978.
E. Ledrain, *Les monuments égyptiens de la Bibliothèque Nationale,* Paris 1879-81.
R. Lepsius, *Denkmäler aus Ägypten und Aethiopien,* Leipzig 1849-59, Leipzig 1897-1913.
J. Lieblein, *Dictionnaire des noms hiéroglyphiques en ordre généalogique et alphabétique,* Christiania 1871.
L. Manniche, *Ancient Egyptian Musical Instruments (MÄS* 34*)*, Munich 1975.
D. Meeks, *Année lexicographique,* Paris 1980 - .
A. M. Migliarini, *Indication succinte des monuments égyptiens du Musée de Florence,* Florence 1859.
P. E. Newberry, *Funerary Statuettes and Model Sarcophagi,* Cairo 1937-57.
The Marquis of Northampton, W. Spiegelberg & P. E. Newberry, *Report on some Excavations in the Theban Necropolis during the Winter of 1898-9,* London 1908.

G. Perrot & C. Chipiez, *Histoire de l'art dans l'antiquité*, Paris 1882.
W. M. F. Petrie, *Shabtis, Illustrated by the Collection in University College London*, London 1935.
K. Piehl, *Inscriptions hiéroglyphiques recueillis en Europe et en Égypte*, Stockholm/Leipzig 1886-95.
P. Pierret, *Recueil d'inscriptions inédites du Musée égyptien du Louvre* (*Études égyptologiques* II, Paris 1874, VIII, Paris 1878).
B. Porter & R. L. B. Moss, *Topographical Bibliography of Ancient Egyptian Hieroglyphic Texts, Reliefs and Paintings*, Oxford 1927 - .
H. Ranke, *Die ägyptischen Personennamen*, Glückstadt 1935 - 77.
I. Rosellini, *Breve notizia degli ogetti di antichità* [&c.], Florence 1830.
I. Rosellini, *I Monumenti dell'Egitto et della Nubia. Monumenti civili*, Pisa 1834.
H. Schäfer, *Principles of Egyptian Art*, Oxford 1974.
E. Schiaparelli, *Museo archeologico di Firenze. Antichità egizie*, Rome 1887.
S. Schott, *Das schöne Fest vom Wüstentale. Festbräuche einer Totenstadt*, Wiesbaden 1952.
J. J. Tylor & F. Ll. Griffith, *The Tombs of Paheri*, London 1894.
J. Vandier, *Musée du Louvre. Le Departement des antiquités égyptiennes. Guide sommaire*, Paris (various years).
A. Varille, *Karnak*, Cairo 1943.
WB = A. Erman & H. Grapow, *Wörterbuch der ägyptischen Sprache*, Leipzig 1926-31.
J. G. Wilkinson, *The Manners and Customs of the Ancient Egyptians*, London 1837; 2nd Series 1841; ed. Birch 1878.
W. Wreszinski, *Atlas zur altägyptischen Kulturgeschichte*, Leipzig 1923.

Ancient Egypt and the East, London
AO *Acta Orientalia*, Copenhagen
AO *Acta Orientalia*, Leiden
ARCE *Newsletter published by the American Research Center in Egypt*, Princeton
ASAE *Annales du Service des Antiquités d'Égypte*, Cairo
BIE *Bulletin de l'Institut d'Égypte*, Cairo
BIFAO *Bulletin de l'Institut français d'archéologie orientale*, Cairo
BMMA *Bulletin of the Metropolitan Museum of Art*, New York
BO *Bibliotheca Orientalis*, Leiden
CdE *Chronique d'Égypte, Bulletin périodique de la Fondation Égyptologique Reine Elisabeth*, Brussels
GM *Göttinger Miszellen*, Göttingen
JEA *Journal of Egyptian Archaeology*, London
JNES *Journal of Near Eastern Studies*, Chicago
Kemi, Revue de philologie et d'archéologie égyptiennes et coptes, Paris
LdA *Lexikon der Ägyptologie*, Wiesbaden
MAS *Münchner ägyptologische Studien*, Munich
Mém. Miss. *Mémoires publiés par les membres de la Mission archeologique française au Caire*, Cairo
MDAIAK *Mitteilungen des deutschen archäologischen Instituts, Abteilung Kairo*, Berlin
MIO *Mitteilungen des Instituts für Orientforschung*, Berlin
Numen, Leiden
OrLovPer, *Orientalia Lovaniensia Periodica*, Louvain

Papyrus [Newsletter published by Den danske Hǿjskole i Ægypten], Copenhagen
RA *Revue archéologique*, Paris
RAC *Reallexikon für Antike und Christentum*, Stuttgart
RdE *Revue d'archéologie, publié par la Societé française d'Égyptologie*, Paris
RT *Recueil de travaux relatifs à la philologie et à l'archéologie égyptiennes et assyriennes*, Paris
SAK *Studien zur altägyptischen Kultur*, Hamburg
Serapis. A Student Forum on the Ancient World, Chicago
SSEA Journal *Journal of the Society for the Study of Egyptian Antiquities*, Toronto
WZKM *Wiener Zeitschrift fur die Kunde des Morgenlandes*, Vienna
ZÄS *Zeitschrift für ägyptische Sprache und Altertumskunde*, Leipzig

I EARLY TRAVELLERS

II EGYPTIAN PROPER NAMES (PRIVATE)

III TITLES

IV DIVINITIES

V GENERAL

VI OBJECTS IN COLLECTIONS

ILLUSTRATIONS

Plates

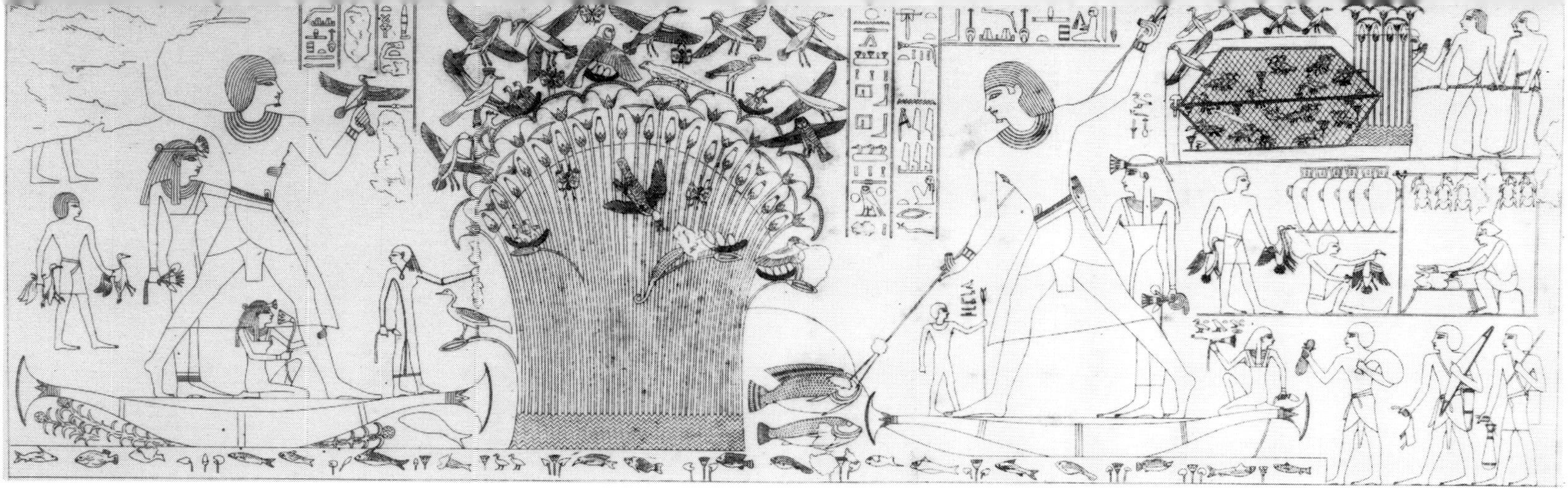

1 TT A5 Fishing and fowling (= Cailliaud, *Voyage à Méroé*, ii, pl. 75[1])

2 TT A5 Vintage (= Cailliaud, *Voyage à Méroé*, ii, pl. 75[2, left])

3 TT A5 Musicians (= Cailliaud, *Voyage à Méroé*, ii, pl. 75[2, right])

PLATE 1

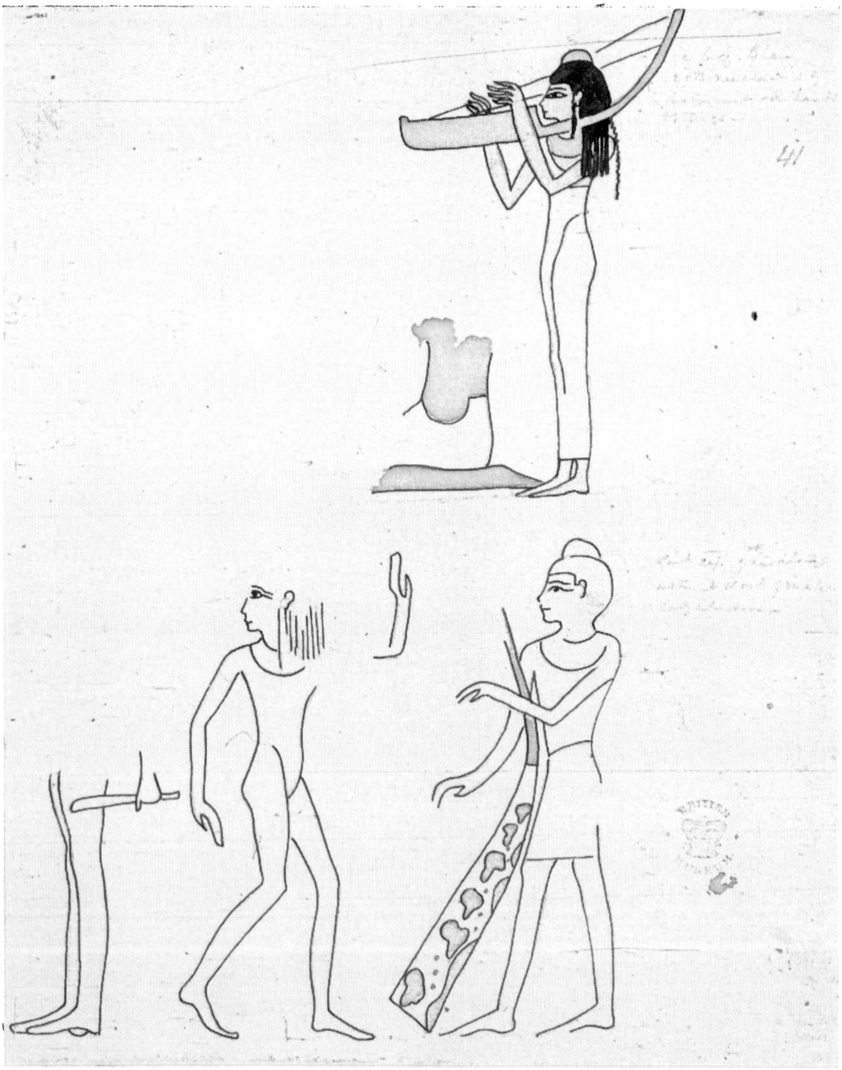

4 TT A5 Musicians (re-drawn from Hay MSS 29822, 41)

5 TT A5 Ladies at banquet (re-drawn from Hay MSS 29822,76)

PLATE 2

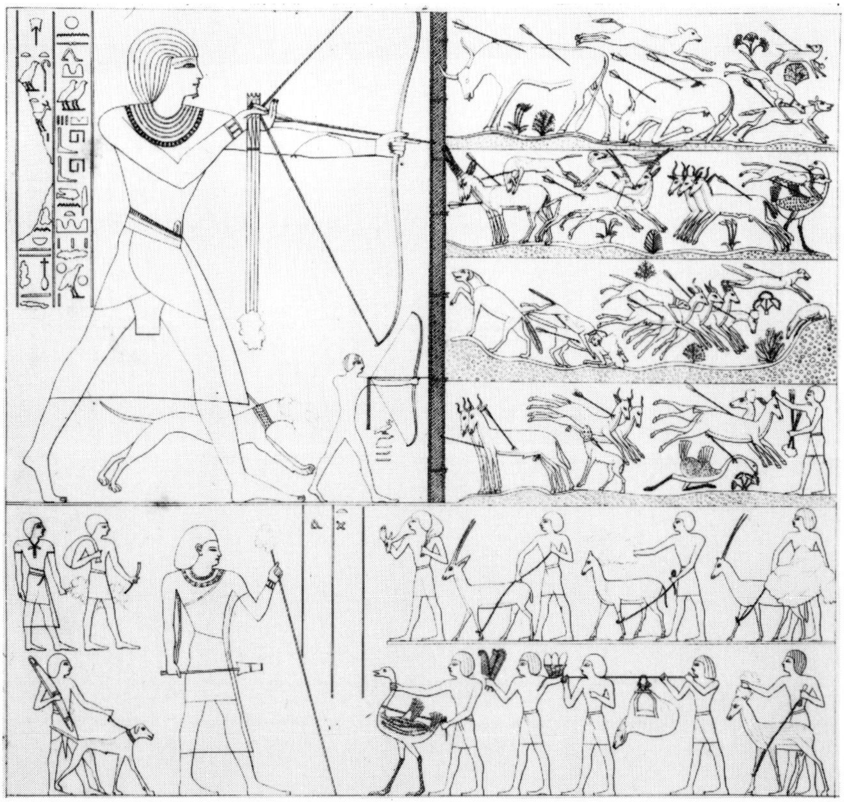

6 TT A5 Hunting in the desert (= Cailliaud, *Voyage à Mêroé*, ii, pl. 74[2])

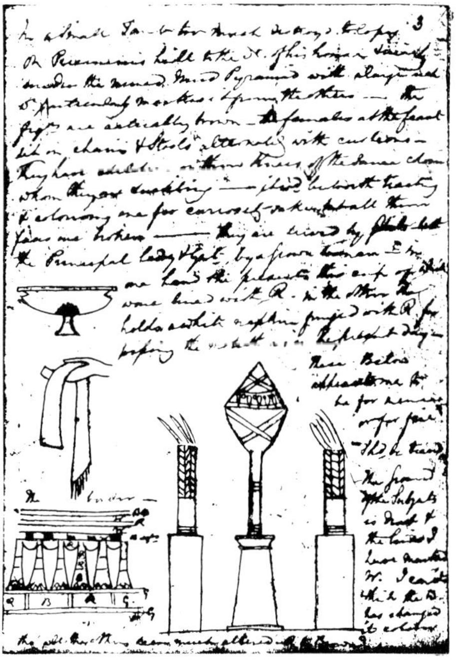

7 TT A11 Details from banquet, and torches (redrawn from Hay MSS 29824,3)

PLATE 3

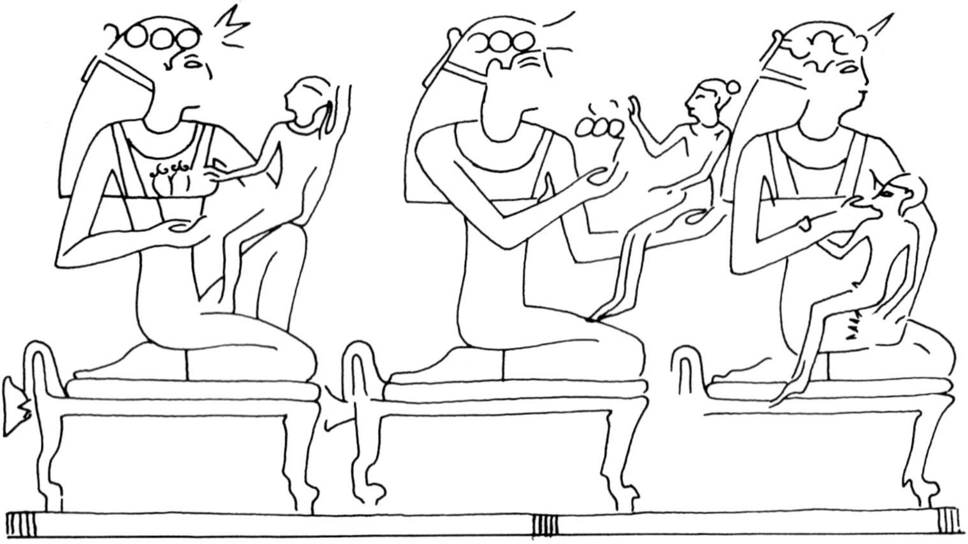

8 TT A11 Nursing women (re-drawn from Hay MSS 29822.45)

8a TT A22(?) Lady at banquet (re-drawn from Hay MSS 29853,107)

PLATE 4

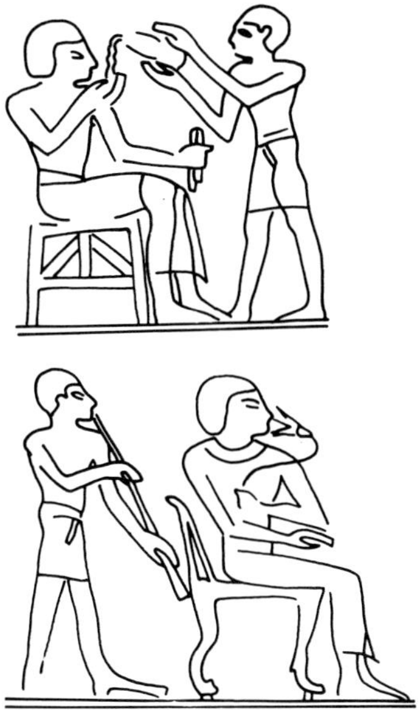

9 TT A22 Men at banquet (re-drawn from Hay MSS 29822,47)

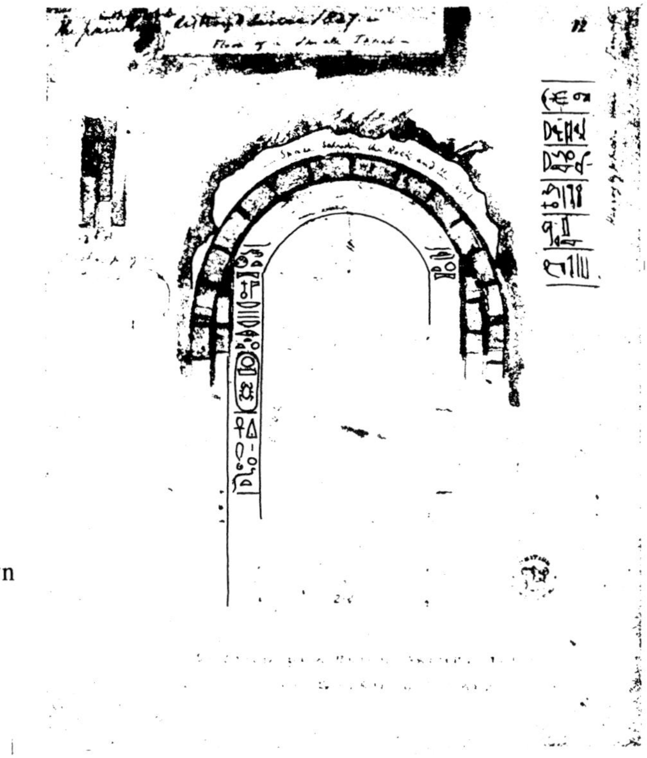

11 TT B2 brick arch (re-drawn from Hay MSS 29821,82)

10 TT A25 Agriculture (re-drawn from Wilkinson MSS v. 107[upper])

12 TT C5 Ladies at banquet (re-drawn from Hay MSS 29816,139–40)

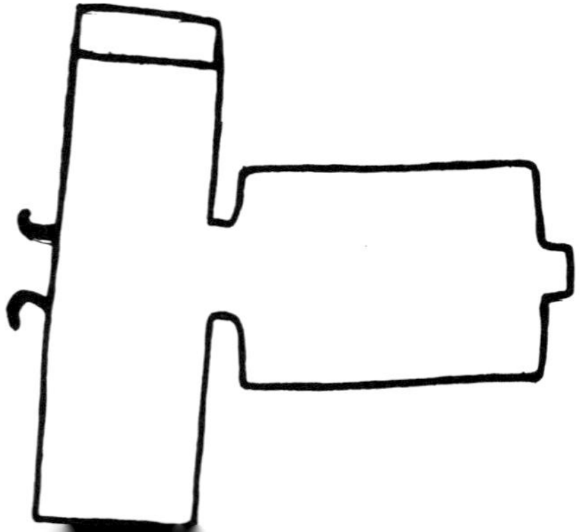

13 TT A4 Plan (re-drawn from Hay MSS 29824,19)

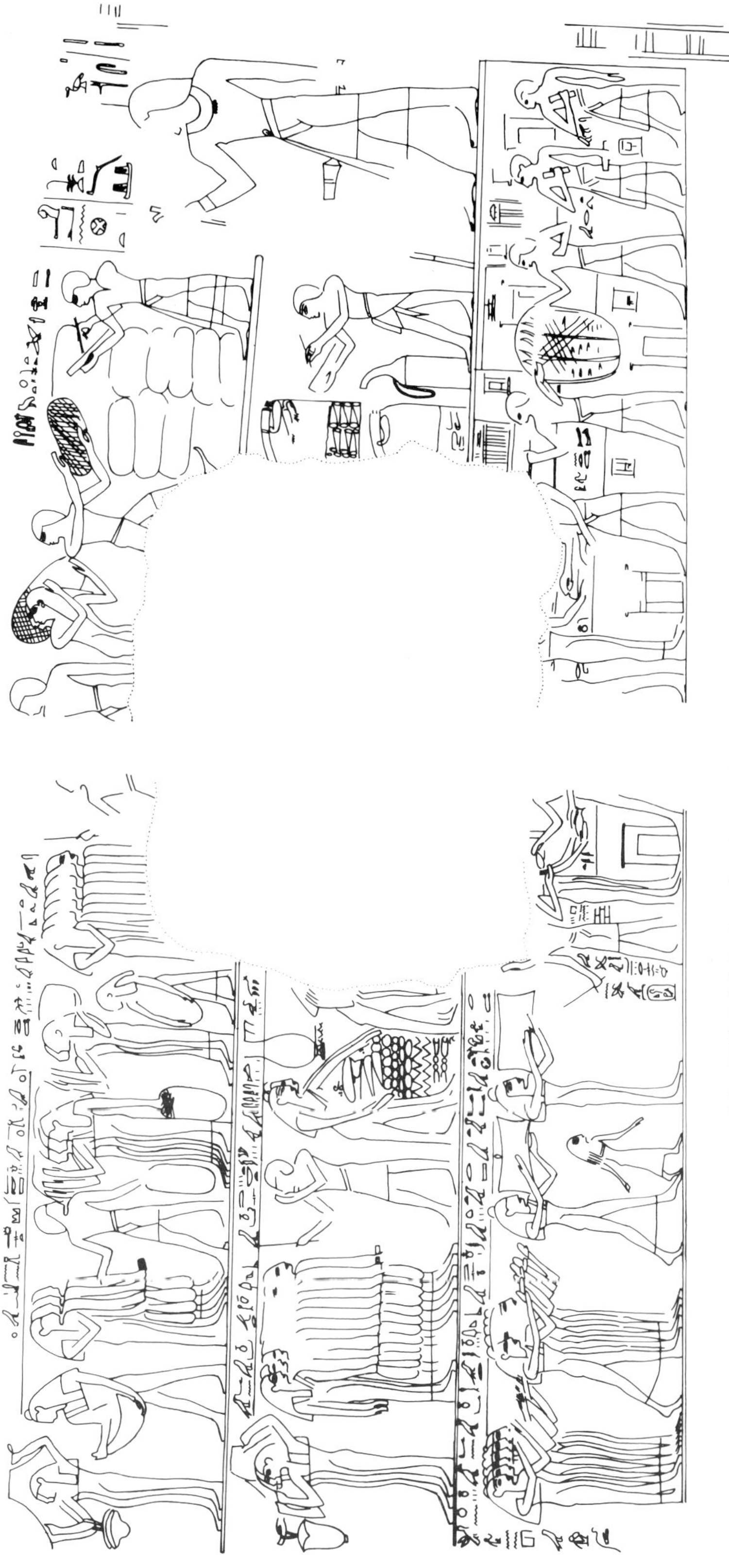

14 TT A4 Market (re-drawn from Hay MSS 29822,21–22)

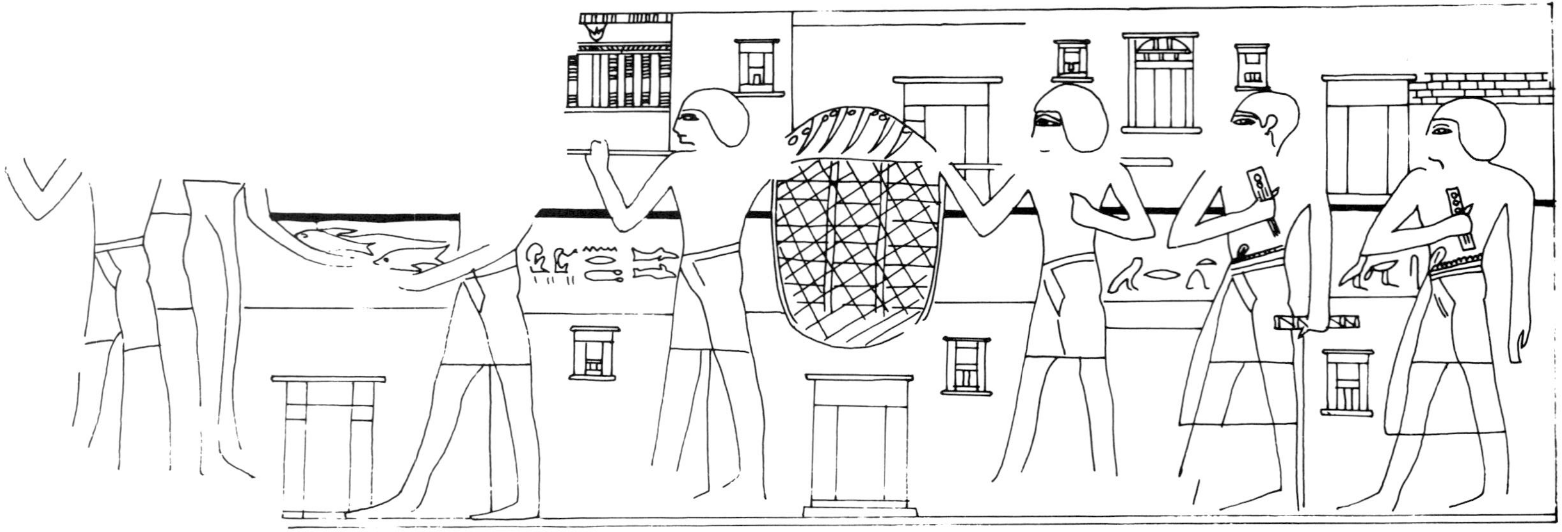

15 TT A4 Street in Thebes (re-drawn from Burton MSS 25644,125)

16 TT A4 A house in Thebes (= Wilkinson, *Manners & Customs*, ed. Birch, No. 131)

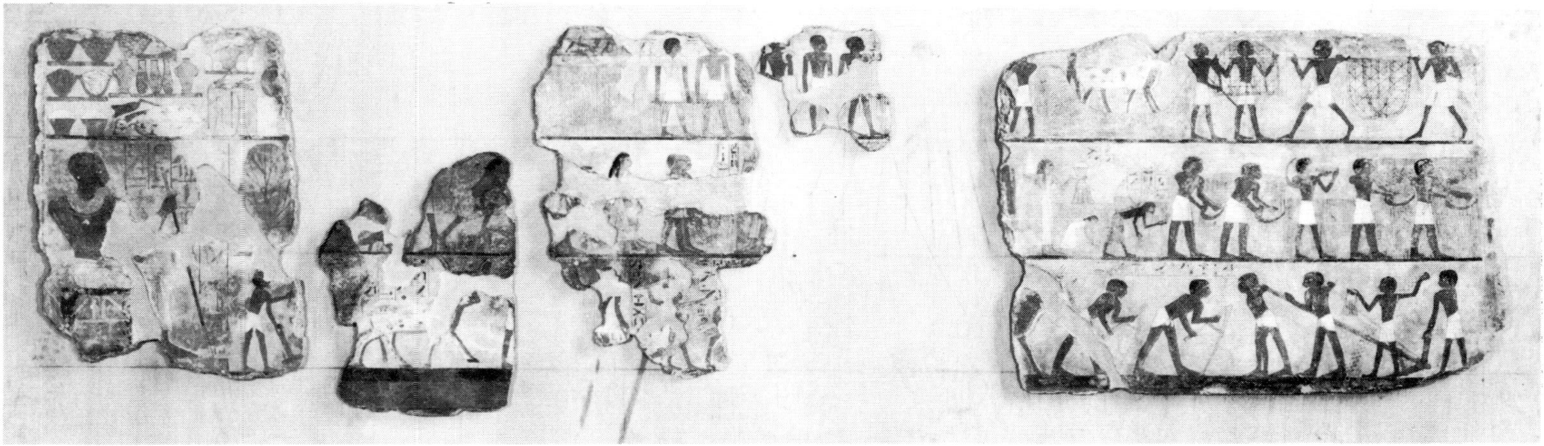

17 TT A4 Agricultural scenes, Louvre N1431

18 TT A4 Grain barges, Louvre N1430

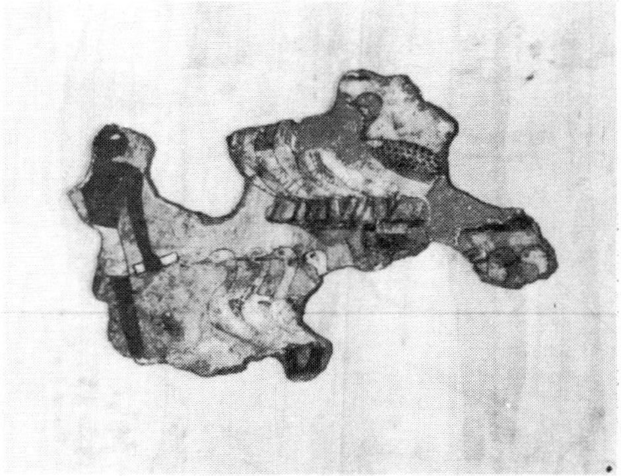

19 TT A4 Geese, Louvre (no number)

PLATE 9

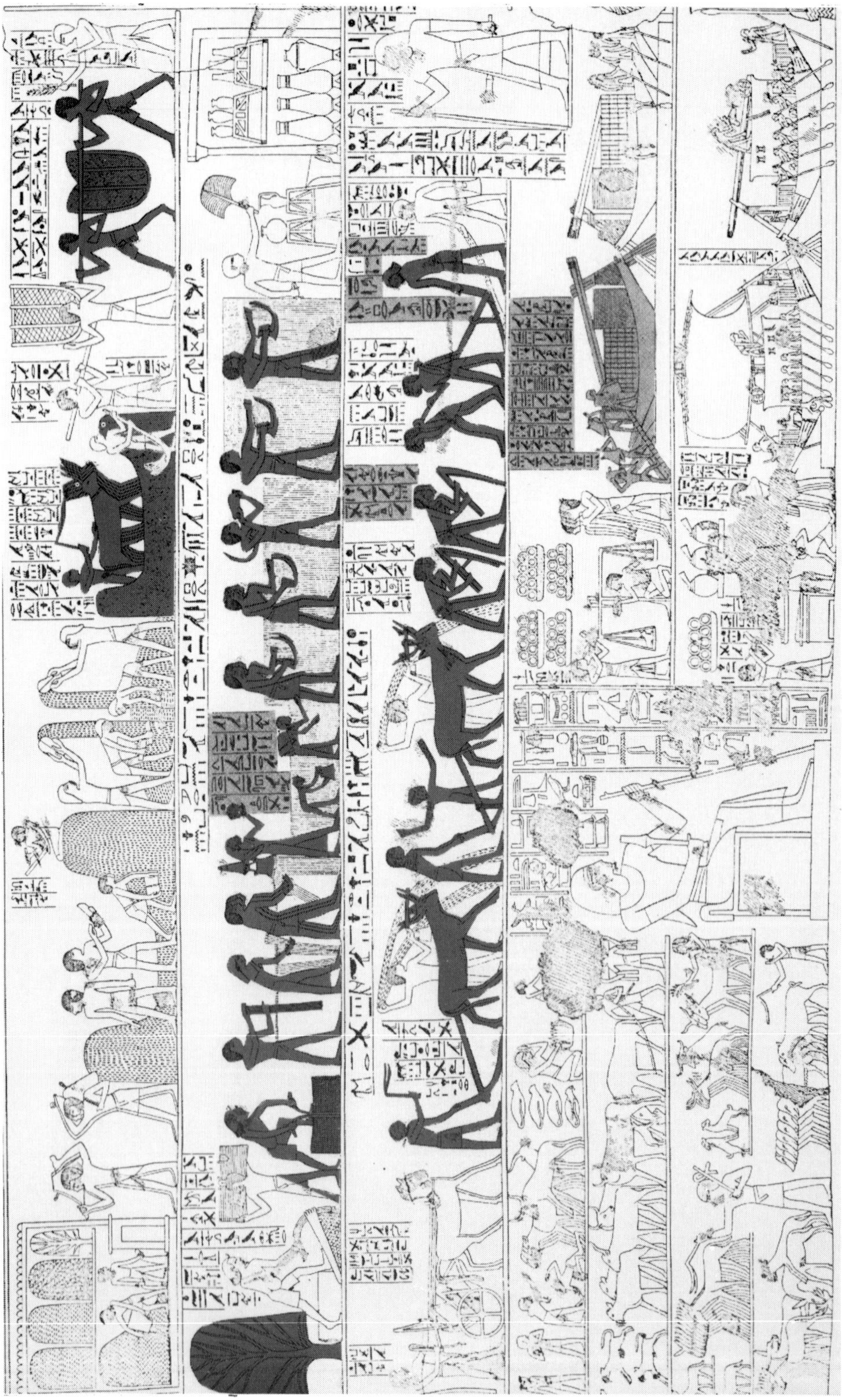

20 Tomb of Paḥeri (= Tylor & Griffith, *Paḥeri*, pl. 3)

PLATE 10

21 TT A4 Banquet and Opening of the Mouth (Burton MSS 25638,48. By permission of the British Library)

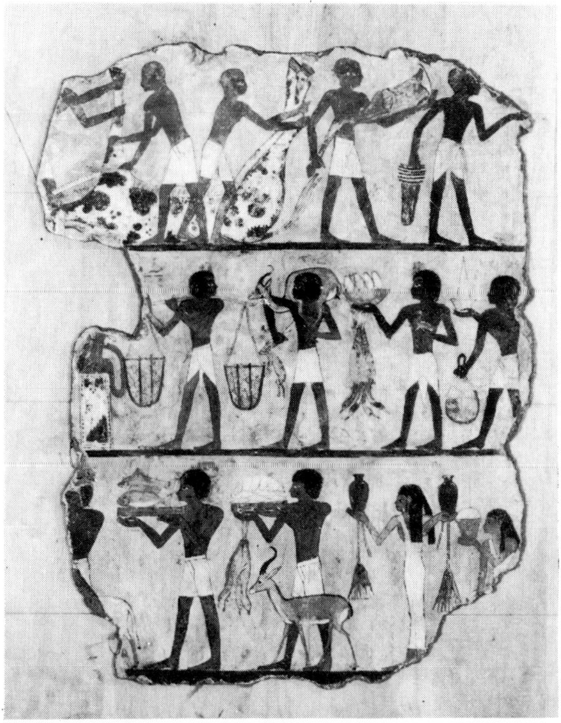

22 TT A4 Butchers and offering bringers, Louvre N1393

PLATE 11

23 TT A4 Funeral procession (re-drawn from Hay Add. MSS 29824,18, 18 verso)

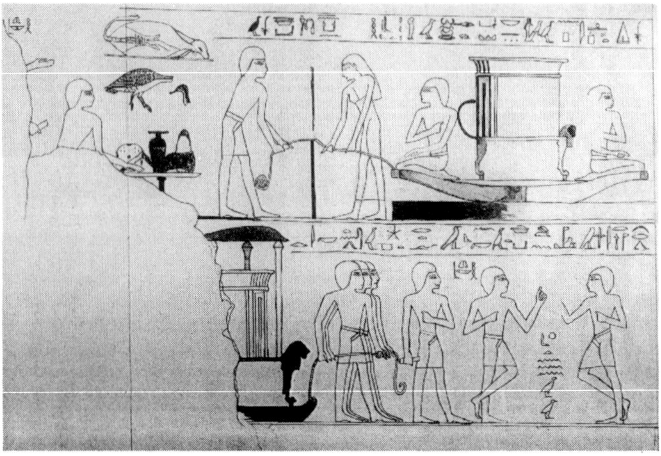

24 TT A4 Detail of the funeral procession as drawn by Hay (Add. MSS 29822,23. By permission of the British Library)

PLATE 12

25 Detail from the funeral procession (re-drawn from Hay Add. MSS 29822,36)

26 TT A4 Man with oars from the funeral procession (re-drawn from Hay Add. MSS 29853,105)

PLATE 13

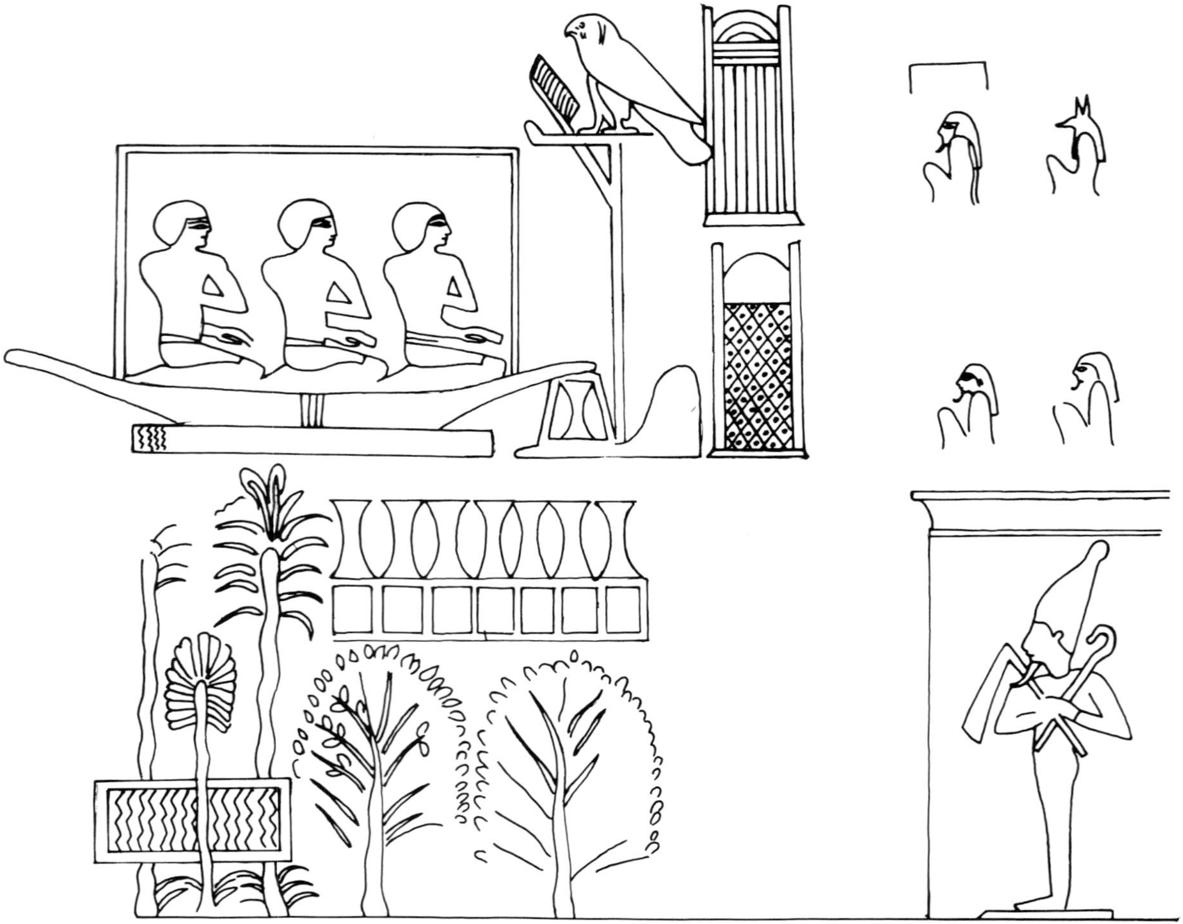

27 TT A4 Details from the funeral procession (re-drawn from Burton Add. MSS 25638,50)

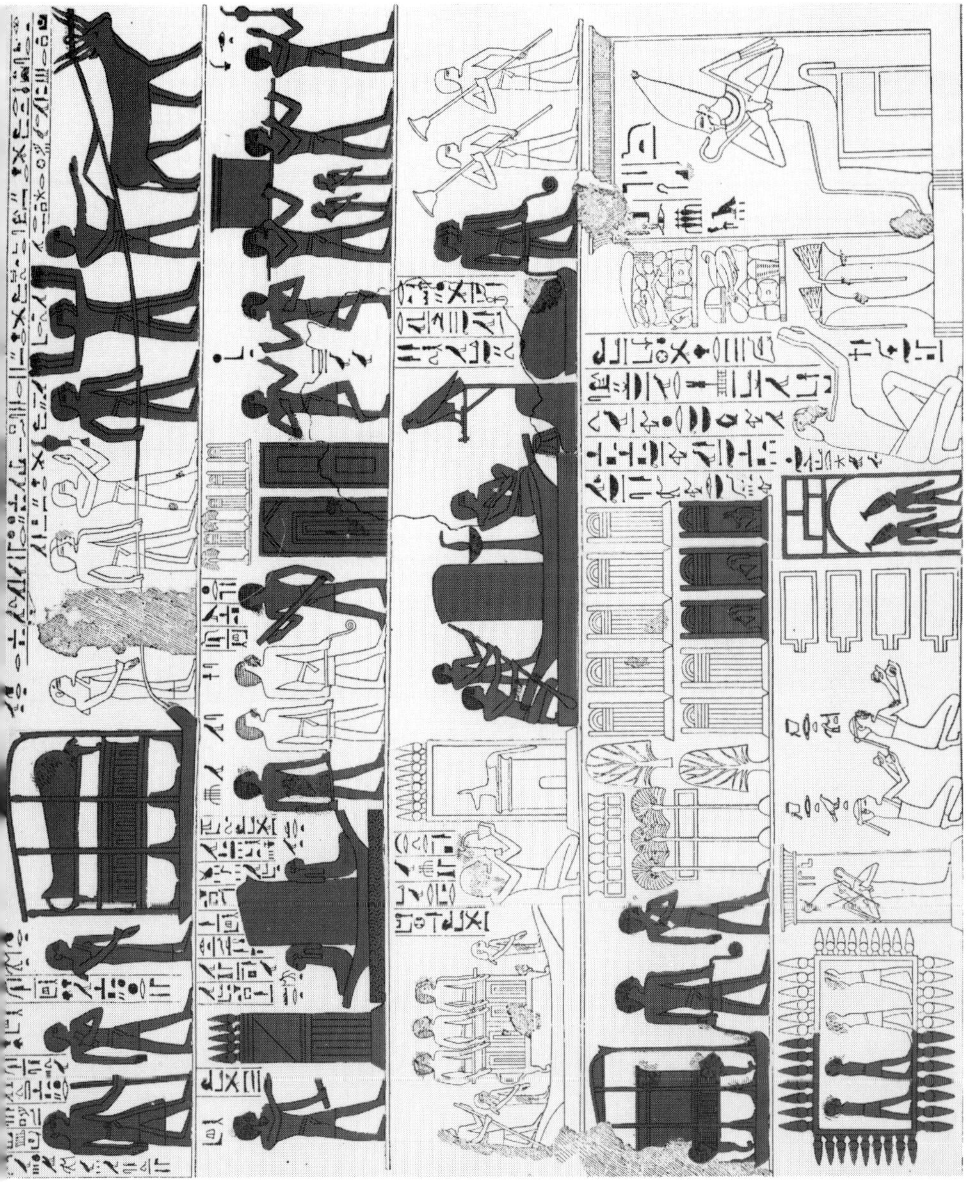

28 Tomb of Paḥeri (Tylor & Griffith, *Paḥeri*, pl. 5)

29 TT A4 The tomb owner and his wife (re-drawn from Hay Add. MSS 29822,38)

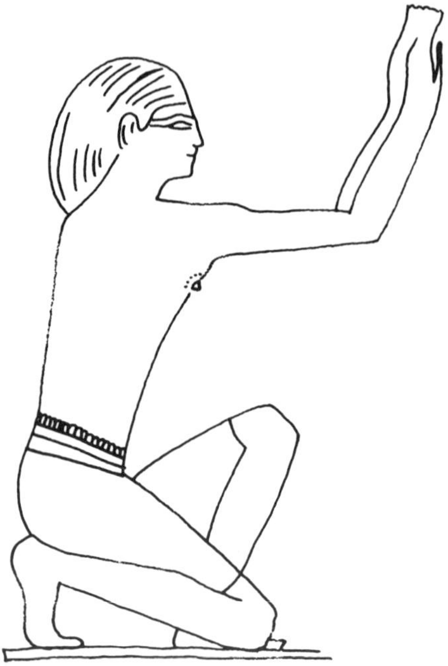

30 TT A4 The tomb owner adoring (re-drawn from Hay Add. MSS 29822,40)

PLATE 16

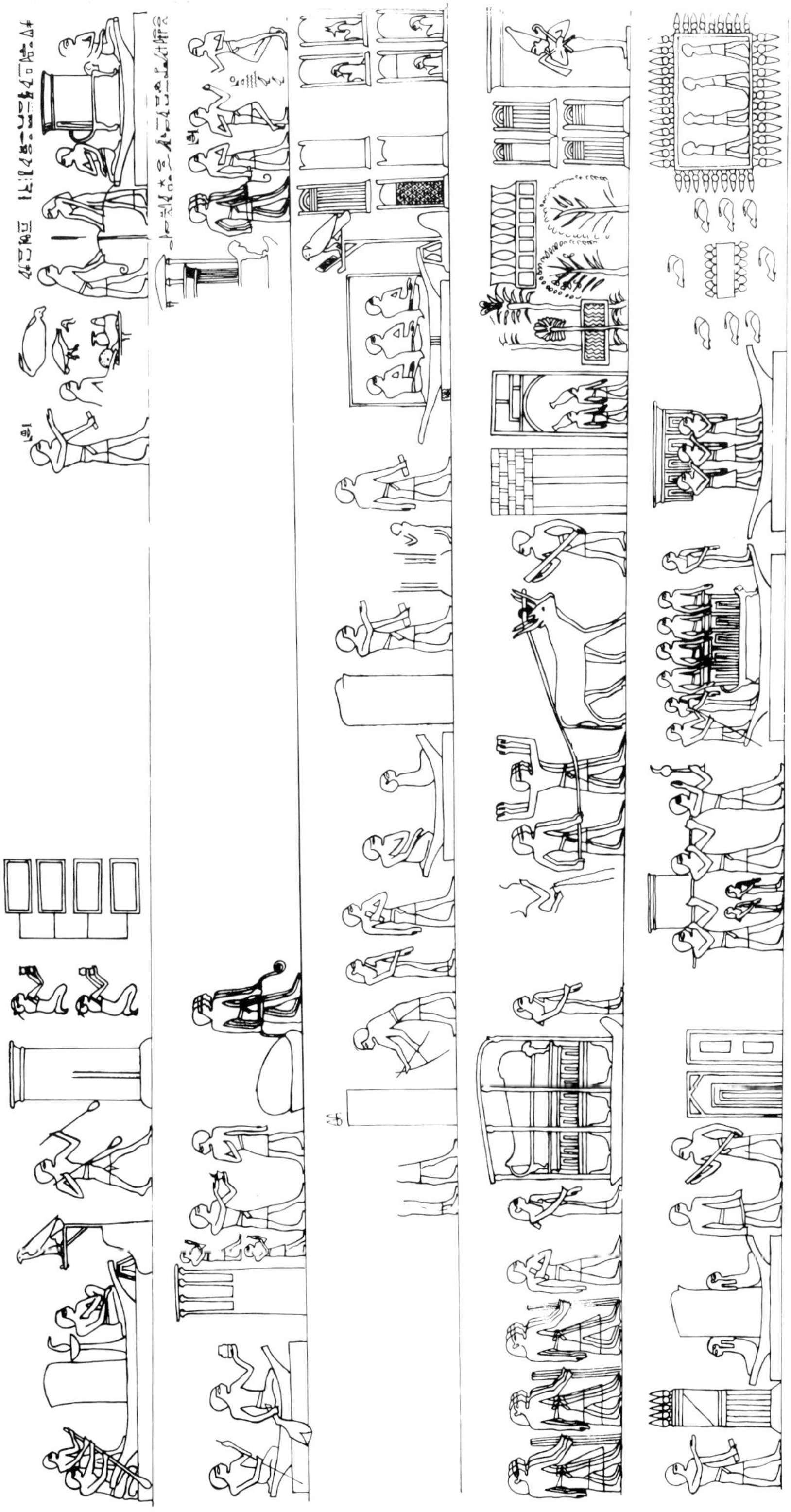

31 TT A4 The funeral procession reconstructed

PLATE 17

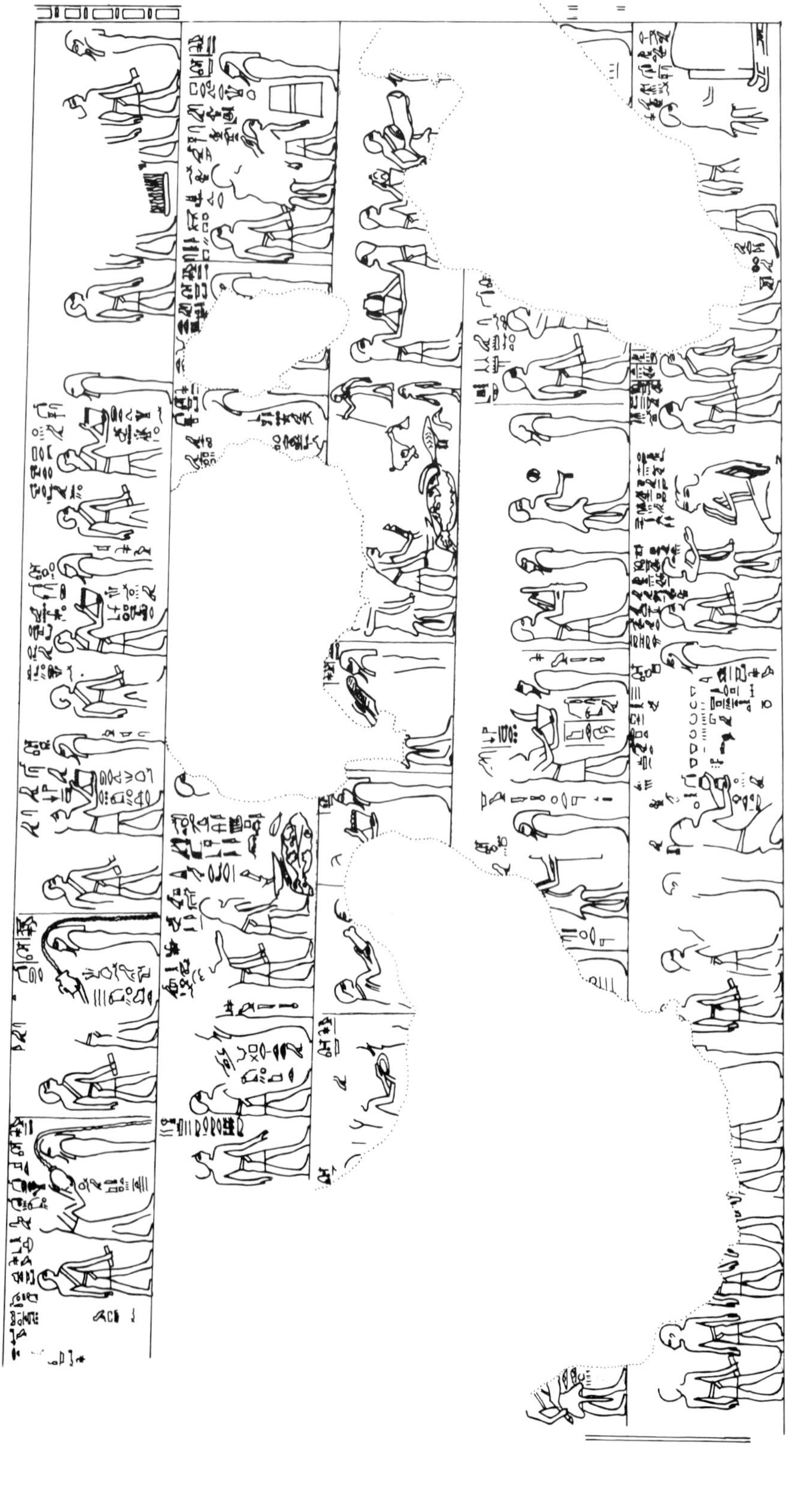

32 TT A4 Opening of the Mouth (re-drawn from Hay Add. MSS 29822,24–32)

PLATE 18

33 The tomb owner and his wife as drawn by Hay (Add. MSS 29822,35. By permission of the British Library)

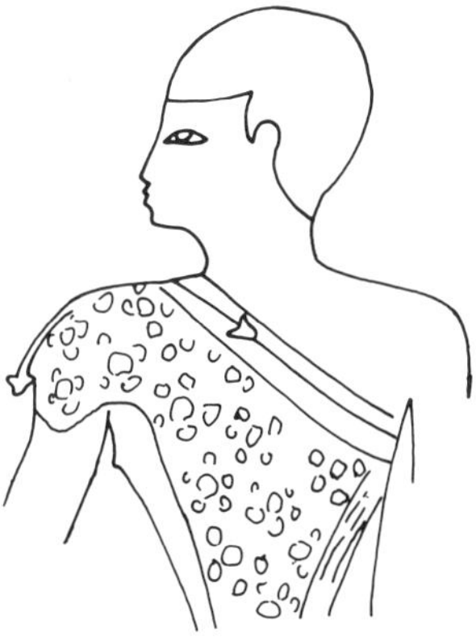

34 TT A4 Priest (re-drawn from Hay Add. MSS 29822,34)

35 Tomb of Paḥeri (= Tylor & Griffith, *Paheri*, pl. 6)

PLATE 19

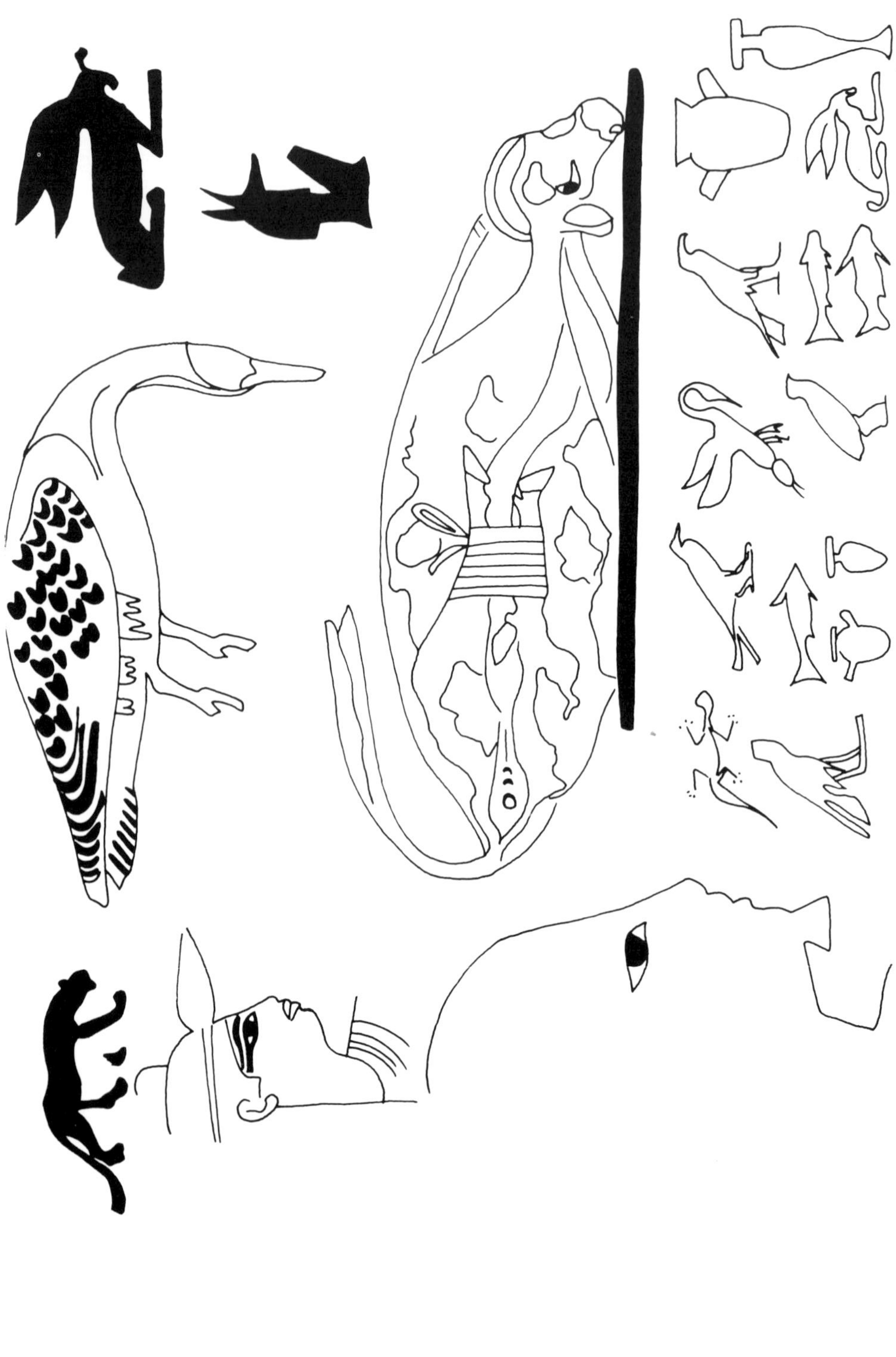

36 TT A4 Miscellaneous drawings (re-drawn from Hay Add. MSS 29853,131)

37 TT A4 Statue of the tomb owner, Rijksmuseum van Oudheden D 51 (Photo Dr M. J. Raven, Rijksmuseum van Oudheden, Leiden)

PLATE 21

38 TT A4 Statue group from the tomb, Louvre A 55

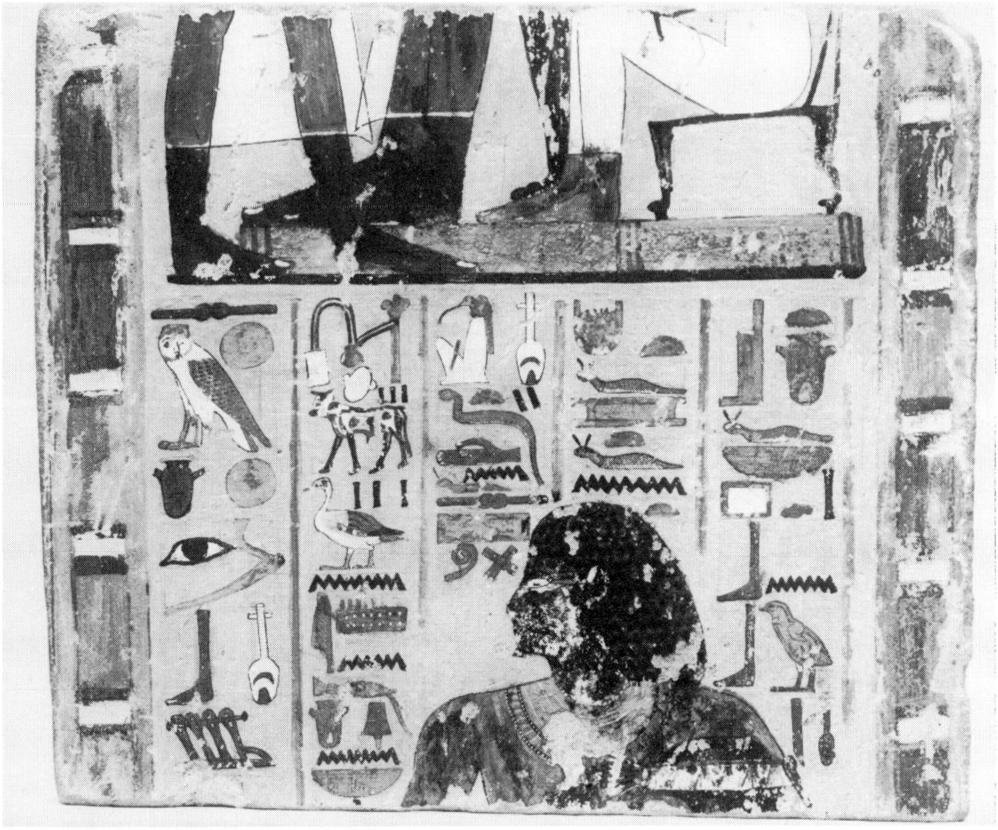

39 TT A6 Jamb(?) from the tomb, MMA Acc. No. 15.2.4 (The Metropolitan Museum of Art, Rogers Fund, 1915)

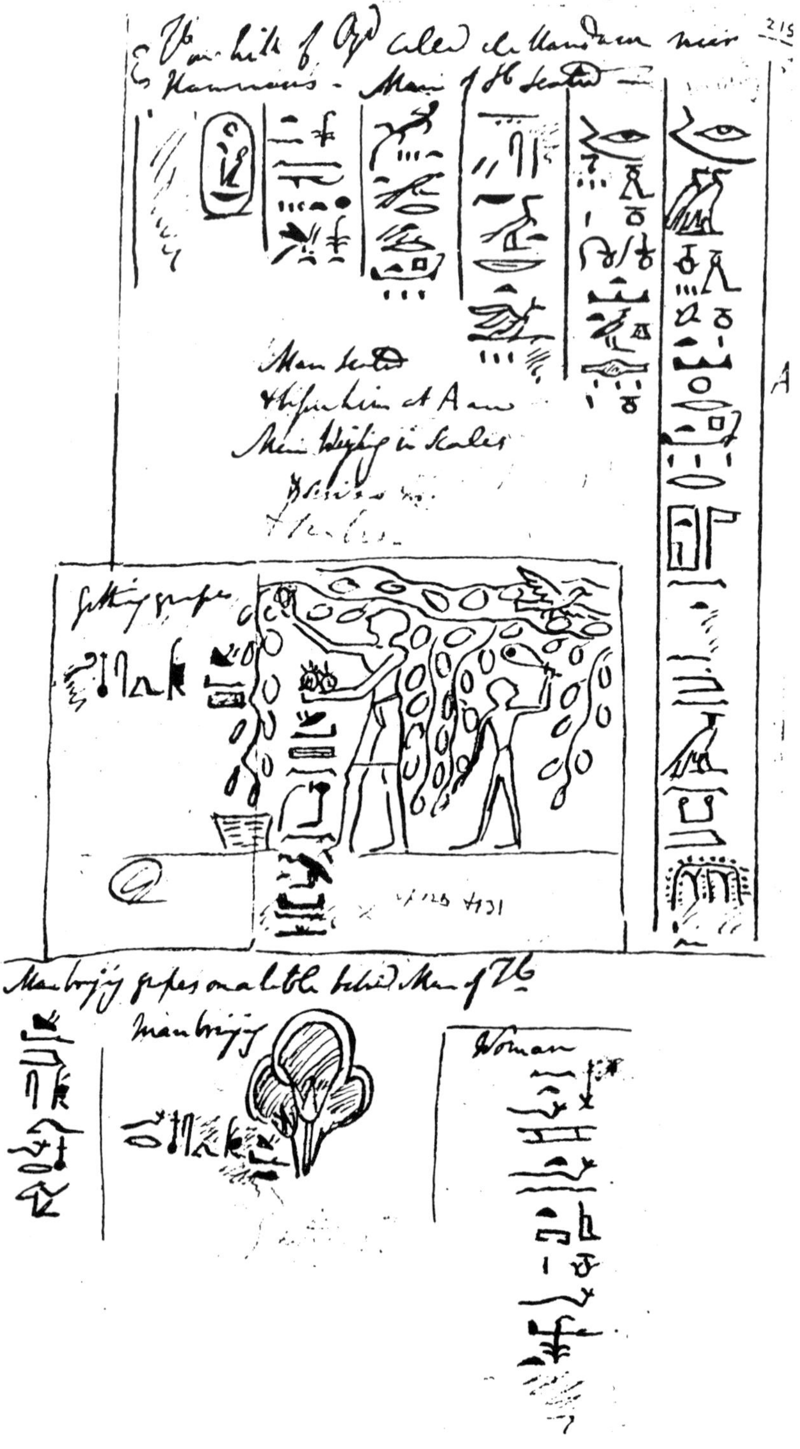

40 Miscellaneous sketches (re-drawn from Wilkinson MSS v. 215. By kind permission of the National Trust)

Part 1. Fowling scene. Part 2. Spearing fish with the bident.
Thebes.
1. An amateur sportsman throwing the stick.
2. His son holding a fresh stick ready, and carrying the game.
3, 4. His daughter, or sisters. 5. Another son carrying the game.
6. A decoy bird, with its nest in the boat.
7. The ichneumon carrying away a young bird from a nest.
8. Two bulti fish speared with the bident of fig. 11.
9, 10. Butterflies and dragon flies.
12. His sister holding a spear.
13. His son holding a spear, and carrying the fish strung upon a water plant.
The cat appears as if begging to be let out of the boat into the thicket.

41 TT A24 Fishing & fowling (= Wilkinson, *Manners & Customs*, ed. Birch, No. 365)

42 TT C4 Feast of the Valley and agriculture (Prudhoe Atlas A.19 a. By kind permission of His Grace, the Duke of Northumberland. Photo courtesy of The Griffith Institute, Ashmolean Museum, Oxford)

43 TT C4 Supervising agriculture (re-drawn from Hay Add. MSS 29852,266–7)

44 TT C4 Agriculture (= Wilkinson, *Manners & Customs*, ed. Birch, No. 468)

45 TT C4 Offering to relatives (re-drawn from Hay Add. MSS 29852,258–64)

PLATE 27

46 TT C4 Miscellaneous sketches; above and opposite (re-drawn from Wilkinson MSS v. 140–1. By kind permission of the National Trust).

PLATE 28

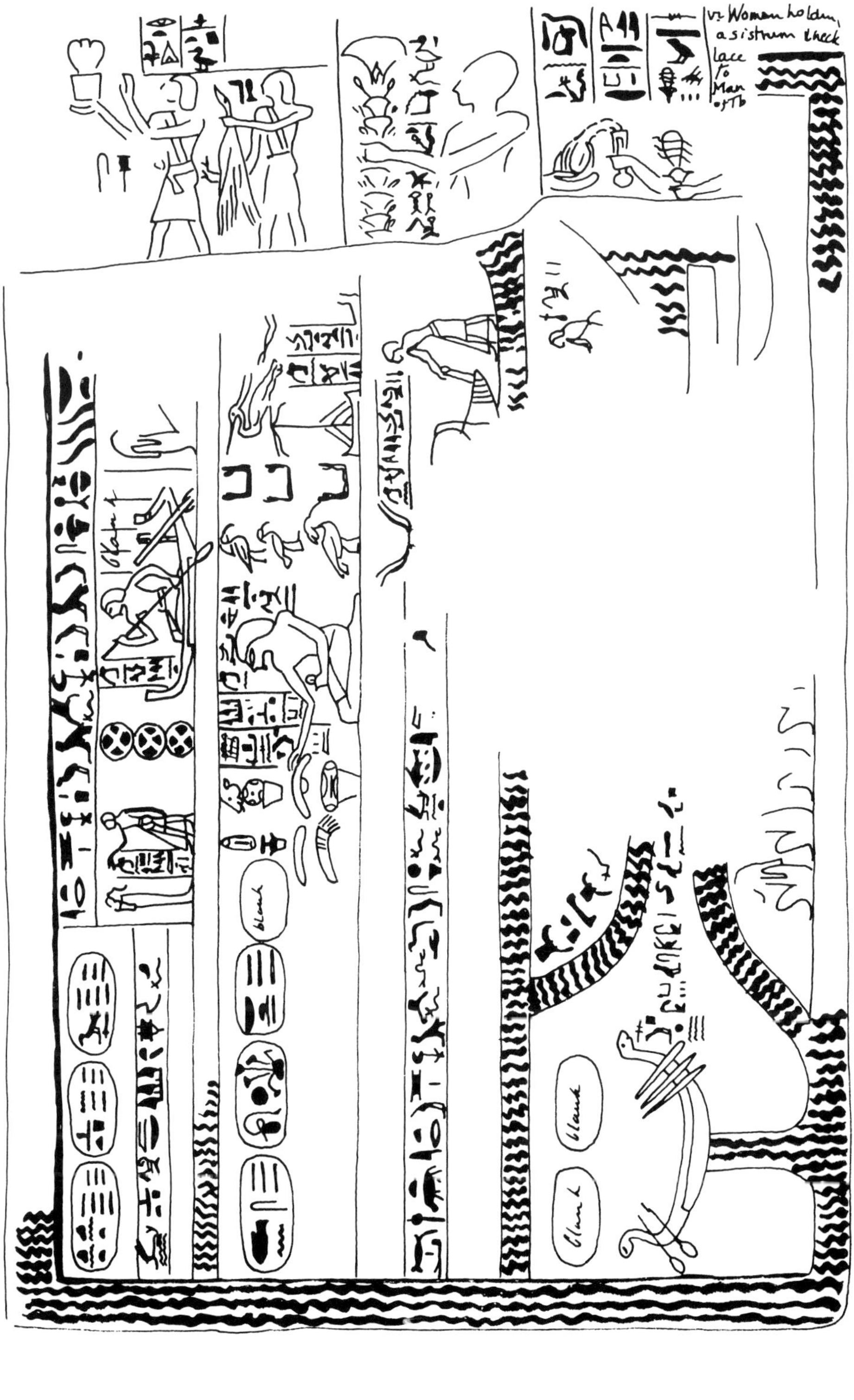

PLATE 29

47 TT C4 Offering bringers with flowers, Florence 2471. (Courtesy of the Soprintendenza archeologica per la Toscana)

48 TT C4 Mourners (re-drawn from Burton Add. MSS 25638,71)

PLATE 31

49 TT C4 Funeral procession (Prudhoe Atlas A.19 b. By kind permission of His Grace, the Duke of Northumberland. Photo courtesy of The Griffith Institute, Ashmolean Museum, Oxford)

50 TT C4 Kite (= Wilkinson, *Manners & Customs*, ed. Birch, No. 634)

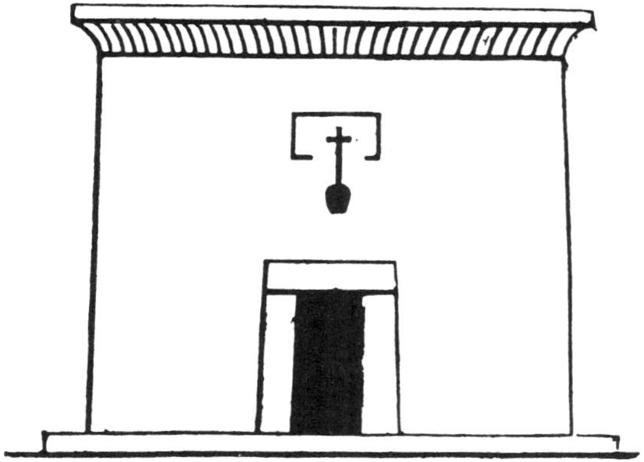

51 TT C4 The embalming house (= Wilkinson, *Manners & Customs*, ed. Birch, No. 134)

52 TT C4 Priests and mummies, Florence 2472. (Courtesy of the Soprintendenza archeologica per la Toscana)

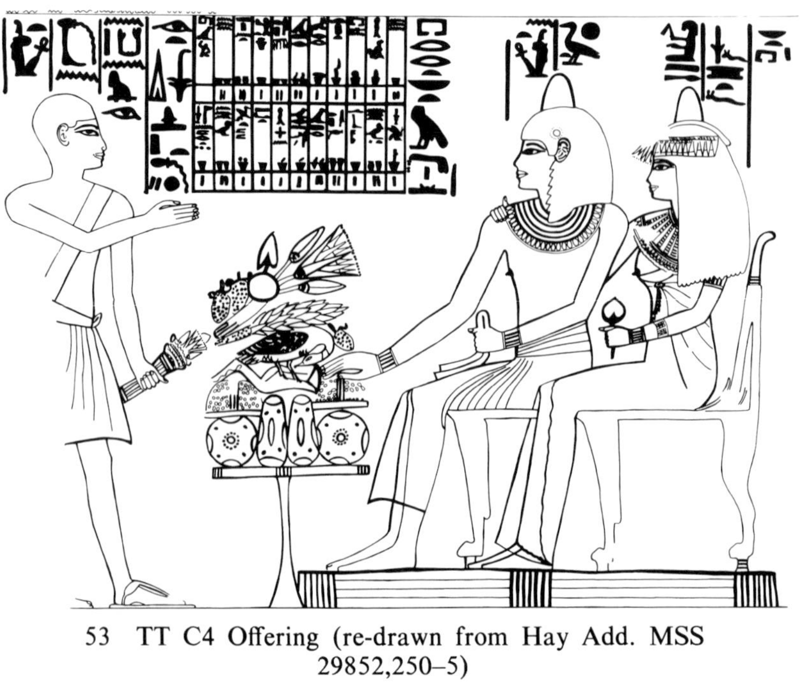

53 TT C4 Offering (re-drawn from Hay Add. MSS 29852,250–5)

54 TT C4 Conducting the tomb owner
(redrawn from Hay Add. MSS 29852,256–7)

55 TT C4 Funerary scene, Florence 2473.
(Courtesy of the Soprintendenza archeologica per la Toscana)

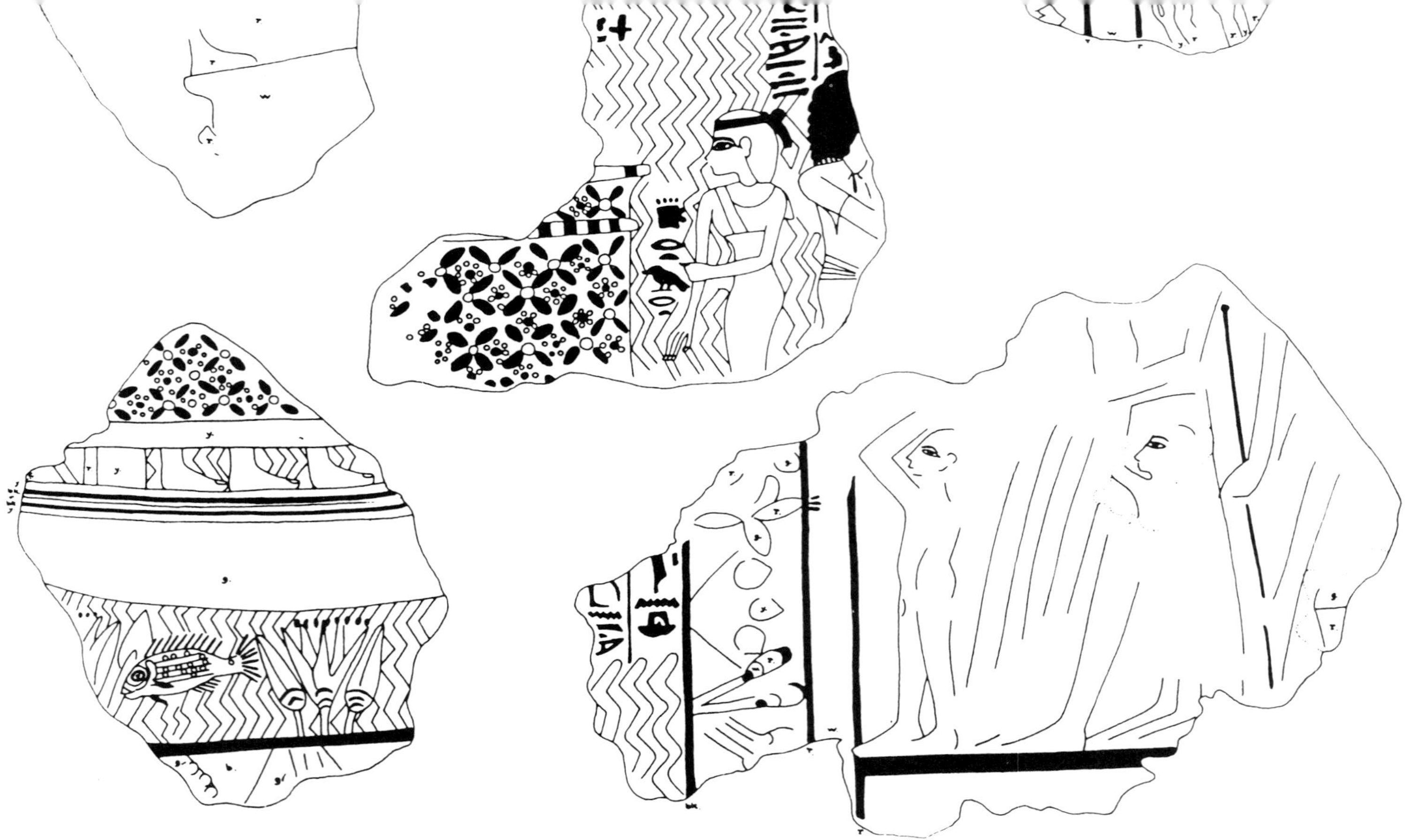

56 TT C4 Fragments found in the tomb (reduced by 50%)

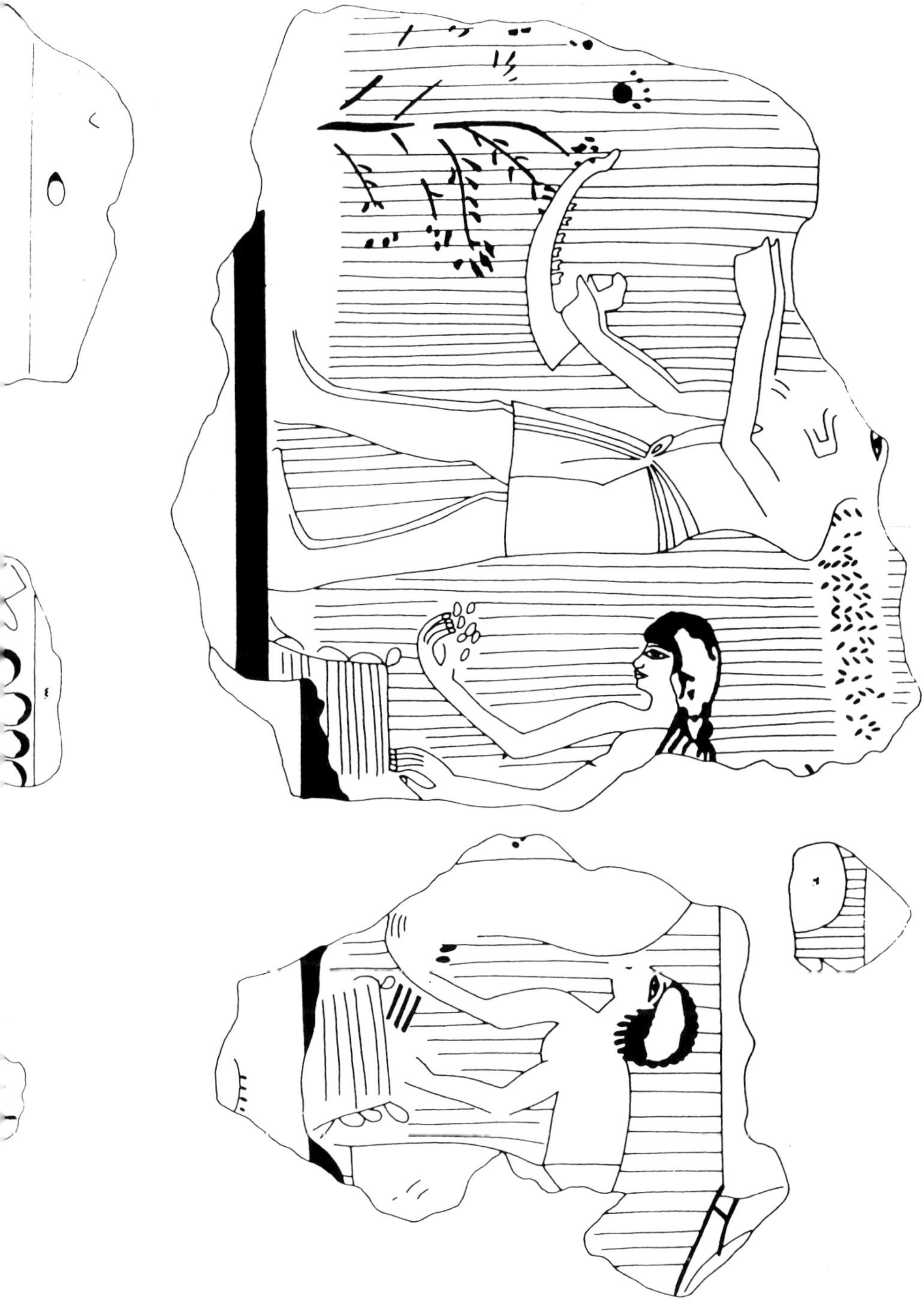

57 TT C4 Fragments found in the tomb (reduced by 50%)

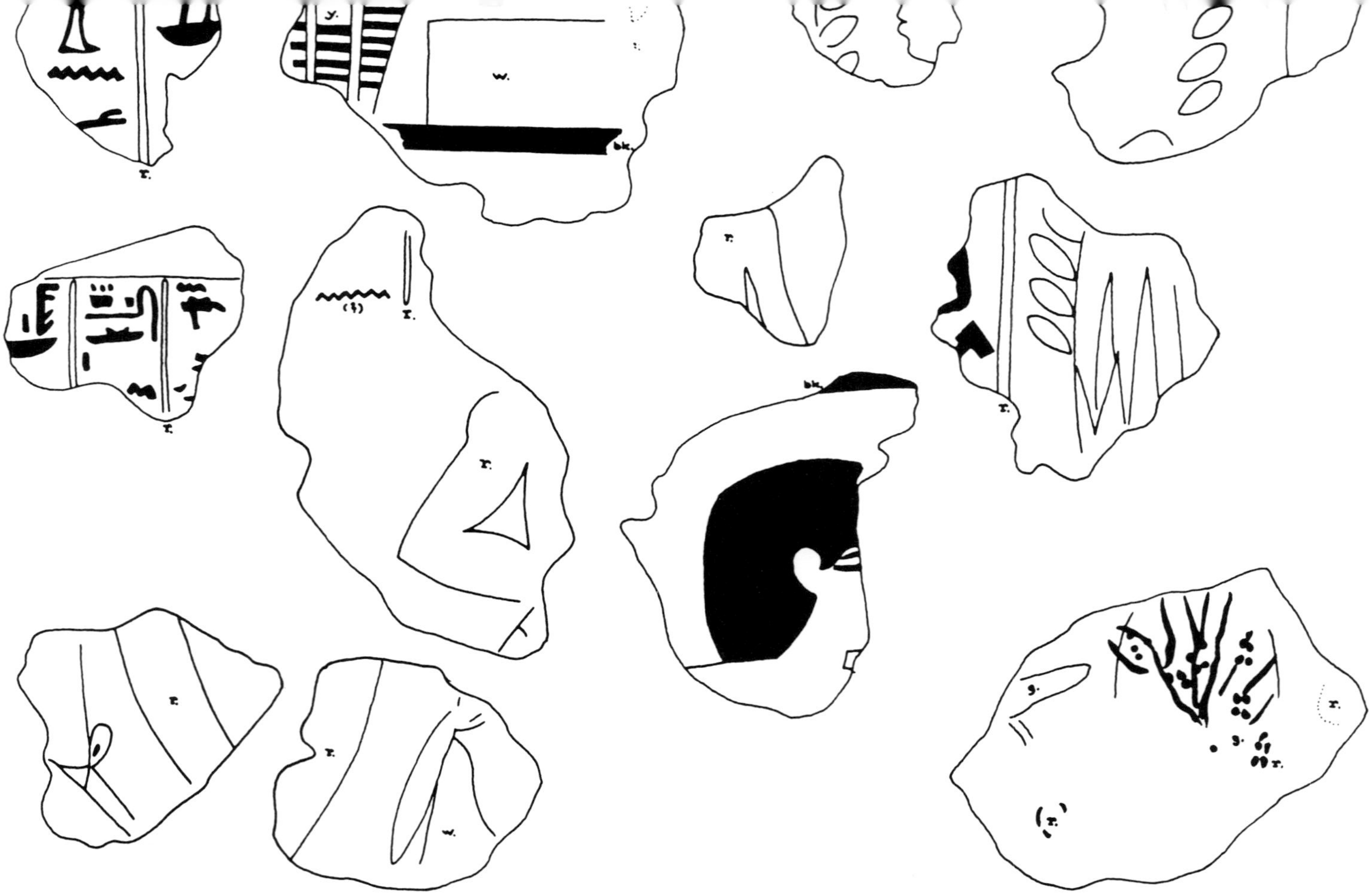

58 TT C4 Fragments found in the tomb (reduced by 28%)

PLATE 36

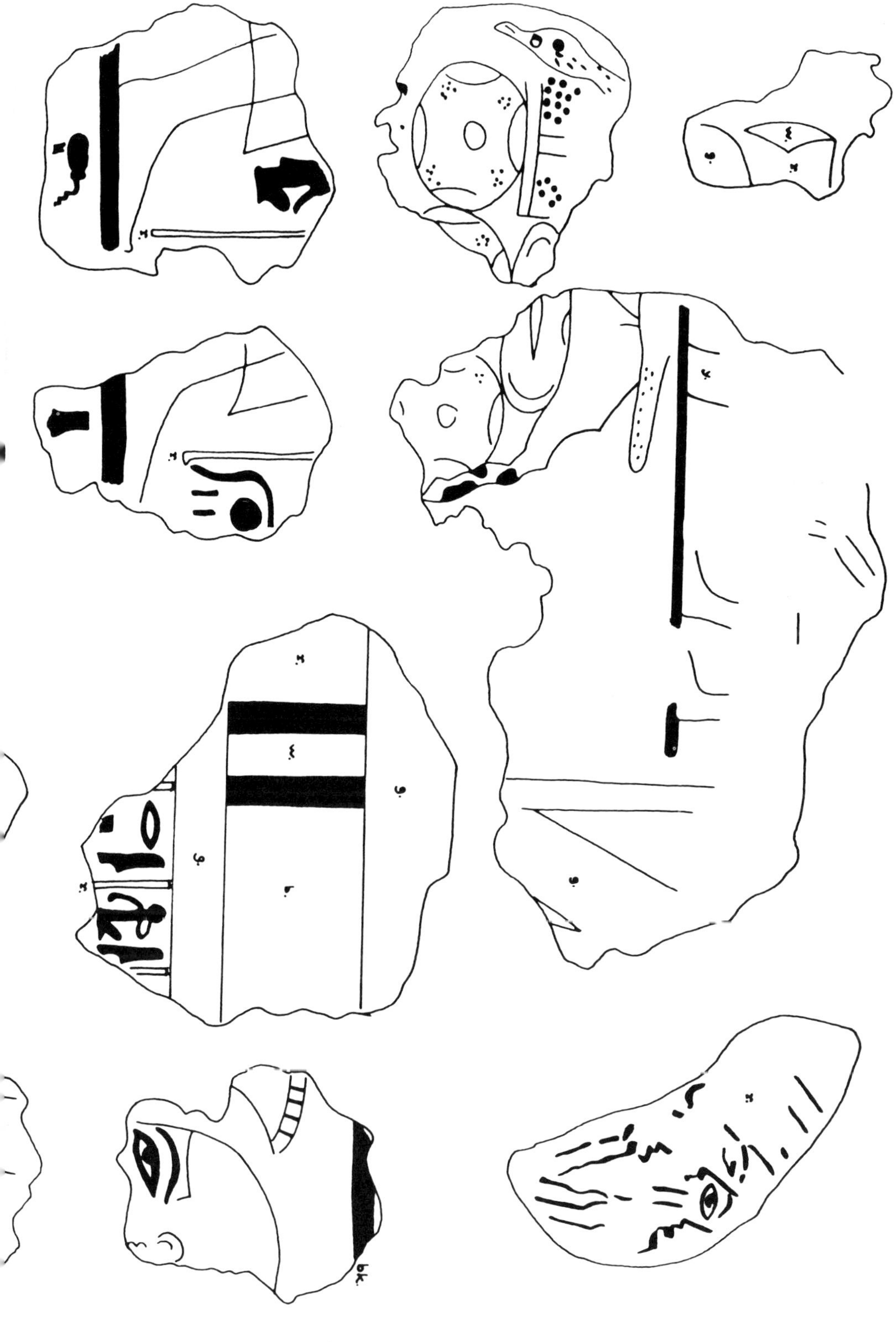

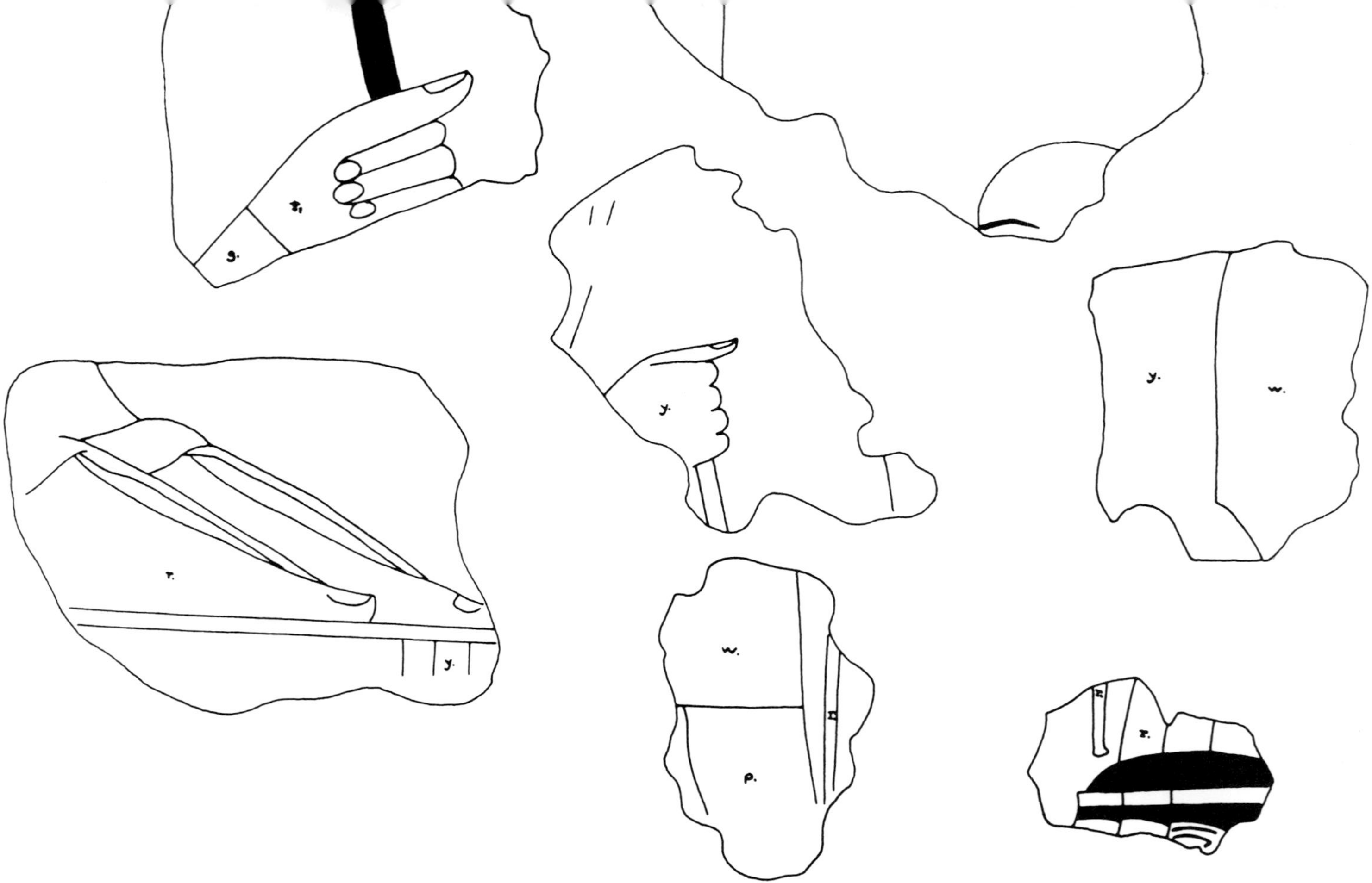

59 TT C4 Fragments found in the tomb (reduced by 28%)

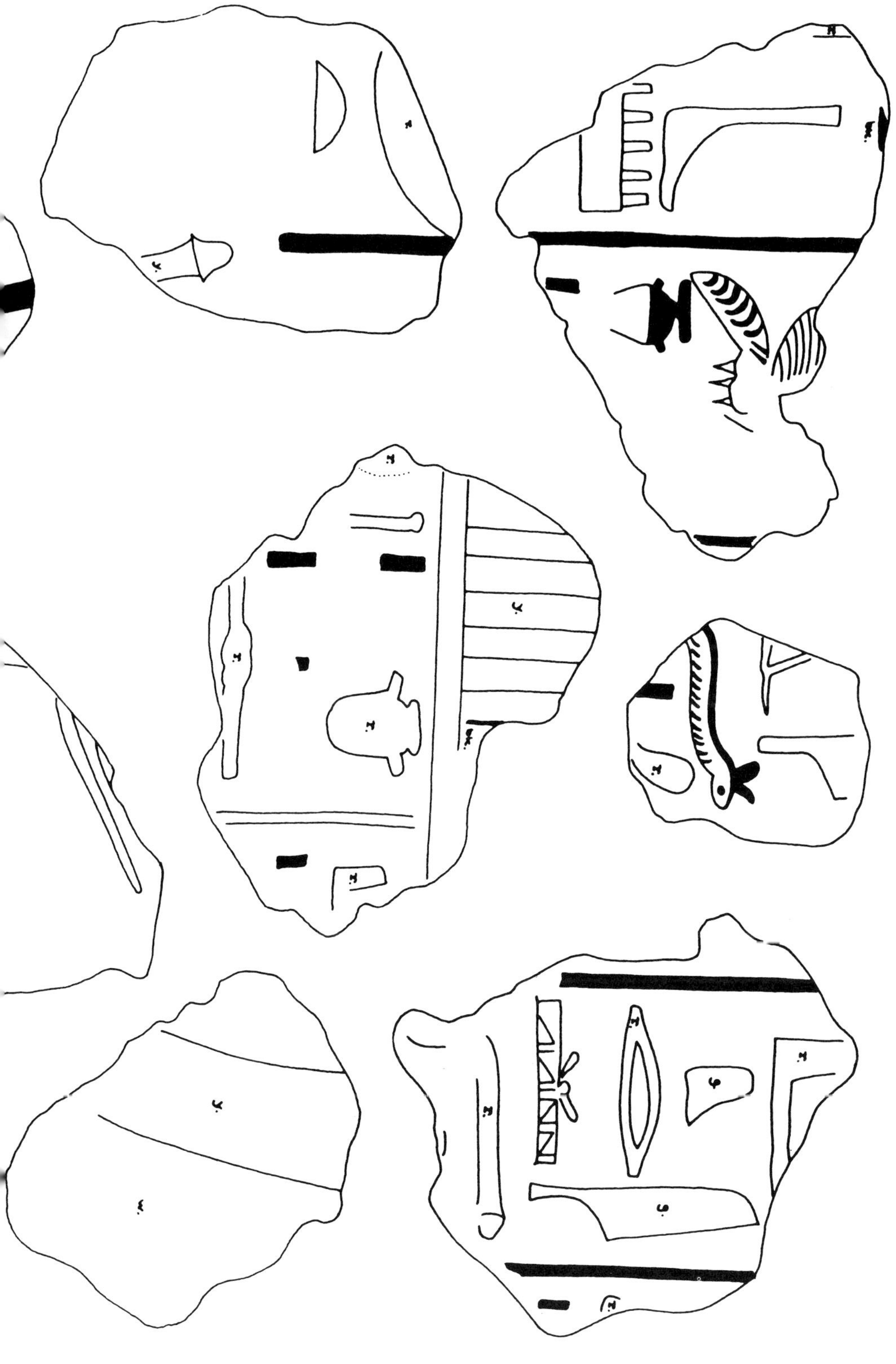

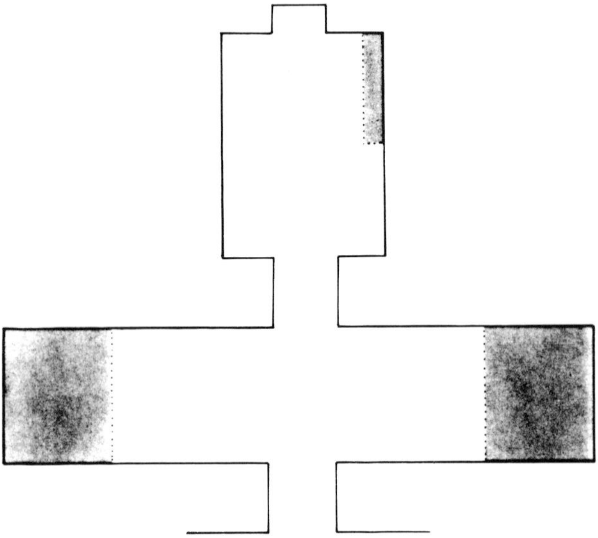

60 [1] TT C4 Plan of the tomb

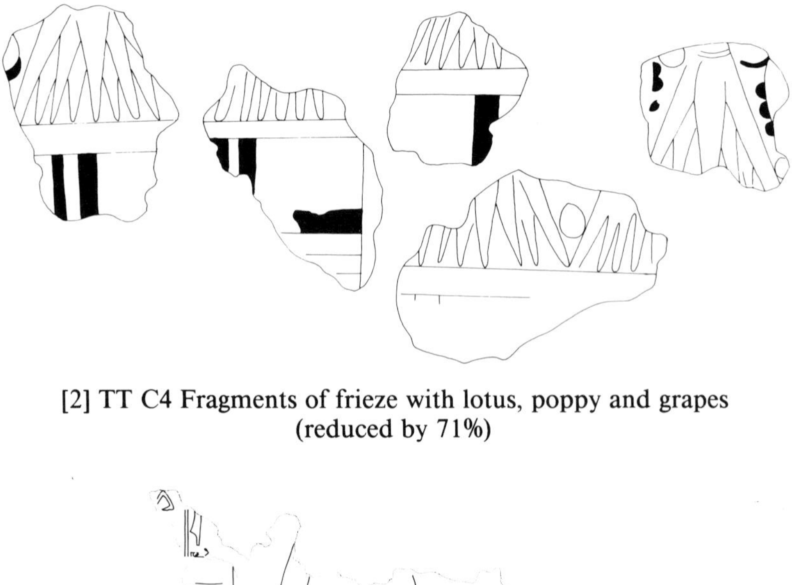

[2] TT C4 Fragments of frieze with lotus, poppy and grapes
(reduced by 71%)

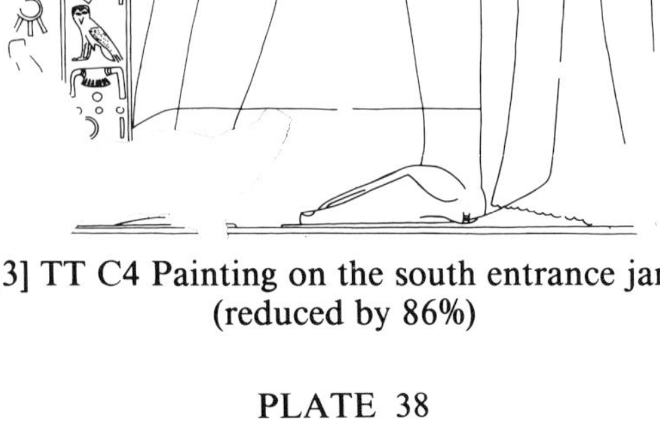

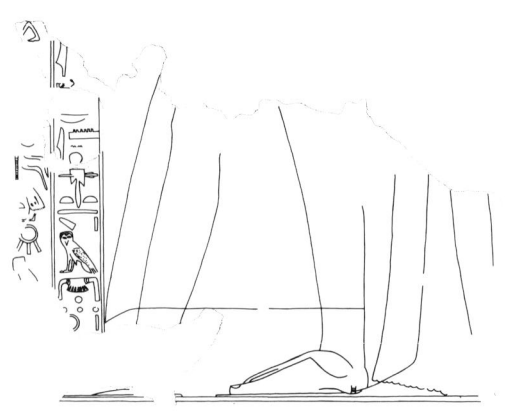

[3] TT C4 Painting on the south entrance jamb
(reduced by 86%)

PLATE 38

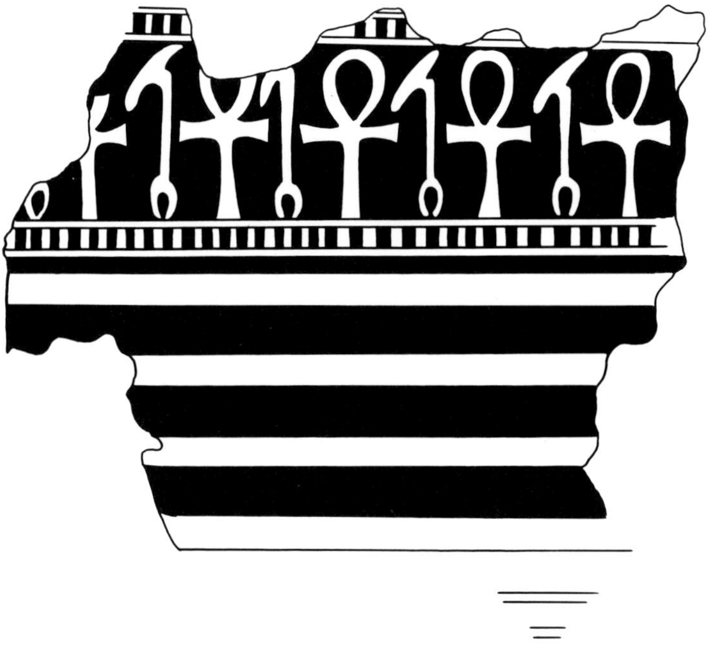

[4] (*top*) TT C4 Painting on the south wall of the inner room (reduced by 72%)

[5] (*left*) TT C4 Painting on the north wall of the inner room (reduced by 72%)

[6] (*above*) TT C4 Western goddess (re-drawn from Wilkinson MSS v.181. By kind permission of the National Trust. Same size)

61 [1] TT C4 View of the tomb below the house of the Baghdady family

[2] TT C4 Funerary cones found in the tomb

[3] TT C4 South entrance jamb showing name of Amūn hacked out and restored

[4] TT C4 Palace façade border on left side wall of hall

[5] TT C4 Two layers of plaster in palace façade border on right front wall of hall

62 [1] TT C4 Kite at lake (fragment found in tomb)

[2] TT C4 Mourners (palimpsest) at lake (fragment found in tomb)

[3] TT C4 Birds among offerings (fragment found in tomb)

[4] TT C4 Fish among offerings (fragment found in tomb)

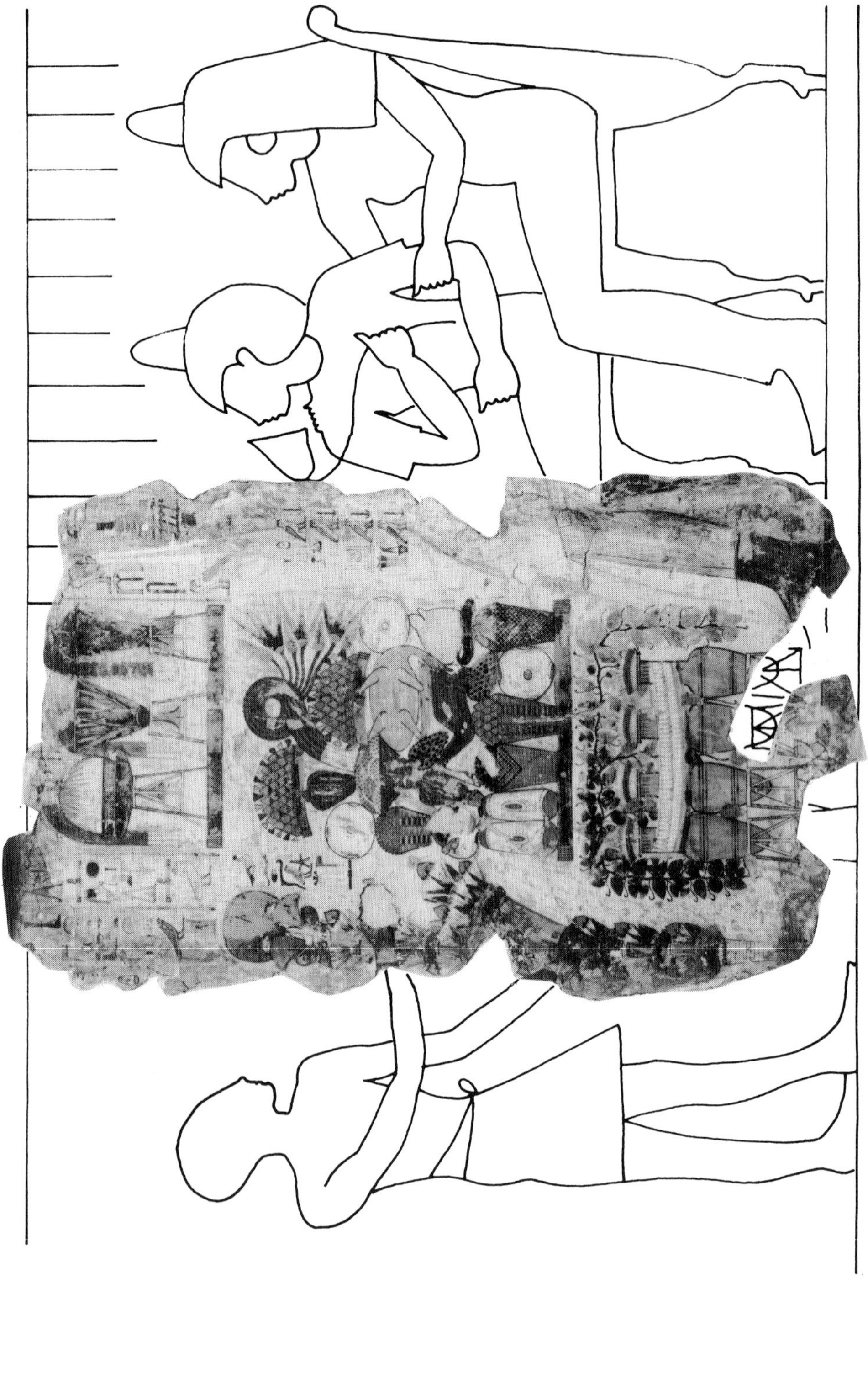

63 BM Tomb. Feast of the Valley

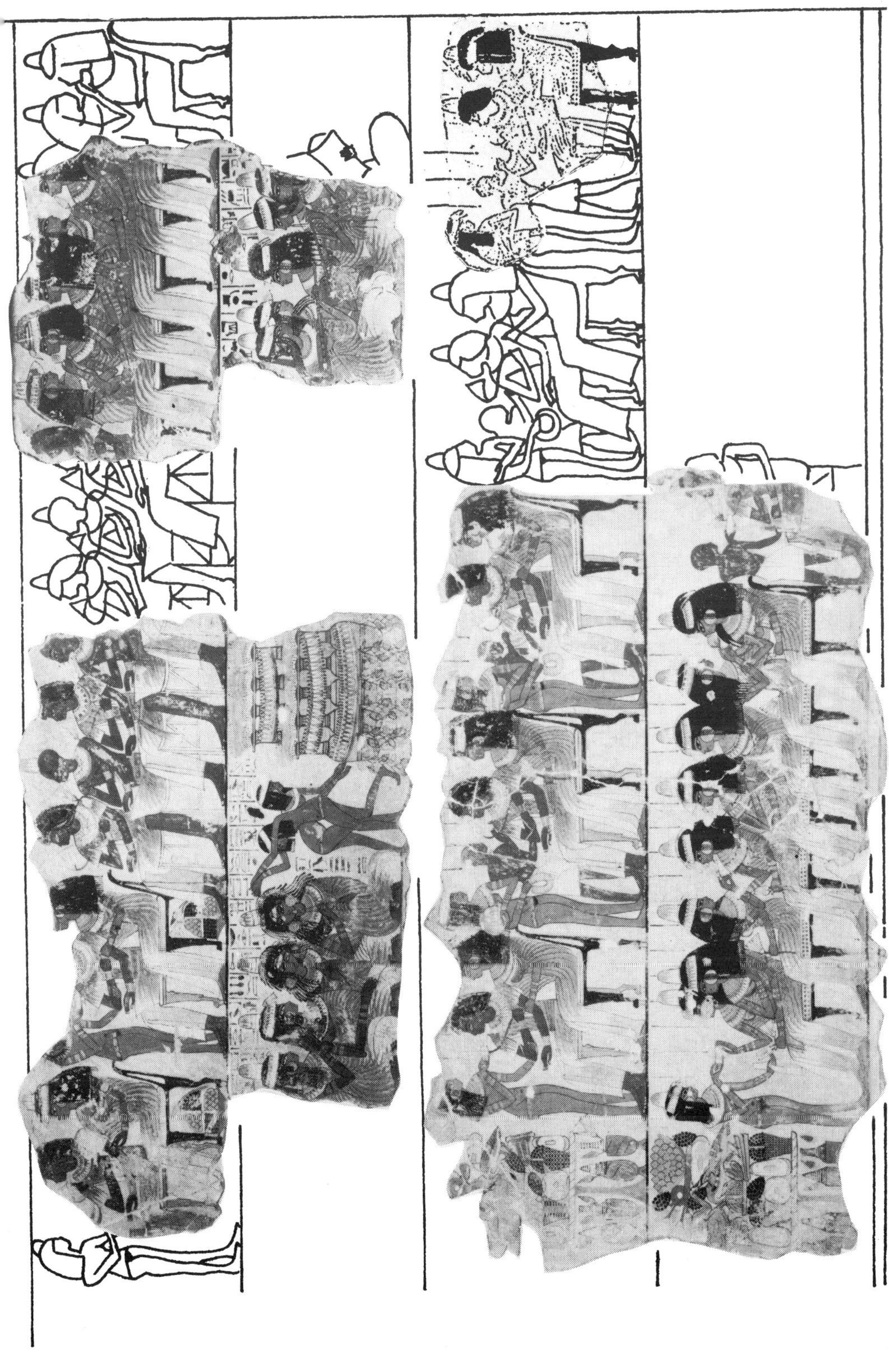

64 BM Tomb. Banquet, including fragment Avignon A51

PLATE 45

65 Detail of banquet, Avignon A51 (Courtesy of Musée Calvet, Avignon)

66 BM Tomb (= *BIE* 34, 1952, fig, 148)

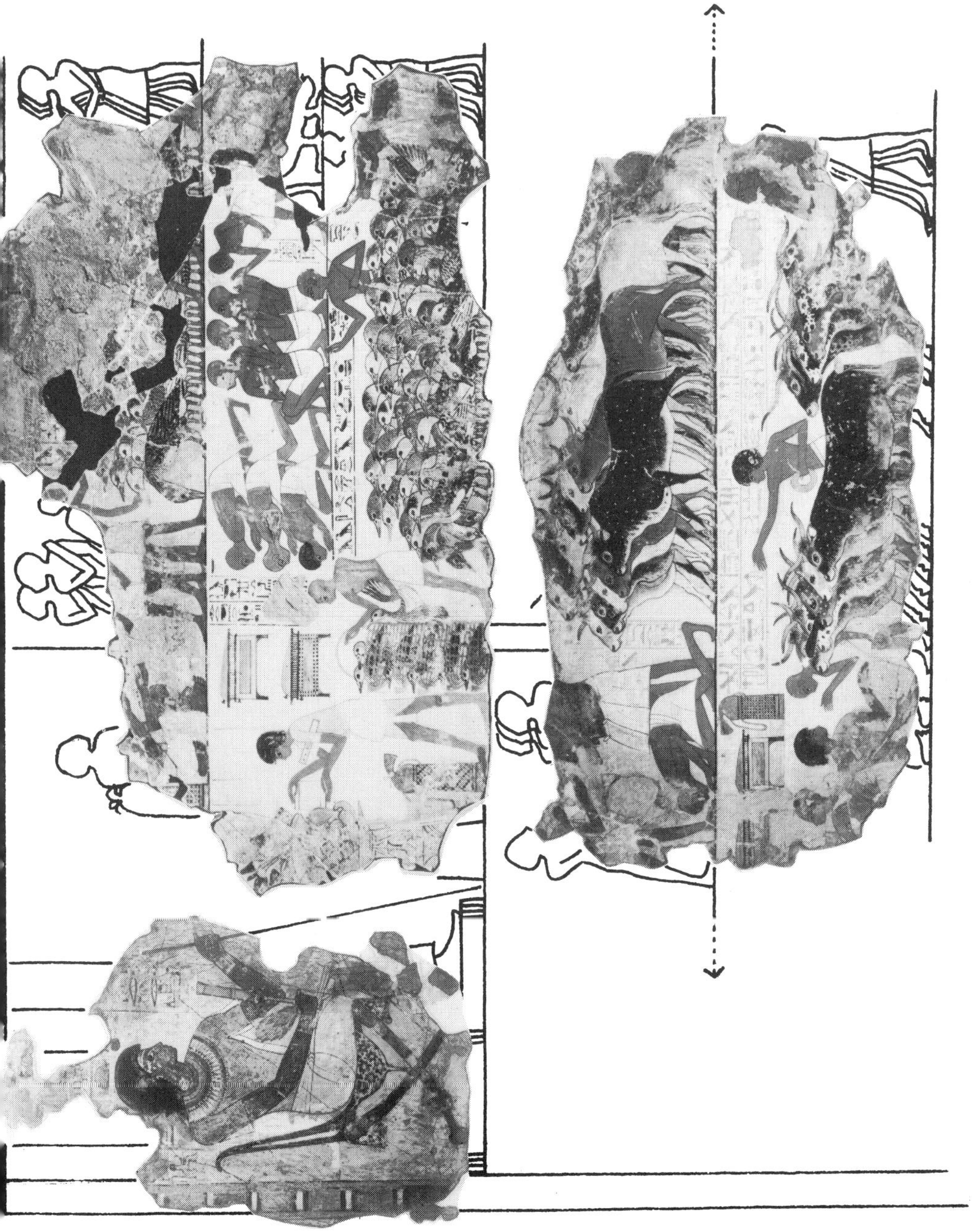

67 BM Tomb. Inspecting cattle and fowl

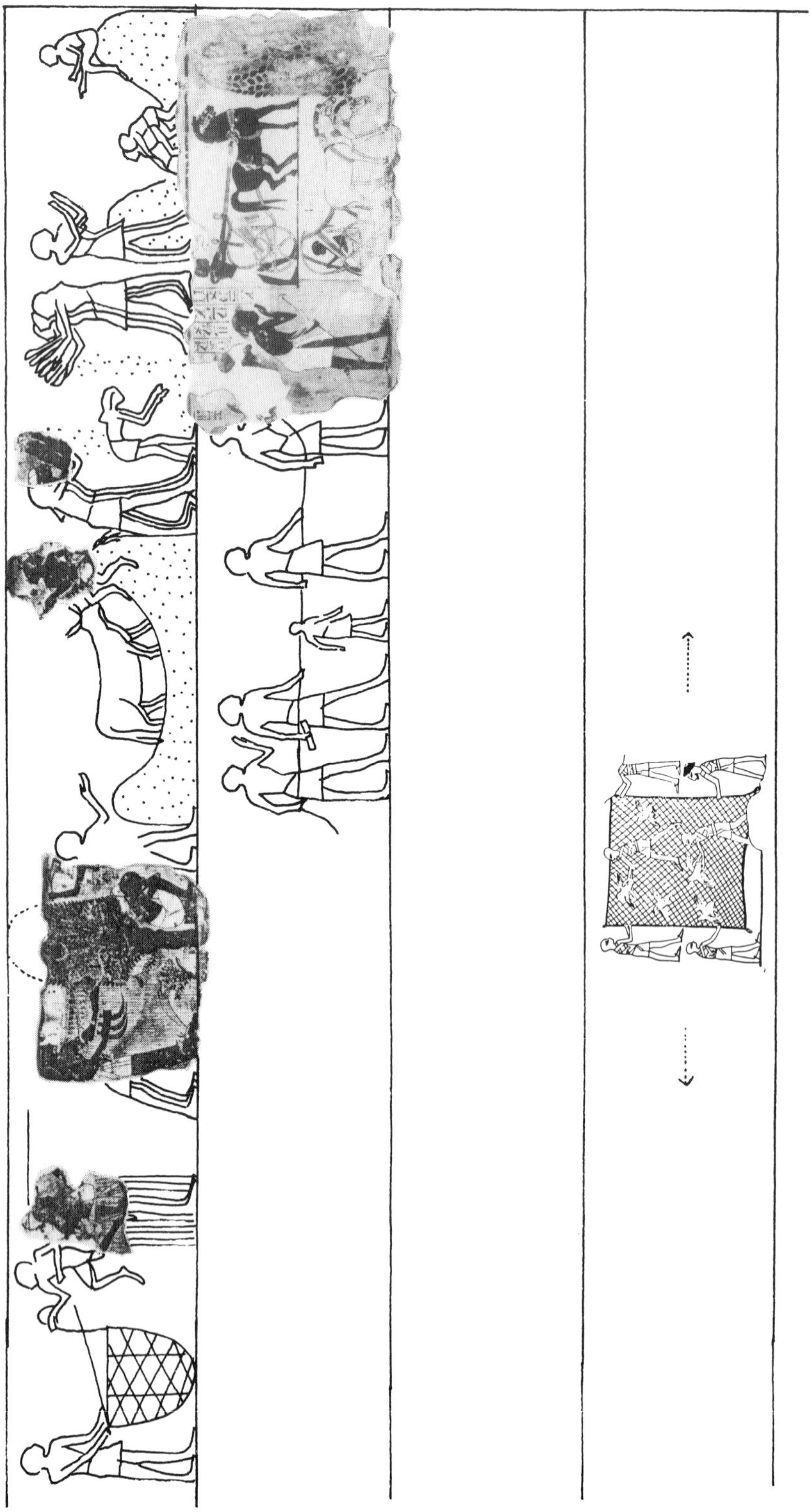

68 BM Tomb. Agriculture, partly reconstructed incorporating fragments in East Berlin. (Courtesy of Staatliche Museen zu Berlin)

69 East Berlin 18529–31. (Courtesy of Staatliche Museen zu Berlin)

70 East Berlin 18539. (Courtesy of Staatliche Museen zu Berlin)

71 East Berlin 18540. (Courtesy of Staatliche Museen zu Berlin)

72 East Berlin 18532. (Courtesy of Staatliche Museen zu Berlin)

PLATE 50

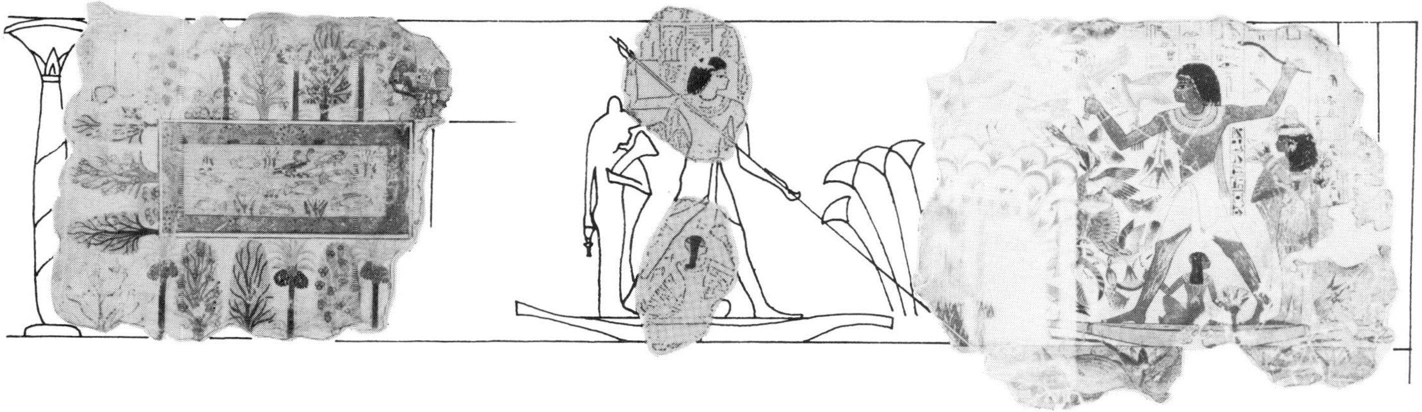

73 BM Tomb. Fishing and fowling, including fragments Ills. 74 and 75 (Courtesy of the British Museum)

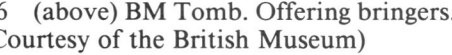

74 (far-left) BM Tomb (= *BIE* 34, 1953, fig. 180)

75 (left) BM Tomb (= *BIE* 34, 1953, fig, 146)

76 (above) BM Tomb. Offering bringers. (Courtesy of the British Museum)

77 East Berlin 18528. (Courtesy of Staatliche Museen zu Berlin)

78 'Bankes' Tomb. Tomb owner offering. (Photo by the author, with permission of the National Trust, Bankes Collection, Kingston Lacy)

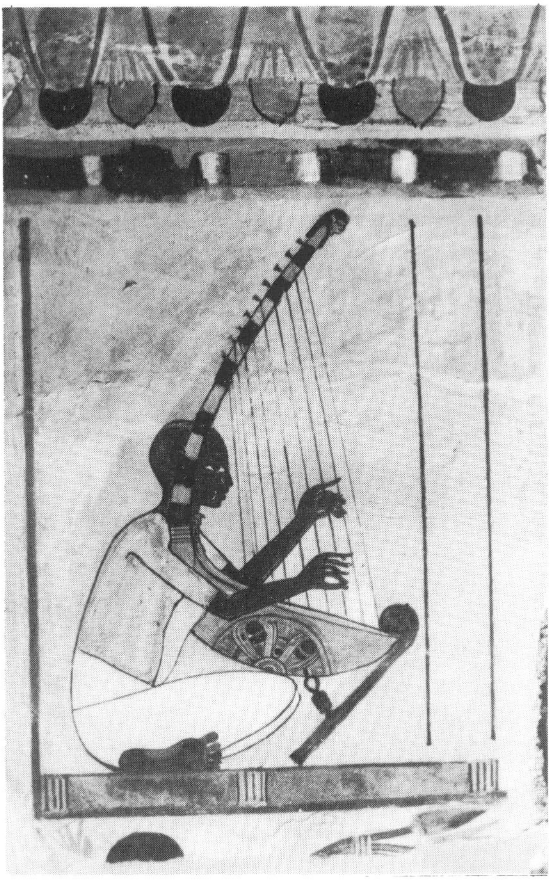

79 'Bankes' Tomb. Harpist. (Photo by the author, with permission of The National Trust, Bankes Collection, Kingston Lacy)

80 'Bankes' tomb. Harpist and lutist. (Photo by the author, with permission of The National Trust, Bankes Collection, Kingston Lacy)

PLATE 53

81 'Bankes' Tomb. Orchestra. (Photo by the author, with permission of The National Trust, Bankes Collection, Kingston Lacy)

82 'Bankes' Tomb. Orchestra (= *Ed. Phil. Journ.* 3, 1820, pl. 10)

83 Fragments from TT 52 (Courtesy of The Brooklyn Museum)

84 Fragments from TT 93(?), Dresden 757a

85 Fragments from TT 93(?), Dresden 757b

86 Fragment from TT 93(?), Dresden 757c

87 Fragment from TT 172, Fitzwilliam Museum E 83.1913. (Photo by the author with the permisson of the Museum)

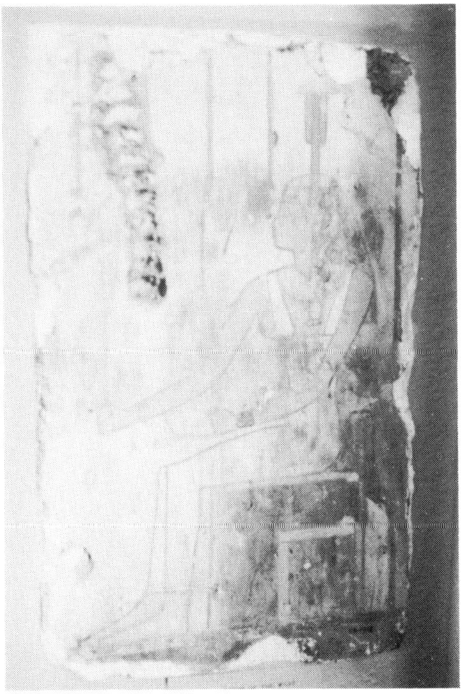

88 Fragment from TT 172, Fitzwilliam Museum E 84.1913. (Photo by the author with the permission of the Museum)

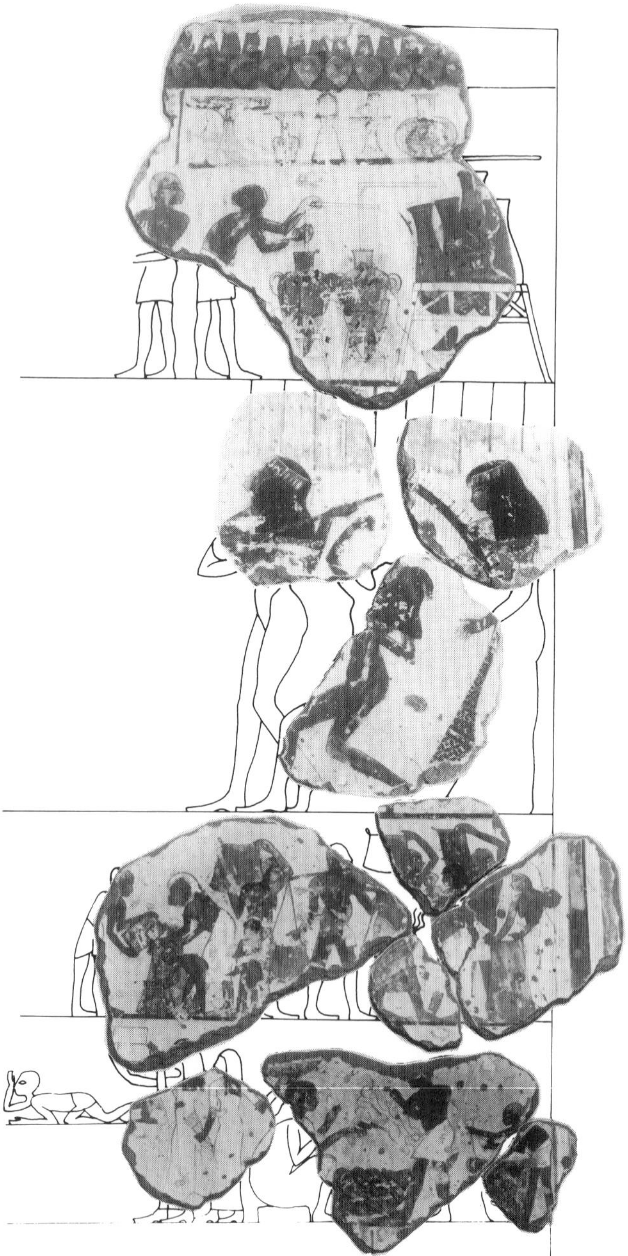

89 Fragments from a tomb, Turin Suppl. 1341–44. (Photographs courtesy of the Soprintendenza per le antichita egizie)

90 Fragment from the same tomb as Ill. 89. (Photographs courtesy of the Soprintendenza per le antichita egizie)

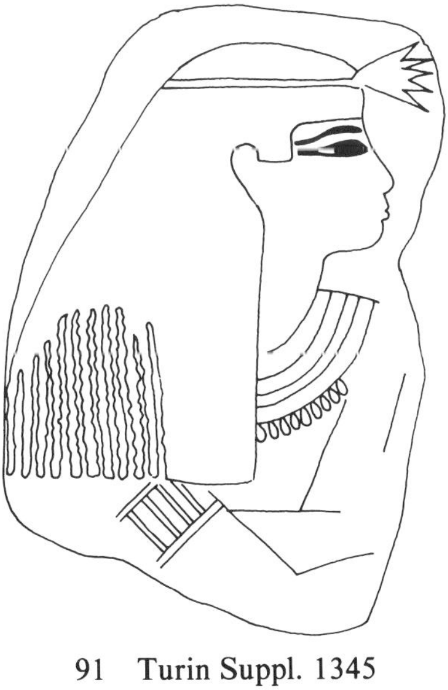

91 Turin Suppl. 1345

92 East Berlin, Ägyptisches Museum 18533
(Courtesy of Staatliche Museen zu Berlin)

93 East Berlin, Ägyptisches Museum 18527
(Courtesy of Staatliche Museen zu Berlin)

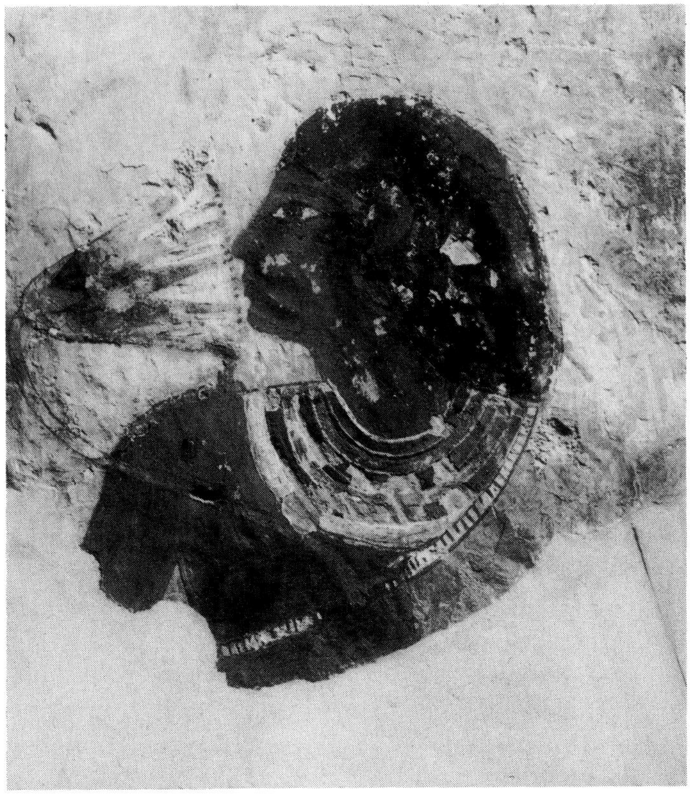

94 The Brooklyn Museum 32.1600. (Courtesy of The Brooklyn Museum)

95 Turin Suppl. 1346

96 Turin Suppl. 1349

PLATE 61

97 East Berlin, Ägyptisches Museum 18547 (Courtesy of Staatliche Museen zu Berlin)

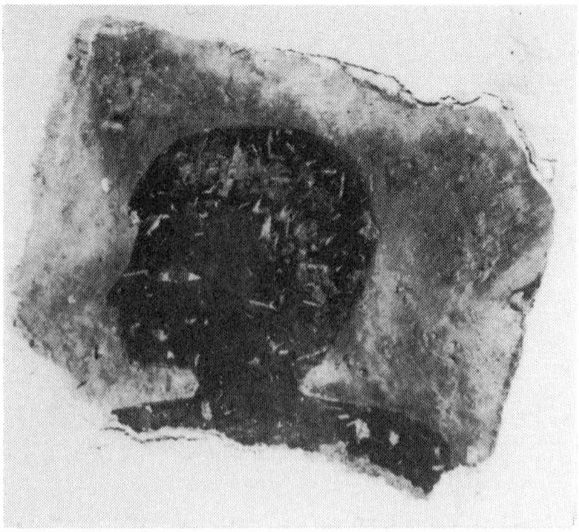

98 East Berlin, Ägyptisches Museum 18549 (Courtesy of Staatliche Museen zu Berlin)

99 Turin Suppl. 1349

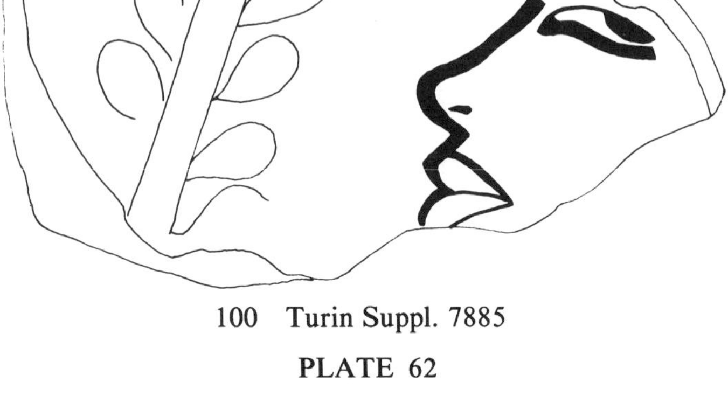

100 Turin Suppl. 7885

101 East Berlin, Agytisches Museum 18535 (Courtesy of Staatliche Museen zu Berlin)

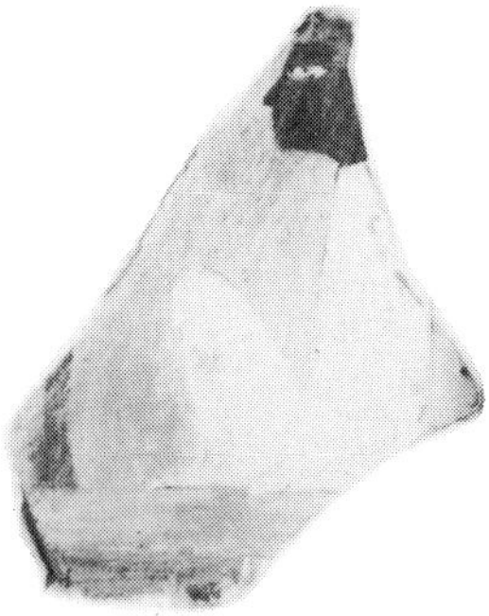

102 East Berlin, Ăgyptisches Museum 18537 (Courtesy of Staatliche Museen zu Berlin)

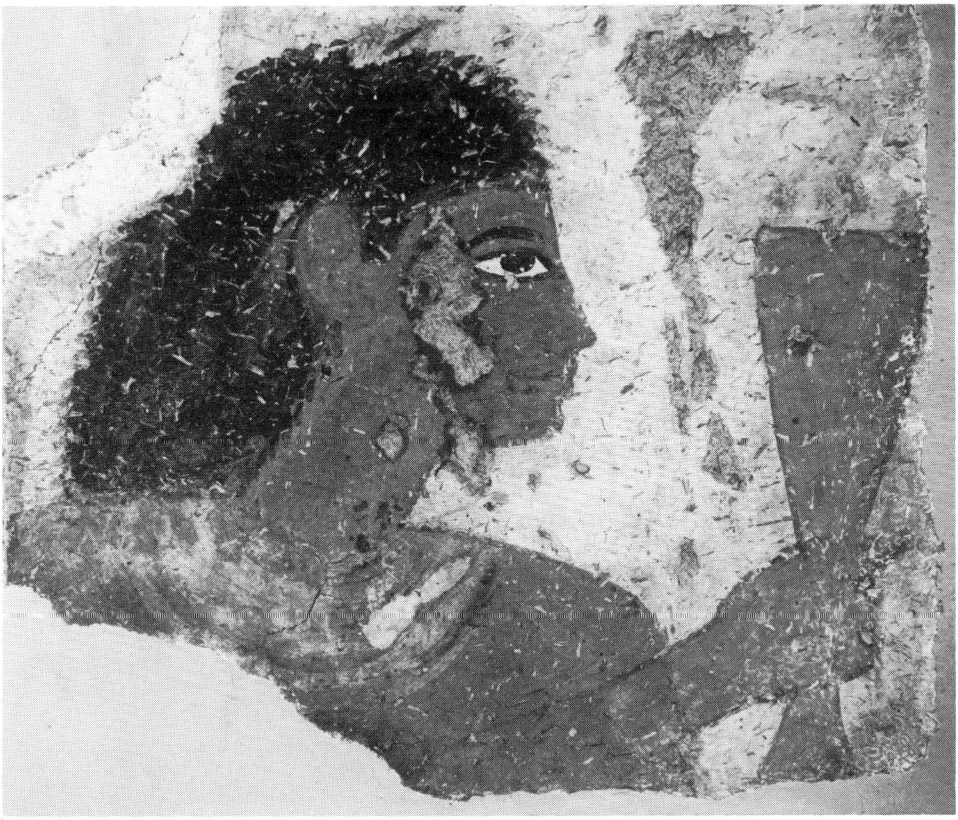

103 Birmingham fragment. (By courtesy of Birmingham Museums and Art Gallery)

104 Turin Suppl. 1349

105 Bristol BRSMG: H 4639. (By courtesy of the City of Bristol Museum and Art Gallery)

PLATE 64

106 East Berlin, Agyptisches Museum 18553 (Courtesy of Staatliche Museen zu Berlin)

107 East Berlin, Ägyptisches Museum 18551 (Courtesy of Staatliche Museen zu Berlin)

108 Bristol BRSMG: H 4637. (By courtesy of the City of Bristol Museum and Art Gallery)

109 Metropolitan Museum of Art 06.1332.1 (Gift of Bashford Dean, 1906. Courtesy of the Museum)

PLATE 66

110 Copenhagen, Ny Carlsberg Glyptotek AIN 1145–6. (Courtesy of the Museum)

ADDENDA

After the completion of the present work an article entitled 'La destruction systématique des tombes thébaines' by Arpag Mekhitarian appeared in the *Festschrift Jean Vercoutter*, Paris 1985, pp. 239-44 with pls. The author is able to throw additional light on the destruction of the tombs during World War II. A box of documents has survived, which belonged to A. Stoppelaere, who worked in the necropolis until 1956. Among the material were photographs of seventy-three fragments of tomb decoration, which had been photographed while with a merchant in Cairo. According to the author the fragments were later confiscated and deposited in the Egyptian Museum in Cairo.

Among the identifiable fragments are three from the banquet scene of TT 38 (Mekhitarian, pl. IIa-c); an offering bringer from a tomb the style of which is reminiscent of TT 15 (Mekhitarian, pl. IVa); a fragment which the present writer has now identified as belonging to the tomb of Nebamūn in the British Museum (cf. above, pp. 150ff, and Mekhitarian, pl. IVb) and which was by Keimer said to have belonged in the de Benzion collection. According to Mekhitarian, one fragment (pl. Va) shows a couple with the woman having the same name as the mother of the owner of TT 87; while yet another (pl. Vb) shows the father and grandfather of Rámosi of TT 55 in a situation similar to the one in TT C4 (our Ill. 54). Whether these two fragments come from the tombs of their sons or from monuments of their own remains an open question. But in view of the fact that TT C4 already has certain unusual features in common with TT 55 (cf. our Ill. 55), it would seem more appropriate to place the fragment published by Mekhitarian somewhere on the painted wall of the tomb of Rámosi himself rather than searching for an allegedly lost tomb of his father.

During a recent visit to the Louvre, and through the kindness of J. L. de Cenival, I was able to examine a number of small fragments in the museum, as well as one larger fragment on display in the galleries. Some of them are without doubt part of the agricultural scene of TT A4 of Wensu (cf. above, pp. 68ff and in particular footnote 7). They show part of a missing upper register with work in and around the granary, as extant in the tomb of Paḥeri.

The two larger fragments show sacks of grain being carried towards the left with the right part of a heap of grain behind one of the groups of figures. Tiny fragments represent a bushel for measuring the grain; the legs of four men who would have been scooping up the grain; heads of two men against the heap of grain; the upper left tip of a heap of grain with part of an inscription:  (cf. the scribe Nebmosi elsewhere in the scene); as well as various minute fragments of the heap of grain and persons who may have belonged in the scene. The two larger fragments are reproduced in Ill. 111a-b.

Among the remaining small fragments are several which are part of banquet scenes:

a) Two fragments from the same scene showing the heads of three male guests with lotus flowers and unguent cones. Over the horizontal dividing line above them a mat is visible (Ill. 112a-b).

b) Two joining fragments showing a squatting male guest with a lotus bud, and, in a lower register, the head of an attendant (Ill. 113a-b).

c) One fragment showing a servant girl holding a shallow cup in one hand and two tiny vases in the other. Under her hands is a basket of fruit(?). Her hair is divided in one thick and a thinner strand (Ill. 114).

d) Two fragments of a banquet orchestra, one showing the lower extremity of a portable, boat-shaped harp and uninscribed columns for hieroglyphs; the other reveals the sound box of a lute (Ill. 115a-b).

A larger fragment at present exhibited in the galleries shows a man fanning jars on a stand and another undoubtedly attending to guests on an adjoining portion of the wall. The pale colours are reminiscent of the colour scheme of another fragment exhibited in the same room from TT A22 (cf. above, pp. 54ff), through proof of a connection between the two is lacking (Ill. 116).

Finally a fragment showing the 'layered' heads of three men facing right are reminiscent of the style of the fragment illustrated in our Ill. 100, that is to say the school of painting dating from the very end of the Eighteenth dynasty (Ill. 117).

111 TT A4 Work in the granary (Louvre)

112 Two fragments from a banquet scene (Louvre)

113 Two joining fragments from a banquet scene (Louvre)

114 Servant girl in a banquet scene (Louvre)

115 Harp and lute from a banquet scene (Louvre)

116 Man fanning jars in a banquet scene (Louvre)

117 Upper part of three men (Louvre)